CRITICAL,

HISTORICAL AND MISCELLANEOUS

ESSAYS.

BY LORD MACAULAY.

WITH A MEMOIR AND INDEX.

IN SIX VOLUMES.

VOL. II.

NEW YORK:
SHELDON AND COMPANY.
BOSTON: GOULD AND LINCOLN.
MDCCCLXI.

RIVERSIDE, CAMBRIDGE:
STEREOTYPED AND PRINTED BY
H. O. HOUGHTON.

CONTENTS

OF

THE SECOND VOLUME.

ESSAYS.

MILL ON GOVERNMENT.[1]

(*Edinburgh Review*, March 1829.)

Of those philosophers who call themselves Utilitarians, and whom others generally call Benthamites, Mr. Mill is, with the exception of the illustrious founder of the sect, by far the most distinguished. The little work now before us contains a summary of the opinions held by this gentleman and his brethren on several subjects most important to society. All the seven essays of which it consists abound in curious matter. But at present we intend to confine our remarks to the Treatise on Government, which stands first in the volume. On some future occasion, we may perhaps attempt to do justice to the rest.

It must be owned that to do justice to any composition of Mr. Mill is not, in the opinion of his admirers, a very easy task. They do not, indeed, place him in the same rank with Mr. Bentham; but the terms in which they extol the disciple, though feeble when compared with the hyperboles of adoration employed by

[1] *Essays on Government, Jurisprudence, the Liberty of the Press, Prisons and Prison Discipline, Colonies, the Law of Nations, and Education.* By James Mill, Esq., author of the History of British India. Reprinted by permission from the Supplement to the Encyclopædia Britannica. (Not for sale.) London, 1828.

them in speaking of the master, are as strong as any sober man would allow himself to use concerning Locke or Bacon. The essay before us is perhaps the most remarkable of the works to which Mr. Mill owes his fame. By the members of his sect, it is considered as perfect and unanswerable. Every part of it is an article of their faith; and the damnatory clauses, in which their creed abounds far beyond any theological symbol with which we are acquainted, are strong and full against all who reject any portion of what is so irrefragably established. No man, they maintain, who has understanding sufficient to carry him through the first proposition of Euclid, can read this master-piece of demonstration and honestly declare that he remains unconvinced.

We have formed a very different opinion of this work. We think that the theory of Mr. Mill rests altogether on false principles, and that even on those false principles he does not reason logically. Nevertheless, we do not think it strange that his speculations should have filled the Utilitarians with admiration. We have been for some time past inclined to suspect that these people, whom some regard as the lights of the world and others as incarnate demons, are in general ordinary men, with narrow understandings and little information. The contempt which they express for elegant literature is evidently the contempt of ignorance. We apprehend that many of them are persons who, having read little or nothing, are delighted to be rescued from the sense of their own inferiority by some teacher who assures them that the studies which they have neglected are of no value, puts five or six phrases into their mouths, lends them an odd number of the Westminster Review, and in a month transforms them into philosophers. Mingled with these smatterers, whose attainments just suffice to elevate them from the insignificance of dunces to the dignity of bores, and to spread dismay among their pious aunts and grandmothers, there are, we well know, many well-meaning men who have really read and thought much; but whose reading and meditation have been almost exclusively confined to one class of subjects; and who, consequently, though they possess much valuable knowledge respecting those subjects, are by no means so well qualified to judge of a great system as if they had taken a more enlarged view of literature and society.

Nothing is more amusing or instructive than to observe the manner in which people who think themselves wiser than all the rest of the world fall into snares which the simple good sense of their neighbours detects and avoids. It is one of the principal tenets of the Utilitarians that sentiment and eloquence serve only to impede the pursuit of truth. They therefore affect a quakerly plainness, or rather a cynical negligence and impurity, of style. The strongest arguments, when clothed in brilliant language, seem to them so much wordy nonsense. In the mean time they surrender their understandings, with a facility found in no other party, to the meanest and most abject sophisms, provided those sophisms come before them disguised with the externals of demonstration. They do not seem to know that logic has its illusions as well as rhetoric, — that a fallacy may lurk in a syllogism as well as in a metaphor.

Mr. Mill is exactly the writer to please people of this description. His arguments are stated with the utmost affectation of precision; his divisions are awfully formal; and his style is generally as dry as that of Euclid's Elements. Whether this be a merit, we must be permitted to doubt. Thus much is certain: that the ages in which the true principles of philosophy were least understood were those in which the ceremonial of logic was most strictly observed, and that the time from which we date the rapid progress of the experimental sciences was also the time at which a less exact and formal way of writing came into use.

The style which the Utilitarians admire suits only those subjects on which it is possible to reason *a priori*. It grew up with the verbal sophistry which flourished during the dark ages. With that sophistry it fell before the Baconian philosophy in the day of the great deliverance of the human mind. The inductive method not only endured but required greater freedom of diction. It was impossible to reason from phenomena up to principles, to mark slight shades of difference in quality, or to estimate the comparative effect of two opposite considerations between which there was no common measure, by means of the naked and meagre jargon of the schoolmen. Of those schoolmen Mr. Mill has inherited both the spirit and the style. He is an Aristotelian of the fifteenth century, born out of due season. We have here an elaborate treatise on Government, from which, but for two or three passing allusions, it would not appear that the author was aware that any governments actually existed among men. Certain propensities of human nature are assumed; and from these premises the whole science of politics is synthetically deduced! We can scarcely persuade ourselves that we are not reading a book written before the time of Bacon and Galileo, — a book written in those days in which physicians reasoned from the nature of heat to the treatment of fever, and astronomers proved syllogistically that the planets could have no independent motion, — because the heavens were incorruptible, and nature abhorred a vacuum!

The reason, too, which Mr. Mill has assigned for taking this course strikes us as most extraordinary.

"Experience," says he, "if we look only at the outside of the facts, appears to be *divided* on this subject. Absolute monarchy, under Neros and Caligulas, under such men as the Emperors of Morocco and Sultans of Turkey, is the scourge of human nature. On the other side, the people of Denmark, tired out with the oppression of an aristocracy, resolved that their king should be absolute; and, under their absolute monarch, are as well governed as any people in Europe."

This Mr. Mill actually gives as a reason for pursuing the *a priori* method. But, in our judgment, the very circumstances which he mentions irresistibly prove that the *a priori* method is altogether unfit for investigations of this kind, and that the only way to arrive at the truth is by induction. *Experience* can never be divided, or even appear to be divided, except with reference to some hypothesis. When we say that one fact is inconsistent with another fact, we mean only that it is inconsistent with *the theory* which we have founded on that other fact. But, if the fact be certain, the unavoidable conclusion is that our theory is false; and, in order to correct it, we must reason back from an enlarged collection of facts to principles.

Now here we have two governments which, by Mr. Mill's own account, come under the same head in his *theoretical* classification. It is evident, therefore, that, by reasoning on that theoretical classification, we shall be brought to the conclusion that these two forms of government must produce the same effects. But Mr. Mill himself tells us that they do not produce the same effects. Hence he infers that the only way to get at truth is to place implicit confidence in that chain of proof *a priori* from which it appears that they must produce the same effects! To believe at once in a theory and in a fact which contradicts it is an exercise of faith sufficiently hard: but to believe in a theory *because* a fact contradicts it is what neither philosopher nor pope ever before required. This, however, is what Mr. Mill demands of us. He seems to think that, if all despots, without exception, governed ill, it would be unnecessary to prove, by a synthetical argument, what would then be sufficiently clear from experience. But, as some despots will be so perverse as to govern well, he finds himself compelled to prove the impossibility of their governing well by that synthetical argument which would have been superfluous had not the facts contradicted it. He reasons *a priori*, because the phenomena are not what, by reasoning *a priori*, he will prove them to be. In other words, he reasons *a priori*, because, by so reasoning, he is certain to arrive at a false conclusion!

In the course of the examination to which we propose to subject the speculations of Mr. Mill we shall have to notice many other curious instances of that turn of mind which the passage above quoted indicates.

The first chapter of his Essay relates to the ends of government. The conception on this subject, he tells us, which exists in the minds of most men is vague and undistinguishing. He first assumes, justly enough, that the end of government is "to increase to the utmost the pleasures, and diminish to the utmost the pains, which men derive from each other." He then proceeds to show, with great form, that "the greatest possible happiness of society is attained by insuring to every man the greatest possible quantity of the produce of his labour." To effect this is, in his opinion, the end of government. It is remarkable that Mr. Mill, with all his affected display of precision, has here given a description of the ends of government far less precise than that which is in the mouths of the vulgar. The first man with whom Mr. Mill may travel in a stage coach will tell him that government exists for the protection of the *persons* and property of men. But Mr. Mill seems to think that the preservation of property is the first and only object. It is true, doubtless, that many of the injuries which are offered to the persons of men proceed from a desire to possess their property. But the practice of vindictive assassination as it has existed in some parts of Europe — the practice of fighting wanton and sanguinary duels, like those of the sixteenth and seventeenth centuries, in which bands of seconds risked their lives as well as the principals; — these practices, and many others which might be named, are evidently injurious to society; and we do not see how a government which tolerated them could be said "to diminish to the utmost the pains which men derive from each other." Therefore, according to Mr. Mill's very correct assumption, such a government would not perfectly accomplish the end of its institution. Yet such a government might, as far as we can perceive, "insure to every man the greatest possible quantity of the produce of his labour." Therefore such a government might, according to Mr. Mill's subsequent doctrine, perfectly accomplish the end of its institution.

The matter is not of much consequence, except as an instance of that slovenliness of thinking which is often concealed beneath a peculiar ostentation of logical neatness.

Having determined the ends, Mr. Mill proceeds to consider the means. For the preservation of property some portion of the community must be intrusted with power. This is Government; and the question is, how are those to whom the necessary power is intrusted to be prevented from abusing it?

Mr. Mill first passes in review the simple forms of government. He allows that it would be inconvenient, if not physically impossible, that the whole community should meet in a mass; it follows, therefore, that the powers of government cannot be directly exercised by the people. But he sees no objection to pure and direct Democracy, except the difficulty which we have mentioned.

"The community," says he, "cannot have an interest opposite to its interests. To affirm this would be a contradiction in terms. The community within itself, and with respect to itself, can have no sinister interest. One community may intend the evil of another; never its own. This is an indubitable proposition, and one of great importance."

Mr. Mill then proceeds to demonstrate that a purely aristocratical form of government is necessarily bad.

"The reason for which government exists is, that one man, if stronger than another, will take from him whatever that other possesses and he desires. But if one man will do this, so will several. And if powers are put into the hands of a comparatively small number, called an aristocracy, — powers which make them stronger than the rest of the community, they will take from the rest of the community as much as they please of the objects of desire. They will thus defeat the very end for which government was instituted. The unfitness, therefore, of an aristocracy to be intrusted with the powers of government, rests on demonstration."

In exactly the same manner Mr. Mill proves absolute monarchy to be a bad form of government.

"If government is founded upon this as a law of human nature, that a man, if able, will take from others any thing which they have and he desires, it is sufficiently evident, that when a man is called a king he does not change his nature; so that when he has got power to enable him to take from every man whatever he pleases, he will take whatever he pleases. To suppose that he will not, is to affirm that government is unnecessary, and that human beings will abstain from injuring one another of their own accord.

"It is very evident that this reasoning extends to every modification of the smaller number. Whenever the powers of government are placed in any hands other than those of the community, whether those of one man, of a few, or of several, those principles of human nature which imply that government is at all necessary, imply that those persons will make use of them to defeat the very end for which government exists."

But is it not possible that a king or an aristocracy may soon be saturated with the objects of their desires, and may then protect the community in the enjoyment of the rest? Mr. Mill answers in the negative. He proves, with great pomp, that every man desires to have the actions of every other correspondent to his will. Others can be induced to conform to our will only by motives derived from pleasure or from pain. The infliction of pain is of course direct injury; and, even if it take the milder course, in order to produce obedience by motives derived from pleasure, the government must confer favours. But, as there is no limit to its desire of obedience, there will be no limit to its disposition to confer favours; and, as it can confer favours only by plundering the people, there will be no limit to its disposition to plunder the people. "It is therefore not true that there is in the mind of a king, or in the minds of an aristocracy, any point of saturation with the objects of desire."

Mr. Mill then proceeds to show that, as monarchical and oligarchical governments can influence men by motives drawn from pain, as well as by motives drawn from pleasure, they will carry their cruelty, as well as their rapacity, to a frightful extent. As he seems greatly to admire his own reasonings on this subject, we think it but fair to let him speak for himself.

"The chain of inference in this case is close and strong to a most unusual degree. A man desires that the actions of other men shall be instantly and accurately correspondent to his will. He desires that the actions of the greatest possible number shall be so. Terror is the grand instrument. Terror can work only through assurance that evil will follow any failure of conformity between the will and the actions willed. Every failure must therefore be punished. As there are no bounds to the mind's desire of its pleasure, there are, of course, no bounds to its desire of perfection in the instruments of that pleasure. There are, therefore, no bounds to its desire of exactness in the conformity between its will and the actions willed; and by consequence to the strength of that terror which is its procuring cause. Every the most minute failure must be visited with the heaviest infliction; and as failure in extreme exactness must frequently happen, the occasions of cruelty must be incessant.

"We have thus arrived at several conclusions of the highest possible importance. We have seen that the principle of human nature, upon which the necessity of government is founded, the propensity of one man to possess himself of the objects of desire at the cost of another, leads on, by infallible sequence, where power over a community is attained, and nothing checks, not only to that degree of plunder which leaves the members (excepting always the recipients and instruments of the plunder) the bare means of subsistence, but to that degree of cruelty which is necessary to keep in existence the most intense terrors."

Now, no man who has the least knowledge of the real state of the world, either in former ages or at the present moment, can possibly be convinced, though he may perhaps be bewildered, by arguments like these. During the last two centuries, some hundreds of absolute princes have reigned in Europe. Is it true, that their cruelty has kept in existence the most intense degree of terror; that their rapacity has left no more than the bare means of subsistence to any of their subjects, their ministers and soldiers excepted? Is this true of all of them? Of one half of them? Of one tenth part of them? Of a single one? Is it true, in the full extent, even of Philip the Second, of Louis the Fifteenth, or of the Emperor Paul? But it is scarcely necessary to quote history. No man of common sense, however ignorant he may be of books, can be imposed on by Mr. Mill's argument; because no man of common sense can live among his fellow-creatures for a day without seeing innumerable facts which contradict it. It is our business, however, to point out its fallacy; and happily the fallacy is not very recondite.

We grant that rulers will take as much as they can of the objects of their desires; and that, when the agency of other men is necessary to that end, they will attempt by all means in their power to enforce the prompt obedience of such men. But what are the objects of human desire? Physical pleasure, no doubt, in part. But the mere appetites which we have in common with the animals would be gratified almost as cheaply and easily as those of the animals are gratified, if nothing were given to taste, to ostentation, or to the affections. How small a portion of the income of a gentleman in easy circumstances is laid out merely in giving pleasurable sensations to the body of the possessor! The greater part even of what is spent on his kitchen and his cellar goes, not to titillate his palate, but to keep up his character for hospitality, to save him from the reproach of meanness in housekeeping, and to cement the ties of good neighbourhood. It is clear that a king or an aristocracy may be supplied to satiety with mere corporal pleasures, at an expense which the rudest and poorest community would scarcely feel.

Those tastes and propensities which belong to us as reasoning and imaginative beings are not indeed so easily gratified. There is, we admit, no point of saturation with objects of desire which come under this head. And therefore the argument of Mr. Mill will be just, unless there be something in the nature of the objects of desire themselves which is inconsistent with it. Now, of these objects there is none which men in general seem to desire more than the good opinion of others. The hatred and contempt of the public are generally felt to be intolerable. It is probable that our regard for the sentiments of our fellow-creatures springs, by association, from a sense of their ability to hurt or to serve us. But, be this as it may, it is notorious that, when the habit of mind of which we speak has once been formed, men feel extremely solicitous about the opinions of those by whom it is most improbable, nay, absolutely impossible, that they should ever be in the slightest degree injured or benefited. The desire of posthumous fame and the dread of posthumous reproach and execration are feelings from the influence of which scarcely any man is perfectly free, and which in many men are powerful and constant motives of action. As we are afraid that, if we handle this part of the argument after our own manner, we shall incur the reproach of sentimentality, a word which, in the sacred language of the Benthamites, is synonymous with idiocy, we will quote what Mr. Mill himself says on the subject, in his Treatise on Jurisprudence.

> "Pains from the moral source are the pains derived from the unfavourable sentiments of mankind. . . . . These pains are capable of rising to a height with which hardly any other pains incident to our nature can be compared. There is a certain degree of unfavourableness in the sentiments of his fellow-creatures, under which hardly any man, not below the standard of humanity, can endure to live.
>
> "The importance of this powerful agency, for the prevention of injurious acts, is too obvious to need to be illustrated. If sufficiently at command, it would almost supersede the use of other means. . . . .
>
> "To know how to direct the unfavourable sentiments of mankind, it is necessary to know in as complete, that is, in as comprehensive, a way as possible, what it is which gives them birth. Without entering into the metaphysics of the question, it is a sufficient practical answer, for the present purpose, to say that the unfavourable sentiments of man are excited by every thing which hurts them."

It is strange that a writer who considers the pain derived from the unfavourable sentiments of others as so acute that, if sufficiently at command, it would supersede the use of the gallows and the tread-mill, should take no notice of this most important restraint when discussing the question of government. We will attempt to deduce a theory of politics in the mathematical form, in which Mr. Mill delights, from the premises with which he has himself furnished us.

Proposition I. Theorem.

No rulers will do any thing which may hurt the people.

This is the thesis to be maintained; and the following we humbly offer to Mr. Mill, as its syllogistic demonstration.

No rulers will do that which produces pain to themselves.

But the unfavourable sentiments of the people will give pain to them.

Therefore no rulers will do any thing which may excite the unfavourable sentiments of the people.

But the unfavourable sentiments of the people are excited by every thing which hurts them.

Therefore no rulers will do any thing which may hurt the people. Which was the thing to be proved.

Having thus, as we think, not unsuccessfully imitated Mr. Mill's logic, we do not see why we should not imitate, what is at least equally perfect in its kind, his self-complacency, and proclaim our Εὕρηκα in his own words: "The chain of inference, in this case, is close and strong to a most unusual degree."

The fact is, that, when men, in treating of things which cannot be circumscribed by precise definitions, adopt this mode of reasoning, when once they begin to talk of power, happiness, misery, pain, pleasure, motives, objects of desire, as they talk of lines and numbers, there is no end to the contradictions and absurdities into which they fall. There is no proposition so monstrously untrue in morals or politics that we will not undertake to prove it, by something which shall sound like a logical demonstration, from admitted principles.

Mr. Mill argues that, if men are not inclined to plunder each other, government is unnecessary; and that, if they are so inclined, the powers of government, when entrusted to a small number of them, will necessarily be abused. Surely it is not by propounding dilemmas of this sort that we are likely to arrive at sound conclusions in any moral science. The whole question is a question of degree. If all men preferred the moderate approbation of their neighbours to any degree of wealth or grandeur, or sensual pleasure, government would be unnecessary. If all men desired wealth so intensely as to be willing to brave the hatred of their fellow-creatures for sixpence, Mr. Mill's argument against monarchies and aristocracies would be true to the full extent. But the fact is, that all men have some desires which impel them to injure their neighbours, and some desires which impel them to benefit their neighbours. Now, if there were a community consisting of two classes of men, one of which should be principally influenced by the one set of motives and the other by the other, government would clearly be necessary to restrain the class which was eager for plunder and careless of reputation: and yet the powers of government might be safely intrusted to the class which was chiefly actuated by the love of approbation. Now, it might with no small plausibility be maintained that, in many countries, *there are* two classes which, in some degree, answer to this description; that the poor compose the class which government is established to restrain, and the people of some property the class to which the powers of government may without danger be confided. It might be said that a man who can barely earn a livelihood by severe labour is under stronger temptations to pillage others than a man who enjoys many luxuries. It might be said that a man who is lost in the crowd is less likely to have the fear of public opinion before his eyes than a man whose station and mode of living render him conspicuous. We do not assert all this. We only say that it was Mr. Mill's business to prove the contrary; and that, not having proved the contrary, he is not entitled to say, "that those principles which imply that government is at all necessary, imply that an aristocracy will make use of its power to defeat the end for which governments exist." This is not true, unless it be true that a rich man is as likely to covet the goods of his neighbours as a poor man, and that a poor man is as likely to be solicitous about the opinions of his neighbours as a rich man.

But we do not see that, by reasoning *a priori* on such subjects as these, it is possible to advance one single step. We know that every man has some desires which he can gratify only by hurting his neighbours, and some which he can gratify only by pleasing them. Mr. Mill has chosen to look only at one-half of human nature, and to reason on the motives which impel men to oppress and despoil others, as if they were the only motives by which men could possibly be influenced. We have already shown that, by taking the other half of the human character, and reasoning on it as if it were the whole, we can bring out a result diametrically opposite to that at which Mr. Mill has arrived. We can, by such a process, easily prove that any form of government is good, or that all government is superfluous.

We must now accompany Mr. Mill on the next stage of his argument. Does any combination of the three simple forms of government afford the requisite securities against the abuse of power? Mr. Mill complains that those who maintain the affirmative generally beg the question; and proceeds to settle the point by proving, after his fashion, that no combination of the three simple forms, or of any two of them, can possibly exist.

"From the principles which we have already laid down it follows that, of the objects of human desire, and, speaking more definitely, of the means to the ends of human desire, namely, wealth and power, each party will endeavour to obtain as much as possible.

"If any expedient presents itself to any of the supposed parties effectual to this end, and not opposed to any preferred object of pursuit, we may infer with certainty that it will be adopted. One effectual expedient is not more effectual than obvious. Any two of the parties, by combining, may swallow up the third. That such combination will take place appears to be as certain as any thing which depends upon human will; because there are strong motives in favour of it, and none that can be conceived in opposition to it. . . . . The mixture of three of the kinds of government, it is thus evident, cannot possibly exist. . . . . It may be proper to inquire whether an union may not be possible of two of them. . . .

"Let us first suppose, that monarchy is united with aristocracy. Their power is equal or not equal. If it is not equal, it follows, as a necessary consequence, from the principles which we have already established, that the stronger will take from the weaker till it engrosses the whole. The only question therefore is, What will happen when the power is equal?

"In the first place, it seems impossible that such equality should ever exist. How is it to be established? or, by what criterion is it to be ascertained? If there is no such criterion, it must, in all cases, be the result of chance. If so, the chances against it are as infinity to one. The idea, therefore, is wholly chimerical and absurd. . . . .

"In this doctrine of the mixture of the simple forms of government is included the celebrated theory of the balance among the component parts of a government. By this it is supposed that, when a government is composed of monarchy, aristocracy, and democracy, they balance one another, and by mutual checks produce good government. A few words will suffice to show that, if any theory deserves the epithets of 'wild, visionary and chimerical,' it is that of the balance. If there are three powers, how is it possible to prevent two of them from combining to swallow up the third?

"The analysis which we have already performed will enable us to trace rapidly the concatenation of causes and effects in this imagined case.

"We have already seen that the interest of the community, considered in the aggregate, or in the democratical point of view, is, that each individual should receive protection; and that the powers which are constituted for that purpose should be employed exclusively for that purpose. . . . . We have also seen that the interest of the king and of the governing aristocracy is directly the reverse. It is to have unlimited power over the rest of the community, and to use it for their own advantage. In the supposed case of the balance of the monarchical, aristocratical, and democratical powers, it cannot be for the interest of either the monarchy or the aristocracy to combine with the democracy; because it is the interest of the democracy, or community at large, that neither the king nor the aristocracy should have one particle of power, or one particle of the wealth of the community, for their own advantage.

"The democracy or community have all possible motives to endeavour to prevent the monarchy and aristocracy from exercising power, or obtaining the wealth of the community for their own advantage. The monarchy and aristocracy have all possible motives for endeavouring to obtain unlimited power over the persons and property of the community. The consequence is inevitable: they have all possible motives for combining to obtain that power."

If any part of this passage be more eminently absurd than another, it is, we think, the argument by which Mr. Mill proves that there cannot be an union of monarchy and aristocracy. Their power, he says, must be equal or not equal. But of equality there is no criterion. Therefore the chances against its existence are as infinity to one. If the power be not equal, then it follows, from the principles of human nature, that the stronger will take from the weaker, till it has engrossed the whole.

Now, if there be no criterion of equality between two portions of power there can be no common measure of portions of power. Therefore it is utterly impossible to compare them together. But where two portions of power are of the same kind, there is no difficulty in ascertaining, sufficiently for all practical purposes, whether they are equal or unequal. It is easy to judge whether two men run equally fast, or can lift equal weights. Two arbitrators, whose joint decision is to be final, and neither of whom can do any thing without the assent of the other, possess equal power. Two electors, each of whom has a vote for a borough, possess, in that respect, equal power. If not, all Mr. Mill's political theories fall to the ground at once. For, if it be impossible to ascertain whether two portions of power are equal, he never can show that, even under a system of universal suffrage, a minority might not carry every thing their own way, against the wishes and interests of the majority.

Where there are two portions of power differing in kind, there is, we admit, no criterion of equality. But then, in such a case, it is absurd to talk, as Mr. Mill does, about the stronger and the weaker. Popularly, indeed, and with reference to some particular objects, these words may very fairly be used. But to use them mathematically is altogether improper. If we are speaking of a boxing-match, we may say that some famous bruiser has greater bodily power than any man in England. If we are speaking of a pantomime, we may say the same of some very agile harlequin. But it would be talking nonsense to say, in general, that the power of Harlequin either exceeded that of the pugilist, or fell short of it.

If Mr. Mill's argument be good as between different branches of a legislature, it is equally good as between sovereign powers. Every government, it may be said, will, if it can, take the objects of its desires from every other. If the French government can subdue England it will do so. If the English government can subdue France it will do so. But the power of England and France is either equal or not equal. The chance that it is not exactly equal is as infinity to one, and may safely be left out of the account; and then the stronger will infallibly take from the weaker till the weaker is altogether enslaved.

Surely the answer to all this hubbub of unmeaning words is the plainest possible. For some purposes France is stronger than England. For some purposes England is stronger than France. For some, neither has any power at all. France has the greater population, England the greater capital; France has the greater army, England the greater fleet. For an expedition to Rio Janeiro or the Philippines, England has the greater power. For a war on the Po or the Danube, France has the greater power. But neither has power sufficient to keep the other in quiet subjection for a month. Invasion would be very perilous; the idea of complete conquest on either side utterly ridiculous. This is the manly and sensible way of discussing such questions. The *ergo*, or rather the *argal*, of Mr. Mill cannot impose on a child. Yet we ought scarcely to say this; for we remember to have heard *a child* ask whether Bonaparte was stronger than an elephant!

Mr. Mill reminds us of those philosophers of the sixteenth century who, having satisfied themselves *a priori* that the rapidity with which bodies descended to the earth varied exactly as their weights, refused to believe the contrary on the evidence of their own eyes and ears. The British constitution, according to Mr. Mill's classification, is a mixture of monarchy and aristocracy; one House of Parliament being composed of hereditary nobles, and the other almost entirely chosen by a privileged class who possess the elective franchise on account of their property, or their connection with certain corporations. Mr. Mill's argument proves that, from the time that these two powers were mingled in our government, that is, from the very first dawn of our history, one or the other must have been constantly encroaching. According to him, moreover, all the encroachments must have been on one side. For the first encroachment could only have been made by the stronger; and that first encroachment would have made the stronger stronger still. It is, therefore, matter of absolute demonstration, that either the Parliament was stronger than the Crown in the reign of Henry VIII., or that the Crown was stronger than the Parliament in 1641. "Hippocrate dira ce que lui plaira," says the girl in Moliere; "mais le cocher est mort." Mr. Mill may say what he pleases; but the English constitution is still alive. That since the Revolution the Parliament has possessed great power in the state, is what nobody will dispute. The King, on the other hand, can create new peers, and can dissolve Parliaments. William sustained severe mortifications from the House of Commons, and was, indeed, unjustifiably oppressed. Anne was desirous to change a ministry which had a majority in both Houses. She watched her moment for a dissolution, created twelve Tory peers, and succeeded. Thirty years later, the House of Commons drove Walpole from his seat. In 1784, George III. was able to keep Mr. Pitt in office in the face of a majority of the House of Commons. In 1804, the apprehension of a defeat in Parliament compelled the same King to part from his most favoured minister. But, in 1807, he was able to do exactly what Anne had done nearly a hundred years before. Now, had the power of the King increased during the intervening century, or had it remained stationary? Is it possible that the one lot among the infinite number should have fallen to us? If not, Mr. Mill has proved that one of the two parties must have been constantly taking from the other. Many of the ablest men in England think that the influence of the Crown has, on the whole, increased since the reign of Anne. Others think that the Parliament has been growing in strength. But of this there is no doubt, that both sides possessed great power then, and possess great power now. Surely, if there were the least truth in the argument of Mr. Mill, it could not possibly be a matter of doubt, at the end of a hundred and twenty years, whether the one side or the other had been the gainer.

But we ask pardon. We forgot that a fact, irreconcilable with Mr. Mill's theory, furnishes, in his opinion, the strongest reason for adhering to the theory. To take up the question in another manner, is it not plain that there may be two bodies, each possessing a perfect and entire power, which cannot be taken from it without its own concurrence? What is the meaning of the words stronger and weaker, when applied to such bodies as these? The one may, indeed, by physical force, altogether destroy the other. But this is not the question. A third party, a general of their own, for example, may, by physical force, subjugate them both. Nor is there any form of government, Mr. Mill's utopian democracy not excepted, secure from such an occurrence. We are speaking of the powers with which the constitution invests the two branches of the legislature; and we ask Mr. Mill how, on his own principles, he can maintain that one of them will be able to encroach on the other, if the consent of the other be necessary to such encroachment?

Mr. Mill tells us that, if a government be composed of the three simple forms, which he will not admit the British constitution to be, two of the component parts will inevitably join against the third. Now, if two of them combine and act as one, this case evidently resolves itself into the last; and all the observations which we have just made will fully apply to it. Mr. Mill says, that "any two of the parties, by combining, may swallow up the third;" and afterwards asks, "How it is possible to prevent two of them from combining to swallow up the third?" Surely Mr. Mill must be aware that in politics two is not always the double of one. If the concurrence of all the three branches of the legislature be necessary to every law, each branch will possess constitutional power sufficient to protect it against any thing but that physical force from which no form of government is secure. Mr. Mill reminds us of the Irishman, who could not be brought to understand how one juryman could possibly starve out eleven others.

But is it certain that two of the branches of the legislature will combine against the third? "It appears to be as certain," says Mr. Mill, "as any thing which depends upon human will; because there are strong motives in favour of it, and none that can be conceived in opposition to it." He subsequently sets forth what these motives are. The interest of the democracy is that each individual should receive protection. The interest of the King and the aristocracy is to have all the power that they can obtain, and to use it for their own ends. Therefore the King and the aristocracy have all possible motives for combining against the people. If our readers will look back to the passage quoted above, they will see that we represent Mr. Mill's argument quite fairly.

Now we should have thought that, without the help of either history or experience, Mr. Mill would have discovered, by the light of his own logic, the fallacy which lurks, and indeed scarcely lurks, under this pretended demonstration. The interest of the King may be opposed to that of the people. But is it identical with that of the aristocracy? In the very page which contains this argument, intended to prove that the King and the aristocracy will coalesce against the people, Mr. Mill attempts to show that there is so strong an opposition of interest between the King and the aristocracy that if the powers of government are divided between them the one will inevitably usurp the power of the other. If so, he is not entitled to conclude that they will combine to destroy the power of the people merely because their interests may be at variance with those of the people. He is bound to show, not merely that in all communities the interest of a king must be opposed to that of the people, but also that, in all communities, it must be more directly opposed to the interest of the people than to the interest of the aristocracy. But he has not shown this. Therefore he has not proved his proposition on his own principles. To quote history would be a mere waste of time. Every schoolboy, whose studies have gone so far as the Abridgments of Goldsmith, can mention instances in which sovereigns have allied themselves with the people against the aristocracy, and in which the nobles have allied themselves with the people against the sovereign. In general, when there are three parties, every one of which has much to fear from the others, it is not found that two of them combine to plunder the third. If such a combination be formed, it scarcely ever effects its purpose. It soon becomes evident which member of the coalition is likely to be the greater gainer by the transaction. He becomes an object of jealousy to his ally, who, in all probability, changes sides, and compels him to restore what he has taken. Everybody knows how Henry VIII. trimmed between Francis and the Emperor Charles. But it is idle to cite examples of the operation of a principle which is illustrated in almost every page of history, ancient or modern, and to which almost every state in Europe has, at one time or another, been indebted for its independence.

Mr. Mill has now, as he conceives, demonstrated that the simple forms of government are bad, and that the mixed forms cannot possibly exist. There is still, however, it seems, a hope for mankind.

> "In the grand discovery of modern times, the system of representation, the solution of all the difficulties, both speculative and practical, will perhaps be found. If it cannot, we seem to be forced upon the extraordinary conclusion, that good government is impossible. For, as there is no individual or combination of individuals, except the community itself, who would not have an interest in bad government if intrusted with its powers, and as the community itself is incapable of exercising those powers, and must intrust them to certain individuals, the conclusion is obvious: the community itself must check those individuals; else they will follow their interest, and produce bad government. But how is it the community can check? The community can act only when assembled; and when assembled, it is incapable of acting. The community, however, can choose representatives."

The next question is — How must the representative body be constituted? Mr. Mill lays down two principles, about which, he says, "it is unlikely that there will be any dispute."

"First, The checking body must have a degree of power sufficient for the business of checking."

"Secondly, It must have an identity of interest with the community. Otherwise, it will make a mischievous use of its power."

The first of these propositions certainly admits of no dispute. As to the second, we shall hereafter take occasion to make some remarks on the sense in which Mr. Mill understands the words "interest of the community."

It does not appear very easy, on Mr. Mill's principles, to find out any mode of making the interest of the representative body identical with that of the constituent body. The plan proposed by Mr. Mill is simply that of very frequent election. "As it appears," says he, "that limiting the duration of their power is a security against the sinister interest of the people's representatives, so it appears that it is the only security of which the nature of the case admits." But all the arguments by which Mr. Mill has proved monarchy and aristocracy to be pernicious will, as it appears to us, equally prove this security to be no security at all. Is it not clear that the representatives, as soon as they are elected, are an aristocracy, with an interest opposed to the interest of the community? Why should they not pass a law for extending the term of their power from one year to ten years, or declare themselves senators for life? If the whole legislative power is given to them, they will be constitutionally competent to do this. If part of the legislative power is withheld from them, to whom is that part given? Is the people to retain it, and to express its assent or dissent in primary assemblies? Mr. Mill himself tells us that the community can only act when assembled, and that, when assembled, it is incapable of acting. Or is it to be provided, as in some of the American republics, that no change in the fundamental laws shall be made without the consent of a convention, specially elected for the purpose? Still the difficulty recurs: Why may not the members of the convention betray their trust, as well as the members of the ordinary legislature? When private men, they may have been zealous for the interests of the community. When candidates, they may have pledged themselves to the cause of the constitution. But, as soon as they are a convention, as soon as they are separated from the people, as soon as the supreme power is put into their hands, commences that interest opposite to the interest of the community which must, according to Mr. Mill, produce measures opposite to the interests of the community. We must find some other means, therefore, of checking this check upon a check; some other prop to carry the tortoise, that carries the elephant, that carries the world.

We know well that there is no real danger in such a case. But there is no danger only because there is no truth in Mr. Mill's principles. If men were what he represents them to be, the letter of the very constitution which he recommends would afford no safeguard against bad government. The real security is this, that legislators will be deterred by the fear of resistance and of infamy from acting in the manner which we have described. But restraints, exactly the same in kind, and differing only in degree, exist in all forms of government. That broad line of distinction which Mr. Mill tries to point out between monarchies and aristocracies on the one side, and democracies on the other, has in fact no existence. In no form of government is there an absolute identity of interest between the people and their rulers. In every form of government, the rulers stand in some awe of the people. The fear of resistance and the sense of shame operate, in a certain degree, on the most absolute kings and the most illiberal oligarchies. And nothing but the fear of resistance and the sense of shame preserves the freedom of the most democratic communities from the encroachments of their annual and biennial delegates.

We have seen how Mr. Mill proposes to render the interest of the representative body identical with that of the constituent body. The next question is, in what manner the interest of the constituent body is to be rendered identical with that of the community. Mr. Mill shows that a minority of the community, consisting even of many thousands, would be a bad constituent body, and, indeed, merely a numerous aristocracy.

"The benefits of the representative system," says he, "are lost, in all cases in which the interests of the choosing body are not the same with those of the community. It is very evident, that if the community itself were the choosing body, the interest of the community and that of the choosing body would be the same."

On these grounds Mr. Mill recommends that all males of mature age, rich and poor, educated and ignorant, shall have votes. But why not the women too? This question has often been asked in parliamentary debate, and has never, to our knowledge, received a plausible answer. Mr. Mill escapes from it as fast as he can. But we shall take the liberty to dwell a little on the words of the oracle. "One thing," says he, "is pretty clear, that all those individuals whose interests are involved in those of other individuals, may be struck off without inconvenience. . . . In this light women may be regarded, the interest of almost all of whom is involved either in that of their fathers, or in that of their husbands."

If we were to content ourselves with saying, in answer to all the arguments in Mr. Mill's essay, that the interest of a king is involved in that of the community, we should be accused, and justly, of talking nonsense. Yet such an assertion would not, as far as we can perceive, be more unreasonable than that which Mr. Mill has here ventured to make. Without adducing one fact, without taking the trouble to perplex the question by one sophism, he placidly dogmatises away the interest of one half of the human race. If there be a word of truth in history, women have always been, and still are, over the greater part of the globe, humble companions, playthings, captives, menials, beasts of burden. Except in a few happy and highly civilised communities, they are strictly in a state of personal slavery. Even in those countries where they are best treated, the laws are generally unfavourable to them, with respect to almost all the points in which they are most deeply interested.

Mr. Mill is not legislating for England or the United States; but for mankind. Is then the interest of a Turk the same with that of the girls who compose his harem? Is the interest of a Chinese the same with that of the woman whom he harnesses to his plough? Is the interest of an Italian the same with that of the daughter whom he devotes to God? The interest of a respectable Englishman may be said, without any impropriety, to be identical with that of his wife. But why is it so? Because human nature is *not* what Mr. Mill conceives it to be; because civilised men, pursuing their own happiness in a social state, are not Yahoos fighting for carrion; because there is a pleasure in being loved and esteemed, as well as in being feared and servilely obeyed. Why does not a gentleman restrict his wife to the bare maintenance which the law would compel him to allow her, that he may have more to spend on his personal pleasures? Because, if he loves her, he has pleasure in seeing her pleased; and because, even if he dislikes her, he is unwilling that the whole neighbourhood should cry shame on his meanness and ill-nature. Why does not the legislature, altogether composed of males, pass a law to deprive women of all civil privileges whatever, and reduce them to the state of slaves? By passing such a law, they would gratify what Mr. Mill tells us is an inseparable part of human nature, the desire to possess unlimited power of inflicting pain upon others. That they do not pass such a law, though they have the power to pass it, and that no man in England wishes to see such a law passed, proves that the desire to possess unlimited power of inflicting pain is not inseparable from human nature.

If there be in this country an identity of interest between the two sexes, it cannot possibly arise from any thing but the pleasure of being loved, and of communicating happiness. For, that it does not spring from the mere instinct of sex, the treatment which women experience over the greater part of the world abundantly proves. And, if it be said that our laws of marriage have produced it, this only removes the argument a step further; for those laws have been made by males. Now, if the kind feelings of one half of the species be a sufficient security for the happiness of the other, why may not the kind feelings of a monarch or an aristocracy be sufficient at least to prevent them from grinding the people to the very utmost of their power?

If Mr. Mill will examine why it is that women are better treated in England than in Persia, he may perhaps find out, in the course of his inquiries, why it is that the Danes are better governed than the subjects of Caligula.

We now come to the most important practical question in the whole essay. Is it desirable that all males arrived at years of discretion should vote for representatives, or should a pecuniary qualification be required? Mr. Mill's opinion is, that the lower the qualification the better; and that the best system is that in which there is none at all.

"The qualification," says he, "must either be such as to embrace the majority of the population, or something less than the majority. Suppose, in the first place, that it embraces the majority, the question is, whether the majority would have an interest in oppressing those who, upon this supposition, would be deprived of political power? If we reduce the calculation to its elements, we shall see that the interest which they would have of this deplorable kind, though it would be something, would not be very great. Each man of the majority, if the majority were constituted the governing body, would have something less than the benefit of oppressing a single man. If the majority were twice as great as the minority, each man of the majority would only have one half the benefit of oppressing a single man. . . . Suppose, in the second place, that the qualification did not admit a body of electors so large as the majority, in that case taking again the calculation in its elements, we shall see that each man would have a benefit equal to that derived from the oppression of more than one man; and that, in proportion as the elective body constituted a smaller and smaller minority, the benefit of misrule to the elective body would be increased, and bad government would be insured."

The first remark which we have to make on this argument is, that, by Mr. Mill's own account, even a government in which every human being should vote would still be defective. For, under a system of universal suffrage, the majority of the electors return the representative, and the majority of the representatives make the law. The whole people may vote, therefore; but only the majority govern. So that, by Mr. Mill's own confession, the most perfect system of government conceivable is one in which the interest of the ruling body to oppress, though not great, is something.

But is Mr. Mill in the right when he says that such an interest could not be very great? We think not. If, indeed, every man in the community possessed an equal share of what Mr. Mill calls the objects of desire, the majority would probably abstain from plundering the minority. A large minority would offer a vigorous resistance; and the property of a small minority would not repay the other members of the community for the trouble of dividing it. But it happens that in all civilised communities there is a small minority of rich men, and a great majority of poor men. If there were a thousand men with ten pounds apiece, it would not be worth while for nine hundred and ninety of them to rob ten, and it would be a bold attempt for six hundred of them to rob four hundred. But, if ten of them had a hundred thousand pounds apiece, the case would be very different. There would then be much to be got, and nothing to be feared.

"That one human being will desire to render the person and property of another subservient to his pleasures, notwithstanding the pain or loss of pleasure which it may occasion to that other individual, is," according to Mr. Mill, "the foundation of government." That the property of the rich minority can be made subservient to the pleasures of the poor majority will scarcely be denied. But Mr. Mill proposes to give the poor majority power over the rich minority. Is it possible to doubt to what, on his own principles such an arrangement must lead?

It may perhaps be said that, in the long run, it is for the interest of the people that property should be secure, and that therefore they will respect it. We answer thus: — It cannot be pretended that it is not for the immediate interest of the people to plunder the rich. Therefore, even if it were quite certain that, in the long run, the people would, as a body, lose by doing so, it would not necessarily follow that the fear of remote ill consequences would overcome the desire of immediate acquisitions. Every individual might flatter himself that the punishment would not fall on him. Mr. Mill himself tells us, in his Essay on Jurisprudence, that no quantity of evil which is remote and uncertain will suffice to prevent crime.

But we are rather inclined to think that it would, on the whole, be for the interest of the majority to plunder the rich. If so, the Utilitarians will say, that the rich *ought* to be plundered. We deny the inference. For, in the first place, if the object of government be the greatest happiness of the greatest number, the intensity of the suffering which a measure inflicts must be taken into consideration, as well as the number of the sufferers. In the next place, we have to notice one most important distinction which Mr. Mill has altogether overlooked. Throughout his essay, he confounds the community with the species. He talks of the greatest happiness of the greatest number: but, when we examine his reasonings, we find that he thinks only of the greatest number of a single generation.

Therefore, even if we were to concede that all those arguments of which we have exposed the fallacy are unanswerable, we might still deny the conclusion at which the essayist arrives. Even if we were to grant that he had found out the form of government which is best for the majority of the people now living on the face of the earth, we might still without inconsistency maintain that form of government to be pernicious to mankind. It would still be incumbent on Mr. Mill to prove that the interest of every generation is identical with the interest of all succeeding generations. And how on his own principles he could do this we are at a loss to conceive.

The case, indeed, is strictly analogous to that of an aristocratic government. In an aristocracy, says Mr. Mill, the few, being invested with the powers of government, can take the objects of their desires from the people. In the same manner, every generation in turn can gratify itself at the expense of posterity, — priority of time, in the latter case, giving an advantage exactly corresponding to that which superiority of station gives in the former. That an aristocracy will abuse its advantage, is, according to Mr. Mill, matter of demonstration. Is it not equally certain that the whole people will do the same; that, if they have the power, they will commit waste of every sort on the estate of mankind, and transmit it to posterity impoverished and desolated?

How is it possible for any person who holds the doctrines of Mr. Mill to doubt that the rich, in a democracy such as that which he recommends, would be pillaged as unmercifully as under a Turkish Pacha? It is no doubt for the interest of the next generation, and it may be for the remote interest of the present generation, that property should be held sacred. And so no doubt it will be for the interest of the next Pacha, and even for that of the present Pacha, if he should hold office long, that the inhabitants of his Pachalik should be encouraged to accumulate wealth. Scarcely any despotic sovereign has plundered his subjects to a large extent without having reason before the end of his reign to regret it. Every body knows how bitterly Louis the Fourteenth, towards the close of his life, lamented his former extravagance. If that magnificent prince had not expended millions on Marli and Versailles, and tens of millions on the aggrandisement of his grandson, he would not have been compelled at last to pay servile court to low-born money-lenders, to humble himself before men on whom, in the days of his pride, he would not have vouchsafed to look, for the means of supporting even his own household. Examples to the same effect might easily be multiplied. But despots, we see, do plunder their subjects, though history and experience tell them that, by prematurely exacting the means of profusion, they are in fact devouring the seed-corn from which the future harvest of revenue is to spring. Why then should we suppose that the people will be deterred from procuring immediate relief and enjoyment by the fear of distant calamities, of calamities which perhaps may not be fully felt till the times of their grand-children?

These conclusions are strictly drawn from Mr. Mill's own principles: and, unlike most of the conclusions which he has himself drawn from those principles, they are not, as far as we know, contradicted by facts. The case of the United States is not in point. In a country where the necessaries of life are cheap and the wages of labour high, where a man who has no capital but his legs and arms may expect to become rich by industry and frugality, it is not very decidedly even for the immediate advantage of the poor to plunder the rich; and the punishment of doing so would very speedily follow the offence. But in countries in which the great majority live from hand to mouth, and in which vast masses of wealth have been accumulated by a comparatively small number, the case is widely different. The immediate want is, at particular seasons, craving, imperious, irresistible. In our own time it has steeled men to the fear of the gallows, and urged them on the point of the bayonet. And, if these men had at their command that gallows and those bayonets which now scarcely restrain them, what is to be expected? Nor is this state of things one which can exist only under a bad government. If there be the least truth in the doctrines of the school to which Mr. Mill belongs, the increase of population will necessarily produce it everywhere. The increase of population is accelerated by good and cheap government. Therefore, the better the government, the greater is the inequality of conditions: and the greater the inequality of conditions, the stronger are the motives which impel the populace to spoliation. As for America, we appeal to the twentieth century.

It is scarcely necessary to discuss the effects which a general spoliation of the rich would produce. It may indeed happen that, where a legal and political system full of abuses is inseparably bound up with the institution of property, a nation may gain by a single convulsion, in which both perish together. The price is fearful. But, if, when the shock is over, a new order of things should arise under which property may enjoy security, the industry of individuals will soon repair the devastation. Thus we entertain no doubt that the Revolution was, on the whole, a most salutary event for France. But would France have gained if, ever since the year 1793, she had been governed by a democratic convention? If Mr. Mill's principles be sound, we say that almost her whole capital would by this time have been annihilated. As soon as the first explosion was beginning to be forgotten, as soon as wealth again began to germinate, as soon as the poor again began to compare their cottages and salads with the hotels and banquets of the rich, there would have been another scramble for property, another maximum, another general confiscation, another reign of terror. Four or five such convulsions following each other, at intervals of ten or twelve years, would reduce the most flourishing countries of Europe to the state of Barbary or the Morea.

The civilised part of the world has now nothing to fear from the hostility of savage nations. Once the deluge of barbarism has passed over it, to destroy and to fertilise; and in the present state of mankind we enjoy a full security against that calamity. That flood will no more return to cover the earth. But is it possible that in the bosom of civilisation itself may be engendered the malady which shall destroy it? Is it possible that institutions may be established which, without the help of earthquake, of famine, of pestilence, or of the foreign sword, may undo the work of so many ages of wisdom and glory, and gradually sweep away taste, literature, science, commerce, manufactures, everything but the rude arts necessary to the support of animal life? Is it possible that, in two or three hundred years, a few lean and half-naked fishermen may divide with owls and foxes the ruins of the greatest European cities — may wash their nets amidst the relics of her gigantic docks, and build their huts out of the capitals of her stately cathedrals? If the principles of Mr. Mill be sound, we say, without hesitation, that the form of government which he recommends will assuredly produce all this. But, if these principles be unsound, if the reasonings by which we have opposed them be just, the higher and middling orders are the natural representatives of the human race. Their interest may be opposed in some things to that of their poorer contemporaries; but it is identical with that of the innumerable generations which are to follow.

Mr. Mill concludes his essay, by answering an objection often made to the project of universal suffrage — that the people do not understand their own interests. We shall not go through his arguments on this subject, because, till he has proved that it is for the interest of the people to respect property, he only makes matters worse by proving that they understand their interests. But we cannot refrain from treating our readers with a delicious *bonne bouche* of wisdom, which he has kept for the last moment.

"The opinions of that class of the people who are below the middle rank are formed, and their minds are directed, by that intelligent, that virtuous rank, who come the most immediately in contact with them, who are in the constant habit of intimate communication with them, to whom they fly for advice and assistance in all their numerous difficulties, upon whom they feel an immediate and daily dependence in health and in sickness, in infancy and in old age, to whom their children look up as models for their imitation, whose opinions they hear daily repeated, and account it their honour to adopt. There can be no doubt that the middle rank, which gives to science, to art, and to legislation itself their most distinguished ornaments, and is the chief source of all that has exalted and refined human nature, is that portion of the community, of which, if the basis of representation were ever so far extended, the opinion would ultimately decide. Of the people beneath them, a vast majority would be sure to be guided by their advice and example."

This single paragraph is sufficient to upset Mr. Mill's theory. Will the people act against their own interest? Or will the middle rank act against its own interest? Or is the interest of the middle rank identical with the interest of the people? If the people act according to the directions of the middle rank, as Mr. Mill says that they assuredly will, one of these three questions must be answered in the affirmative. But, if any one of the three be answered in the affirmative, his whole system falls to the ground. If the interest of the middle rank be identical with that of the people, why should not the powers of government be intrusted to that rank? If the powers of government were intrusted to that rank, there would evidently be an aristocracy of wealth; and "to constitute an aristocracy of wealth, though it were a very numerous one, would," according to Mr. Mill, "leave the community without protection, and exposed to all the evils of unbridled power." Will not the same motives which induce the middle classes to abuse one kind of power induce them to abuse another? If their interest be the same with that of the people they will govern the people well. If it be opposite to that of the people they will advise the people ill. The system of universal suffrage, therefore, according to Mr. Mill's own account, is only a device for doing circuitously what a representative system, with a pretty high qualification, would do directly.

So ends this celebrated Essay. And such is this philosophy for which the experience of three thousand years is to be discarded; this philosophy, the professors of which speak as if it had guided the world to the knowledge of navigation and alphabetical writing; as if, before its dawn, the inhabitants of Europe had lived in caverns and eaten each other! We are sick, it seems, like the children of Israel, of the objects of our old and legitimate worship. We pine for a new idolatry. All that is costly and all that is ornamental in our intellectual treasures must be delivered up, and cast into the furnace — and there comes out this Calf!

Our readers can scarcely mistake our object in writing this article. They will not suspect us of any disposition to advocate the cause of absolute monarchy, or of any narrow form of oligarchy, or to exaggerate the evils of popular government. Our object at present is, not so much to attack or defend any particular system of polity, as to expose the vices of a kind of reasoning utterly unfit for moral and political discussions; of a kind of reasoning which may so readily be turned to purposes of falsehood that it ought to receive no quarter, even when by accident it may be employed on the side of truth.

Our objection to the essay of Mr. Mill is fundamental. We believe that it is utterly impossible to deduce the science of government from the principles of human nature.

What proposition is there respecting human nature which is absolutely and universally true? We know of only one: and that is not only true, but identical; that men always act from self-interest. This truism the Utilitarians proclaim with as much pride as if it were new, and as much zeal as if it were important. But in fact, when explained, it means only that men, if they can, will do as they choose. When we see the actions of a man we know with certainty what he thinks his interest to be. But it is impossible to reason with certainty from what *we* take to be his interest to his actions. One man goes without a dinner that he may add a shilling to a hundred thousand pounds: another runs in debt to give balls and masquerades. One man cuts his father's throat to get possession of his old clothes: another hazards his own life to save that of an enemy. One man volunteers on a forlorn hope: another is drummed out of a regiment for cowardice. Each of these men has, no doubt, acted from self-interest. But we gain nothing by knowing this, except the pleasure, if it be one, of multiplying useless words. In fact, this principle is just as recondite and just as important as the great truth that whatever is, is. If a philosopher were always to state facts in the following form — "There is a shower: but whatever is, is; therefore, there is a shower," — his reasoning would be perfectly sound; but we do not apprehend that it would materially enlarge the circle of human knowledge. And it is equally idle to attribute any importance to a proposition which, when interpreted, means only that a man had rather do what he had rather do.

If the doctrine, that men always act from self-interest, be laid down in any other sense than this — if the meaning of the word self-interest be narrowed so as to exclude any one of the motives which may by possibility act on any human being, — the proposition ceases to be identical; but at the same time it ceases to be true.

What we have said of the word "self-interest" applies to all the synonymes and circumlocutions which are employed to convey the same meaning; pain and pleasure, happiness and misery, objects of desire, and so forth.

The whole art of Mr. Mill's essay consists in one simple trick of legerdemain. It consists in using words of the sort which we have been describing first in one sense and then in another. Men will take the objects of their desire if they can. Unquestionably: — but this is an identical proposition: for an object of desire means merely a thing which a man will procure if he can. Nothing can possibly be inferred from a maxim of this kind. When we see a man take something we shall know that it was an object of his desire. But till then we have no means of judging with certainty what he desires or what he will take. The general proposition, however, having been admitted, Mr. Mill proceeds to reason as if men had no desires but those which can be gratified only by spoliation and oppression. It then becomes easy to deduce doctrines of vast importance from the original axiom. The only misfortune is, that by thus narrowing the meaning of the word desire the axiom becomes false, and all the doctrines consequent upon it are false likewise.

When we pass beyond those maxims which it is impossible to deny without a contradiction in terms, and which, therefore, do not enable us to advance a single step in practical knowledge, we do not believe that it is possible to lay down a single general rule respecting the motives which influence human actions. There is nothing which may not, by association or by comparison, become an object either of desire or of aversion. The fear of death is generally considered as one of the strongest of our feelings. It is the most formidable sanction which legislators have been able to devise. Yet it is notorious that, as Lord Bacon has observed, there is no passion by which that fear has not been often overcome. Physical pain is indisputably an evil;

yet it has been often endured, and even welcomed. Innumerable martyrs have exulted in torments which made the spectators shudder; and, to use a more homely illustration, there are few wives who do not long to be mothers.

Is the love of approbation a stronger motive than the love of wealth? It is impossible to answer this question generally even in the case of an individual with whom we are very intimate. We often say, indeed, that a man loves fame more than money or money more than fame. But this is said in a loose and popular sense; for there is scarcely a man who would not endure a few sneers for a great sum of money, if he were in pecuniary distress; and scarcely a man, on the other hand, who, if he were in flourishing circumstances, would expose himself to the hatred and contempt of the public for a trifle. In order, therefore, to return a precise answer even about a single human being, we must know what is the amount of the sacrifice of reputation demanded and of the pecuniary advantage offered, and in what situation the person to whom the temptation is proposed stands at the time. But, when the question is propounded generally about the whole species, the impossibility of answering is still more evident. Man differs from man; generation from generation; nation from nation. Education, station, sex, age, accidental associations, produce infinite shades of variety.

Now, the only mode in which we can conceive it possible to deduce a theory of government from the principles of human nature is this. We must find out what are the motives which, in a particular form of government, impel rulers to bad measures, and what are those which impel them to good measures. We must then compare the effect of the two classes of motives; and, according as we find the one or the other to prevail, we must pronounce the form of government in question good or bad.

Now let it be supposed that, in aristocratical and monarchical states, the desire of wealth and other desires of the same class always tend to produce misgovernment, and that the love of approbation and other kindred feelings always tend to produce good government. Then, if it be impossible, as we have shown that it is, to pronounce generally which of the two classes of motives is the more influential, it is impossible to find out, *a priori*, whether a monarchical or aristocratical form of government be good or bad.

Mr. Mill has avoided the difficulty of making the comparison, by very coolly putting all the weights into one of the scales, — by reasoning as if no human being had ever sympathised with the feelings, been gratified by the thanks, or been galled by the execrations, of another.

The case, as we have put it, is decisive against Mr. Mill; and yet we have put it in a manner far too favourable to him. For, in fact, it is impossible to lay it down as a general rule that the love of wealth in a sovereign always produces misgovernment, or the love of approbation good government. A patient and far-sighted ruler, for example, who is less desirous of raising a great sum immediately than of securing an unencumbered and progressive revenue, will, by taking off restraints from trade and giving perfect security to property, encourage accumulation and entice capital from foreign countries. The commercial policy of Prussia, which is perhaps superior to that of any country in the world, and which puts to shame the absurdities of our republican brethren on the other side of the Atlantic, has probably sprung from the desire of an absolute ruler to enrich himself. On the other hand, when the popular estimate of virtues and vices is erroneous, which is too often the case, the love of approbation leads sovereigns to spend the wealth of the nation on useless shows, or to engage in wanton and destructive wars. If then we can neither compare the strength of two motives, nor determine with certainty to what description of actions either motive will lead, how can we possibly deduce a theory of government from the nature of man?

How, then, are we to arrive at just conclusions on a subject so important to the happiness of mankind? Surely by that method which, in every experimental science to which it has been applied, has signally increased the power and knowledge of our species, — by that method for which our new philosophers would substitute quibbles scarcely worthy of the barbarous respondents and opponents of the middle ages, — by the method of Induction; — by observing the present state of the world, — by assiduously studying the history of past ages, — by sifting the evidence of facts, — by carefully combining and contrasting those which are authentic, — by generalising with judgment and diffidence, — by perpetually bringing the theory which we have constructed to the test of new facts, — by correcting, or altogether abandoning it, according as those new facts prove it to be partially or fundamentally unsound. Proceeding thus, — patiently, — diligently, — candidly, — we may hope to form a system as far inferior in pretension to that which we have been examining and as far superior to it in real utility as the prescriptions of a great physician, varying with every stage of every malady and with the constitution of every patient, to the pill of the advertising quack which is to cure all human beings, in all climates, of all diseases.

This is that noble Science of Politics, which is equally removed from the barren theories of the Utilitarian sophists, and from the petty craft, so often mistaken for statesmanship by minds grown narrow in habits of intrigue, jobbing, and official etiquette; — which of all sciences is the most important to the welfare of nations, — which of all sciences most tends to expand and invigorate the mind, — which draws nutriment and ornament from every part of philosophy and literature, and dispenses in return nutriment and ornament to all. We are sorry and surprised when we see men of good intentions and good natural abilities abandon this healthful and generous study to pore over speculations like those which we have been examining. And we should heartily rejoice to find that our remarks had induced any person of this description to employ, in researches of real utility, the talents and industry which are now wasted on verbal sophisms, wretched of their wretched kind.

As to the greater part of the sect, it is, we apprehend, of little consequence what they study or under whom. It would be more amusing, to be sure, and more reputable, if they would take up the old republican cant and declaim about Brutus and Timoleon, the duty of killing tyrants and the blessedness of dying for liberty. But, on the whole, they might have chosen worse. They may as well be Utilitarians as jockeys or dandies. And, though quibbling about self-interest and motives, and objects of desire, and the greatest happiness of the greatest number, is but a poor employment for a grown man, it certainly hurts the health less than hard drinking and the fortune less than high play; it is not much more laughable than phrenology, and is immeasurably more humane than cock-fighting.

WESTMINSTER REVIEWER'S DEFENCE OF MILL.[1]

(*Edinburgh Review*, June 1829.)

WE have had great reason, we think, to be gratified by the success of our late attack on the Utilitarians. We could publish a long list of the cures which it has wrought in cases previously considered as hopeless. Delicacy forbids us to divulge names; but we cannot refrain from alluding to two remarkable instances. A respectable lady writes to inform us that her son, who was plucked at Cambridge last January, has not been heard to call Sir James Mackintosh a poor ignorant fool more than twice since the appearance of our article. A distinguished political writer in the Westminster and Parliamentary Reviews has borrowed Hume's History, and has actually got as far as the battle of Agincourt. He assures us that he takes great pleasure in his new study, and that he is very impatient to learn how Scotland and England became one kingdom. But the greatest compliment that we have received is that Mr. Bentham himself should have condescended to take the field in defence of Mr. Mill. We have not been in the habit of reviewing reviews; but, as Mr. Bentham is a truly great man, and as his party have thought fit to announce in puffs and placards that this

1 *The Westminster Review. No. XXI. Article XVI. Edinburgh Review. No. XCVII. Article on Mill's Essays on Government, &c.*

article is written by him, and contains not only an answer to our attacks, but a development of the "greatest happiness principle," with the latest improvements of the author, we shall for once depart from our general rule. However the conflict may terminate, we shall at least not have been vanquished by an ignoble hand.

Of Mr. Bentham himself we shall endeavour, even while defending ourselves against his reproaches, to speak with the respect to which his venerable age, his genius, and his public services entitle him. If any harsh expression should escape us, we trust that he will attribute it to inadvertence, to the momentary warmth of controversy, — to anything, in short, rather than to a design of affronting him. Though we have nothing in common with the crew of Hurds and Boswells, who, either from interested motives, or from the habit of intellectual servility and dependence, pamper and vitiate his appetite with the noxious sweetness of their undiscerning praise, we are not perhaps less competent than they to appreciate his merit, or less sincerely disposed to acknowledge it. Though we may sometimes think his reasonings on moral and political questions feeble and sophistical — though we may sometimes smile at his extraordinary language — we can never be weary of admiring the amplitude of his comprehension, the keenness of his penetration, the exuberant fertility with which his mind pours forth arguments and illustrations. However sharply he may speak of us, we can never cease to revere in him the father of the philosophy of Jurisprudence. He has a full right to all the privileges of a great inventor; and, in our court of criticism, those privileges will never be pleaded in vain. But they are limited in the same manner in which, fortunately for the ends of justice, the privileges of the peerage are now limited. The advantage is personal and incommunicable. A nobleman can now no longer cover with his protection every lackey who follows his heels, or every bully who draws in his quarrel: and, highly as we respect the exalted rank which Mr. Bentham holds among the writers of our time, yet when, for the due maintenance of literary police, we shall think it necessary to confute sophists, or to bring pretenders to shame, we shall not depart from the ordinary course of our proceedings because the offenders call themselves Benthamites.

Whether Mr. Mill has much reason to thank Mr. Bentham for undertaking his defence, our readers, when they have finished this article, will perhaps be inclined to doubt. Great as Mr. Bentham's talents are, he has, we think, shown an undue confidence in them. He should have considered how dangerous it is for any man, however eloquent and ingenious he may be, to attack or defend a book without reading it: and we feel quite convinced that Mr. Bentham would never have written the article before us if he had, before he began, perused our review with attention, and compared it with Mr. Mill's Essay.

He has utterly mistaken our object and meaning. He seems to think that we have undertaken to set up some theory of government in opposition to that of Mr. Mill. But we distinctly disclaimed any such design. From the beginning to the end of our article, there is not, as far as we remember, a single sentence which, when fairly construed, can be considered as indicating any such design. If such an expression can be found, it has been dropped by inadvertence. Our object was to prove, not that monarchy and aristocracy are good, but that Mr. Mill had not proved them to be bad; not that democracy is bad, but that Mr. Mill had not proved it to be good. The points in issue are these: whether the famous Essay on Government be, as it has been called, a perfect solution of the great political problem, or a series of sophisms and blunders; and whether the sect which, while it glories in the precision of its logic, extols this Essay as a masterpiece of demonstration, be a sect deserving of the respect or of the derision of mankind. These, we say, are the issues; and on these we with full confidence put ourselves on the country.

It is not necessary, for the purposes of this investigation, that we should state what our political creed is, or whether we have any political creed at all. A man who cannot act the most trivial part in a farce has a right to hiss Romeo Coates: a man who does not know a vein from an artery may caution a simple neighbour against the advertisements of Dr. Eady. A complete theory of government would indeed be a noble present to mankind; but it is a present which we do not hope and do not pretend that we can offer. If, however, we cannot lay the foundation, it is something to clear away the rubbish; if we cannot set up truth, it is something to pull down error. Even if the subjects of which the Utilitarians treat were subjects of less fearful importance, we should think it no small service to the cause of good sense and good taste to point out the contrast between their magnificent pretensions and their miserable performances. Some of them have, however, thought fit to display their ingenuity on questions of the most momentous kind, and on questions concerning which men cannot reason ill with impunity. We think it, under these circumstances, an absolute duty to expose the fallacy of their arguments. It is no matter of pride or of pleasure. To read their works is the most soporific employment that we know; and a man ought no more to be proud of refuting them than of having two legs. We must now come to close quarters with Mr. Bentham, whom, we need not say, we do not mean to include in this observation. He charges us with maintaining,—

"First, 'That it is not true that all despots govern ill;'—whereon the world is in a mistake, and the Whigs have the true light. And for proof, principally,—that the King of Denmark is not Caligula. To which the answer is, that the King of Denmark is not a despot. He was put in his present situation by the people turning the scale in his favour in a balanced contest between himself and the nobility. And it is quite clear that the same power would turn the scale the other way the moment a King of Denmark should take into his head to be Caligula. It is of little consequence by what congeries of letters the Majesty of Denmark is typified in the royal press of Copenhagen, while the real fact is that the sword of the people is suspended over his head, in case of ill-behaviour, as effectually as in other countries where more noise is made upon the subject. Every body believes the sovereign of Denmark to be a good and virtuous gentleman; but there is no more superhuman merit in his being so than in the case of a rural squire who does not shoot his land-steward or quarter his wife with his yeomanry sabre.

"It is true that there are partial exceptions to the rule, that all men use power as badly as they dare. There may have been such things as amiable negro-drivers and sentimental masters of press-gangs; and here and there, among the odd freaks of human nature, there may have been specimens of men who were 'No tyrants, though bred up to tyranny.' But it would be as wise to recommend wolves for nurses at the Foundling on the credit of Romulus and Remus as to substitute the exception for the general fact, and advise mankind to take to trusting to arbitrary power on the credit of these specimens."

Now, in the first place, we never cited the case of Denmark to prove that all despots do not govern ill. We cited it to prove that Mr. Mill did not know how to reason. Mr. Mill gave it as a reason for deducing the theory of government from the general laws of human nature that the King of Denmark was not Caligula. This we said, and we still say, was absurd.

In the second place, it was not we, but Mr. Mill, who said that the King of Denmark was a despot. His words are these: — "The people of Denmark, tired out with the oppression of an aristocracy, resolved that their king should be absolute; and under their absolute monarch are as well governed as any people in Europe." We leave Mr. Bentham to settle with Mr. Mill the distinction between a despot and an absolute king.

In the third place, Mr. Bentham says that there was in Denmark a balanced contest between the king and the nobility. We find some difficulty in believing that Mr. Bentham seriously means to say this, when we consider that Mr. Mill has demonstrated the chance to be as infinity to one against the existence of such a balanced contest.

Fourthly, Mr. Bentham says that in this balanced contest the people turned the scale in favour of the king against the aristocracy. But Mr. Mill has demonstrated that it cannot possibly be for the interest of the monarchy and democracy to join against the aristocracy; and that, wherever the three parties exist, the king and the aristocracy will combine against the people. This, Mr. Mill assures us, is as certain as anything which depends upon human will.

Fifthly, Mr. Bentham says that, if the King of Denmark were to oppress his people, the people and nobles would combine against the king. But Mr. Mill has proved that it can never be for the interest of the aristocracy to combine with the democracy against the king. It is evidently Mr. Bentham's opinion, that "monarchy, aristocracy, and democracy may balance each other, and by mutual checks produce good government." But this is the very theory which Mr. Mill pronounces to be the wildest, the most visionary, the most chimerical ever broached on the subject of government.

We have no dispute on these heads with Mr. Bentham. On the contrary, we think his explanation true — or, at least, true in part; and we heartily thank him for lending us his assistance to demolish the essay of his follower. His wit and his sarcasm are sport to us; but they are death to his unhappy disciple.

Mr. Bentham seems to imagine that we have said something implying an opinion favourable to despotism. We can scarcely suppose that, as he has not condescended to read that portion of our work which he undertook to answer, he can have bestowed much attention on its general character. Had he done so he would, we think, scarcely have entertained such a suspicion. Mr. Mill asserts, and pretends to prove, that under no despotic government does any human being, except the tools of the sovereign, possess more than the necessaries of life, and that the most intense degree of terror is kept up by constant cruelty. This, we say, is untrue. It is not merely a rule to which there are exceptions: but it is not the rule. Despotism is bad; but it is scarcely anywhere so bad as Mr. Mill says that it is everywhere. This we are sure Mr. Bentham will allow. If a man were to say that five hundred thousand people die every year in London of dram-drinking, he would not assert a proposition more monstrously false than Mr. Mill's. Would it be just to charge us with defending intoxication because we might say that such a man was grossly in the wrong?

We say with Mr. Bentham that despotism is a bad thing. We say with Mr. Bentham that the exceptions do not destroy the authority of the rule. But this we say — that a single exception overthrows an argument which either does not prove the rule at all, or else proves the rule to be *true without exceptions;* and such an argument is Mr. Mill's argument against despotism. In this respect there is a great difference between rules drawn from experience and rules deduced *a priori.* We might believe that there had been a fall of snow last August, and yet not think it likely that there would be snow next August. A single occurrence opposed to our general experience would tell for very little in our calculation of the chances. But, if we could once satisfy ourselves that in *any* single right-angled triangle the square of the hypothenuse might be less than the squares of the sides, we must reject the forty-seventh proposition of Euclid altogether. We willingly adopt Mr. Bentham's lively illustration about the wolf; and we will say in passing that it gives us real pleasure to see how little old age has diminished the gaiety of this eminent man. We can assure him that his merriment gives us far more pleasure on his account than pain on our own. We say with him, Keep the wolf out of the nursery, in spite of the story of Romulus and Remus. But, if the shepherd who saw the wolf licking and suckling those famous twins were, after telling this story to his companions, to assert that it was an infallible rule that no wolf ever had spared, or ever would spare, any living thing which might fall in its way — that its nature was carnivorous — and that it could not possibly disobey its nature, we think that the hearers might have been excused for staring. It may be strange, but is not inconsistent, that a wolf which has eaten ninety-nine children should spare the hundredth. But the fact that a wolf has once spared a child is sufficient to show that there must be some flaw in the chain of reasoning purporting to prove that wolves cannot possibly spare children.

Mr. Bentham proceeds to attack another position which he conceives us to maintain: —

> "Secondly, That a government not under the control of the community (for there is no question upon any other) '*may soon be saturated.*' Tell it not in Bow-street, whisper it not in Hatton-garden — that there is a plan for preventing injustice by 'saturation.' With what peals of unearthly merriment would Minos, Æacus, and Rhadamanthus be aroused upon their benches, if the 'light wings of saffron and of blue' should bear this theory into their grim domains! Why do not the owners of pocket-handkerchiefs try to 'saturate?' Why does not the cheated publican beg leave to check the gulosity of his defrauder with a *repetatur haustus*, and the pummelled plaintiff neutralise the malice of his adversary, by requesting to have the rest of the beating in presence of the court, — if it is not that such conduct would run counter to all the conclusions of experience, and be the procreation of the mischief it affected to destroy? Woful is the man whose wealth depends on his having more than somebody else can be persuaded to take from Him; and woful also is the people that is in such a case!"

Now this is certainly very pleasant writing: but there is no great difficulty in answering the argument. The real reason which makes it absurd to think of preventing theft by pensioning off thieves is this, that there is no limit to the number of thieves. If there were only a hundred thieves in a place, and we were quite sure that no person not already addicted to theft would take to it, it might become a question whether to keep the thieves from dishonesty by raising them above distress would not be a better course than to employ officers against them. But the actual cases are not parallel. Every man who chooses can become a thief; but a man cannot become a king or a member of the aristocracy whenever he chooses. The number of the depredators is limited; and therefore the amount of depredation, so far as physical pleasures are concerned, must be limited also. Now, we made the remark which Mr. Bentham censures with reference to physical pleasures only. The pleasures of ostentation, of taste, of revenge, and other pleasures of the same description, have, we distinctly allowed, no limit. Our words are these: — "A king or an aristocracy may be supplied to satiety with *corporal pleasures*, at an expense which the rudest and poorest community would scarcely feel." Does Mr. Bentham deny this? If he does, we leave him to Mr. Mill. "What," says that philosopher, in his Essay on Education, "what are the ordinary pursuits of wealth and power, which kindle to such a height the ardour of mankind? Not the mere love of eating and of drinking, or all the physical objects together which wealth can purchase or power command. With these every man is in the long run speedily satisfied." What the difference is between being speedily satisfied and being soon saturated, we leave Mr. Bentham and Mr. Mill to settle together.

The word 'saturation,' however, seems to provoke Mr. Bentham's mirth. It certainly did not strike us as very pure English; but, as Mr. Mill used it, we supposed it to be good Benthamese. With the latter language we are not critically acquainted, though, as it has many roots in common with our mother tongue, we can contrive, by the help of a converted Utilitarian, who attends us in the capacity of Moonshee, to make out a little. But Mr. Bentham's authority is of course decisive; and we bow to it.

Mr. Bentham next represents us as maintaining: —

"Thirdly, That 'though there may be some tastes and propensities that have no point of saturation, there exists a sufficient check in the desire of the good opinion of others.' The misfortune of this argument is, that no man cares for the good opinion of those he has been accustomed to wrong. If oysters have opinions, it is probable they think very ill of those who eat them in August; but small is the effect upon the autumnal glutton that engulfs their gentle substances within his own. The planter and the slave-driver care just as much about negro opinion, as the epicure about the sentiments of oysters. M. Ude throwing live eels into the fire as a kindly method of divesting them of the unsavoury oil that lodges beneath their skins, is not more convinced of the immense aggregate of good which arises to the lordlier parts of the creation, than is the gentle peer who strips his fellow man of country and of family for a wild-fowl slain. The goodly land-owner, who lives by morsels squeezed indiscriminately from the waxy hands of the cobbler and the polluted ones of the nightman, is in no small degree the object of both hatred and contempt; but it is to be feared that he is a long way from feeling them to be intolerable. The principle of '*At mihi plaudo ipse domi, simul ac nummos contemplor in arcâ*,' is sufficient to make a wide interval between the opinions of the plaintiff and defendant in such cases. In short, to banish law and leave all plaintiffs to trust to the desire of reputation on the opposite side, would only be transporting the theory of the Whigs from the House of Commons to Westminster Hall."

Now, in the first place, we never maintained the proposition which Mr. Bentham puts into our mouths. We said, and say, that there is a *certain* check to the rapacity and cruelty of men, in their desire of the good opinion of others. We never said that it was sufficient. Let Mr. Mill show it to be insufficient. It is enough for us to prove that there is a set-off against the principle from which Mr. Mill deduces the whole theory of government. The balance may be, and, we believe, will be, against despotism and the narrower forms of aristocracy. But what is this to the correctness or incorrectness of Mr. Mill's accounts? The question is not, whether the motives which lead rulers to behave ill are stronger than those which lead them to behave well; — but, whether we ought to form a theory of government by looking *only* at the motives which lead rulers to behave ill and never noticing those which lead them to behave well.

Absolute rulers, says Mr. Bentham, do not care for the good opinion of their subjects; for no man cares for the good opinion of those whom he has been accustomed to wrong. By Mr. Bentham's leave, this is a plain begging of the question. The point at issue is this: — Will kings and nobles wrong the people? The argument in favour of kings and nobles is this: — they will not wrong the people, because they care for the good opinion of the people. But this argument Mr. Bentham meets thus: — they will not care for the good opinion of the people, because they are accustomed to wrong the people.

Here Mr. Mill differs, as usual, from Mr. Bentham. "The greatest princes," says he, in his Essay on Education, "the most despotical masters of human destiny, when asked what they aim at by their wars and conquests, would answer, if sincere, as Frederick of Prussia answered, *pour faire parler de soi*; — to occupy a large space in the admiration of mankind." Putting Mr. Mill's and Mr. Bentham's principles together, we might make out very easily that "the greatest princes, the most despotical masters of human destiny," would never abuse their power.

A man who has been long accustomed to injure people must also have been long accustomed to do without their love, and to endure their aversion. Such a man may not miss the pleasure of popularity; for men seldom miss a pleasure which they have long denied themselves. An old tyrant does without popularity just as an old water-drinker does without wine. But, though it is perfectly true that men who for the good of their health have long abstained from wine feel the want of it very little, it would be absurd to infer that men will always abstain from wine when their health requires that they should do so. And it would be equally absurd to say, because men who have been accustomed to oppress care little for popularity, that men will therefore necessarily prefer the pleasures of oppression to those of popularity.

Then, again, a man may be accustomed to wrong people in one point and not in another. He may care for their good opinion with regard to one point and not with regard to another. The Regent Orleans laughed at charges of impiety, libertinism, extravagance, idleness, disgraceful promotions. But the slightest allusion to the charge of poisoning threw him into convulsions. Louis the Fifteenth braved the hatred and contempt of his subjects during many years of the most odious and imbecile misgovernment. But, when a report was spread that he used human blood for his baths, he was almost driven mad by it. Surely Mr. Bentham's position "that no man cares for the good opinion of those whom he has been accustomed to wrong" would be objectionable, as far too sweeping and indiscriminate, even if it did not involve, as in the present case we have shown that it does, a direct begging of the question at issue.

Mr. Bentham proceeds: —

"Fourthly, The Edinburgh Reviewers are of opinion, that 'it might, with no small plausibility, be maintained, that in many countries, there are two classes which, in some degree, answer to this description;' [viz.] 'that the poor compose the class which government is established to restrain; and the people of some property the class to which the powers of government may without danger be confided.'

"They take great pains, it is true, to say this and not to say it. They shuffle and creep about, to secure a hole to escape at, if 'what they do not assert' should be found in any degree inconvenient. A man might waste his life in trying to find out whether the Misses of the *Edinburgh* mean to say Yes or No in their political coquetry. But whichever way the lovely spinsters may decide, it is diametrically opposed to history and the evidence of facts, that the poor *are* the class whom there is any difficulty in restraining. It is not the poor but the rich that have a propensity to take the property of other people. There is no instance upon earth of the poor having combined to take away the property of the rich; and all the instances habitually brought forward in support of it are gross misrepresentations, founded upon the most necessary acts of self-defence on the part of the most numerous classes. Such a misrepresentation is the common one of the Agrarian law; which was nothing but an attempt on the part of the Roman people to get back some part of what had been taken from them by undisguised robbery. Such another is the stock example of the French Revolution, appealed to by the *Edinburgh Review* in the actual case. It is utterly untrue that the French Revolution took place because 'the poor began to compare their cottages and salads with the hotels and banquets of the rich;' it took place because they were robbed of their cottages and salads to support the hotels and banquets of their oppressors. It is utterly untrue that there was either a scramble for property or a general confiscation; the classes who took part with the foreign invaders lost their property, as they would have done here, and ought to do everywhere. All these are the vulgar errors of the man on the lion's back, — which the lion will set to rights when he can tell his own story. History is nothing but the relation of the sufferings of the poor from the rich; except precisely so far as the numerous classes of the community have contrived to keep the virtual power in their hands, or in other words, to establish free governments. If a poor man injures the rich, the law is instantly at his heels; the injuries of the rich towards the poor are always inflicted *by* the law. And to enable the rich to do this to any extent that may be practicable or prudent, there is clearly one postulate required, which is, that the rich shall make the law."

This passage is alone sufficient to prove that Mr. Bentham has not taken the trouble to read our article from beginning to end. We are quite sure that he would not stoop to misrepresent it. And, if he had read it with any attention, he would have perceived that all this coquetry, this hesitation, this Yes and No, this saying and not saying, is simply an exercise of the undeniable right which in controversy belongs to the defensive side — to the side which proposes to establish nothing. The affirmative of the issue and the burden of the proof are with Mr. Mill, not with us. We are not bound, perhaps we are not able, to show that the form of government which he recommends is bad. It is quite enough if we can show that he does not prove it to be good. In his proof, among many other flaws, is this — He says, that if men are not inclined to plunder each other, government is unnecessary, and that, if men are so inclined, kings and aristocracies will plunder the people. Now this, we say, is a fallacy. That *some* men will plunder their neighbours if they can, is a sufficient reason for the existence of governments. But it is not demonstrated that kings and aristocracies will plunder the people, unless it be true that *all* men will plunder their neighbours if they can. Men are placed in very different situations. Some have all the bodily pleasures that they desire, and many other pleasures besides, without plundering anybody. Others can scarcely obtain their daily bread without plundering. It may be true, but surely it is not self-evident, that the former class is under as strong temptations to plunder as the latter. Mr. Mill was therefore bound to prove it. That he has not proved it is one of thirty or forty fatal errors in his argument. It is not necessary that we should express an opinion or even have an opinion on the subject. Perhaps we are in a state of perfect scepticism: but what then? Are we the theory-makers? When we bring before the world a theory of government, it will be time to call upon us to offer proof at every step. At present we stand on our undoubted logical right. We concede nothing; and we deny nothing. We say to the Utilitarian theorists: — When you prove your doctrine, we will believe it; and, till you prove it, we will not believe it.

Mr. Bentham has quite misunderstood what we said about the French Revolution. We never alluded to that event for the purpose of proving that the poor were inclined to rob the rich. Mr. Mill's principles of human nature furnished us with that part of our argument ready-made. We alluded to the French Revolution for the purpose of illustrating the effects which general spoliation produces on society, not for the purpose of showing that general spoliation will take place under a democracy. We allowed distinctly that, in the peculiar circumstances of the French monarchy, the Revolution, though accompanied by a great shock to the institution of property, was a blessing. Surely Mr. Bentham will not maintain that the injury produced by the deluge of assignats and by the maximum fell only on the emigrants, — or that there were not many emigrants who would have staid and lived peaceably under any government if their persons and property had been secure.

We never said that the French Revolution took place because the poor began to compare their cottages and salads with the hotels and banquets of the rich.

We were not speaking about *the causes* of the Revolution, or thinking about them. This we said, and say, that, if a democratic government had been established in France, the poor, when they began to compare their cottages and salads with the hotels and banquets of the rich, would, on the supposition that Mr. Mill's principles are sound, have plundered the rich, and repeated without provocation all the severities and confiscations which, at the time of the Revolution, were committed with provocation. We say that Mr. Mill's favourite form of government would, if his own views of human nature be just, make those violent convulsions and transfers of property which now rarely happen, except, as in the case of the French Revolution, when the people are maddened by oppression, events of annual or biennial occurrence. We gave no opinion of our own. We give none now. We say that this proposition may be proved from Mr. Mill's own premises, by steps strictly analogous to those by which he proves monarchy and aristocracy to be bad forms of government. To say this, is not to say that the proposition is true. For we hold both Mr. Mill's premises and his deduction to be unsound throughout.

Mr. Bentham challenges us to prove from history that the people will plunder the rich. What does history say to Mr. Mill's doctrine, that absolute kings will always plunder their subjects so unmercifully as to leave nothing but a bare subsistence to any except their own creatures? If experience is to be the test, Mr. Mill's theory is unsound. If Mr. Mill's reasoning *a priori* be sound, the people in a democracy will plunder the rich. Let us use one weight and one measure. Let us not throw history aside when we are proving a theory, and take it up again when we have to refute an objection founded on the principles of that theory.

We have not done, however, with Mr. Bentham's charges against us.

"Among other specimens of their ingenuity, they think they embarrass the subject by asking why, on the principles in question, women should not have votes as well as men. *And why not?*

'Gentle shepherd, tell me why. —'

If the mode of election was what it ought to be, there would be no more difficulty in women voting for a representative in Parliament than for a director at the India House. The world will find out at some time that the readiest way to secure justice on some points is to be just on all: — that the whole is easier to accomplish than the part; and that, whenever the camel is driven through the eye of the needle, it would be simple folly and debility that would leave a hoof behind."

Why, says or sings Mr. Bentham, should not women vote? It may seem uncivil in us to turn a deaf ear to his Arcadian warblings. But we submit, with great deference, that it is not *our* business to tell him why. We fully agree with him that the principle of female suffrage is not so palpably absurd that a chain of reasoning ought to be pronounced unsound merely because it leads to female suffrage. We say that every argument which tells in favour of the universal suffrage of the males tells equally in favour of female suffrage. Mr. Mill, however, wishes to see all men vote, but says that it is unnecessary that women should vote; and for making this distinction *he* gives as a reason an assertion which, in the first place, is not true, and which, in the next place, would, if true, overset his whole theory of human nature; namely, that the interest of the women is identical with that of the men. We side with Mr. Bentham, so far at least as this: that, when we join to drive the camel through the needle, he shall go through hoof and all. We at present desire to be excused from driving the camel. It is Mr. Mill who leaves the hoof behind. But we should think it uncourteous to reproach him in the language which Mr. Bentham, in the exercise of his paternal authority over the sect, thinks himself entitled to employ.

> "Another of their perverted ingenuities is, that 'they are rather inclined to think,' that it would, on the whole, be for the interest of the majority to plunder the rich; and if so, the Utilitarians will say that the rich *ought* to be plundered. On which it is sufficient to reply, that for the majority to plunder the rich would amount to a declaration that nobody should be rich; which, as all men wish to be rich, would involve a suicide of hope. And as nobody has shown a fragment of reason why such a proceeding should be for the general happiness, it does not follow that the 'Utilitarians' would recommend it. The Edinburgh Reviewers have a waiting gentlewoman's ideas of 'Utilitarianism.' It is unsupported by anything but the pitiable 'We are rather inclined to think'—and is utterly contradicted by the whole course of history and human experience besides,—that there is either danger or possibility of such a consummation as the majority agreeing on the plunder of the rich. There have been instances in human memory, of their agreeing to plunder rich oppressors, rich traitors, rich enemies,—but the rich *simpliciter* never. It is as true now as in the days of Harrington, that 'a people never will, nor ever can, never did, nor ever shall, take up arms for levelling.' All the commotions in the world have been for something else; and 'levelling' is brought forward as the blind to conceal what the other was."

We say, again and again, that we are on the defensive. We do not think it necessary to prove that a quack medicine is poison. Let the vendor prove it to be sanative. We do not pretend to show that universal suffrage is an evil. Let its advocates show it to be a good. Mr. Mill tells us that, if power be given for short terms to representatives elected by all the males of mature age, it will then be for the interest of those representatives to promote the greatest happiness of the greatest number. To prove this, it is necessary that he should prove three propositions: first, that the interest of such a representative body will be identical with the interest of the constituent body; secondly, that the interest of the constituent body will be identical with that of the community; thirdly, that the interest of one generation of a community is identical with that of all succeeding generations. The two first propositions Mr. Mill attempts to prove, and fails. The last he does not even attempt to prove. We therefore refuse our assent to his conclusions. Is this unreasonable?

We never even dreamed, what Mr. Bentham conceives us to have maintained, that it could be for the greatest happiness of *mankind* to plunder the rich. But we are "rather inclined to think," though doubtingly and with a disposition to yield to conviction, that it may be for the pecuniary interest of the majority of a single generation in a thickly-peopled country to plunder the rich. Why we are inclined to think so we will explain, whenever we send a theory of government to an Encyclopædia. At present we are bound to say only that we think so, and shall think so till somebody shows us a reason for thinking otherwise.

Mr. Bentham's answer to us is simple assertion. He must not think that we mean any discourtesy by meeting it with a simple denial. The fact is, that almost all the governments that have ever existed in the civilised world have been, in part at least, monarchical and aristocratical. The first government constituted on principles approaching to those which the Utilitarians hold was, we think, that of the United States. That the poor have never combined to plunder the rich in the governments of the old world, no more proves that they might not combine to plunder the rich under a system of universal suffrage, than the fact that the English kings of the House of Brunswick have not been Neros and Domitians proves that sovereigns may safely be intrusted with absolute power. Of what the people would do in a state of perfect sovereignty we can judge only by indications, which, though rarely of much moment in themselves, and though always suppressed with little difficulty, are yet of great significance, and resemble those by which our domestic animals sometimes remind us that they are of kin with the fiercest monsters of the forest. It would not be wise to reason from the behaviour of a dog crouching under the lash, which is the case of the Italian people, or from the behaviour of a dog pampered with the best morsels of a plentiful kitchen, which is the case of the people of America, to the behaviour of a wolf, which is nothing but a dog run wild, after a week's fast among the snows of the Pyrenees. No commotion, says Mr. Bentham, was ever really produced by the wish of levelling: the wish has been put forward as a blind; but something else has been the real object. Grant all this. But why has levelling been put forward as a blind in times of commotion to conceal the real objects of the agitators? Is it with declarations which involve "a suicide of hope" that men attempt to allure others? Was famine, pestilence, slavery, ever held out to attract the people? If levelling has been made a pretence for disturbances, the argument against Mr. Bentham's doctrine is as strong as if it had been the real object of disturbances.

But the great objection which Mr. Bentham makes to our review, still remains to be noticed: —

"The pith of the charge against the author of the Essays is, that he has written 'an elaborate Treatise on Government,' and 'deduced the whole science from the assumption of certain propensities of human nature.' Now, in the name of Sir Richard Birnie and all saints, from what else *should* it be deduced? What did ever anybody imagine to be the end, object, and design of government *as it ought to be* but the same operation, on an extended scale, which that meritorious chief magistrate conducts on a limited one at Bow-street; to wit, the preventing one man from injuring another? Imagine, then, that the Whiggery of Bow-street were to rise up against the proposition that their science was to be deduced from 'certain propensities of human nature,' and thereon were to ratiocinate as follows:—

"'How then are we to arrive at just conclusions on a subject so important to the happiness of mankind? Surely by that method, which, in every experimental science to which it has been applied, has signally increased the power and knowledge of our species,—by that method for which our new philosophers would substitute quibbles scarcely worthy of the barbarous respondents and opponents of the middle ages,—by the method of induction,—by observing the present state of the world,—by assiduously studying the history of past ages,—by sifting the evidence of facts,—by carefully combining and contrasting those which are authentic,—by generalising with judgment and diffidence,—by perpetually bringing the theory which we have constructed to the test of new facts,—by correcting, or altogether abandoning it, according as those new facts prove it to be partially or fundamentally unsound. Proceeding thus,—patiently, diligently, candidly, we may hope to form a system as far inferior in pretension to that which we have been examining, and as far superior to it in real utility, as the prescriptions of a great physician, varying with every stage of every malady, and with the constitution of every patient, to the pill of the advertising quack, which is to cure all human beings, in all climates, of all diseases.'"

"Fancy now,—only fancy,—the delivery of these wise words at Bow-street; and think how speedily the practical catchpolls would reply, that all this might be very fine, but as far as they had studied history, the naked story was, after all, that numbers of men had a propensity to thieving, and their business was to catch them; that they, too, had been sifters of facts; and, to say the truth, their simple opinion was, that their brethren of the red waistcoat — though they should be sorry to think ill of any man — had somehow contracted a leaning to the other side, and were more bent on puzzling the case for the benefit of the defendants, than on doing the duty of good officers and true. Such would, beyond all doubt, be the sentence passed on such trimmers in the microcosm of Bow-street. It might not absolutely follow that they were in a plot to rob the goldsmiths' shops, or to set fire to the House of Commons; but it would be quite clear that they had got *a feeling*, — that they were in process of siding with the thieves, — and that it was not to them that any man must look who was anxious that pantries should be safe."

This is all very witty; but it does not touch us. On the present occasion, we cannot but flatter ourselves that we bear a much greater resemblance to a practical catchpoll than either Mr. Mill or Mr. Bentham. It would, to be sure, be very absurd in a magistrate, discussing the arrangements of a police-office, to spout in the style either of our article or Mr. Bentham's; but, in substance, he would proceed, if he were a man of sense, exactly as *we* recommend. He would, on being appointed to provide for the security of property in a town, study attentively the state of the town. He would learn at what places, at what times, and under what circumstances, theft and outrage were most frequent. Are the streets, he would ask, most infested with thieves at sunset or at midnight? Are there any public places of resort which give peculiar facilities to pickpockets? Are there any districts completely inhabited by a lawless population? Which are the flash-houses, and which the shops of receivers? Having made himself master of the facts he would act accordingly. A strong detachment of officers might be necessary for Petticoat Lane; another for the pit entrance of Covent Garden Theatre. Grosvenor Square and Hamilton Place would require little or no protection.

Exactly thus should we reason about government. Lombardy is oppressed by tyrants; and constitutional checks, such as may produce security to the people, are required. It is, so to speak, one of the resorts of thieves; and there is great need of police-officers. Denmark resembles one of those respectable streets in which it is scarcely necessary to station a catchpoll, because the inhabitants would at once join to seize a thief. Yet, even in such a street, we should wish to see an officer appear now and then, as his occasional superintendence would render the security more complete. And even Denmark, we think, would be better off under a constitutional form of government.

Mr. Mill proceeds like a director of police, who, without asking a single question about the state of his district, should give his orders thus: — "My maxim is, that every man will take what he can. Every man in London would be a thief, but for the thief-takers. This is an undeniable principle of human nature. Some of my predecessors have wasted their time in inquiring about particular pawnbrokers, and particular alehouses. Experience is altogether divided. Of people placed in exactly the same situation, I see that one steals, and that another would sooner burn his hand off. *Therefore* I trust to the laws of human nature alone, and pronounce all men thieves alike. Let every body, high and low, be watched. Let Townsend take particular care that the Duke of Wellington does not steal the silk handkerchief of the lord in waiting at the levee. A person has lost a watch. Go to Lord Fitzwilliam and search him for it; he is as great a receiver of stolen goods as Ikey Solomons himself. Don't tell me about his rank, and character, and fortune. He is a man; and a man does not change his nature when he is called a lord.[1] Either men will steal or they will not steal. If they will not, why do I sit here? If they will, his lordship must be a thief." The Whiggery of Bow Street would perhaps rise up against this wisdom. Would Mr. Bentham think that the Whiggery of Bow Street was in the wrong?

We blamed Mr. Mill for deducing his theory of government from the principles of human nature. "In the name of Sir Richard Birnie and all saints," cries Mr. Bentham, "from what else should it be deduced?" In spite of this solemn adjuration, we shall venture to answer Mr. Bentham's question by another. How does he arrive at those principles of human nature from which he proposes to deduce the science of government? We think that we may venture to put an answer into his mouth; for in truth there is but one possible answer. He will say — By experience. But what is the extent of this experience? Is it an experience which includes experience of the conduct of men intrusted with the powers of government; or is it exclusive of that experience? If it includes experience of the manner in which men act when intrusted with the powers of government, then those principles of human nature from which the science of government is to be deduced can only be known after going through that inductive process by which we propose to arrive at the science of government. Our knowledge of human nature, instead of being prior in order to our knowl-

1 "If Government is founded upon this, as a law of human nature, that a man, if able, will take from others anything which they have and he desires, it is sufficiently evident that when a man is called a king, he does not change his nature: so that, when he has power to take what he pleases, he will take what he pleases. To suppose that he will not, is to affirm that government is unnecessary, and that human beings will abstain from injuring one another of their own accord. — MILL *on Government.*

edge of the science of government, will be posterior to it. And it would be correct to say, that by means of the science of government, and of other kindred sciences — the science of education, for example, which falls under exactly the same principle — we arrive at the science of human nature.

If, on the other hand, we are to deduce the theory of government from principles of human nature, in arriving at which principles we have not taken into the account the manner in which men act when invested with the powers of government, then those principles must be defective. They have not been formed by a sufficiently copious induction. We are reasoning, from what a man does in one situation, to what he will do in another. Sometimes we may be quite justified in reasoning thus. When we have no means of acquiring information about the particular case before us, we are compelled to resort to cases which bear some resemblance to it. But the most satisfactory course is to obtain information about the particular case; and, whenever this can be obtained, it ought to be obtained. When first the yellow fever broke out, a physician might be justified in treating it as he had been accustomed to treat those complaints which, on the whole, had the most symptoms in common with it. But what should we think of a physician who should now tell us that he deduced his treatment of yellow fever from the general theory of pathology? Surely we should ask him, Whether, in constructing his theory of pathology, he had or had not taken into the account the facts which had been ascertained respecting the yellow fever? If he had, then it would be more correct to say that he had arrived at the principles of pathology partly by his experience of cases of yellow fever than that he had deduced his treatment of yellow fever from the principles of pathology. If he had not, he should not prescribe for us. If we had the yellow fever, we should prefer a man who had never treated any cases but cases of yellow fever to a man who had walked the hospitals of London and Paris for years, but who knew nothing of our particular disease.

Let Lord Bacon speak for us: "Inductionem censemus eam esse demonstrandi formam, quæ sensum tuetur, et naturam premit, et operibus imminet, ac fere immiscetur. Itaque ordo quoque demonstrandi plane invertitur. Adhuc enim res ita geri consuevit, ut a sensu et particularibus primo loco ad maxime generalia advoletur, tanquam ad polos fixos, circa quos disputationes vertantur; ab illis cætera, per media, deriventur; viâ certe compendiariâ, sed præcipiti, et ad naturam imperviâ, ad disputationes proclivi et accommodatâ. At, secundum nos, axiomata continenter et gradatim excitantur, ut non, nisi postremo loco, ad maxime generalia veniatur." Can any words more exactly describe the political reasonings of Mr. Mill than those in which Lord Bacon thus describes the logomachies of the schoolmen? Mr. Mill springs at once to a general principle of the widest extent, and from that general principle deduces syllogistically every thing which is included in it. We say with Bacon — "non, nisi postremo loco, ad maxime generalia veniatur." In the present inquiry, the science of human nature is the "maxime generale." To this the Utilitarian rushes at once, and from this he deduces a hundred sciences. But the true philosopher, the inductive reasoner, travels up to it slowly, through those hundred sciences, of which the science of government is one.

As we have lying before us that incomparable volume, the noblest and most useful of all the works of the human reason, the Novum Organum, we will transcribe a few lines, in which the Utilitarian philosophy is portrayed to the life.

"Syllogismus ad *principia* scientiarum non adhibetur, ad media axiomata frustra adhibetur, cum sit subtilitati naturæ longe impar. Assensum itaque constringit, non res. Syllogismus ex propositionibus constat, propositiones ex verbis, verba notionum tesseræ sunt. Itaque si notiones ipsæ, id quod basis rei est, confusæ sint, et temerè a rebus abstractæ, nihil in iis quæ superstruuntur est firmitudinis. Itaque spes est una in Inductione vera. In notionibus nil sani est, nec in Logicis nec in physicis. Non substantia, non qualitas, agere, pati, ipsum esse, bonæ notiones sunt; multo minus grave, leve, densum, tenue, humidum, siccum, generatio, corruptio, attrahere, fugare, elementum, materia, forma, et id genus, sed omnes phantasticæ et male terminatæ."

Substitute for the "substantia," the "generatio," the "corruptio," the "elementum," the "materia" of the old schoolmen, Mr. Mill's pain, pleasure, interest, power, objects of desire, — and the words of Bacon will seem to suit the current year as well as the beginning of the seventeenth century.

We have now gone through the objections that Mr. Bentham makes to our article: and we submit ourselves on all the charges to the judgment of the public.

The rest of Mr. Bentham's article consists of an exposition of the Utilitarian principle, or, as he decrees that it shall be called, the "greatest happiness principle." He seems to think that we have been assailing it. We never said a syllable against it. We spoke slightingly of the Utilitarian sect, as we thought of them, and think of them; but it was not for holding this doctrine that we blamed them. In attacking them we no more meant to attack the "greatest happiness principle" than when we say that Mahometanism is a false religion we mean to deny the unity of God, which is the first article of the Mahometan creed; — no more than Mr. Bentham, when he sneers at the Whigs, means to blame them for denying the divine right of kings. We reasoned throughout our article on the supposition that the end of government was to produce the greatest happiness to mankind.

Mr. Bentham gives an account of the manner in which he arrived at the discovery of the "greatest happiness principle." He then proceeds to describe the effects which, as he conceives, that discovery is producing in language so rhetorical and ardent that, if it had been written by any other person, a genuine Utilitarian would certainly have thrown down the book in disgust.

"The only rivals of any note to the new principle which were brought forward, were those known by the names of the 'moral sense,' and the 'original contract.' The new principle superseded the first of these, by presenting it with a guide for its decisions; and the other, by making it unnecessary to resort to a remote and imaginary contract for what was clearly the business of every man and every hour. Throughout the whole horizon of morals and of politics, the consequences were glorious and vast. It might be said without danger of exaggeration, that they who sat in darkness had seen a great light. The mists in which mankind had jousted against each other were swept away, as when the sun of astronomical science arose in the full development of the principle of gravitation. If the object of legislation was the greatest happiness, *morality* was the promotion of the same end by the conduct of the individual; and by analogy, the happiness of the world was the morality of nations.

". . . . . . All the sublime obscurities, which had haunted the mind of man from the first formation of society, — the phantoms whose steps had been on earth, and their heads among the clouds, — marshalled themselves at the sound of this new principle of connection and of union, and stood a regulated band, where all was order, symmetry, and force. What men had struggled for and bled, while they saw it but as through a glass darkly, was made the object of substantial knowledge and lively apprehension. The bones of sages and of patriots stirred within their tombs, that what they dimly saw and followed had become the world's common heritage. And the great result was wrought by no supernatural means, nor produced by any unparallelable concatenation of events. It was foretold by no oracles, and ushered by no portents; but was brought about by the quiet and reiterated exercise of God's first gift of common sense."

Mr. Bentham's discovery does not, as we think we shall be able to show, approach in importance to that of gravitation, to which he compares it. At all events, Mr. Bentham seems to us to act much as Sir Isaac Newton would have done if he had gone about boasting that he was the first person who taught bricklayers not to jump off scaffolds and break their legs.

Does Mr. Bentham profess to hold out any new motive which may induce men to promote the happiness of the species to which they belong? Not at all. He distinctly admits that, if he is asked why government should attempt to produce the greatest possible happiness, he can give no answer.

"The real answer," says he, "appeared to be, that men at large *ought* not to allow a government to afflict them with more evil or less good than they can help. What *a government* ought to do is a mysterious and searching question, which those may answer who know what it means; but what other men ought to do is a question of no mystery at all. The word *ought*, if it means anything, must have reference to some kind of interest or motives; and what interest a government has in doing right, when it happens to be interested in doing wrong, is a question for the schoolmen. The fact appears to be, that *ought* is not predicable of governments. The question is not why governments are bound not to do this or that, but why *other men* should let them if they can help it. The point is not to determine why the lion should not eat sheep, but why men should not eat their own mutton if they can."

The principle of Mr. Bentham, if we understand it, is this, that mankind ought to act so as to produce their greatest happiness. The word *ought*, he tells us, has no meaning, unless it be used with reference to some interest. But the interest of a man is synonymous with his greatest happiness:—and therefore to say that a man ought to do a thing, is to say that it is for his greatest happiness to do it. And to say that mankind *ought* to act so as to produce their greatest happiness, is to say that the greatest happiness is the greatest happiness — and this is all!

Does Mr. Bentham's principle tend to make any man wish for anything for which he would not have wished, or do any thing which he would not have done, if the principle had never been heard of? If not, it is an utterly useless principle. Now, every man pursues his own happiness or interest — call it which you will. If his happiness coincides with the happiness of the species, then, whether he ever heard of the "greatest happiness principle" or not, he will, to the best of his knowledge and ability, attempt to produce the greatest happiness of the species. But, if what he thinks his happiness be inconsistent with the greatest happiness of mankind, will this new principle convert him to another frame of mind? Mr. Bentham himself allows, as we have seen, that he can give no reason why a man should promote the greatest happiness of others if their greatest happiness be inconsistent with what he thinks his own. We should very much like to know how the Utilitarian principle would run when reduced to one plain imperative proposition? Will it run thus — pursue your own happiness? This is superfluous. Every man pursues it, according to his light, and always has pursued it, and always must pursue it. To say that a man has done any thing, is to say that he thought it for his happiness to do it. Will the principle run thus — pursue the greatest happiness of mankind, whether it be your own greatest happiness or not? This is absurd and impossible; and Bentham himself allows it to be so. But, if the principle be not stated in one of these two ways, we cannot imagine how it is to be stated at all. Stated in one of these ways, it is an identical proposition, — true, but utterly barren of consequences. Stated in the other way, it is a contradiction in terms. Mr. Bentham has distinctly declined the absurdity. Are we then to suppose that he adopts the truism?

There are thus, it seems, two great truths which the Utilitarian philosophy is to communicate to mankind — two truths which are to produce a revolution in morals, in laws, in governments, in literature, in the whole system of life. The first of these is speculative; the second is practical. The speculative truth is, that the greatest happiness is the greatest happiness. The practical rule is very simple; for it imports merely that men should never omit, when they wish for any thing, to wish for it, or when they do any thing, to do it! It is a great comfort to us to think that we readily assented to the former of these great doctrines as soon as it was stated to us; and that we have long endeavoured, as far as human frailty would permit, to conform to the latter in our practice. We are, however, inclined to suspect that the calamities of the human race have been owing, less to their not knowing that happiness was happiness, than to their not knowing how to obtain it — less to their neglecting to do what they did, than to their not being able to do what they wished, or not wishing to do what they ought.

Thus frivolous, thus useless is this philosophy,—"controversiarum ferax, operum effœta, ad garriendum prompta, ad generandum invalida."[1] The humble mechanic who discovers some slight improvement in the construction of safety lamps or steam-vessels does more for the happiness of mankind than the "magnificent principle," as Mr. Bentham calls it, will do in ten thousand years. The mechanic teaches us how we may in a small degree be better off than we were. The Utilitarian advises us with great pomp to be as well off as we can.

The doctrine of a moral sense may be very unphilosophical; but we do not think that it can be proved to be pernicious. Men did not entertain certain desires and aversions because they believed in a moral sense, but they gave the name of moral sense to a feeling which they found in their minds, however it came there. If they had given it no name at all it would still have influenced their actions; and it will not be very easy to demonstrate that it has influenced their actions the more because they have called it the moral sense. The theory of the original contract is a fiction, and a very absurd fiction; but in practice it meant, what the "greatest happiness principle," if ever it becomes a watchword of political warfare, will mean — that is to say, whatever served the turn of those who used it. Both the one expression and the other sound very well in debating clubs; but in the real conflicts of life our passions and interests bid them stand aside and know their place. The "greatest happiness principle" has always been latent under the words, social contract, jus-

[1] Bacon, *Novum Organum.*

tice, benevolence, patriotism, liberty, and so forth, just as far as it was for the happiness, real or imagined, of those who used these words to promote the greatest happiness of mankind. And of this we may be sure, that the words "greatest happiness" will never, in any man's mouth, mean more than the greatest happiness of others which is consistent with what he thinks his own. The project of mending a bad world by teaching people to give new names to old things reminds us of Walter Shandy's scheme for compensating the loss of his son's nose by christening him Trismegistus. What society wants is a new motive — not a new cant. If Mr. Bentham can find out any argument yet undiscovered which may induce men to pursue the general happiness, he will indeed be a great benefactor to our species. But those whose happiness is identical with the general happiness are even now promoting the general happiness to the very best of their power and knowledge; and Mr. Bentham himself confesses that he has no means of persuading those whose happiness is not identical with the general happiness to act upon his principle. Is not this, then, darkening counsel by words without knowledge? If the only fruit of the "magnificent principle" is to be, that the oppressors and pilferers of the next generation are to talk of seeking the greatest happiness of the greatest number, just as the same class of men have talked in our time of seeking to uphold the Protestant constitution — just as they talked under Anne of seeking the good of the Church, and under Cromwell of seeking the Lord — where is the gain? Is not every great question already enveloped in a sufficiently dark cloud of unmeaning words? Is it so difficult for a man to cant some one or more of the good old English cants which his father and grandfather canted before him, that he must learn, in the schools of the Utilitarians, a new sleight of tongue, to make fools clap and wise men sneer? Let our countrymen keep their eyes on the neophytes of this sect, and see whether we turn out to be mistaken in the prediction which we now hazard. It will before long be found, we prophesy, that, as the corruption of a dunce is the generation of an Utilitarian, so is the corruption of an Utilitarian the generation of a jobber.

The most elevated station that the "greatest happiness principle" is ever likely to attain is this, that it may be a fashionable phrase among newspaper writers and members of parliament — that it may succeed to the dignity which has been enjoyed by the "original contract," by the "constitution of 1688," and other expressions of the same kind. We do not apprehend that it is a less flexible cant than those which have preceded it, or that it will less easily furnish a pretext for any design for which a pretext may be required. The "original contract" meant in the Convention Parliament the co-ordinate authority of the Three Estates. If there were to be a radical insurrection to-morrow, the "original contract" would stand just as well for annual parliaments and universal suffrage. The "Glorious Constitution," again, has meant everything in turn: the Habeas Corpus Act, the Suspension of the Habeas Corpus Act, the Test Act, the Repeal of the Test Act. There has not been for many years a single important measure which has not been unconstitutional with its opponents, and which its supporters have not maintained to be agreeable to the true spirit of the constitution. Is it easier to ascertain what is for the greatest happiness of the human race than what is the constitution of England? If not, the "greatest happiness principle" will be what the "principles of the constitution" are, a thing to be appealed to by everybody, and understood by everybody in the sense which suits him best. It will mean cheap bread, dear bread, free trade, protecting duties, annual parliaments, septennial parliaments, universal suffrage, Old Sarum, trial by jury, martial law — everything, in short, good, bad, or indifferent, of which any person, from rapacity or from benevolence, chooses to undertake the defence. It will mean six-and-eightpence with the attorney, tithes at the rectory, and game-laws at the manor-house. The Statute of Uses, in appearance the most sweeping legislative reform in our history, was said to have produced no other effect than that of adding three words to a conveyance. The universal admission of Mr. Bentham's great principle would, as far as we can see, produce no other effect than that those orators who, while waiting for a meaning, gain time (like bankers paying in sixpences during a run) by uttering words that mean nothing would substitute "the greatest happiness," or rather, as the longer phrase, the greatest happiness of the greatest number," for "under existing circumstances," — "now that I am on my legs," — and "Mr. Speaker, I, for one, am free to say." In fact, principles of this sort resemble those forms which are sold by law-stationers, with blanks for the names of parties, and for the special circumstances of every case — mere customary headings and conclusions, which are equally at the command of the most honest and of the most unrighteous claimant. It is on the filling up that everything depends.

The "greatest happiness principle" of Mr. Bentham is included in the Christian morality; and, to our thinking, it is there exhibited in an infinitely more sound and philosophical form than in the Utilitarian speculations. For in the New Testament it is neither an identical proposition, nor a contradiction in terms; and, as laid down by Mr. Bentham, it must be either the one or the other. "Do as you would be done by: Love your neighbour as yourself:" these are the precepts of Jesus Christ. Understood in an enlarged sense, these precepts are, in fact, a direction to every man to promote the greatest happiness of the greatest number. But this direction would be utterly unmeaning, as it actually is in Mr. Bentham's philosophy, unless it were accompanied by a sanction. In the Christian scheme, accordingly, it is accompanied by a sanction of immense force. To a man whose greatest happiness in this world is inconsistent with the greatest happiness of the greatest number is held out the prospect of an infinite happiness hereafter, from which he excludes himself by wronging his fellow-creatures here.

This is practical philosophy, as practical as that on which penal legislation is founded. A man is told to do something which otherwise he would not do, and is furnished with a new motive for doing it. Mr. Bentham has no new motive to furnish his disciples with. He has talents sufficient to effect any thing that can be effected. But to induce men to act without an inducement is too much, even for him. He should reflect that the whole vast world of morals cannot be moved unless the mover can obtain some stand for his engines beyond it. He acts as Archimedes would have done, if he had attempted to move the earth by a lever fixed on the earth. The action and reaction neutralise each other. The artist labours, and the world remains at rest. Mr. Bentham can only tell us to do something which we have always been doing, and should still have continued to do, if we had never heard of the "greatest happiness principle" — or else to do something which we have no conceivable motive for doing, and therefore shall not do. Mr. Bentham's principle is at best no more than the golden rule of the Gospel without its sanction. Whatever evils, therefore, have existed in societies in which the authority of the Gospel is recognised may, *a fortiori*, as it appears to us, exist in societies in which the Utilitarian principle is recognised. We do not apprehend that it is more difficult for a tyrant or a persecutor to persuade himself and others that in putting to death those who oppose his power or differ from his opinions he is pursuing "the greatest happiness," than that he is doing as he would be done by. But religion gives him a motive for doing as he would be done by: and Mr. Bentham furnishes him no motive to induce him to promote the general happiness. If, on the other hand, Mr. Bentham's principle mean only that every man should pursue his own greatest happiness, he merely asserts what everybody knows, and recommends what everybody does.

It is not upon this "greatest happiness principle" that the fame of Mr. Bentham will rest. He has not taught people to pursue their own happiness; for that they always did. He has not taught them to promote the happiness of others, at the expense of their own; for that they will not and cannot do. But he has taught them *how*, in some most important points, to promote their own happiness; and, if his school had emulated him as successfully in this respect as in the trick of passing off truisms for discoveries, the name of Benthamite would have been no word for the scoffer. But few of those who consider themselves as in a more especial manner his followers have anything in common with him but his faults. The whole science of Jurispru dence is his. He has done much for political economy; but we are not aware that in either department any improvement has been made by members of his sect. He discovered truths; all that *they* have done has been to make those truths unpopular. He investigated the philosophy of law; he could teach them only to snarl at lawyers.

We entertain no apprehensions of danger to the institutions of this country from the Utilitarians. Our fears are of a different kind. We dread the odium and discredit of their alliance. We wish to see a broad and clear line drawn between the judicious friends of practical reform and a sect which, having derived all its influence from the countenance which they have imprudently bestowed upon it, hates them with the deadly hatred of ingratitude. There is not, and we firmly believe that there never was, in this country a party so unpopular. They have already made the science of political economy — a science of vast importance to the welfare of nations — an object of disgust to the majority of the community. The question of parliamentary reform will share the same fate if once an association be formed in the public mind between Reform and Utilitarianism.

We bear no enmity to any member of the sect; and for Mr. Bentham we entertain very high admiration. We know that among his followers there are some well-intentioned men, and some men of talents: but we cannot say that we think the logic on which they pride themselves likely to improve their heads, or the scheme of morality which they have adopted likely to improve their hearts. Their theory of morals, however, well deserves an article to itself; and perhaps, on some future occasion, we may discuss it more fully than time and space at present allow.

The preceding article was written, and was actually in types, when a letter from Mr. Bentham appeared in the newspapers, importing that, "though he had furnished the Westminster Review with some *memoranda* respecting 'the greatest happiness principle,' he had nothing to do with the remarks on our former article." We are truly happy to find that this illustrious man had so small a share in a performance which, for his sake, we have treated with far greater lenity than it deserved. The mistake, however, does not in the least affect any part of our arguments; and we have therefore thought it unnecessary to cancel or cast anew any of the foregoing pages. Indeed, we are not sorry that the world should see how respectfully we were disposed to treat a great man, even when we considered him as the author of a very weak and very unfair attack on ourselves. We wish, however, to intimate to the actual writer of that attack that our civilities were intended for the author of the "Preuves Judiciaires," and the "Defence of Usury"—and not for him. We cannot conclude, indeed, without expressing a wish—though we fear it has but little chance of reaching Mr. Bentham—that he would endeavour to find better editors for his compositions. If M. Dumont had not been a *rédacteur* of a different description from some of his successors, Mr. Bentham would never have attained the distinction of even giving his name to a sect.

UTILITARIAN THEORY OF GOVERNMENT.[1]

(*Edinburgh Review*, October 1829.)

We have long been of opinion that the Utilitarians have owed all their influence to a mere delusion — that, while professing to have submitted their minds to an intellectual discipline of peculiar severity, to have discarded all sentimentality, and to have acquired consummate skill in the art of reasoning, they are decidedly inferior to the mass of educated men in the very qualities in which they conceive themselves to excel. They have undoubtedly freed themselves from the dominion of some absurd notions. But their struggle for intellectual emancipation has ended, as injudicious and violent struggles for political emancipation too often end, in a mere change of tyrants. Indeed, we are not sure that we do not prefer the venerable nonsense which holds prescriptive sway over the ultra-Tory to the upstart dynasty of prejudices and sophisms by which the revolutionists of the moral world have suffered themselves to be enslaved.

The Utilitarians have sometimes been abused as intolerant, arrogant, irreligious, — as enemies of literature, of the fine arts, and of the domestic charities.

1 *Westminster Review*, (*XXII. Art.* 16,) *on the Strictures of the Edinburgh Review* (*XCVIII. Art.* 1) *on the Utilitarian Theory of Government, and the "Greatest Happiness Principle."*

They have been reviled for some things of which they were guilty, and for some of which they were innocent. But scarcely anybody seems to have perceived that almost all their peculiar faults arise from the utter want both of comprehensiveness and of precision in their mode of reasoning. We have, for some time past, been convinced that this was really the case; and that, whenever their philosophy should be boldly and unsparingly scrutinised, the world would see that it had been under a mistake respecting them.

We have made the experiment; and it has succeeded far beyond our most sanguine expectations. A chosen champion of the School has come forth against us. A specimen of his logical abilities now lies before us; and we pledge ourselves to show that no prebendary at an anti-Catholic meeting, no true-blue baronet after the third bottle at a Pitt Club, ever displayed such utter incapacity of comprehending or answering an argument as appears in the speculations of this Utilitarian apostle; that he does not understand our meaning, or Mr. Mill's meaning, or Mr. Bentham's meaning, or his own meaning; and that the various parts of his system — if the name of system can be so misapplied — directly contradict each other.

Having shown this, we intend to leave him in undisputed possession of whatever advantage he may derive from the last word. We propose only to convince the public that there is nothing in the far-famed logic of the Utilitarians of which any plain man has reason to be afraid; that this logic will impose on no man who dares to look it in the face.

The Westminster Reviewer begins by charging us with having misrepresented an important part of Mr. Mill's argument.

"The first extract given by the Edinburgh Reviewers from the essay was an insulated passage, purposely despoiled of what had preceded and what followed. The author had been observing, that 'some profound and benevolent investigators of human affairs had adopted the conclusion that, of all the possible forms of government, absolute monarchy is the best.' This is what the reviewers have omitted at the beginning. He then adds, as in the extract, that 'Experience, *if we look only at the outside of the facts*, appears to be divided on this subject;' there are Caligulas in one place, and kings of Denmark in another. 'As the surface of history affords, therefore, no certain principle of decision, *we must go beyond the surface*, and penetrate to the springs within.' This is what the reviewers have omitted at the end."

It is perfectly true that our quotation from Mr. Mill's essay was, like most other quotations, preceded and followed by something which we did not quote. But, if the Westminster Reviewer means to say that either what preceded or what followed would, if quoted, have shown that we put a wrong interpretation on the passage which was extracted, he does not understand Mr. Mill rightly.

Mr. Mill undoubtedly says that, "as the surface of history affords no certain principle of decision, we must go beyond the surface, and penetrate to the springs within." But these expressions will admit of several interpretations. In what sense, then, does Mr. Mill use them? If he means that we ought to inspect the facts with close attention, he means what is rational. But, if he means that we ought to leave the facts, with all their apparent inconsistencies, unexplained — to lay down a general principle of the widest extent, and to deduce doctrines from that principle by syllogistic argument, without pausing to consider whether those doctrines be or be not consistent with the facts, — then he means what is irrational; and this is clearly what he does mean: for he immediately begins, without offering the least explanation of the contradictory appearances which he has himself described, to go beyond the surface in the following manner: — "That one human being will desire to render the person and property of another subservient to his pleasures, notwithstanding the pain or loss of pleasure which it may occasion to that other individual, is the foundation of government. The desire of the object implies the desire of the power necessary to accomplish the object." And thus he proceeds to deduce consequences directly inconsistent with what he has himself stated respecting the situation of the Danish people.

If we assume that the object of government is the preservation of the persons and property of men, then we must hold that, wherever that object is attained, there the principle of good government exists. If that object be attained both in Denmark and in the United States of America, then that which makes government good must exist, under whatever disguise of title or name, both in Denmark and in the United States. If men lived in fear for their lives and their possessions under Nero and under the National Convention, it follows that the causes from which misgovernment proceeds existed both in the despotism of Rome and in the democracy of France. What, then, is that which, being found in Denmark and in the United States, and not being found in the Roman Empire or under the administration of Robespierre, renders governments, widely differing in their external form, practically good? Be it what it may, it certainly is not that which Mr. Mill proves *a priori* that it must be, — a democratic representative assembly. For the Danes have no such assembly.

The latent principle of good government ought to

be tracked, as it appears to us, in the same manner in which Lord Bacon proposed to track the principle of Heat. Make as large a list as possible, said that great man, of those bodies in which, however widely they differ from each other in appearance, we perceive heat; and as large a list as possible of those which, while they bear a general resemblance to hot bodies, are nevertheless not hot. Observe the different degrees of heat in different hot bodies; and then, if there be something which is found in all hot bodies, and of which the increase or diminution is always accompanied by an increase or diminution of heat, we may hope that we have really discovered the object of our search. In the same manner we ought to examine the constitution of all those communities in which, under whatever form, the blessings of good government are enjoyed; and to discover, if possible, in what they resemble each other, and in what they all differ from those societies in which the object of government is not attained. By proceeding thus we shall arrive, not indeed at a perfect theory of government, but at a theory which will be of great practical use, and which the experience of every successive generation will probably bring nearer and nearer to perfection.

The inconsistencies into which Mr. Mill has been betrayed by taking a different course ought to serve as a warning to all speculators. Because Denmark is well governed by a monarch who, in appearance at least, is absolute, Mr. Mill thinks that the only mode of arriving at the true principles of government is to deduce them *a priori* from the laws of human nature. And what conclusion does he bring out by this deduction? We will give it in his own words: — "In the grand discovery of modern times, the system of representation, the solution of all the difficulties, both speculative and practical, will perhaps be found. If it cannot, we seem to be forced upon the extraordinary conclusion that good government is impossible." That the Danes are well governed without a representation is a reason for deducing the theory of government from a general principle from which it necessarily follows that good government is impossible without a representation! We have done our best to put this question plainly; and we think that, if the Westminster Reviewer will read over what we have written twice or thrice with patience and attention, some glimpse of our meaning will break in even on his mind.

Some objections follow, so frivolous and unfair, that we are almost ashamed to notice them.

> "When it was said that there was in Denmark a balanced contest between the king and the nobility, what was said was, that there was a balanced contest, but it did not last. It was balanced till something put an end to the balance; and so is everything else That such a balance will not last, is precisely what Mr. Mill had demonstrated."

Mr. Mill, we positively affirm, pretends to demonstrate, not merely that a balanced contest between the king and the aristocracy will not last, but that the chances are as infinity to one against the existence of such a balanced contest. This is a mere question of fact. We quote the words of the essay, and defy the Westminster Reviewer to impeach our accuracy: —

> "It seems impossible that such equality should ever exist. How is it to be established? Or by what criterion is it to be ascertained? If there is no such criterion, it must, in all cases, be the result of chance. If so, the chances against it are as infinity to one."

The Reviewer has confounded the division of power

with the balance or equal division of power. Mr. Mill says that the division of power can never exist long, because it is next to impossible that the equal division of power should ever exist at all.

"When Mr. Mill asserted that it cannot be for the interest of either the monarchy or the aristocracy to combine with the democracy, it is plain he did not assert that if the monarchy and aristocracy were in doubtful contest with each other, they would not, either of them, accept of the assistance of the democracy. He spoke of their taking the side of the democracy; not of their allowing the democracy to take side with themselves."

If Mr. Mill meant any thing, he must have meant this — that the monarchy and the aristocracy will never forget their enmity to the democracy in their enmity to each other.

"The monarchy and aristocracy," says he, "have all possible motives for endeavouring to obtain unlimited power over the persons and property of the community. The consequence is inevitable. They have all possible motives for combining to obtain that power, and unless the people have power enough to be a match for both they have no protection. The balance, therefore, is a thing the existence of which upon the best possible evidence is to be regarded as impossible."

If Mr. Mill meant only what the Westminster Reviewer conceives him to have meant, his argument would leave the popular theory of the balance quite untouched. For it is the very theory of the balance that the help of the people will be solicited by the nobles when hard pressed by the king, and by the king when hard pressed by the nobles; and that, as the price of giving alternate support to the crown and the aristocracy, they will obtain something for themselves, as the Reviewer admits that they have done in Denmark. If Mr. Mill admits this, he admits the only theory of the balance of which we ever heard — that very theory which he has declared to be wild and chimerical. If he denies it, he is at issue with the Westminster Reviewer as to the phenomena of the Danish government.

We now come to a more important passage. Our opponent has discovered, as he conceives, a radical error which runs through our whole argument, and vitiates every part of it. We suspect that we shall spoil his triumph.

"Mr. Mill never asserted '*that under no despotic government does any human being, except the tools of the sovereign, possess more than the necessaries of life, and that the most intense degree of terror is kept up by constant cruelty.*' He said that absolute power leads to such results, 'by infallible sequence, where power over a community is attained, *and nothing checks.*' The critic on the Mount never made a more palpable misquotation.

"The spirit of this misquotation runs through every part of the reply of the Edinburgh Review that relates to the Essay on Government; and is repeated in as many shapes as the Roman pork. The whole description of 'Mr. Mill's argument against despotism,' — including the illustration from right-angled triangles and the square of the hypothenuse, — is founded on this invention of saying what an author has not said, and leaving unsaid what he has."

We thought, and still think, for reasons which our readers will soon understand, that we represented Mr. Mill's principle quite fairly, and according to the rule of law and common sense, *ut res magis valeat quam pereat.* Let us, however, give him all the advantage of the explanation tendered by his advocate, and see what he will gain by it.

The Utilitarian doctrine then is, not that despots and aristocracies will always plunder and oppress the people to the last point, but that they will do so if nothing checks them.

In the first place, it is quite clear that the doctrine

thus stated is of no use at all, unless the force of the checks be estimated. The first law of motion is, that a ball once projected will fly on to all eternity with undiminished velocity, unless something checks. The fact is, that a ball stops in a few seconds after proceeding a few yards with very variable motion. Every man would wring his child's neck and pick his friend's pocket if nothing checked him. In fact, the principle thus stated means only that governments will oppress unless they abstain from oppressing. This is quite true, we own. But we might with equal propriety turn the maxim round, and lay it down, as the fundamental principle of government, that all rulers will govern well, unless some motive interferes to keep them from doing so.

If there be, as the Westminster Reviewer acknowledges, certain checks which, under political institutions the most arbitrary in seeming, sometimes produce good government, and almost always place some restraint on the rapacity and cruelty of the powerful, surely the knowledge of those checks, of their nature, and of their effect, must be a most important part of the science of government. Does Mr. Mill say any thing upon this part of the subject? Not one word.

The line of defence now taken by the Utilitarians evidently degrades Mr. Mill's theory of government from the rank which, till within the last few months, was claimed for it by the whole sect. It is no longer a practical system, fit to guide statesmen, but merely a barren exercise of the intellect, like those propositions in mechanics in which the effect of friction and of the resistance of the air is left out of the question; and which, therefore, though correctly deduced from the premises, are in practice utterly false. For, if Mr.

Mill professes to prove only that absolute monarchy and aristocracy are pernicious without checks, — if he allows that there are checks which produce good government even under absolute monarchs and aristocracies, — and if he omits to tell us what those checks are, and what effects they produce under different circumstances, — he surely gives us no information which can be of real utility.

But the fact is, — and it is most extraordinary that the Westminster Reviewer should not have perceived it, — that, if once the existence of checks on the abuse of power in monarchies and aristocracies be admitted, the whole of Mr. Mill's theory falls to the ground at once. This is so palpable, that, in spite of the opinion of the Westminster Reviewer, we must acquit Mr. Mill of having intended to make such an admission. We still think that the words, "where power over a community is attained, and nothing checks," must not be understood to mean that under a monarchical or aristocratical form of government there can really be any check which can in any degree mitigate the wretchedness of the people.

For all possible checks may be classed under two general heads, — want of will, and want of power. Now, if a king or an aristocracy, having the power to plunder and oppress the people, can want the will, all Mr. Mill's principles of human nature must be pronounced unsound. He tells us, "that the desire to possess unlimited power of inflicting pain upon others, is an inseparable part of human nature;" and that "a chain of inference, close and strong to a most unusual degree," leads to the conclusion that those who possess this power will always desire to use it. It is plain, therefore, that, if Mr. Mill's principles be sound, the check on a monarchical or an aristocratical government will not be the want of will to oppress.

If a king or an aristocracy, having, as Mr. Mill tells us that they always must have, the will to oppress the people with the utmost severity, want the power, then the government, by whatever name it may be called, must be virtually a mixed government or a pure democracy: for it is quite clear that the people possess some power in the state — some means of influencing the nominal rulers. But Mr. Mill has demonstrated that no mixed government can possibly exist, or at least that such a government must come to a very speedy end; therefore, every country in which people not in the service of the government have, for any length of time, been permitted to accumulate more than the bare means of subsistence must be a pure democracy. That is to say, France before the revolution, and Ireland during the last century, were pure democracies. Prussia, Austria, Russia, all the governments of the civilised world, are pure democracies. If this be not a *reductio ad absurdum*, we do not know what is.

The errors of Mr. Mill proceed principally from that radical vice in his reasoning which, in our last number, we described in the words of Lord Bacon. The Westminster Reviewer is unable to discover the meaning of our extracts from the *Novum Organum*, and expresses himself as follows:

> "The quotations from Lord Bacon are misapplications, such as anybody may make to any thing he dislikes. There is no more resemblance between pain, pleasure, motives, &c., and *substantia*, *generatio*, *corruptio*, *elementum*, *materia*, — than between lines, angles, magnitudes, &c., and the same."

It would perhaps be unreasonable to expect that a

writer who cannot understand his own English should understand Lord Bacon's Latin. We will therefore attempt to make our meaning clearer.

What Lord Bacon blames in the schoolmen of his time is this, — that they reasoned syllogistically on words which had not been defined with precision; such as moist, dry, generation, corruption, and so forth. Mr. Mill's error is exactly of the same kind. He reasons syllogistically about power, pleasure, and pain, without attaching any definite notion to any one of those words. There is no more resemblance, says the Westminster Reviewer, between pain and *substantia* than between pain and a line or an angle. By his permission, in the very point to which Lord Bacon's observation applies, Mr. Mill's subjects do resemble the *substantia* and *elementum* of the schoolmen and differ from the lines and magnitudes of Euclid. We can reason *a priori* on mathematics, because we can define with an exactitude which precludes all possibility of confusion. If a mathematician were to admit the least laxity into his notions, if he were to allow himself to be deluded by the vague sense which words bear in popular use, or by the aspect of an ill-drawn diagram, if he were to forget in his reasonings that a point was indivisible, or that the definition of a line excluded breadth, there would be no end to his blunders. The schoolmen tried to reason mathematically about things which had not been, and perhaps could not be, defined with mathematical accuracy. We know the result. Mr. Mill has in our time attempted to do the same. He talks of power, for example, as if the meaning of the word power were as determinate as the meaning of the word circle. But, when we analyse his speculations, we find that his notion of power is, in the words of Bacon, "*phantastica et male terminata.*"

There are two senses in which we may use the word *power*, and those words which denote the various distributions of power, as, for example, *monarchy ;* — the one sense popular and superficial, — the other more scientific and accurate. Mr. Mill, since he chose to reason *a priori*, ought to have clearly pointed out in which sense he intended to use words of this kind, and to have adhered inflexibly to the sense on which he fixed. Instead of doing this, he flies backwards and forwards from the one sense to the other, and brings out conclusions at last which suit neither.

The state of those two communities to which he has himself referred — the kingdom of Denmark and the empire of Rome — may serve to illustrate our meaning. Looking merely at the surface of things, we should call Denmark a despotic monarchy, and the Roman world, in the first century after Christ, an aristocratical republic. Caligula was, in theory, nothing more than a magistrate elected by the senate, and subject to the senate. That irresponsible dignity which, in the most limited monarchies of our time, is ascribed to the person of the sovereign never belonged to the earlier Cæsars. The sentence of death which the great council of the commonwealth passed on Nero was strictly according to the theory of the constitution. Yet, in fact, the power of the Roman emperors approached nearer to absolute dominion than that of any prince in modern Europe. On the other hand, the King of Denmark, in theory the most despotic of princes, would in practice find it most perilous to indulge in cruelty and licentiousness. Nor is there, we believe, at the present moment a single sovereign in our part of the world who has so much real power over the lives of his subjects as Robespierre, while he lodged at a chandler's and dined at a restaurateur's, exercised over the lives of those whom he called his fellow-citizens.

Mr. Mill and the Westminster Reviewer seem to agree that there cannot long exist in any society a division of power between a monarch, an aristocracy, and the people, or between any two of them. However the power be distributed, one of the three parties will, according to them, inevitably monopolise the whole. Now, what is here meant by power? If Mr. Mill speaks of the external semblance of power, — of power recognised by the theory of the constitution, — he is palpably wrong. In England, for example, we have had for ages the name and form of a mixed government, if nothing more. Indeed, Mr. Mill himself owns that there are appearances which have given colour to the theory of the balance, though he maintains that these appearances are delusive. But, if he uses the word power in a deeper and philosophical sense, he is, if possible, still more in the wrong than on the former supposition. For, if he had considered in what the power of one human being over other human beings must ultimately consist, he would have perceived, not only that there are mixed governments in the world, but that all the governments in the world, and all the governments which can even be conceived as existing in the world, are virtually mixed.

If a king possessed the lamp of Aladdin, — if he governed by the help of a genius who carried away the daughters and wives of his subjects through the air to the royal *Parc-aux-cerfs*, and turned into stone every man who wagged a finger against his majesty's government, there would indeed be an unmixed despotism. But, fortunately, a ruler can be gratified only by means of his subjects. His power depends on their obedience; and, as any three or four of them are more than a match for him by himself, he can only enforce the unwilling obedience of some by means of the willing obedience of others.

Take any of those who are popularly called absolute princes — Napoleon for example. Could Napoleon have walked through Paris, cutting off the head of one person in every house which he passed? Certainly not without the assistance of an army. If not, why not? Because the people had sufficient physical power to resist him, and would have put forth that power in defence of their lives and of the lives of their children. In other words, there was a portion of power in the democracy under Napoleon. Napoleon might probably have indulged himself in such an atrocious freak of power if his army would have seconded him. But, if his army had taken part with the people, he would have found himself utterly helpless; and, even if they had obeyed his orders against the people, they would not have suffered him to decimate their own body. In other words, there was a portion of power in the hands of a minority of the people, that is to say, in the hands of an aristocracy, under the reign of Napoleon.

To come nearer home, — Mr. Mill tells us that it is a mistake to imagine that the English government is mixed. He holds, we suppose, with all the politicians of the Utilitarian school, that it is purely aristocratical. There certainly is an aristocracy in England; and we are afraid that their power is greater than it ought to be. They have power enough to keep up the game-laws and corn-laws; but they have not power enough to subject the bodies of men of the lowest class to wanton outrage at their pleasure. Suppose that they were to make a law that any gentleman of two thousand a-year might have a day-labourer or a pauper flogged with a cat-of-nine-tails whenever the whim might take him. It is quite clear that the first day on which such flagellation should be administered would be the last day of the English aristocracy. In this point, and in many other points which might be named, the commonalty in our island enjoy a security quite as complete as if they exercised the right of universal suffrage. We say, therefore, that the English people have in their own hands a sufficient guarantee that in some points the aristocracy will conform to their wishes; — in other words, they have a certain portion of power over the aristocracy. Therefore the English government is mixed.

Wherever a king or an oligarchy refrains from the last extremity of rapacity and tyranny through fear of the resistance of the people, there the constitution, whatever it may be called, is in some measure democratical. The admixture of democratic power may be slight. It may be much slighter than it ought to be; but some admixture there is. Wherever a numerical minority, by means of superior wealth or intelligence, of political concert, or of military discipline, exercises a greater influence on the society than any other equal number of persons, — there, whatever the form of government may be called, a mixture of aristocracy does in fact exist. And, wherever a single man, from whatever cause, is so necessary to the community, or to any portion of it, that he possesses more power than any other man, there is a mixture of monarchy. This is the philosophical classification of governments: and if we use this classification we shall find, not only that there are mixed governments, but that all governments are, and must always be, mixed. But we may safely challenge Mr. Mill to give any definition of power, or to make any classification of governments, which shall bear him out in his assertion that a lasting division of authority is impracticable.

It is evidently on the real distribution of power, and not on names and badges, that the happiness of nations must depend. The representative system, though doubtless a great and precious discovery in politics, is only one of the many modes in which the democratic part of the community can efficiently check the governing few. That certain men have been chosen as deputies of the people, — that there is a piece of paper stating such deputies to possess certain powers, — these circumstances in themselves constitute no security for good government. Such a constitution nominally existed in France; while, in fact, an oligarchy of committees and clubs trampled at once on the electors and the elected. Representation is a very happy contrivance for enabling large bodies of men to exert their power with less risk of disorder than there would otherwise be. But, assuredly, it does not of itself give power. Unless a representative assembly is sure of being supported in the last resort by the physical strength of large masses who have spirit to defend the constitution and sense to defend it in concert, the mob of the town in which it meets may overawe it; — the howls of the listeners in its gallery may silence its deliberations; — an able and daring individual may dissolve it. And, if that sense and that spirit of which we speak be diffused through a society, then, even without a representative assembly, that society will enjoy many of the blessings of good government.

Which is the better able to defend himself; a strong man with nothing but his fists, or a paralytic cripple encumbered with a sword which he cannot lift? Such, we believe, is the difference between Denmark and some new republics in which the constitutional forms of the United States have been most sedulously imitated.

Look at the Long Parliament on the day on which Charles came to seize the five members: and look at it again on the day when Cromwell stamped with his foot on its floor. On which day was its apparent power the greater? On which day was its real power the less? Nominally subject, it was able to defy the sovereign. Nominally sovereign, it was turned out of doors by its servant.

Constitutions are in politics what paper money is in commerce. They afford great facilities and conveniences. But we must not attribute to them that value which really belongs to what they represent. They are not power, but symbols of power, and will, in an emergency, prove altogether useless unless the power for which they stand be forthcoming. The real power by which the community is governed is made up of all the means which all its members possess of giving pleasure or pain to each other.

Great light may be thrown on the nature of a circulating medium by the phenomena of a state of barter. And in the same manner it may be useful to those who wish to comprehend the nature and operation of the outward signs of power to look at communities in which no such signs exist; for example, at the great community of nations. There we find nothing analogous to a constitution: but do we not find a government? We do in fact find government in its purest, and simplest, and most intelligible form. We see one portion of power acting directly on another portion of power. We see a certain police kept up; the weak to a certain degree protected; the strong to a certain degree restrained. We see the principle of the balance in constant operation. We see the whole system sometimes undisturbed by any attempt at encroachment for twenty or thirty years at a time; and all this is produced without a legislative assembly, or an executive magistracy — without tribunals — without any code which deserves the name; solely by the mutual hopes and fears of the various members of the federation. In the community of nations, the first appeal is to physical force. In communities of men, forms of government serve to put off that appeal, and often render it unnecessary. But it is still open to the oppressed or the ambitious.

Of course, we do not mean to deny that a form of government will, after it has existed for a long time, materially affect the real distribution of power throughout the community. This is because those who administer a government, with their dependents, form a compact and disciplined body, which, acting methodically and in concert, is more powerful than any other equally numerous body which is inferior in organisation. The power of rulers is not, as superficial observers sometimes seem to think, a thing *sui generis*. It is exactly similar in kind, though generally superior in amount, to that of any set of conspirators who plot to overthrow it. We have seen in our time the most extensive and the best organised conspiracy that ever existed — a conspiracy which possessed all the elements of real power in so great a degree that it was able to cope with a strong government, and to triumph over it — the Catholic Association. An Utilitarian would tell us, we suppose, that the Irish Catholics had no portion of political power whatever on the first day of the late Session of Parliament.

Let us really go beyond the surface of facts: let us, in the sound sense of the words, penetrate to the springs within; and the deeper we go the more reason shall we find to smile at those theorists who hold that the sole hope of the human race is in a rule-of-three sum and a ballot-box.

We must now return to the Westminster Reviewer. The following paragraph is an excellent specimen of his peculiar mode of understanding and answering arguments.

"The reply to the argument against 'saturation,' supplies its own answer. The reason why it is of no use to try to 'saturate' is precisely what the Edinburgh Reviewers have suggested, — '*that there is no limit to the number of thieves.*' There are the thieves, and the thieves' cousins, — with their men-servants, their maid-servants, and their little ones, to the fortieth generation. It is true, that 'a man cannot become a king or a member of the aristocracy whenever he chooses;' but if there is to be no limit to the depredators except their own inclination to increase and multiply, the situation of those who are to suffer is as wretched as it needs be. It is impossible to define what *are* 'corporal pleasures.' A Duchess of Cleveland was a 'corporal pleasure.' The most disgraceful period in the history of any nation — that of the Restoration — presents an instance of the length to which it is possible to go in an attempt to 'saturate' with pleasures of this kind."

To reason with such a writer is like talking to a deaf man who catches at a stray word, makes answer beside the mark, and is led further and further into error by every attempt to explain. Yet, that our readers may fully appreciate the abilities of the new philosophers, we shall take the trouble to go over some of our ground again.

Mr. Mill attempts to prove that there is no point of

saturation with the objects of human desire. He then takes it for granted that men have no objects of desire but those which can be obtained only at the expense of the happiness of others. Hence he infers that absolute monarchs and aristocracies will necessarily oppress and pillage the people to a frightful extent.

We answered in substance thus. There are two kinds of objects of desire; those which give mere bodily pleasure, and those which please through the medium of associations. Objects of the former class, it is true, a man cannot obtain without depriving somebody else of a share. But then with these every man is soon satisfied. A king or an aristocracy cannot spend any very large portion of the national wealth on the mere pleasures of sense. With the pleasures which belong to us as reasoning and imaginative beings we are never satiated, it is true: but then, on the other hand, many of those pleasures can be obtained without injury to any person, and some of them can be obtained only by doing good to others.

The Westminster Reviewer, in his former attack on us, laughed at us for saying that a king or an aristocracy could not be easily satiated with the pleasures of sense, and asked why the same course was not tried with thieves. We were not a little surprised at so silly an objection from the pen, as we imagined, of Mr. Bentham. We returned, however, a very simple answer. There is no limit to the number of thieves. Any man who chooses can steal: but a man cannot become a member of the aristocracy or a king whenever he chooses. To satiate one thief, is to tempt twenty other people to steal. But by satiating one king or five hundred nobles with bodily pleasures we do not produce more kings or more nobles. The answer of the Westminster Reviewer we have quoted above; and it will amply repay our readers for the trouble of examining it. We never read any passage which indicated notions so vague and confused. The number of the thieves, says our Utilitarian, is not limited. For there are the dependents and friends of the king and of the nobles. Is it possible that he should not perceive that this comes under a different head? The bodily pleasures which a man in power dispenses among his creatures are bodily pleasures as respects his creatures, no doubt. But the pleasure which he derives from bestowing them is not a bodily pleasure. It is one of those pleasures which belong to him as a reasoning and imaginative being. No man of common understanding can have failed to perceive that, when we said that a king or an aristocracy might easily be supplied to satiety with sensual pleasures, we were speaking of sensual pleasures directly enjoyed by themselves. But "it is impossible," says the Reviewer, "to define what are corporal pleasures." Our brother would indeed, we suspect, find it a difficult task; nor, if we are to judge of his genius for classification from the specimen which immediately follows, would we advise him to make the attempt. "A Duchess of Cleveland was a corporal pleasure." And to this wise remark is appended a note, setting forth that Charles the Second gave to the Duchess of Cleveland the money which he ought to have spent on the war with Holland. We scarcely know how to answer a man who unites so much pretension to so much ignorance. There are, among the many Utilitarians who talk about Hume, Condillac, and Hartley, a few who have read those writers. Let the Reviewer ask one of these what he thinks on the subject. We shall not undertake to whip a pupil of so little promise through his first course of metaphysics. We shall, therefore, only say — leaving him to guess and wonder what we can mean — that, in our opinion, the Duchess of Cleveland was not a merely corporal pleasure, — that the feeling which leads a prince to prefer one woman to all others, and to lavish the wealth of kingdoms on her, is a feeling which can only be explained by the law of association.

But we are tired, and even more ashamed than tired, of exposing these blunders. The whole article is of a piece. One passage, however, we must select, because it contains a very gross misrepresentation.

"'*They never alluded to the French Revolution for the purpose of proving that the poor were inclined to rob the rich.*' They only said, 'as soon as the poor *again* began to compare their cottages and salads with the hotels and banquets of the rich, there would have been another scramble for property, another general confiscation,' &c."

We said that, *if Mr. Mill's principles of human nature were correct*, there would have been another scramble for property, and another confiscation. We particularly pointed this out in our last article. We showed the Westminster Reviewer that he had misunderstood us. We dwelt particularly on the condition which was introduced into our statement. We said that we had not given, and did not mean to give, any opinion of our own. And, after this, the Westminster Reviewer thinks proper to repeat his former misrepresentation, without taking the least notice of that qualification to which we, in the most marked manner, called his attention.

We hasten on to the most curious part of the article under our consideration — the defence of the "greatest happiness principle." The Reviewer charges us with having quite mistaken its nature.

"All that they have established is, that they do not understand it. Instead of the truism of the Whigs, 'that the greatest happiness is the greatest happiness,' what Mr. Bentham had demonstrated, or at all events had laid such foundations that there was no trouble in demonstrating, was, that the greatest happiness of the individual was in the long run to be obtained by pursuing the greatest happiness of the aggregate."

It was distinctly admitted by the Westminster Reviewer, as we remarked in our last article, that he could give no answer to the question, — why governments should attempt to produce the greatest possible happiness? The Reviewer replies thus: —

"Nothing of the kind will be admitted at all. In the passage thus selected to be tacked to the other, the question started was, concerning 'the object of government;' in which government was spoken of as an operation, not as anything that is capable of feeling pleasure or pain. In this sense it is true enough, that *ought* is not predicable of governments."

We will quote, once again, the passage which we quoted in our last Number; and we really hope that our brother critic will feel something like shame while he peruses it.

"The real answer appeared to be, that men at large *ought* not to allow a government to afflict them with more evil or less good, than they can help. What a *government* ought to do is a mysterious and searching question which those may answer who know what it means; but what other men ought to do is a question of no mystery at all. The word *ought*, if it means anything, must have reference to some kind of interest or motives; and what interest a government has in doing right, when it happens to be interested in doing wrong, is a question for the schoolmen. The fact appears to be that *ought* is not predicable of governments. The question is not, why governments are bound not to do this or that, but why other men should let them if they can help it. The point is not to determine why the lion should not eat sheep, but why men should not eat their own mutton if they can."

We defy the Westminster Reviewer to reconcile this passage with the "general happiness principle" as he now states it. He tells us that he meant by government, not the people invested with the powers of government, but a mere *operation* incapable of feeling pleasure or pain. We say, that he meant the people invested with the powers of government, and nothing else. It is true that *ought* is not predicable of an operation. But who would ever dream of raising any question about the *duties* of an operation? What did the Reviewer mean by saying, that a government could not be interested in doing right because it was interested in doing wrong? Can an operation be interested in either? And what did he mean by his comparison about the lion? Is a lion an operation incapable of pain or pleasure? And what did he mean by the expression, "other men," so obviously opposed to the word "government?" But let the public judge between us. It is superfluous to argue a point so clear.

The Reviewer does indeed seem to feel that his expressions cannot be explained away, and attempts to shuffle out of the difficulty by owning, that "the double meaning of the word government was not got clear of without confusion." He has now, at all events, he assures us, made himself master of Mr. Bentham's philosophy. The real and genuine "greatest happiness principle" is, that the greatest happiness of every individual is identical with the greatest happiness of society; and all other "greatest happiness principles" whatever are counterfeits. "This," says he, "is the spirit of Mr. Bentham's principle; and if there is anything opposed to it in any former statement it may be corrected by the present."

Assuredly, if a fair and honourable opponent had,

in discussing a question so abstruse as that concerning the origin of moral obligation, made some unguarded admission inconsistent with the spirit of his doctrines, we should not be inclined to triumph over him. But no tenderness is due to a writer who, in the very act of confessing his blunders, insults those by whom his blunders have been detected, and accuses them of misunderstanding what, in fact, he has himself mis-stated.

The whole of this transaction illustrates excellently the real character of this sect. A paper comes forth, professing to contain a full developement of the "greatest happiness principle," with the latest improvements of Mr. Bentham. The writer boasts that his article has the honour of being the announcement and the organ of this wonderful discovery, which is to make "the bones of sages and patriots stir within their tombs." This "magnificent principle" is then stated thus: Mankind ought to pursue their greatest happiness. But there are persons whose interest is opposed to the greatest happiness of mankind. *Ought* is not predicable of such persons. For the word *ought* has no meaning unless it be used with reference to some interest.

We answered, with much more lenity than we should have shown to such nonsense, had it not proceeded, as we supposed, from Mr. Bentham, that interest was synonymous with greatest happiness; and that, therefore, if the word *ought* has no meaning, unless used with reference to interest, then, to say that mankind ought to pursue their greatest happiness, is simply to say, that the greatest happiness is the greatest happiness; that every individual pursues his own happiness; that either what he thinks is happiness must coincide with the greatest happiness of society or not; that, if what he thinks his happiness coincides with the greatest happiness of society, he will attempt to promote the greatest happiness of society whether he ever heard of the "greatest happiness principle" or not; and that, by the admission of the Westminster Reviewer, if his happiness is inconsistent with the greatest happiness of society, there is no reason why he should promote the greatest happiness of society. Now, that there are individuals who think that for their happiness which is not for the greatest happiness of society is evident. The Westminster Reviewer allowed that some of these individuals were in the right; and did not pretend to give any reason which could induce any one of them to think himself in the wrong. So that the "magnificent principle" turned out to be, either a truism or a contradiction in terms; either this maxim—"Do what you do;" or this maxim, "Do what you cannot do."

The Westminster Reviewer had the wit to see that he could not defend this palpable nonsense; but, instead of manfully owning that he had misunderstood the whole nature of the "greatest happiness principle" in the summer, and had obtained new light during the autumn, he attempts to withdraw the former principle unobserved, and to substitute another, directly opposed to it, in its place; clamouring all the time against our unfairness, like one who, while changing the cards, diverts the attention of the table from his sleight of hand by vociferating charges of foul play against other people.

The "greatest happiness principle" for the present quarter is then this,—that every individual will best promote his own happiness in this world, religious considerations being left out of the question, by promoting the greatest happiness of the whole species. And this principle, we are told, holds good with respect to kings and aristocracies as well as with other people.

"It is certain that the individual operators in any government, if they were thoroughly intelligent and entered into a perfect calculation of all existing chances, would seek for their own happiness in the promotion of the general; which brings them, if they knew it, under Mr. Bentham's rule. The mistake of supposing the contrary, lies in confounding criminals who have had the luck to escape punishment with those who have the risk still before them. Suppose, for instance, a member of the House of Commons were at this moment to debate within himself, whether it would be for his ultimate happiness to begin, according to his ability, to misgovern. If he could be sure of being as lucky as some that are dead and gone, there might be difficulty in finding him an answer. But he is *not* sure; and never can be, till he is dead. He does not know that he is not close upon the moment when misgovernment such as he is tempted to contemplate, will be made a terrible example of. It is not fair to pick out the instance of the thief that has died unhanged. The question is, whether thieving is at this moment an advisable trade to begin with all the possibilities of hanging not got over? This is the spirit of Mr. Bentham's principle; and if there is any thing opposed to it in any former statement, it may be corrected by the present."

We hope that we have now at last got to the real "magnificent principle," — to the principle which is really to make "the bones of the sages and patriots stir." What effect it may produce on the bones of the dead we shall not pretend to decide; but we are sure that it will do very little for the happiness of the living.

In the first place, nothing is more certain than this, that the Utilitarian theory of government, as developed in Mr. Mill's Essay and in all the other works on the subject which have been put forth by the sect, rests on these two principles, — that men follow their interest, and that the interest of individuals may be, and in fact perpetually is, opposed to the interest of society. Unless these two principles be granted, Mr. Mill's Essay does not contain one sound sentence. All his arguments against monarchy and aristocracy, all his arguments in favour of democracy, nay, the very argument by which he shows that there is any necessity for having government at all, must be rejected as utterly worthless.

This is so palpable that even the Westminster Reviewer, though not the most clear-sighted of men, could not help seeing it. Accordingly, he attempts to guard himself against the objection, after the manner of such reasoners, by committing two blunders instead of one. "All this," says he, "only shows that the members of a government would do well if they were all-wise;" and he proceeds to tell us that, as rulers are not all-wise, they will invariably act against this principle wherever they can, so that the democratical checks will still be necessary to produce good government.

No form which human folly takes is so richly and exquisitely laughable as the spectacle of an Utilitarian in a dilemma. What earthly good can there be in a principle upon which no man will act until he is all-wise? A certain most important doctrine, we are told, has been demonstrated so clearly that it ought to be the foundation of the science of government. And yet the whole frame of government is to be constituted exactly as if this fundamental doctrine were false, and on the supposition that no human being will ever act as if he believed it to be true!

The whole argument of the Utilitarians in favour of universal suffrage proceeds on the supposition that even the rudest and most uneducated men cannot, for any length of time, be deluded into acting against their own true interest. Yet now they tell us that, in all aristocratical communities, the higher and more educated class will, not occasionally, but invariably, act against its own interest. Now, the only use of proving anything, as far as we can see, is that people may believe it. To say that a man does what he believes to be against his happiness is a contradiction in terms. If, therefore, government and laws are to be constituted on the supposition on which Mr. Mill's Essay is founded, that all individuals will, whenever they have power over others put into their hands, act in opposition to the general happiness, then government and laws must be constituted on the supposition that no individual believes, or ever will believe, his own happiness to be identical with the happiness of society. That is to say, government and laws are to be constituted on the supposition that no human being will ever be satisfied by Mr. Bentham's proof of his "greatest happiness principle," — a supposition which may be true enough, but which says little, we think, for the principle in question.

But where has this principle been demonstrated? We are curious, we confess, to see this demonstration which is to change the face of the world and yet is to convince nobody. The most amusing circumstance is that the Westminster Reviewer himself does not seem to know whether the principle has been demonstrated or not. "Mr. Bentham," he says, "has demonstrated it, or at all events has laid such foundations that there is no trouble in demonstrating it." Surely it is rather strange that such a matter should be left in doubt. The Reviewer proposed, in his former article, a slight verbal emendation in the statement of the principle; he then announced that the principle had received its last improvement; and gloried in the circumstance that the Westminster Review had been selected as the organ of that improvement. Did it never occur to him that one slight improvement to a doctrine is to prove it?

Mr. Bentham has not demonstrated the "greatest happiness principle," as now stated. He is far too wise a man to think of demonstrating any such thing. In those sections of his *Introduction to the Principles of Morals and Legislation*, to which the Reviewer refers us in his note, there is not a word of the kind. Mr. Bentham says, most truly, that there are no occasions in which a man has not *some* motives for consulting the happiness of other men; and he proceeds to set forth what those motives are — sympathy on all occasions, and the love of reputation on most occasions. This is the very doctrine which we have been maintaining against Mr. Mill and the Westminster Reviewer. The principal charge which we brought against Mr. Mill was, that those motives to which Mr. Bentham ascribes so much influence were quite left out of consideration in his theory. The Westminster Reviewer, in the very article now before us, abuses us for saying, in the spirit, and almost in the words of Mr. Bentham, that "there is a certain check to the rapacity and cruelty of men in their desire of the good opinion of others." But does this principle, in which we fully agree with Mr. Bentham, go the length of the new "greatest happiness principle?" The question is, not whether men have *some* motives for promoting the greatest happiness, but whether the *stronger* motives be those which impel them to promote the greatest happiness. That this would always be the case if men knew their own worldly interests is the assertion of the Reviewer. As he expresses some doubt whether Mr. Bentham has demonstrated this or not, we would advise him to set the point at rest by giving his own demonstration.

The Reviewer has not attempted to give a general confirmation of the "greatest happiness principle;" but he has tried to prove that it holds good in one or two particular cases. And even in those particular cases he has utterly failed. A man, says he, who calculated the chances fairly would perceive that it would be for his greatest happiness to abstain from stealing; for a thief runs a greater risk of being hanged than an honest man.

It would have been wise, we think, in the Westminster Reviewer, before he entered on a discussion of this sort, to settle in what human happiness consists. Each of the ancient sects of philosophy held some tenet on this subject which served for a distinguishing badge. The *summum bonum* of the Utilitarians, as far as we can judge from the passage which we are now considering, is the not being hanged.

That it is an unpleasant thing to be hanged, we most willingly concede to our brother. But that the whole question of happiness or misery resolves itself into this single point, we cannot so easily admit. We must look at the thing purchased as well as the price paid for it. A thief, assuredly, runs a greater risk of being hanged than a labourer; and so an officer in the army runs a greater risk of being shot than a banker's clerk; and a governor of India runs a greater risk of dying of cholera than a lord of the bedchamber. But does it therefore follow that every man, whatever his habits or feelings may be, would, if he knew his own happiness, become a clerk rather than a cornet, or goldstick in waiting rather than governor of India?

Nothing can be more absurd than to suppose, like the Westminster Reviewer, that thieves steal only because they do not calculate the chances of being hanged as correctly as honest men. It never seems to have occurred to him as possible that a man may so greatly prefer the life of a thief to the life of a labourer that he may determine to brave the risk of detection and punishment, though he may even think that risk greater than it really is. And how, on Utilitarian principles, is such a man to be convinced that he is in the wrong? "You will be found out." — "Undoubtedly." — "You will be hanged within two years." — "I expect to be hanged within one year." — "Then why do you pursue this lawless mode of life?" — Because I would rather live for one year with plenty of money, dressed like a gentleman, eating and drinking of the best, frequenting public places, and visiting a dashing mistress, than break stones on the road, or sit down to the loom, with the certainty of attaining a good old age. It is my humour. Are you answered?"

A king, says the Reviewer again, would govern well, if he were wise, for fear of provoking his subjects to insurrection. Therefore, the true happiness of a king is identical with the greatest happiness of society. Tell Charles II. that, if he will be constant to his queen, sober at table, regular at prayers, frugal in his expenses, active in the transaction of business, if he will drive the herd of slaves, buffoons, and procurers from Whitehall, and make the happiness of his people the rule of his conduct, he will have a much greater chance of reigning in comfort to an advanced age; that his profusion and tyranny have exasperated his subjects, and may, perhaps, bring him to an end as terrible as his father's. He might answer, that he saw the danger, but that life was not worth having without ease and vicious pleasures. And what has our philosopher to say? Does he not see that it is no more possible to reason a man out of liking a short life and a merry one more than a long life and a dull one than to reason a Greenlander out of his train oil? We may say that the tastes of the thief and the tyrant differ from ours; but what right have we to say, looking at this world alone, that they do not pursue their greatest happiness very judiciously?

It is the grossest ignorance of human nature to suppose that another man calculates the chances differently from us, merely because he does what, in his place, we should not do. Every man has tastes and propensities, which he is disposed to gratify at a risk and expense which people of different temperaments and habits think extravagant. "Why," says Horace, "does one brother like to lounge in the forum, to play in the Campus, and to anoint himself in the baths, so well, that he would not put himself out of his way for all the wealth of the richest plantations of the East; while the other toils from sunrise to sunset for the purpose of increasing his fortune?" Horace attributes the diversity to the influence of the Genius and the natal star: and eighteen hundred years have taught us only to disguise our ignorance beneath a more philosophical language.

We think, therefore, that the Westminster Reviewer, even if we admit his calculation of the chances to be right, does not make out his case. But he appears to us to miscalculate chances more grossly than any person who ever acted or speculated in this world. "It is for the happiness," says he, "of a member of the House of Commons to govern well; for he never can tell that he is not close on the moment when misgovernment will be terribly punished: if he was sure that he should be as lucky as his predecessors, it might be for his happiness to misgovern; but he is not sure." Certainly a member of Parliament is not sure that he shall not be torn in pieces by a mob, or guillotined by a revolutionary tribunal for his opposition to reform. Nor is the Westminster Reviewer sure that he shall not be hanged for writing in favour of universal suffrage. We may have democratical massacres. We may also have aristocratical proscriptions. It is not very likely, thank God, that we should see either. But the radical, we think, runs as much danger as the aristocrat. As to our friend the Westminster Reviewer, he, it must be owned, has as good a right as any man on his side, "*Antonî gladios contemnere.*" But take the man whose votes, ever since he has sate in Parliament, have been the most uniformly bad, and oppose him to the man whose votes have been the most uniformly good. The Westminster Reviewer would probably select Mr. Sadler and Mr. Hume. Now, does any rational man think, — will the Westminster Reviewer himself say, — that Mr. Sadler runs more risk of coming to a miserable end on account of his public conduct than Mr. Hume? Mr. Sadler does not know that he is not close on the moment when he will be made an example of; for Mr. Sadler knows, if possible, less about the future than about the past. But he has no more reason to expect that he shall be made an example of than to expect that London will be swallowed up by an earthquake next spring; and it would be as foolish in him to act on the former supposition as on the latter. There is a risk; for there is a risk of every thing which does not involve a contradiction; but it is a risk from which no man in his wits would give a shilling to be insured. Yet our Westminster Reviewer tells us that this risk alone, apart from all considerations of religion, honour, or benevolence, would, as a matter of mere calculation, induce a wise member of the House of Commons to refuse any emoluments which might be offered him as the price of his support to pernicious measures.

We have hitherto been examining cases proposed by our opponent. It is now our turn to propose one; and we beg that he will spare no wisdom in solving it.

A thief is condemned to be hanged. On the eve of the day fixed for the execution a turnkey enters his cell and tells him that all is safe, that he has only to slip out, that his friends are waiting in the neighbourhood with disguises, and that a passage is taken for him in an American packet. Now, it is clearly for the greatest happiness of society that the thief should be hanged and the corrupt turnkey exposed and punished. Will the Westminster Reviewer tell us that it is for the greatest happiness of the thief to summon the head jailer and tell the whole story? Now, either it is for the greatest happiness of a thief to be hanged or it is not. If it is, then the argument, by which the Westminster Reviewer attempts to prove that men do not promote their own happiness by thieving, falls to the ground. If it is not, then there are men whose greatest happiness is at variance with the greatest happiness of the community.

To sum up our arguments shortly, we say that the "greatest happiness principle," as now stated, is diametrically opposed to the principle stated in the Westminster Review three months ago.

We say that, if the "greatest happiness principle," as now stated, be sound, Mr. Mill's Essay, and all other works concerning Government which, like that Essay, proceed on the supposition that individuals may have an interest opposed to the greatest happiness of society, are fundamentally erroneous.

We say that those who hold this principle to be sound must be prepared to maintain, either that monarchs and aristocracies may be trusted to govern the community, or else that men cannot be trusted to follow their own interest when that interest is demonstrated to them.

We say that, if men cannot be trusted to follow their own interest when that interest has been demonstrated to them, then the Utilitarian arguments in favour of universal suffrage are good for nothing.

We say that the "greatest happiness principle" has not been proved; that it cannot be generally proved; that even in the particular cases selected by the Reviewer it is not clear that the principle is true; and that many cases might be stated in which the common sense of mankind would at once pronounce it to be false.

We now leave the Westminster Reviewer to alter and amend his "magnificent principle" as he thinks best. Unlimited, it is false. Properly limited, it will be barren. The "greatest happiness principle" of the 1st of July, as far as we could discern its meaning through a cloud of rodomontade, was an idle truism. The "greatest happiness principle" of the 1st of October is, in the phrase of the American newspapers, "important if true." But unhappily it is not true. It is not our business to conjecture what new maxim is to make the bones of sages and patriots stir on the 1st of December. We can only say that, unless it be something infinitely more ingenious than its two predecessors, we shall leave it unmolested. The Westminster Reviewer may, if he pleases, indulge himself like

Sultan Schahriar with espousing a rapid succession of virgin theories. But we must beg to be excused from playing the part of the vizier who regularly attended on the day after the wedding to strangle the new Sultana.

The Westminster Reviewer charges us with urging it as an objection to the "greatest happiness principle" that "it is included in the Christian morality." This is a mere fiction of his own. We never attacked the morality of the Gospel. We blamed the Utilitarians for claiming the credit of a discovery, when they had merely stolen that morality, and spoiled it in the stealing. They have taken the precept of Christ and left the motive; and they demand the praise of a most wonderful and beneficial invention, when all that they have done has been to make a most useful maxim useless by separating it from its sanction. On religious principles it is true that every individual will best promote his own happiness by promoting the happiness of others. But if religious considerations be left out of the question it is not true. If we do not reason on the supposition of a future state, where is the motive? If we do reason on that supposition, where is the discovery?

The Westminster Reviewer tells us that "we wish to see the science of Government unsettled because we see no prospect of a settlement which accords with our interests." His angry eagerness to have questions settled resembles that of a judge in one of Dryden's plays — the Amphitryon, we think — who wishes to decide a cause after hearing only one party, and, when he has been at last compelled to listen to the statement of the defendant, flies into a passion, and exclaims, "There now, sir! See what you have done. The case was quite clear a minute ago; and you must come and puzzle it!" He is the zealot of a sect. We are searchers after truth. He wishes to have the question settled. We wish to have it sifted first. The querulous manner in which we have been blamed for attacking Mr. Mill's system, and propounding no system of our own, reminds us of the horror with which that shallow dogmatist, Epicurus, the worst parts of whose nonsense the Utilitarians have attempted to revive, shrank from the keen and searching scepticism of the second Academy.

It is not our fault that an experimental science of vast extent does not admit of being settled by a short demonstration; — that the subtilty of nature, in the moral as in the physical world, triumphs over the subtilty of syllogism. The quack, who declares on affidavit that, by using his pills and attending to his printed directions, hundreds who had been dismissed incurable from the hospitals have renewed their youth like the eagles, may, perhaps, think that Sir Henry Halford, when he feels the pulses of patients, inquires about their symptoms, and prescribes a different remedy to each, is unsettling the science of medicine for the sake of a fee.

If, in the course of this controversy, we have refrained from expressing any opinion respecting the political institutions of England, it is not because we have not an opinion or because we shrink from avowing it. The Utilitarians, indeed, conscious that their boasted theory of government would not bear investigation, were desirous to turn the dispute about Mr. Mill's Essay into a dispute about the Whig party, rotten boroughs, unpaid magistrates, and ex-officio informations. When we blamed them for talking nonsense, they cried out that they were insulted for being reformers, — just as poor Ancient Pistol swore that the scars which he had received from the cudgel of Fluellen were got in the Gallia wars. We, however, did not think it desirable to mix up political questions, about which the public mind is violently agitated, with a great problem in moral philosophy.

Our notions about Government are not, however, altogether unsettled. We have an opinion about parliamentary reform, though we have not arrived at that opinion by the royal road which Mr. Mill has opened for the explorers of political science. As we are taking leave, probably for the last time, of this controversy, we will state very concisely what our doctrines are. On some future occasion we may, perhaps, explain and defend them at length.

Our fervent wish, and we will add our sanguine hope, is that we may see such a reform of the House of Commons as may render its votes the express image of the opinion of the middle orders of Britain. A pecuniary qualification we think absolutely necessary; and, in settling its amount, our object would be to draw the line in such a manner that every decent farmer and shopkeeper might possess the elective franchise. We should wish to see an end put to all the advantages which particular forms of property possess over other forms, and particular portions of property over other equal portions. And this would content us. Such a reform would, according to Mr. Mill, establish an aristocracy of wealth, and leave the community without protection and exposed to all the evils of unbridled power. Most willingly would we stake the whole controversy between us on the success of the experiment which we propose.

SOUTHEY'S COLLOQUIES.[1]

(*Edinburgh Review*, January 1830.)

It would be scarcely possible for a man of Mr. Southey's talents and acquirements to write two volumes so large as those before us, which should be wholly destitute of information and amusement. Yet we do not remember to have read with so little satisfaction any equal quantity of matter, written by any man of real abilities. We have, for some time past, observed with great regret the strange infatuation which leads the Poet Laureate to abandon those departments of literature in which he might excel, and to lecture the public on sciences of which he has still the very alphabet to learn. He has now, we think, done his worst. The subject which he has at last undertaken to treat is one which demands all the highest intellectual and moral qualities of a philosophical statesman, an understanding at once comprehensive and acute, a heart at once upright and charitable. Mr. Southey brings to the task two faculties which were never, we believe, vouchsafed in measure so copious to any human being, the faculty of believing without a reason, and the faculty of hating without a provocation.

1 *Sir Thomas More; or, Colloquies on the Progress and Prospects of Society.* By Robert Southey, Esq., LL.D., Poet Laureate. 2 vols. 8vo. London: 1829.

It is, indeed, most extraordinary, that a mind like Mr. Southey's, a mind richly endowed in many respects by nature, and highly cultivated by study, a mind which has exercised considerable influence on the most enlightened generation of the most enlightened people that ever existed, should be utterly destitute of the power of discerning truth from falsehood. Yet such is the fact. Government is to Mr. Southey one of the fine arts. He judges of a theory, of a public measure, of a religion or a political party, of a peace or a war, as men judge of a picture or a statue, by the effect produced on his imagination. A chain of associations is to him what a chain of reasoning is to other men; and what he calls his opinions are in fact merely his tastes.

Part of this description might perhaps apply to a much greater man, Mr. Burke. But Mr. Burke assuredly possessed an understanding admirably fitted for the investigation of truth, an understanding stronger than that of any statesman, active or speculative, of the eighteenth century, stronger than every thing, except his own fierce and ungovernable sensibility. Hence he generally chose his side like a fanatic, and defended it like a philosopher. His conduct on the most important occasions of his life, at the time of the impeachment of Hastings for example, and at the time of the French Revolution, seems to have been prompted by those feelings and motives which Mr. Coleridge has so happily described,

> "Stormy pity, and the cherish'd lure
> Of pomp, and proud precipitance of soul."

Hindostan, with its vast cities, its gorgeous pagodas, its infinite swarms of dusky population, its long-descended dynasties, its stately etiquette, excited in a mind so capacious, so imaginative, and so susceptible, the most intense interest. The peculiarities of the costume, of the manners, and of the laws, the very mystery which hung over the language and origin of the people, seized his imagination. To plead under the ancient arches of Westminster Hall, in the name of the English people, at the bar of the English nobles, for great nations and kings separated from him by half the world, seemed to him the height of human glory. Again, it is not difficult to perceive that his hostility to the French Revolution principally arose from the vexation which he felt at having all his old political associations disturbed, at seeing the well known landmarks of states obliterated, and the names and distinctions with which the history of Europe had been filled for ages at once swept away. He felt like an antiquary whose shield had been scoured, or a connoisseur who found his Titian retouched. But, however he came by an opinion, he had no sooner got it than he did his best to make out a legitimate title to it. His reason, like a spirit in the service of an enchanter, though spell-bound, was still mighty. It did whatever work his passions and his imagination might impose. But it did that work, however arduous, with marvellous dexterity and vigour. His course was not determined by argument; but he could defend the wildest course by arguments more plausible than those by which common men support opinions which they have adopted after the fullest deliberation. Reason has scarcely ever displayed, even in those well constituted minds of which she occupies the throne, so much power and energy as in the lowest offices of that imperial servitude.

Now in the mind of Mr. Southey reason has no place at all, as either leader or follower, as either sovereign or slave. He does not seem to know what an argument is. He never uses arguments himself. He never troubles himself to answer the arguments of his opponents. It has never occurred to him, that a man ought to be able to give some better account of the way in which he has arrived at his opinions than merely that it is his will and pleasure to hold them. It has never occurred to him that there is a difference between assertion and demonstration, that a rumour does not always prove a fact, that a single fact, when proved, is hardly foundation enough for a theory, that two contradictory propositions cannot be undeniable truths, that to beg the question is not the way to settle it, or that when an objection is raised, it ought to be met with something more convincing than "scoundrel" and "blockhead."

It would be absurd to read the works of such a writer for political instruction. The utmost that can be expected from any system promulgated by him is that it may be splendid and affecting, that it may suggest sublime and pleasing images. His scheme of philosophy is a mere day-dream, a poetical creation, like the Domdaniel cavern, the Swerga, or Padalon; and indeed it bears no inconsiderable resemblance to those gorgeous visions. Like them, it has something of invention, grandeur, and brilliancy. But, like them, it is grotesque and extravagant, and perpetually violates even that conventional probability which is essential to the effect of works of art.

The warmest admirers of Mr. Southey will scarcely, we think, deny that his success has almost always borne an inverse proportion to the degree in which his undertakings have required a logical head. His poems, taken in the mass, stand far higher than his prose works. His official Odes indeed, among which the

Vision of Judgment must be classed, are, for the most part, worse than Pye's and as bad as Cibber's; nor do we think him generally happy in short pieces. But his longer poems, though full of faults, are nevertheless very extraordinary productions. We doubt greatly whether they will be read fifty years hence; but that, if they are read, they will be admired, we have no doubt whatever.

But, though in general we prefer Mr. Southey's poetry to his prose, we must make one exception. The Life of Nelson is, beyond all doubt, the most perfect and the most delightful of his works. The fact is, as his poems most abundantly prove, that he is by no means so skilful in designing as in filling up. It was therefore an advantage to him to be furnished with an outline of characters and events, and to have no other task to perform than that of touching the cold sketch into life. No writer, perhaps, ever lived, whose talents so precisely qualified him to write the history of the great naval warrior. There were no fine riddles of the human heart to read, no theories to propound, no hidden causes to develope, no remote consequences to predict. The character of the hero lay on the surface. The exploits were brilliant and picturesque. The necessity of adhering to the real course of events saved Mr. Southey from those faults which deform the original plan of almost every one of his poems, and which even his innumerable beauties of detail scarcely redeem. The subject did not require the exercise of those reasoning powers the want of which is the blemish of his prose. It would not be easy to find, in all literary history, an instance of a more exact hit between wind and water. John Wesley and the Peninsular War were subjects of a very different kind, subjects which required all the qualities of a philosophic historian. In Mr. Southey's works on these subjects, he has, on the whole, failed. Yet there are charming specimens of the art of narration in both of them. The Life of Wesley will probably live. Defective as it is, it contains the only popular account of a most remarkable moral revolution, and of a man whose eloquence and logical acuteness might have made him eminent in literature, whose genius for government was not inferior to that of Richelieu, and who, whatever his errors may have been, devoted all his powers, in defiance of obloquy and derision, to what he sincerely considered as the highest good of his species. The History of the Peninsular War is already dead: indeed, the second volume was dead-born. The glory of producing an imperishable record of that great conflict seems to be reserved for Colonel Napier.

The Book of the Church contains some stories very prettily told. The rest is mere rubbish. The adventure was manifestly one which could be achieved only by a profound thinker, and one in which even a profound thinker might have failed, unless his passions had been kept under strict control. But in all those works in which Mr. Southey has completely abandoned narration, and has undertaken to argue moral and political questions, his failure has been complete and ignominious. On such occasions his writings are rescued from utter contempt and derision solely by the beauty and purity of the English. We find, we confess, so great a charm in Mr. Southey's style that, even when he writes nonsense, we generally read it with pleasure, except indeed when he tries to be droll. A more insufferable jester never existed. He very often attempts to be humorous, and yet we do not remember a single occasion on which he has succeeded farther than to be quaintly and flippantly dull. In one of his works he tells us that Bishop Spratt was very properly so called, inasmuch as he was a very small poet. And in the book now before us he cannot quote Francis Bugg, the renegade Quaker, without a remark on his unsavoury name. A wise man might talk folly like this by his own fireside; but that any human being, after having made such a joke, should write it down, and copy it out, and transmit it to the printer, and correct the proof-sheets, and send it forth into the world, is enough to make us ashamed of our species.

The extraordinary bitterness of spirit which Mr. Southey manifests towards his opponents is, no doubt, in a great measure to be attributed to the manner in which he forms his opinions. Differences of taste, it has often been remarked, produce greater exasperation than differences on points of science. But this is not all. A peculiar austerity marks almost all Mr. Southey's judgments of men and actions. We are far from blaming him for fixing on a high standard of morals, and for applying that standard to every case. But rigour ought to be accompanied by discernment; and of discernment Mr. Southey seems to be utterly destitute. His mode of judging is monkish. It is exactly what we should expect from a stern old Benedictine, who had been preserved from many ordinary frailties by the restraints of his situation. No man out of a cloister ever wrote about love, for example, so coldly and at the same time so grossly. His descriptions of it are just what we should hear from a recluse who knew the passion only from the details of the confessional. Almost all his heroes make love either like Seraphim or like cattle. He seems to have no notion of any thing between the Platonic passion of the Glendoveer who gazes with rapture on his mistress's leprosy, and the brutal appetite of Arvalan and Roderick. In Roderick, indeed, the two characters are united. He is first all clay, and then all spirit. He goes forth a Tarquin, and comes back too ethereal to be married. The only love scene, as far as we can recollect, in Madoc, consists of the delicate attentions which a savage, who has drunk too much of the Prince's excellent metheglin, offers to Goervyl. It would be the labour of a week to find, in all the vast mass of Mr. Southey's poetry, a single passage indicating any sympathy with those feelings which have consecrated the shades of Vaucluse and the rocks of Meillerie.

Indeed, if we except some very pleasing images of paternal tenderness and filial duty, there is scarcely any thing soft or humane in Mr. Southey's poetry. What theologians call the spiritual sins are his cardinal virtues, hatred, pride, and the insatiable thirst of vengeance. These passions he disguises under the name of duties; he purifies them from the alloy of vulgar interests; he ennobles them by uniting them with energy, fortitude, and a severe sanctity of manners; and he then holds them up to the admiration of mankind. This is the spirit of Thalaba, of Ladurlad, of Adosinda, of Roderick after his conversion. It is the spirit which, in all his writings, Mr. Southey appears to affect. "I do well to be angry," seems to be the predominant feeling of his mind. Almost the only mark of charity which he vouchsafes to his opponents is to pray for their reformation; and this he does in terms not unlike those in which we can imagine a Portuguese priest interceding with Heaven for a Jew, delivered over to the secular arm after a relapse.

We have always heard, and fully believe, that Mr. Southey is a very amiable and humane man; nor do we intend to apply to him personally any of the remarks which we have made on the spirit of his writings. Such are the caprices of human nature. Even Uncle Toby troubled himself very little about the French grenadiers who fell on the glacis of Namur. And Mr. Southey, when he takes up his pen, changes his nature as much as Captain Shandy, when he girt on his sword. The only opponents to whom the Laureate gives quarter are those in whom he finds something of his own character reflected. He seems to have an instinctive antipathy for calm, moderate men, for men who shun extremes, and who render reasons. He has treated Mr. Owen of Lanark, for example, with infinitely more respect than he has shown to Mr. Hallam or to Dr. Lingard; and this for no reason that we can discover, except that Mr. Owen is more unreasonably and hopelessly in the wrong than any speculator of our time.

Mr. Southey's political system is just what we might expect from a man who regards politics, not as matter of science, but as matter of taste and feeling. All his schemes of government have been inconsistent with themselves. In his youth he was a republican; yet, as he tells us in his preface to these Colloquies, he was even then opposed to the Catholic Claims. He is now a violent Ultra-Tory. Yet, while he maintains, with vehemence approaching to ferocity, all the sterner and harsher parts of the Ultra-Tory theory of government, the baser and dirtier part of that theory disgusts him. Exclusion, persecution, severe punishments for libellers and demagogues, proscriptions, massacres, civil war, if necessary, rather than any concession to a discontented people; these are the measures which he seems inclined to recommend. A severe and gloomy tyranny, crushing opposition, silencing remonstrance, drilling the minds of the people into unreasoning obedience, has in it something of grandeur which delights his imagination. But there is nothing fine in the shabby tricks and jobs of office; and Mr. Southey, accordingly, has no toleration for them. When a Jacobin, he did not perceive that his system led logically, and would have led practically, to the removal of religious distinctions. He now commits a similar error. He renounces the abject and paltry part of the creed of his party, without perceiving that it is also an essential part of that creed. He would have tyranny and purity together; though the most superficial observation might have shown him that there can be no tyranny without corruption.

It is high time, however, that we should proceed to the consideration of the work which is our more immediate subject, and which, indeed, illustrates in almost every page our general remarks on Mr. Southey's writings. In the preface, we are informed that the author, notwithstanding some statements to the contrary, was always opposed to the Catholic Claims. We fully believe this; both because we are sure that Mr. Southey is incapable of publishing a deliberate falsehood, and because his assertion is in itself probable. We should have expected that, even in his wildest paroxysms of democratic enthusiasm, Mr. Southey would have felt no wish to see a simple remedy applied to a great practical evil. We should have expected that, the only measure which all the great statesmen of two generations have agreed with each other in supporting would be the only measure which Mr. Southey would have agreed with himself in opposing. He has passed from one extreme of political opinion to another, as Satan in Milton went round the globe, contriving constantly to "ride with darkness." Wherever the thickest shadow of the night may at any moment chance to fall, there is Mr. Southey. It is not every body who could have so dexterously avoided blundering on the daylight in the course of a journey to the antipodes.

Mr. Southey has not been fortunate in the plan of any of his fictitious narratives. But he has never failed so conspicuously as in the work before us; except, indeed, in the wretched Vision of Judgment. In November, 1817, it seems the Laureate was sitting over his newspaper, and meditating about the death of the Princess Charlotte. An elderly person of very dignified aspect makes his appearance, announces himself as a stranger from a distant country, and apologizes very politely for not having provided himself with letters of introduction. Mr. Southey supposes his visitor to be some American gentleman who has come to see the lakes and the lake-poets, and accordingly proceeds to perform, with that grace, which only long practice can give, all the duties which authors owe to starers. He assures his guest that some of the most agreeable visits which he has received have been from Americans, and that he knows men among them whose talents and virtues would do honour to any country. In passing we may observe, to the honour of Mr. Southey, that, though he evidently has no liking for the American institutions, he never speaks of the people of the United States with that pitiful affectation of contempt by which some members of his party have done more than wars or tariffs can do to excite mutual enmity between two communities formed for mutual friendship. Great as the faults of his mind are, paltry spite like this has no place in it. Indeed it is scarcely conceivable that a man of his sensibility and his imagination should look without pleasure and national pride on the vigorous and splendid youth of a great people, whose veins are filled with our blood, whose minds are nourished with our literature, and on whom is entailed the rich inheritance of our civilisation, our freedom, and our glory.

But we must return to Mr. Southey's study at Keswick. The visitor informs the hospitable poet that he is not an American but a spirit. Mr. Southey, with more frankness than civility, tells him that he is a very queer one. The stranger holds out his hand. It has neither weight nor substance. Mr. Southey upon this becomes more serious; his hair stands on end; and he adjures the spectre to tell him what he is, and why he comes. The ghost turns out to be Sir Thomas More. The traces of martyrdom, it seems, are worn in the other world, as stars and ribands are worn in this. Sir Thomas shows the poet a red streak round his neck, brighter than a ruby, and informs him that Cranmer wears a suit of flames in paradise, the right hand glove, we suppose, of peculiar brilliancy.

Sir Thomas pays but a short visit on this occasion, but promises to cultivate the new acquaintance which he has formed, and, after begging that his visit may be kept secret from Mrs. Southey, vanishes into air.

The rest of the book consists of conversations between Mr. Southey and the spirit about trade, currency, Catholic emancipation, periodical literature, female nunneries, butchers, snuff, book-stalls, and a hundred other subjects. Mr. Southey very hospitably takes an opportunity to escort the ghost round the lakes, and directs his attention to the most beautiful points of view. Why a spirit was to be evoked for the purpose of talking over such matters and seeing such sights, why the vicar of the parish, a blue-stocking from London, or an American, such as Mr. Southey at first supposed the aërial visitor to be, might not have done as well, we are unable to conceive. Sir Thomas tells Mr. Southey nothing about future events, and indeed absolutely disclaims the gift of prescience. He has learned to talk modern English. He has read all the new publications, and loves a jest as well as when he jested with the executioner, though we cannot say that the quality of his wit has materially improved in Paradise. His powers of reasoning, too, are by no means in as great vigour as when he sate on the woolsack; and though he boasts that he is "divested of all those passions which cloud the intellects and warp the understandings of men," we think him, we must confess, far less stoical than formerly. As to revelations, he tells Mr. Southey at the outset to expect none from him. The Laureate expresses some doubts, which assuredly will not raise him in the opinion of our modern millennarians, as to the divine authority of the Apocalypse. But the ghost preserves an impenetrable silence. As far as we remember, only one hint about the employment of disembodied spirits escapes him. He encourages Mr. Southey to hope that there is a Paradise Press, at which all the valuable publications of Mr. Murray and Mr. Colburn are reprinted as regularly as at Philadelphia; and delicately insinuates that Thalaba and the Curse of Kehama are among the number. What a contrast does this absurd fiction present to those charming narratives which Plato and Cicero prefixed to their dialogues! What cost in machinery, yet what poverty of effect! A ghost brought in to say what any man might have said! The glorified spirit of a great statesman and philosopher dawdling, like a bilious old nabob at a watering place, over quarterly reviews and novels, dropping in to pay long calls, making excursions in search of the picturesque! The scene of St. George and St. Dennis in the Pucelle is hardly more ridiculous. We know what Voltaire meant. Nobody, however, can suppose that Mr. Southey means to make game of the mysteries of a higher state of existence. The fact is that, in the work before us, in the Vision of Judgement, and in some of his other pieces, his mode of treating the most solemn subjects differs from that of open scoffers only as the extravagant representations of sacred persons and things in some grotesque Italian paintings differ from the caricatures which Carlile exposes in the front of his shop. We interpret the particular act by the general character. What in the window of a convicted blasphemer we call blasphemous, we call only absurd and ill judged in an altar-piece.

We now come to the conversations which pass between Mr. Southey and Sir Thomas More, or rather between two Southeys, equally eloquent, equally angry, equally unreasonable, and equally given to talking about what they do not understand.[1] Perhaps we could not select a better instance of the spirit which pervades the whole book than the passages in which Mr. Southey gives his opinion of the manufacturing system. There is nothing which he hates so bitterly. It is, according to him, a system more tyrannical than that of the feudal ages, a system of actual servitude, a system which destroys the bodies and degrades the

[1] A passage in which some expressions used by Mr. Southey were misrepresented, certainly without any unfair intention, has been here omitted.

minds of those who are engaged in it. He expresses a hope that the competition of other nations may drive us out of the field; that our foreign trade may decline; and that we may thus enjoy a restoration of national sanity and strength. But he seems to think that the extermination of the whole manufacturing population would be a blessing, if the evil could be removed in no other way.

Mr. Southey does not bring forward a single fact in support of these views; and, as it seems to us, there are facts which lead to a very different conclusion. In the first place, the poor-rate is very decidedly lower in the manufacturing than in the agricultural districts. If Mr. Southey will look over the Parliamentary returns on this subject, he will find that the amount of parochial relief required by the labourers in the different counties of England is almost exactly in inverse proportion to the degree in which the manufacturing system has been introduced into those counties. The returns for the years ending in March 1825, and in March 1828, are now before us. In the former year we find the poor-rate highest in Sussex, about twenty shillings to every inhabitant. Then come Buckinghamshire, Essex, Suffolk, Bedfordshire, Huntingdonshire, Kent, and Norfolk. In all these the rate is above fifteen shillings a head. We will not go through the whole. Even in Westmoreland and the North Riding of Yorkshire, the rate is at more than eight shillings. In Cumberland and Monmouthshire, the most fortunate of all the agricultural districts, it is at six shillings. But in the West Riding of Yorkshire, it is as low as five shillings; and when we come to Lancashire, we find it at four shillings, one fifth of what it is in Sussex. The returns of the year ending in March 1828 are a little, and but a little, more unfavourable to the manufacturing districts. Lancashire, even in that season of distress, required a smaller poor-rate than any other district, and little more than one fourth of the poor-rate raised in Sussex. Cumberland alone, of the agricultural districts, was as well off as the West Riding of Yorkshire. These facts seem to indicate that the manufacturer is both in a more comfortable and in a less dependent situation than the agricultural labourer.

As to the effect of the manufacturing system on the bodily health, we must beg leave to estimate it by a standard far too low and vulgar for a mind so imaginative as that of Mr. Southey, the proportion of births and deaths. We know that, during the growth of this atrocious system, this new misery, to use the phrases of Mr. Southey, this new enormity, this birth of a portentous age, this pest which no man can approve whose heart is not seared or whose understanding has not been darkened, there has been a great diminution of mortality, and that this diminution has been greater in the manufacturing towns than any where else. The mortality still is, as it always was, greater in towns than in the country. But the difference has diminished in an extraordinary degree. There is the best reason to believe that the annual mortality of Manchester, about the middle of the last century, was one in twenty-eight. It is now reckoned at one in forty-five. In Glasgow and Leeds a similar improvement has taken place. Nay, the rate of mortality in those three great capitals of the manufacturing districts is now considerably less than it was, fifty years ago, over England and Wales taken together, open country and all. We might with some plausibility maintain that the people live longer because they are better fed, better lodged, better clothed, and better attended in sickness, and that these improvements are owing to that increase of national wealth which the manufacturing system has produced.

Much more might be said on the subject. But to what end? It is not from bills of mortality and statistical tables that Mr. Southey has learned his political creed. He cannot stoop to study the history of the system which he abuses, to strike the balance between the good and evil which it has produced, to compare district with district, or generation with generation. We will give his own reason for his opinion, the only reason which he gives for it, in his own words:—

"We remained awhile in silence looking upon the assemblage of dwellings below. Here, and in the adjoining hamlet of Millbeck, the effects of manufactures and of agriculture may be seen and compared. The old cottages are such as the poet and the painter equally delight in beholding. Substantially built of the native stone without mortar, dirtied with no white lime, and their long low roofs covered with slate, if they had been raised by the magic of some indigenous Amphion's music, the materials could not have adjusted themselves more beautifully in accord with the surrounding scene; and time has still further harmonized them with weather-stains, lichens, and moss, short grasses, and short fern, and stone-plants of various kinds. The ornamented chimneys, round or square, less adorned than those which, like little turrets, crest the houses of the Portuguese peasantry; and yet not less happily suited to their place, the hedge of clipt box beneath the windows, the rose-bushes beside the door, the little patch of flower-ground, with its tall holly-hocks in front; the garden beside, the bee-hives, and the orchard with its bank of daffodils and snow-drops, the earliest and the profusest in these parts, indicate in the owners some portion of ease and leisure, some regard to neatness and comfort, some sense of natural, and innocent, and healthful enjoyment. The new cottages of the manufacturers are upon the manufacturing pattern — naked, and in a row.

"'How is it,' said I, 'that every thing which is connected with manufactures presents such features of unqualified deformity? From the largest of Mammon's temples down to the poorest hovel in which his helotry are stalled, these edifices have all one character. Time will not mellow them; nature will neither clothe nor conceal them; and they will remain always as offensive to the eye as to the mind.'"

Here is wisdom. Here are the principles on which nations are to be governed. Rose-bushes and poor-rates, rather than steam-engines and independence. Mortality and cottages with weather-stains, rather than health and long life with edifices which time cannot mellow. We are told, that our age has invented atrocities beyond the imagination of our fathers; that society has been brought into a state compared with which extermination would be a blessing; and all because the dwellings of cotton-spinners are naked and rectangular. Mr. Southey has found out a way, he tells us, in which the effects of manufactures and agriculture may be compared. And what is this way? To stand on a hill, to look at a cottage and a factory, and to see which is the prettier. Does Mr. Southey think that the body of the English peasantry live, or ever lived, in substantial or ornamented cottages, with box-hedges, flower-gardens, bee-hives, and orchards? If not, what is his parallel worth? We despise those mock philosophers, who think that they serve the cause of science by depreciating literature and the fine arts. But if any thing could excuse their narrowness of mind it would be such a book as this. It is not strange that, when one enthusiast makes the picturesque the test of political good, another should feel inclined to proscribe altogether the pleasures of taste and imagination.

Thus it is that Mr. Southey reasons about matters

with which he thinks himself perfectly conversant. We cannot, therefore, be surprised to find that he commits extraordinary blunders when he writes on points of which he acknowledges himself to be ignorant. He confesses that he is not versed in political economy, and that he has neither liking nor aptitude for it; and he then proceeds to read the public a lecture concerning it which fully bears out his confession.

"All wealth," says Sir Thomas More, "in former times was tangible. It consisted in land, money, or chattels, which were either of real or conventional value."

Montesinos, as Mr. Southey somewhat affectedly calls himself, answers thus: —

"Jewels, for example, and pictures, as in Holland, where indeed at one time tulip bulbs answered the same purpose."

"That bubble," says Sir Thomas, "was one of those contagious insanities to which communities are subject. All wealth was real, till the extent of commerce rendered a paper currency necessary; which differed from precious stones and pictures in this important point, that there was no limit to its production."

"We regard it," says Montesinos, "as the representative of real wealth; and, therefore, limited always to the amount of what it represents."

"Pursue that notion," answers the ghost, "and you will be in the dark presently. Your provincial banknotes, which constitute almost wholly the circulating medium of certain districts, pass current to-day. To-morrow tidings may come that the house which issued them has stopt payment, and what do they represent then? You will find them the shadow of a shade."

We scarcely know at which end to begin to disentangle this knot of absurdities. We might ask, why it should be a greater proof of insanity in men to set a high value on rare tulips than on rare stones, which are neither more useful nor more beautiful? We might ask how it can be said that there is no limit to the production of paper money, when a man is hanged if he issues any in the name of another, and is forced to cash what he issues in his own? But Mr. Southey's error lies deeper still. "All wealth," says he, "was tangible and real till paper currency was introduced." Now, was there ever, since men emerged from a state of utter barbarism, an age in which there were no debts? Is not a debt, while the solvency of the debtor is undoubted, always reckoned as part of the wealth of the creditor? Yet is it tangible and real wealth? Does it cease to be wealth, because there is the security of a written acknowledgment for it? And what else is paper currency? Did Mr. Southey ever read a bank-note? If he did, he would see that it is a written acknowledgment of a debt, and a promise to pay that debt. The promise may be violated: the debt may remain unpaid: those to whom it was due may suffer: but this is a risk not confined to cases of paper currency: it is a risk inseparable from the relation of debtor and creditor. Every man who sells goods for any thing but ready money runs the risk of finding that what he considered as part of his wealth one day is nothing at all the next day. Mr. Southey refers to the picture-galleries of Holland. The pictures were undoubtedly real and tangible possessions. But surely it might happen that a burgomaster might owe a picture-dealer a thousand guilders for a Teniers. What in this case corresponds to our paper money is not the picture, which is tangible, but the claim of the picture-dealer on his customer for the price of the picture; and this claim is not tangible. Now, would not the picture-dealer consider this claim as part of his wealth? Would not a tradesman who knew of the claim give credit to the picture-dealer the more readily on account of the claim? The burgomaster might be ruined. If so, would not those consequences follow which, as Mr. Southey tells us, were never heard of till paper money came into use? Yesterday this claim was worth a thousand guilders. To-day what is it? The shadow of a shade.

It is true that, the more readily claims of this sort are transferred from hand to hand, the more extensive will be the injury produced by a single failure. The laws of all nations sanction, in certain cases, the transfer of rights not yet reduced into possession. Mr. Southey would scarcely wish, we should think, that all indorsements of bills and notes should be declared invalid. Yet even if this were done, the transfer of claims would imperceptibly take place, to a very great extent. When the baker trusts the butcher, for example, he is in fact, though not in form, trusting the butcher's customers. A man who owes large bills to tradesmen, and fails to pay them, almost always produces distress through a very wide circle of people with whom he never dealt.

In short, what Mr. Southey takes for a difference in kind is only a difference of form and degree. In every society men have claims on the property of others. In every society there is a possibility that some debtors may not be able to fulfil their obligations. In every society, therefore, there is wealth which is not tangible, and which may become the shadow of a shade.

Mr. Southey then proceeds to a dissertation on the national debt, which he considers in a new and most consolatory light, as a clear addition to the income of the country.

"You can understand," says Sir Thomas, "that it constitutes a great part of the national wealth."

"So large a part," answers Montesinos, "that the interest amounted, during the prosperous time of agriculture, to as much as the rental of all the land in Great Britain; and at present to the rental of all lands, all houses, and all other fixed property put together."

The Ghost and the Laureate agree that it is very desirable that there should be so secure and advantageous a deposit for wealth as the funds afford. Sir Thomas then proceeds: —

"Another and far more momentous benefit must not be overlooked; the expenditure of an annual interest, equalling, as you have stated, the present rental of all fixed property."

"That expenditure," quoth Montesinos, "gives employment to half the industry in the kingdom, and feeds half the mouths. Take, indeed, the weight of the national debt from this great and complicated social machine, and the wheels must stop."

From this passage we should have been inclined to think that Mr. Southey supposes the dividends to be a free gift periodically sent down from heaven to the fundholders, as quails and manna were sent to the Israelites; were it not that he has vouchsafed, in the following question and answer, to give the public some information which, we believe, was very little needed.

"Whence comes the interest?" says Sir Thomas.

"It is raised," answers Montesinos, "by taxation."

Now, has Mr. Southey ever considered what would

be done with this sum if it were not paid as interest to the national creditor? If he would think over this matter for a short time, we suspect that the "momentous benefit" of which he talks would appear to him to shrink strangely in amount. A fundholder, we will suppose, spends dividends amounting to five hundred pounds a year; and his ten nearest neighbours pay fifty pounds each to the tax-gatherer, for the purpose of discharging the interest of the national debt. If the debt were wiped out, a measure, be it understood, which we by no means recommend, the fundholder would cease to spend his five hundred pounds a year. He would no longer give employment to industry, or put food into the mouths of labourers. This Mr. Southey thinks a fearful evil. But is there no mitigating circumstances? Each of the ten neighbours of our fundholder has fifty pounds a year more than formerly. Each of them will, as it seems to our feeble understandings, employ more industry and feed more mouths than formerly. The sum is exactly the same. It is in different hands. But on what grounds does Mr. Southey call upon us to believe that it is in the hands of men who will spend it less liberally or less judiciously? He seems to think that nobody but a fundholder can employ the poor; that, if a tax is remitted, those who formerly used to pay it proceed immediately to dig holes in the earth, and to bury the sum which the government had been accustomed to take; that no money can set industry in motion till such money has been taken by the tax-gatherer out of one man's pocket and put into another man's pocket. We really wish that Mr. Southey would try to prove this principle, which is indeed the foundation of his whole theory of finance: for we think it right to hint to him that our hard-hearted and unimaginative generation will expect some more satisfactory reason than the only one with which he has yet favoured it, namely, a similitude touching evaporation and dew.

Both the theory and the illustration, indeed, are old friends of ours. In every season of distress which we can remember, Mr. Southey has been proclaiming that it is not from economy, but from increased taxation, that the country must expect relief; and he still, we find, places the undoubting faith of a political Diafoirus, in his

"Resaignare, repurgare, et reclysterizare."

"A people," he tells us, "may be too rich, but a government cannot be so."

"A state," says he, "cannot have more wealth at its command than may be employed for the general good, a liberal expenditure in national works being one of the surest means of promoting national prosperity; and the benefit being still more obvious, of an expenditure directed to the purposes of national improvement. But a people may be too rich."

We fully admit that a state cannot have at its command more wealth than may be employed for the general good. But neither can individuals, or bodies of individuals, have at their command more wealth than may be employed for the general good. If there be no limit to the sum which may be usefully laid out in public works and national improvement, then wealth, whether in the hands of private men or of the government, may always, if the possessors choose to spend it usefully, be usefully spent. The only ground, therefore, on which Mr. Southey can possibly maintain that a government cannot be too rich, but that a people may be too rich, must be this, that governments are more likely to spend their money on good objects than private individuals.

But what is useful expenditure? "A liberal expenditure in national works," says Mr. Southey, "is one of the surest means for promoting national prosperity." What does he mean by national prosperity? Does he mean the wealth of the state? If so, his reasoning runs thus: The more wealth a state has the better; for the more wealth a state has the more wealth it will have. This is surely something like that fallacy, which is ungallantly termed a lady's reason. If by national prosperity he means the wealth of the people, of how gross a contradiction is Mr. Southey guilty. A people, he tells us, may be too rich: a government cannot: foı a government can employ its riches in making the people richer. The wealth of the people is to be taken from them, because they have too much, and laid out in works, which will yield them more.

We are really at a loss to determine whether Mr. Southey's reason for recommending large taxation is that it will make the people rich, or that it will make them poor. But we are sure that, if his object is to make them rich, he takes the wrong course. There are two or three principles respecting public works, which, as an experience of vast extent proves, may be trusted in almost every case.

It scarcely ever happens that any private man or body of men will invest property in a canal, a tunnel, or a bridge, but from an expectation that the outlay will be profitable to them. No work of this sort can be profitable to private speculators, unless the public be willing to pay for the use of it. The public will not pay of their own accord for what yields no profit or convenience to them. There is thus a direct and obvious connection between the motive which induces individuals to undertake such a work, and the utility of the work.

Can we find any such connection in the case of a public work executed by a government? If it is useful, are the individuals who rule the country richer? If it is useless, are they poorer? A public man may be solicitous for his credit. But is not he likely to gain more credit by an useless display of ostentatious architecture in a great town than by the best road or the best canal in some remote province? The fame of public works is a much less certain test of their utility than the amount of toll collected at them. In a corrupt age, there will be direct embezzlement. In the purest age, there will be abundance of jobbing. Never were the statesmen of any country more sensitive to public opinion, and more spotless in pecuniary transactions, than those who have of late governed England. Yet we have only to look at the buildings recently erected in London for a proof of our rule. In a bad age, the fate of the public is to be robbed outright. In a good age, it is merely to have the dearest and the worst of every thing.

Buildings for state purposes the state must erect. And here we think that, in general, the state ought to stop. We firmly believe that five hundred thousand pounds subscribed by individuals for rail-roads or canals would produce more advantage to the public than five millions voted by Parliament for the same purpose. There are certain old saws about the master's eye and about every body's business, in which we place very great faith.

There is, we have said, no consistency in Mr. Southey's political system. But if there be in his political system any leading principle, any one error which diverges more widely and variously than any other, it is that of which his theory about national works is a ramification. He conceives that the business of the magistrate is, not merely to see that the persons and property of the people are secure from attack, but that he ought to be a jack-of-all-trades, architect, engineer, schoolmaster, merchant, theologian, a Lady Bountiful in every parish, a Paul Pry in every house, spying, eaves-dropping, relieving, admonishing, spending our money for us, and choosing our opinions for us. His principle is, if we understand it rightly, that no man can do any thing so well for himself as his rulers, be they who they may, can do it for him, and that a government approaches nearer and nearer to perfection, in proportion as it interferes more and more with the habits and notions of individuals.

He seems to be fully convinced that it is in the power of government to relieve all the distresses under which the lower orders labour. Nay, he considers doubt on this subject as impious. We cannot refrain from quoting his argument on this subject. It is a perfect jewel of logic.

"'Many thousands in your metropolis,' says Sir Thomas More, 'rise every morning without knowing how they are to subsist during the day; as many of them, where they are to lay their heads at night. All men, even the vicious themselves, know that wickedness leads to misery: but many, even among the good and the wise, have yet to learn that misery is almost as often the cause of wickedness.'

"'There are many,' says Montesinos, 'who know this, but believe that it is not in the power of human institutions to prevent this misery. They see the effect, but regard the causes as inseparable from the condition of human nature.'

"'As surely as God is good,' replies Sir Thomas, 'so surely there is no such thing as necessary evil. For, by the religious mind, sickness, and pain, and death, are not to be accounted evils.' "

Now if sickness, pain, and death, are not evils, we cannot understand why it should be an evil that thousands should rise without knowing how they are to subsist. The only evil of hunger is that it produces first pain, then sickness, and finally death. If it did not produce these, it would be no calamity. If these are not evils, it is no calamity. We will propose a very plain dilemma: either physical pain is an evil, or it is not an evil. If it is an evil, then there is necessary evil in the universe: if it is not, why should the poor be delivered from it?

Mr. Southey entertains as exaggerated a notion of the wisdom of governments as of their power. He speaks with the greatest disgust of the respect now paid to public opinion. That opinion is, according to him, to be distrusted and dreaded; its usurpation ought to be vigorously resisted; and the practice of yielding to it is likely to ruin the country. To maintain police is, according to him, only one of the ends of government. The duties of a ruler are patriarchal and paternal. He ought to consider the moral discipline of the people as his first object, to establish a religion, to train the whole community in that religion, and to consider all dissenters as his own enemies.

" 'Nothing,' says Sir Thomas, 'is more certain, than that religion is the basis upon which civil government rests; that from religion power derives its authority, laws their efficacy, and both their zeal and sanction; and it is necessary that this religion be established as for the security of the state, and for the welfare of the people, who would otherwise be moved to and fro with every wind of doctrine. A state is secure in proportion as the people are attached to its institutions: it is, therefore, the first and plainest rule of sound policy, that the people be trained up in the way they should go. The state that neglects this prepares its own destruction; and they who train them in any other way are undermining it. Nothing in abstract science can be more certain than these positions are.'

"'All of which,' answers Montesinos, 'are nevertheless denied by our professors of the arts Babblative and Scribblative: some in the audacity of evil designs, and others in the glorious assurance of impenetrable ignorance.'"

The greater part of the two volumes before us is merely an amplification of these paragraphs. What does Mr. Southey mean by saying that religion is demonstrably the basis of civil government? He cannot surely mean that men have no motives except those derived from religion for establishing and supporting civil government, that no temporal advantage is derived from civil government, that men would experience no temporal inconvenience from living in a state of anarchy? If he allows, as we think he must allow, that it is for the good of mankind in this world to have civil government, and that the great majority of mankind have always thought it for their good in this world to have civil government, we then have a basis for government quite distinct from religion. It is true that the Christian religion sanctions government, as it sanctions every thing which promotes the happiness and virtue of our species. But we are at a loss to conceive in what sense religion can be said to be the basis of government, in which religion is not also the basis of the practices of eating, drinking, and lighting fires in cold weather. Nothing in history is more certain than that government has existed, has received some obedience, and has given some protection, in times in which it derived no support from religion, in times in which there was no religion that influenced the hearts and lives of men. It was not from dread of Tartarus, or from belief in the Elysian fields, that an Athenian wished to have some institutions which might keep Orestes from filching his cloak, or Midias from breaking his head. "It is from religion," says Mr. Southey, "that power derives its authority, and laws their efficacy." From what religion does our power over the Hindoos derive its authority, or the law in virtue of which we hang Brahmins its efficacy? For thousands of years civil government has existed in almost every corner of the world, in ages of priestcraft, in ages of fanaticism, in ages of Epicurean indifference, in ages of enlightened piety. However pure or impure the faith of the people might be, whether they adored a beneficent or a malignant power, whether they thought the soul mortal or immortal, they have, as soon as they ceased to be absolute savages, found out their need of civil government, and instituted it accordingly. It is as universal as the practice of cookery. Yet, it is as certain, says Mr. Southey, as any thing in abstract science, that government is founded on religion. We should like to know what notion Mr. Southey has of the demonstrations of abstract science. A very vague one, we suspect.

The proof proceeds. As religion is the basis of government, and as the state is secure in proportion as the people are attached to public institutions, it is therefore, says Mr. Southey, the first rule of policy, that the government should train the people in the way in which they should go; and it is plain that those who train them in any other way are undermining the state.

Now it does not appear to us to be the first object that people should always believe in the established religion and be attached to the established government. A religion may be false. A government may be oppressive. And whatever support government gives to false religions, or religion to oppressive governments, we consider as a clear evil.

The maxim, that governments ought to train the people in the way in which they should go, sounds well. But is there any reason for believing that a government is more likely to lead the people in the right way than the people to fall into the right way of themselves? Have there not been governments which were blind leaders of the blind? Are there not still such governments? Can it be laid down as a general rule that the movement of political and religious truth is rather downwards from the government to the people than upwards from the people to the government? These are questions which it is of importance to have clearly resolved. Mr. Southey declaims against public opinion, which is now, he tells us, usurping supreme power. Formerly, according to him, the laws governed; now public opinion governs. What are laws but expressions of the opinion of some class which has power over the rest of the community? By what was the world ever governed but by the opinion of some person or persons? By what else can it ever be governed? What are all systems, religious, political, or scientific, but opinions resting on evidence more or less satisfactory? The question is not between human opinion and some higher and more certain mode of arriving at truth, but between opinion and opinion, between the opinions of one man and another, or of one class and another, or of one generation and another. Public opinion is not infallible; but can Mr. Southey construct any institutions which shall secure to us the guidance of an infallible opinion? Can Mr. Southey select any family, any profession, any class, in short, distinguished by any plain badge from the rest of the community, whose opinion is more likely to be just than this much abused public opinion? Would he choose the peers, for example? Or the two hundred tallest men in the country? Or the poor Knights of Windsor? Or children who are born with cauls? Or the seventh sons of seventh sons? We cannot suppose that he would recommend popular election; for that is merely an appeal to public opinion. And to say that society ought to be governed by the opinion of the wisest and best, though true, is useless. Whose opinion is to decide, who are the wisest and best?

Mr. Southey and many other respectable people seem to think that, when they have once proved the moral and religious training of the people to be a most important object, it follows, of course, that it is an object which the government ought to pursue. They forget that we have to consider, not merely the goodness of the end, but also the fitness of the means. Neither in the natural nor in the political body have all members the same office. There is surely no contradiction in saying that a certain section of the community may be quite competent to protect the persons and property of the rest, yet quite unfit to direct our opinions, or to superintend our private habits.

So strong is the interest of a ruler to protect his subjects against all depredations and outrages except his own, so clear and simple are the means by which this end is to be effected, that men are probably better off under the worst governments in the world than they would be in a state of anarchy. Even when the appointment of magistrates has been left to chance, as in the Italian Republics, things have gone on far better than if there had been no magistrates at all, and if every man had done what seemed right in his own eyes. But we see no reason for thinking that the opinions of the magistrate on speculative questions are more likely to be right than those of any other man. None of the modes by which a magistrate is appointed, popular election, the accident of the lot, or the accident of birth, affords, as far as we can perceive, much security for his being wiser than any of his neighbours. The chance of his being wiser than all his neighbours together is still smaller. Now we cannot understand how it can be laid down that it is the duty and the right of one class to direct the opinions of another, unless it can be proved that the former class is more likely to form just opinions than the latter.

The duties of government would be, as Mr. Southey says that they are, paternal, if a government were necessarily as much superior in wisdom to a people as the most foolish father, for a time, is to the most intelligent child, and if a government loved a people as fathers generally love their children. But there is no reason to believe that a government will have either the paternal warmth of affection or the paternal superiority of intellect. Mr. Southey might as well say that the duties of the shoemaker are paternal, and that it is an usurpation in any man not of the craft to say that his shoes are bad and to insist on having better. The division of labour would be no blessing, if those by whom a thing is done were to pay no attention to the opinion of those for whom it is done. The shoemaker, in the Relapse, tells Lord Foppington that his lordship is mistaken in supposing that his shoe pinches. "It does not pinch; it cannot pinch; I know my business; and I never made a better shoe." This is the way in which Mr. Southey would have a government treat a people who usurp the privilege of thinking. Nay, the shoemaker of Vanbrugh has the advantage in the comparison. He contented himself with regulating his customer's shoes, about which he had peculiar means of information, and did not presume to dictate about the coat and hat. But Mr. Southey would have the rulers of a country prescribe opinions to the people, not only about politics, but about matters concerning which a government has no peculiar sources of information, and concerning which any man in the streets may know as much and think as justly as the King, namely religion and morals.

Men are never so likely to settle a question rightly as when they discuss it freely. A government can interfere in discussion only by making it less free than it would otherwise be. Men are most likely to form just opinions when they have no other wish than to know the truth, and are exempt from all influence, either of hope or fear. Government, as government, can bring nothing but the influence of hopes and fears to support its doctrines. It carries on controversy, not with reasons, but with threats and bribes. If it employs reasons, it does so, not in virtue of any powers which belong to it as a government. Thus, instead of a contest between argument and argument, we have a contest between argument and force. Instead of a contest in which truth, from the natural constitution of the human mind, has a decided advantage over falsehood, we have a contest in which truth can be victorious only by accident.

And what, after all, is the security which this training gives to governments? Mr. Southey would scarcely propose that discussion should be more effectually shackled, that public opinion should be more strictly disciplined into conformity with established institutions, than in Spain and Italy. Yet we know that the restraints which exist in Spain and Italy have not prevented atheism from spreading among the educated classes, and especially among those whose office it is to minister at the altars of God. All our readers know how, at the time of the French Revolution, priest after priest came forward to declare that his doctrine, his ministry, his whole life, had been a lie, a mummery during which he could scarcely compose his countenance sufficiently to carry on the imposture. This was the case of a false, or at least of a grossly corrupted religion. Let us take then the case of all others most favourable to Mr. Southey's argument. Let us take that form of religion which he holds to be the purest, the system of the Arminian part of the Church of England. Let us take the form of government which he most admires and regrets, the government of England in the time of Charles the First. Would he wish to see a closer connection between church and state than then existed? Would he wish for more powerful ecclesiastical tribunals? for a more zealous king? for a more active primate? Would he wish to see a more complete monopoly of public instruction given to the Established Church? Could any government do more to train the people in the way in which he would have them go? And in what did all this training end? The Report of the state of the Province of Canterbury, delivered by Laud to his master at the close of 1639, represents the Church of England as in the highest and most palmy state. So effectually had the government pursued that policy which Mr. Southey wishes to see revived that there was scarcely the least appearance of dissent. Most of the bishops stated that all was well among their flocks. Seven or eight persons in the diocese of Peterborough had seemed refractory to the church, but had made ample submission. In Norfolk and Suffolk all whom there had been reason to suspect had made profession of conformity, and appeared to observe it strictly. It is confessed that there was a little difficulty in bringing some of the vulgar in Suffolk to take the sacrament at the rails in the chancel. This was the only open instance of non-conformity which the vigilant eye of Laud could detect in all the dioceses of his twenty-one suffragans, on the very eve of a revolution in which primate, and church, and monarch, and monarchy were to perish together.

At which time would Mr. Southey pronounce the constitution more secure; in 1639, when Laud presented this Report to Charles; or now, when thousands of meetings openly collect millions of dissenters, when designs against the tithes are openly avowed, when books attacking not only the Establishment, but the first principles of Christianity, are openly sold in the streets? The signs of discontent, he tells us, are stronger in England now than in France when the States-General met: and hence he would have us infer that a revolution like that of France may be at hand. Does he not know that the danger of states is to be estimated, not by what breaks out of the public mind, but by what stays in it? Can he conceive any thing more terrible than the situation of a government which rules without apprehension over a people of hypocrites, which is flattered by the press and cursed in the inner chambers, which exults in the attachment and obedience of its subjects, and knows not that those subjects are leagued against it in a free-masonry of hatred, the sign of which is every day conveyed in the glance of ten thousand eyes, the pressure of ten thousand hands, and the tone of ten thousand voices? Profound and ingenious policy! Instead of curing the disease, to remove those symptoms by which alone its nature can be known! To leave the serpent his deadly sting, and deprive him only of his warning rattle!

When the people whom Charles had so assiduously trained in the good way had rewarded his paternal care by cutting off his head, a new kind of training came into fashion. Another government arose which, like the former, considered religion as its surest basis, and the religious discipline of the people as its first duty. Sanguinary laws were enacted against libertinism; profane pictures were burned: drapery was put on indecorous statues; the theatres were shut up; fast-days were numerous; and the Parliament resolved that no person should be admitted into any public employment, unless the House should be first satisfied of his vital godliness. We know what was the end of this training. We know that it ended in impiety, in filthy and heartless sensuality, in the dissolution of all ties of honour and morality. We know that at this very day scriptural phrases, scriptural names, perhaps some scriptural doctrines, excite disgust and ridicule, solely because they are associated with the austerity of that period.

Thus has the experiment of training the people in established forms of religion been twice tried in England on a large scale, once by Charles and Laud, and once by the Puritans. The High Tories of our time still entertain many of the feelings and opinions of Charles and Laud, though in a mitigated form; nor is it difficult to see that the heirs of the Puritans are still amongst us. It would be desirable that each of these parties should remember how little advantage or honour it formerly derived from the closest alliance with power, that it fell by the support of rulers, and rose by their opposition, that of the two systems that in which the people were at any time drilled was always at that time the unpopular system, that the training of the High Church ended in the reign of the Puritans, and that the training of the Puritans ended in the reign of the harlots.

This was quite natural. Nothing is so galling to a people not broken in from the birth as a paternal, or, in other words, a meddling government, a government which tells them what to read, and say, and eat, and drink, and wear. Our fathers could not bear it two hundred years ago; and we are not more patient than they. Mr. Southey thinks that the yoke of the church is dropping off because it is loose. We feel convinced that it is borne only because it is easy, and that, in the instant in which an attempt is made to tighten it, it will be flung away. It will be neither the first nor the strongest yoke that has been broken asunder and trampled under foot in the day of the vengeance of England.

How far Mr. Southey would have the government carry its measures for training the people in the doctrines of the church, we are unable to discover. In one passage Sir Thomas More asks with great vehemence,

"Is it possible that your laws should suffer the unbelievers to exist as a party? Vetitum est adeo sceleris nihil?"

Montesinos answers. "They avow themselves in defiance of the laws. The fashionable doctrine which the press at this time maintains is, that this is a matter in which the laws ought not to interfere, every man having a right, both to form what opinion he pleases upon religious subjects, and to promulgate that opinion."

It is clear, therefore, that Mr. Southey would not give full and perfect toleration to infidelity. In another passage, however, he observes with some truth, though too sweepingly, that "any degree of intolerance short of that full extent which the Papal Church exercises where it has the power, acts upon the opinions which it is intended to suppress, like pruning upon vigorous plants; they grow the stronger for it." These two passages, put together, would lead us to the conclusion that, in Mr. Southey's opinion, the utmost severity ever employed by the Roman Catholic Church in the days of its greatest power ought to be employed against unbelievers in England; in plain words, that Carlile and his shopmen ought to be burned in Smithfield, and that every person who, when called upon, should decline to make a solemn profession of Christianity ought to suffer the same fate. We do not, however, believe that Mr. Southey would recommend such a course, though his language would, according to all the rules of logic, justify us in supposing this to be his meaning. His opinions form no system at all. He never sees, at one glance, more of a question than will furnish matter for one flowing and well turned sentence; so that it would be the height of unfairness to charge him personally with holding a doctrine, merely because that doctrine is deducible, though by the closest and most accurate reasoning, from the premises which he has laid down. We are, therefore, left completely in the dark as to Mr. Southey's opinions about toleration. Immediately after censuring the government for not punishing infidels, he proceeds to discuss the question of the Catholic disabilities, now, thank God, removed, and defends them on the ground that the Catholic doctrines tend to persecution, and that the Catholics persecuted when they had power.

"They must persecute," says he, "if they believe their own creed, for conscience-sake; and if they do not believe it, they must persecute for policy; because it is only by intolerance that so corrupt and injurious a system can be upheld."

That unbelievers should not be persecuted is an instance of national depravity at which the glorified spirits stand aghast. Yet a sect of Christians is to be excluded from power, because those who formerly held the same opinions were guilty of persecution. We have said that we do not very well know what Mr. Southey's opinion about toleration is. But, on the whole, we take it to be this, that everybody is to tolerate him, and that he is to tolerate nobody.

We will not be deterred by any fear of misrepresentation from expressing our hearty approbation of the mild, wise, and eminently Christian manner in which the Church and the Government have lately acted with respect to blasphemous publications. We praise them for not having thought it necessary to encircle a religion pure, merciful, and philosophical, a religion to the evidence of which the highest intellects have yielded, with the defences of a false and bloody superstition. The ark of God was never taken till it was surrounded by the arms of earthly defenders. In captivity, its sanctity was sufficient to vindicate it from insult, and to lay the hostile fiend prostrate on the threshold of his own temple. The real security of Christianity is to be found in its benevolent morality, in its exquisite adaptation to the human heart, in the facility with which its scheme accommodates itself to the capacity of every human intellect, in the consolation which it bears to the house of mourning, in the light with which it brightens the great mystery of the grave. To such a system it can bring no addition of dignity or of strength, that it is part and parcel of the common law. It is not now for the first time left to rely on the force of its own evidences and the attractions of its own beauty. Its sublime theology confounded the Grecian schools in the fair conflict of reason with reason. The bravest and wisest of the Cæsars found their arms and their policy unavailing, when opposed to the weapons that were not carnal and the kingdom that was not of this world. The victory which Porphyry and Diocletian failed to gain is not, to all appearance, reserved for any of those who have, in this age, directed their attacks against the last restraint of the powerful and the last hope of the wretched. The whole history of Christianity shows, that she is in far greater danger of being corrupted by the alliance of power, than of being crushed by its opposition. Those who thrust temporal sovereignty upon her treat her as their prototypes treated her author. They bow the knee, and spit upon her; they cry "Hail!" and smite her on the cheek; they put a sceptre in her hand, but it is a fragile reed; they crown her, but it is with thorns; they cover with purple the wounds which their own hands have inflicted on her; and inscribe magnificent titles over the cross on which they have fixed her to perish in ignominy and pain.

The general view which Mr. Southey takes of the prospects of society is very gloomy; but we comfort ourselves with the consideration that Mr. Southey is no prophet. He foretold, we remember, on the very eve of the abolition of the Test and Corporation Acts, that these hateful laws were immortal, and that pious minds would long be gratified by seeing the most solemn religious rite of the Church profaned for the purpose of upholding her political supremacy. In the book before us, he says that Catholics cannot possibly be admitted into Parliament until those whom Johnson called "the bottomless Whigs" come into power. While the book was in the press, the prophecy was falsified; and a Tory of the Tories, Mr. Southey's own favourite hero, won and wore that noblest wreath, "Ob cives servatos."

The signs of the times, Mr. Southey tells us, are very threatening. His fears for the country would decidedly preponderate over his hopes, but for his firm reliance on the mercy of God. Now, as we know that God has once suffered the civilised world to be overrun by savages, and the Christian religion to be corrupted by doctrines which made it, for some ages, almost as bad as Paganism, we cannot think it inconsistent with his attributes that similar calamities should again befal mankind.

We look, however, on the state of the world, and of this kingdom in particular, with much greater satisfaction and with better hopes. Mr. Southey speaks with contempt of those who think the savage state happier than the social. On this subject, he says, Rousseau never imposed on him even in his youth. But he conceives that a community which has advanced a little way in civilisation is happier than one which has made greater progress. The Britons in the time of Cæsar were happier, he suspects, than the English of the nineteenth century. On the whole, he selects the generation which preceded the Reformation as that in which the people of this country were better off than at any time before or since.

This opinion rests on nothing, as far as we can see, except his own individual associations. He is a man of letters; and a life destitute of literary pleasures seems insipid to him. He abhors the spirit of the present generation, the severity of its studies, the boldness of its inquiries, and the disdain with which it regards some old prejudices by which his own mind is held in bondage. He dislikes an utterly unenlightened age; he dislikes an investigating and reforming age. The first twenty years of the sixteenth century would have exactly suited him. They furnished just the quantity of intellectual excitement which he requires. The learned few read and wrote largely. A scholar was held in high estimation. But the rabble did not presume to think; and even the most inquiring and independent of the educated classes paid more reverence to authority, and less to reason, than is usual in our time. This is a state of things in which Mr. Southey would have found himself quite comfortable; and, accordingly, he pronounces it the happiest state of things ever known in the world.

The savages were wretched, says Mr. Southey; but the people in the time of Sir Thomas More were happier than either they or we. Now we think it quite certain that we have the advantage over the contemporaries of Sir Thomas More, in every point in which they had any advantage over savages.

Mr. Southey does not even pretend to maintain that the people in the sixteenth century were better lodged or clothed than at present. He seems to admit that in these respects there has been some little improvement. It is indeed a matter about which scarcely any doubt can exist in the most perverse mind that the improvements of machinery have lowered the price of manufactured articles, and have brought within the reach of the poorest some conveniences which Sir Thomas More or his master could not have obtained at any price.

The labouring classes, however, were, according to Mr. Southey, better fed three hundred years ago than at present. We believe that he is completely in error on this point. The condition of servants in noble and wealthy families, and of scholars at the Universities, must surely have been better in those times than that of day-labourers; and we are sure that it was not better than that of our workhouse paupers. From the household book of the Northumberland family, we find that in one of the greatest establishments of the kingdom the servants lived very much as common sailors live now. In the reign of Edward the Sixth the state of the students at Cambridge is described to us, on the very best authority, as most wretched. Many of them dined on pottage made of a farthing's worth of beef with a little salt and oatmeal, and literally nothing else. This account we have from a contemporary master of St. John's. Our parish poor now eat wheaten bread. In the sixteenth century the labourer was glad to get barley, and was often forced to content himself with poorer fare. In Harrison's introduction to Holinshed we have an account of the state of our working population in the "golden days," as Mr. Southey calls them, "of good Queen Bess." "The gentilitie," says he, "commonly provide themselves sufficiently of wheat for their own tables, whylest their household and poore neighbours in some shires are inforced to content themselves with rye or barleie; yea, and in time of dearth, many with bread made eyther of beanes, peason, or otes, or of altogether, and some acornes among. I will not say that this extremity is oft so well to be seen in time of plentie as of dearth; but if I should I could easily bring my trial: for albeit there be much more grounde eared nowe almost in everye place then hathe beene of late yeares, yet such a price of corne continueth in eache towne and markete, without any just cause, that the artificer and poore labouring man is not able to reach unto it, but is driven to content himself with horse-corne." We should like to see what the effect would be of putting any parish in England now on allowance of "horse-corne." The helotry of Mammon are not, in our day, so easily enforced to content themselves as the peasantry of that happy period, as Mr. Southey considers it, which elapsed between the fall of the feudal and the rise of the commercial tyranny.

"The people," says Mr. Southey, "are worse fed than when they were fishers." And yet in another place he complains that they will not eat fish. "They have contracted," says he, "I know not how, some obstinate prejudice against a kind of food at once wholesome and delicate, and every where to be obtained cheaply and in abundance, were the demand for it as general as it ought to be." It is true that the lower orders have an obstinate prejudice against fish. But hunger has no such obstinate prejudices. If what was formerly a common diet is now eaten only in times of severe pressure, the inference is plain. The people must be fed with what they at least think better food than that of their ancestors.

The advice and medicine which the poorest labourer

can now obtain, in disease, or after an accident, is far superior to what Henry the Eighth could have commanded. Scarcely any part of the country is out of the reach of practitioners who are probably not so far inferior to Sir Henry Halford as they are superior to Dr. Butts. That there has been a great improvement in this respect, Mr. Southey allows. Indeed he could not well have denied it. "But," says he, "the evils for which these sciences are the palliative, have increased since the time of the Druids, in a proportion that heavily overweighs the benefit of improved therapeutics." We know nothing either of the diseases or the remedies of the Druids. But we are quite sure that the improvement of medicine has far more than kept pace with the increase of disease during the last three centuries. This is proved by the best possible evidence. The term of human life is decidedly longer in England than in any former age, respecting which we possess any information on which we can rely. All the rants in the world about picturesque cottages and temples of Mammon will not shake this argument. No test of the physical well-being of society can be named so decisive as that which is furnished by bills of mortality. That the lives of the people of this country have been gradually lengthening during the course of several generations, is as certain as any fact in statistics; and that the lives of men should become longer and longer, while their bodily condition during life is becoming worse and worse, is utterly incredible.

Let our readers think over these circumstances. Let them take into the account the sweating sickness and the plague. Let them take into the account that fearful disease which first made its appearance in the generation to which Mr. Southey assigns the palm of felicity, and raged through Europe with a fury at which the physician stood aghast, and before which the people were swept away by myriads. Let them consider the state of the northern counties, constantly the scene of robberies, rapes, massacres, and conflagrations. Let them add to all this the fact that seventy-two thousand persons suffered death by the hands of the executioner during the reign of Henry the Eighth, and judge between the nineteenth and the sixteenth century.

We do not say that the lower orders in England do not suffer severe hardships. But, in spite of Mr. Southey's assertions, and in spite of the assertions of a class of politicians, who, differing from Mr. Southey in every other point, agree with him in this, we are inclined to doubt whether the labouring classes here really suffer greater physical distress than the labouring classes of the most flourishing countries of the Continent.

It will scarcely be maintained that the lazzaroni who sleep under the porticoes of Naples, or the beggars who besiege the convents of Spain, are in a happier situation than the English commonalty. The distress which has lately been experienced in the northern part of Germany, one of the best governed and most prosperous regions of Europe, surpasses, if we have been correctly informed, any thing which has of late years been known among us. In Norway and Sweden the peasantry are constantly compelled to mix bark with their bread; and even this expedient has not always preserved whole families and neighbourhoods from perishing together of famine. An experiment has lately been tried in the kingdom of the Netherlands, which has been cited to prove the possibility of establishing agricultural colonies on the waste lands of England, but which proves to our minds nothing so clearly as this, that the rate of subsistence to which the labouring classes are reduced in the Netherlands is miserably low, and very far inferior to that of the English paupers. No distress which the people here have endured for centuries approaches to that which has been felt by the French in our own time. The beginning of the year 1817 was a time of great distress in this island. But the state of the lowest classes here was luxury compared with that of the people of France. We find in Magendie's "Journal de Physiologie Expérimentale" a paper on a point of physiology connected with the distress of that season. It appears that the inhabitants of six departments, Aix, Jura, Doubs, Haute Saone, Vosges, and Saone-et-Loire, were reduced first to oatmeal and potatoes, and at last to nettles, bean-stalks, and other kinds of herbage fit only for cattle; that when the next harvest enabled them to eat barley-bread, many of them died from intemperate indulgence in what they thought an exquisite repast; and that a dropsy of a peculiar description was produced by the hard fare of the year. Dead bodies were found on the roads and in the fields. A single surgeon dissected six of these, and found the stomach shrunk, and filled with the unwholesome aliments which hunger had driven men to share with beasts. Such extremity of distress as this is never heard of in England, or even in Ireland. We are, on the whole, inclined to think, though we would speak with diffidence on a point on which it would be rash to pronounce a positive judgment without a much longer and closer investigation than we have bestowed upon it, that the labouring classes of this island, though they have their grievances and distresses, some produced by their own improvidence, some by the errors of their rulers, are on the whole better off as to physical comforts than the inhabitants of any equally extensive district of the old world. For this very reason, suffering is more acutely felt and more loudly bewailed here than elsewhere. We must take into the account the liberty of discussion, and the strong interest which the opponents of a ministry always have to exaggerate the extent of the public disasters. There are countries in which the people quietly endure distress that here would shake the foundations of the state, countries in which the inhabitants of a whole province turn out to eat grass with less clamour than one Spitalfields weaver would make here, if the overseers were to put him on barley-bread. In those new commonwealths in which a civilised population has at its command a boundless extent of the richest soil, the condition of the labourer is probably happier than in any society which has lasted for many centuries. But in the old world we must confess ourselves unable to find any satisfactory record of any great nation, past or present, in which the working classes have been in a more comfortable situation than in England during the last thirty years. When this island was thinly peopled, it was barbarous: there was little capital; and that little was insecure. It is now the richest and the most highly civilised spot in the world; but the population is dense. Thus we have never known that golden age which the lower orders in the United States are now enjoying. We have never known an age of liberty, of order, and of education, an age in which the mechanical sciences were carried to a great height, yet in which the people were not sufficiently numerous to cultivate even the most fertile valleys. But, when we compare our own condition with that of our ancestors, we think it clear that the advantages arising from the progress of civilisation have far more than counterbalanced the disadvantages arising from the progress of population. While our numbers have increased tenfold, our wealth has increased a hundred-fold. Though there are so many more people to share the wealth now existing in the country than there were in the sixteenth century, it seems certain that a greater share falls to almost every individual than fell to the share of any of the corresponding class in the sixteenth century. The King keeps a more splendid court. The establishments of the nobles are more magnificent. The esquires are richer; the merchants are richer; the shopkeepers are richer. The serving-man, the artisan, and the husbandman, have a more copious and palatable supply of food, better clothing, and better furniture. This is no reason for tolerating abuses, or for neglecting any means of ameliorating the condition of our poorer countrymen. But it is a reason against telling them, as some of our philosophers are constantly telling them, that they are the most wretched people who ever existed on the face of the earth.

We have already adverted to Mr. Southey's amusing doctrine about national wealth. A state, says he, cannot be too rich; but a people may be too rich. His reason for thinking this is extremely curious.

"A people may be too rich, because it is the tendency of the commercial, and more especially of the manufacturing system, to collect wealth rather than to diffuse it. Where wealth is necessarily employed in any of the speculations of trade, its increase is in proportion to its amount. Great capitalists become like pikes in a fish-pond, who devour the weaker fish; and it is but too certain, that the poverty of one part of the people seems to increase in the same ratio as the riches of another. There are examples of this in history. In Portugal, when the high tide of wealth flowed in from the conquests in Africa and the East, the effect of that great influx was not more visible in the augmented splendour of the court, and the luxury of the higher ranks, than in the distress of the people."

Mr. Southey's instance is not a very fortunate one. The wealth which did so little for the Portuguese was not the fruit either of manufactures or of commerce carried on by private individuals. It was the wealth, not of the people, but of the government and its creatures, of those who, as Mr. Southey thinks, can never be too rich. The fact is that Mr. Southey's proposition is opposed to all history, and to the phænomena which surround us on every side. England is the richest country in Europe, the most commercial country, and the country in which manufactures flourish most. Russia and Poland are the poorest countries in Europe. They have scarcely any trade, and none but the rudest manufactures. Is wealth more diffused in Russia and Poland than in England? There are individuals in Russia and Poland whose incomes are probably equal to those of our richest countrymen. It may be doubted whether there are not, in those countries, as many fortunes of eighty thousand a year as here. But are there as many fortunes of two thousand a year, or of one thousand a year? There are parishes in England which contain more people of between three hundred and three thousand pounds a year than could be found in all the dominions of the Emperor Nicholas. The neat and commodious houses which have been built in London and its vicinity, for people of this class, within the last thirty years would of themselves form a city larger than the capitals of some European kingdoms. And this is the state of society in which the great proprietors have devoured a smaller!

The cure which Mr. Southey thinks that he has discovered is worthy of the sagacity which he has shown in detecting the evil. The calamities arising from the collection of wealth in the hands of a few capitalists are to be remedied by collecting it in the hands of one great capitalist, who has no conceivable motive to use it better than other capitalists, the all-devouring state.

It is not strange that, differing so widely from Mr. Southey as to the past progress of society, we should differ from him also as to its probable destiny. He thinks, that to all outward appearance, the country is hastening to destruction; but he relies firmly on the goodness of God. We do not see either the piety or the rationality of thus confidently expecting that the Supreme Being will interfere to disturb the common succession of causes and effects. We, too, rely on his goodness, on his goodness as manifested, not in extraordinary interpositions, but in those general laws which it has pleased him to establish in the physical and in the moral world. We rely on the natural tendency of the human intellect to truth, and on the natural tendency of society to improvement. We know no well authenticated instance of a people which has decidedly retrograded in civilisation and prosperity, except from the influence of violent and terrible calamities, such as those which laid the Roman empire in ruins, or those which, about the beginning of the sixteenth century, desolated Italy. We know of no country which, at the end of fifty years of peace, and tolerably good government, has been less prosperous than at the beginning of that period. The political importance of a state may decline, as the balance of power is disturbed by the introduction of new forces. Thus the influence of Holland and of Spain is much diminished. But are Holland and Spain poorer than formerly? We doubt it. Other countries have outrun them. But we suspect that they have been positively, though not relatively, advancing. We suspect that Holland is richer than when she sent her navies up the Thames, that Spain is richer than when a French king was brought captive to the footstool of Charles the Fifth.

History is full of the signs of this natural progress of society. We see in almost every part of the annals of mankind how the industry of individuals, struggling up against wars, taxes, famines, conflagrations, mischievous prohibitions, and more mischievous protections, creates faster than governments can squander, and repairs whatever invaders can destroy. We see the wealth of nations increasing, and all the arts of life approaching nearer and nearer to perfection, in spite of the grossest corruption and the wildest profusion on the part of rulers.

The present moment is one of great distress. But how small will that distress appear when we think over the history of the last forty years; a war, compared with which all other wars sink into insignificance; taxation, such as the most heavily taxed people of former times could not have conceived; a debt larger than all the public debts that ever existed in the world added together; the food of the people studiously rendered dear; the currency imprudently debased, and imprudently restored. Yet is the country poorer than in 1790? We firmly believe that, in spite of all the misgovernment of her rulers, she has been almost constantly becoming richer and richer. Now and then there has been a stoppage, now and then a short retrogression; but as to the general tendency there can be no doubt. A single breaker may recede; but the tide is evidently coming in.

If we were to prophesy that in the year 1930 a population of fifty millions, better fed, clad, and lodged than the English of our time, will cover these islands, that Sussex and Huntingdonshire will be wealthier than the wealthiest parts of the West Riding of Yorkshire now are, that cultivation, rich as that of a flower-garden, will be carried up to the very tops of Ben Nevis and Helvellyn, that machines constructed on principles yet undiscovered will be in every house, that there will be no highways but railroads, no travelling but by steam, that our debt, vast as it seems to us, will appear to our great-grandchildren a trifling encumbrance, which might easily be paid off in a year or two, many people would think us insane. We prophesy nothing; but this we say: If any person had told the Parliament which met in perplexity and terror after the crash in 1720 that in 1830 the wealth of England would surpass all their wildest dreams, that the annual revenue would equal the principal of that debt which they considered as an intolerable burden, that for one man of ten thousand pounds then living there would be five men of fifty thousand pounds, that London would be twice as large and twice as populous, and that nevertheless the rate of mortality would have diminished to one half of what it then was, that the post-office would bring more into the exchequer than the excise and customs had brought in together under Charles the Second, that stage-coaches would run from London to York in twenty-four hours, that men would be in the habit of sailing without wind, and would be beginning to ride without horses, our ancestors would have given as much credit to the prediction as they gave to Gulliver's Travels. Yet the prediction would have been true; and they would have perceived that it was not altogether absurd, if they had considered that the country was then raising every year a sum which would have purchased the fee-simple of the revenue of the Plantagenets, ten times what supported the government of Elizabeth, three times what, in the time of Oliver Cromwell, had been thought intolerably oppressive. To almost all men the state of things under which they have been used to live seems to be the necessary state of things. We have heard it said that five per cent. is the natural interest of money, that twelve is the natural number of a jury, that forty shillings is the natural qualification of a county voter. Hence it is that, though in every age everybody knows that up to his own time progressive improvement has been taking place, nobody seems to reckon on any improvement during the next generation. We cannot absolutely prove that those are in error who tell us that society has reached a turning point, that we have seen our best days. But so said all who came before us, and with just as much apparent reason. "A million a year will beggar us," said the patriots of 1640. "Two millions a year will grind the country to powder," was the cry in 1660, "Six millions a year, and a debt of fifty millions!" exclaimed Swift; "the high allies have been the ruin of us." "A hundred and forty millions of debt!" said Junius; "well may we say that we owe Lord Chatham more than we shall ever pay, if we owe him such a load as this." "Two hundred and forty millions of debt!" cried all the statesmen of 1783 in chorus; "what abilities, or what economy on the part of a minister, can save a country so burdened?" We know that if, since 1783, no fresh debt had been incurred, the increased resources of the country would have enabled us to defray that debt at which Pitt, Fox, and Burke stood aghast, nay, to defray it over and over again, and that with much lighter taxation than what we have actually borne. On what principle is it that, when we see nothing but improvement behind us, we are to expect nothing but deterioration before us?

It is not by the intermeddling of Mr. Southey's idol, the omniscient and omnipotent State, but by the prudence and energy of the people, that England has hitherto been carried forward in civilisation; and it is to the same prudence and the same energy that we now look with comfort and good hope. Our rulers will best promote the improvement of the nation by strictly confining themselves to their own legitimate duties, by leaving capital to find its most lucrative course, commodities their fair price, industry and intelligence their natural reward, idleness and folly their natural punishment, by maintaining peace, by defending property, by diminishing the price of law, and by observing strict economy in every department of the state. Let the Government do this: the People will assuredly do the rest.

MR. ROBERT MONTGOMERY.[1]

(*Edinburgh Review*, April 1830.)

THE wise men of antiquity loved to convey instruction under the covering of apologue; and though this practice is generally thought childish, we shall make no apology for adopting it on the present occasion. A generation which has bought eleven editions of a poem by Mr. Robert Montgomery may well condescend to listen to a fable of Pilpay.

A pious Brahmin, it is written, made a vow that on a certain day he would sacrifice a sheep, and on the appointed morning he went forth to buy one. There lived in his neighbourhood three rogues who knew of his vow, and laid a scheme for profiting by it. The first met him and said, "Oh Brahmin, wilt thou buy a sheep? I have one fit for sacrifice." "It is for that very purpose," said the holy man, "that I came forth this day." Then the impostor opened a bag, and brought out of it an unclean beast, an ugly dog, lame and blind. Thereon the Brahmin cried out, "Wretch, who touchest things impure, and utterest things untrue, callest thou that cur a sheep?" "Truly," answered the other, "it is a sheep of the finest fleece, and of the

[1] 1. *The Omnipresence of the Deity: a Poem.* By ROBERT MONTGOMERY. Eleventh Edition. London: 1830.

2. *Satan: a Poem.* By ROBERT MONTGOMERY. Second Edition. London: 1830.

sweetest flesh. Oh Brahmin, it will be an offering most acceptable to the gods." "Friend," said the Brahmin, "either thou or I must be blind."

Just then one of the accomplices came up. "Praised be the gods," said this second rogue, "that I have been saved the trouble of going to the market for a sheep! This is such a sheep as I wanted. For how much wilt thou sell it?" When the Brahmin heard this, his mind waved to and fro, like one swinging in the air at a holy festival. "Sir," said he to the new comer, "take heed what thou dost; this is no sheep, but an unclean cur." "Oh Brahmin," said the new comer, "thou art drunk or mad!"

At this time the third confederate drew near. "Let us ask this man," said the Brahmin, "what the creature is, and I will stand by what he shall say." To this the others agreed; and the Brahmin called out, "Oh stranger, what dost thou call this beast?" "Surely, oh Brahmin," said the knave, "it is a fine sheep." Then the Brahmin said, "Surely the gods have taken away my senses;" and he asked pardon of him who carried the dog, and bought it for a measure of rice and a pot of ghee, and offered it up to the gods, who, being wroth at this unclean sacrifice, smote him with a sore disease in all his joints.

Thus, or nearly thus, if we remember rightly, runs the story of the Sanscrit Æsop. The moral, like the moral of every fable that is worth the telling, lies on the surface. The writer evidently means to caution us against the practices of puffers, a class of people who have more than once talked the public into the most absurd errors, but who surely never played a more curious or a more difficult trick than when they passed Mr. Robert Montgomery off upon the world as a great poet.

In an age in which there are so few readers that a writer cannot subsist on the sum arising from the sale of his works, no man who has not an independent fortune can devote himself to literary pursuits, unless he is assisted by patronage. In such an age, accordingly, men of letters too often pass their lives in dangling at the heels of the wealthy and powerful; and all the faults which dependence tends to produce, pass into their character. They become the parasites and slaves of the great. It is melancholy to think how many of the highest and most exquisitely formed of human intellects have been condemned to the ignominious labour of disposing the commonplaces of adulation in new forms and brightening them into new splendour. Horace invoking Augustus in the most enthusiastic language of religious veneration, Statius flattering a tyrant, and the minion of a tyrant, for a morsel of bread, Ariosto versifying the whole genealogy of a niggardly patron, Tasso extolling the heroic virtues of the wretched creature who locked him up in a mad-house, these are but a few of the instances which might easily be given of the degradation to which those must submit who, not possessing a competent fortune, are resolved to write when there are scarcely any who read.

This evil the progress of the human mind tends to remove. As a taste for books becomes more and more common, the patronage of individuals becomes less and less necessary. In the middle of the last century a marked change took place. The tone of literary men, both in this country and in France, became higher and more independent. Pope boasted that he was the "one poet" who had "pleased by manly ways;" he derided the soft dedications with which Halifax had been fed, asserted his own superiority over the pensioned Boileau, and gloried in being not the follower, but the friend, of nobles and princes. The explanation of all this is very simple. Pope was the first Englishman who, by the mere sale of his writings, realised a sum which enabled him to live in comfort and in perfect independence. Johnson extols him for the magnanimity which he showed in inscribing his Iliad not to a minister or a peer, but to Congreve. In our time this would scarcely be a subject for praise. Nobody is astonished when Mr. Moore pays a compliment of this kind to Sir Walter Scott, or Sir Walter Scott to Mr. Moore. The idea of either of those gentlemen looking out for some lord who would be likely to give him a few guineas in return for a fulsome dedication seems laughably incongruous. Yet this is exactly what Dryden or Otway would have done; and it would be hard to blame them for it. Otway is said to have been choked with a piece of bread which he devoured in the rage of hunger; and, whether this story be true or false, he was beyond all question miserably poor. Dryden, at near seventy, when at the head of the literary men of England, without equal or second, received three hundred pounds for his Fables, a collection of ten thousand verses, and of such verses as no man then living, except himself, could have produced. Pope, at thirty, had laid up between six and seven thousand pounds, the fruits of his poetry. It was not, we suspect, because he had a higher spirit or a more scrupulous conscience than his predecessors, but because he had a larger income, that he kept up the dignity of the literary character so much better than they had done.

From the time of Pope to the present day the readers have been constantly becoming more and more numerous, and the writers, consequently, more and more independent. It is assuredly a great evil that men, fitted by their talents and acquirements to enlighten and charm the world, should be reduced to the necessity of flattering wicked and foolish patrons in return for the sustenance of life. But, though we heartily rejoice that this evil is removed, we cannot but see with concern that another evil has succeeded to it. The public is now the patron, and a most liberal patron. All that the rich and powerful bestowed on authors from the the time of Mæcenas to that of Harley would not, we apprehend, make up a sum equal to that which has been paid by English booksellers to authors during the last fifty years. Men of letters have accordingly ceased to court individuals, and have begun to court the public. They formerly used flattery. They now use puffing.

Whether the old or the new vice be the worse, whether those who formerly lavished insincere praise on others, or those who now contrive by every art of beggary and bribery to stun the public with praises of themselves, disgrace their vocation the more deeply, we shall not attempt to decide. But of this we are sure, that it is high time to make a stand against the new trickery. The puffing of books is now so shamefully and so successfully carried on that it is the duty of all who are anxious for the purity of the national taste, or for the honour of the literary character, to join in discountenancing the practice. All the pens that ever were employed in magnifying Bish's lucky office, Romanis's fleecy hosiery, Packwood's razor strops, and Rowland's Kalydor, all the placard-bearers of Dr. Eady, all the wall-chalkers of Day and Martin, seem to have taken service with the poets and novelists of this generation. Devices which in the lowest trades are considered as disreputable are adopted without scruple, and improved upon with a despicable ingenuity, by people engaged in a pursuit which never was and never will be considered as a mere trade by any man of honour and virtue. A butcher of the higher class disdains to ticket his meat. A mercer of the higher class would be ashamed to hang up papers in his window inviting the passers-by to look at the stock of a bankrupt, all of the first quality, and going for half the value. We expect some reserve, some decent pride, in our hatter and our bootmaker. But no artifice by which notoriety can be obtained is thought too abject for a man of letters.

It is amusing to think over the history of most of the publications which have had a run during the last few years. The publisher is often the publisher of some periodical work. In this periodical work the first flourish of trumpets is sounded. The peal is then echoed and re-echoed by all the other periodical works over which the publisher, or the author, or the author's coterie, may have any influence. The newspapers are for a fortnight filled with puffs of all the various kinds which Sheridan enumerated, direct, oblique, and collusive. Sometimes the praise is laid on thick for simple-minded people. "Pathetic," "sublime," "splendid," "graceful," "brilliant wit," "exquisite humour," and other phrases equally flattering, fall, in a shower as thick and as sweet as the sugar-plums at a Roman carnival. Sometimes greater art is used. A sinecure has been offered to the writer if he would suppress his work, or if he would even soften down a few of his incomparable portraits. A distinguished military and political character has challenged the inimitable satirist of the vices of the great; and the puffer is glad to learn that the parties have been bound over to keep the peace. Sometimes it is thought expedient that the puffer should put on a grave face, and utter his panegyric in the form of admonition. "Such attacks on private character cannot be too much condemned. Even the exuberant wit of our author, and the irresistible power of his withering sarcasm, are no excuses for that utter disregard which he manifests for the feelings of others. We cannot but wonder that a writer of such transcendent talents, a writer who is evidently no stranger to the kindly charities and sensibilities of our nature, should show so little tenderness to the foibles of noble and distinguished individuals, with whom it is clear, from every page of his work, that he must have been constantly mingling in society." These are but tame and feeble imitations of the paragraphs with which the daily papers are filled whenever an attorney's clerk or an apothecary's assistant undertakes to tell the public in bad English and worse French, how people tie their neckcloths and eat their dinners in Grosvenor Square. The editors of the higher and more respectable newspapers usually prefix the words "Advertisement," or "From a Correspondent," to such paragraphs. But this makes little difference. The panegyric is extracted, and the significant heading omitted. The fulsome eulogy makes its appearance on the covers of all the Reviews and Magazines, with "Times" or "Globe" affixed, though the editors of the Times and the Globe have no more to do with it than with Mr. Goss's way of making old rakes young again.

That people who live by personal slander should practise these arts is not surprising. Those who stoop to write calumnious books may well stoop to puff them;

and that the basest of all trades should be carried on in the basest of all manners is quite proper and as it should be. But how any man who has the least self-respect, the least regard for his own personal dignity, can condescend to persecute the public with this Rag-fair importunity, we do not understand. Extreme poverty may, indeed, in some degree, be an excuse for employing these shifts, as it may be an excuse for stealing a leg of mutton. But we really think that a man of spirit and delicacy would quite as soon satisfy his wants in the one way as in the other.

It is no excuse for an author that the praises of journalists are procured by the money or influence of his publishers, and not by his own. It is his business to take such precautions as may prevent others from doing what must degrade him. It is for his honour as a gentleman, and, if he is really a man of talents, it will eventually be for his honour and interest as a writer, that his works should come before the public recommended by their own merits alone, and should be discussed with perfect freedom. If his objects be really such as he may own without shame, he will find that they will, in the long run, be better attained by suffering the voice of criticism to be fairly heard. At present, we too often see a writer attempting to obtain literary fame as Shakspeare's usurper obtains sovereignty. The publisher plays Buckingham to the author's Richard. Some few creatures of the conspiracy are dexterously disposed here and there in the crowd. It is the business of these hirelings to throw up their caps, and clap their hands, and utter their *vivas*. The rabble at first stare and wonder, and at last join in shouting for shouting's sake; and thus a crown is placed on a head which has no right to it, by the huzzas of a few servile dependents.

The opinion of the great body of the reading public is very materially influenced even by the unsupported assertions of those who assume a right to criticize. Nor is the public altogether to blame on this account. Most even of those who have really a great enjoyment in reading are in the same state, with respect to a book, in which a man who has never given particular attention to the art of painting is with respect to a picture. Every man who has the least sensibility or imagination derives a certain pleasure from pictures. Yet a man of the highest and finest intellect might, unless he had formed his taste by contemplating the best pictures, be easily persuaded by a knot of connoisseurs that the worst daub in Somerset House was a miracle of art. If he deserves to be laughed at, it is not for his ignorance of pictures, but for his ignorance of men. He knows that there is a delicacy of taste in painting which he does not possess, that he cannot distinguish hands, as practised judges distinguish them, that he is not familiar with the finest models, that he has never looked at them with close attention, and that, when the general effect of a piece has pleased him or displeased him, he has never troubled himself to ascertain why. When, therefore, people, whom he thinks more competent to judge than himself, and of whose sincerity he entertains no doubt, assure him that a particular work is exquisitely beautiful, he takes it for granted that they must be in the right. He returns to the examination, resolved to find or imagine beauties ; and, if he can work himself up into something like admiration, he exults in his own proficiency.

Just such is the manner in which nine readers out of ten judge of a book. They are ashamed to dislike what men who speak as having authority declare to be good. At present, however contemptible a poem or a novel may be, there is not the least difficulty in procuring favourable notices of it from all sorts of publications, daily, weekly, and monthly. In the mean time, little or nothing is said on the other side. The author and the publisher are interested in crying up the book. Nobody has any very strong interest in crying it down. Those who are best fitted to guide the public opinion think it beneath them to expose mere nonsense, and comfort themselves by reflecting that such popularity cannot last. This contemptuous lenity has been carried too far. It is perfectly true that reputations which have been forced into an unnatural bloom fade almost as soon as they have expanded; nor have we any apprehensions that puffing will ever raise any scribbler to the rank of a classic. It is indeed amusing to turn over some late volumes of periodical works, and to see how many immortal productions have, within a few months, been gathered to the Poems of Blackmore and the novels of Mrs. Behn; how many "profound views of human nature," and "exquisite delineations of fashionable manners," and "vernal, and sunny, and refreshing thoughts," and "high imaginings," and "young breathings," and "embodyings," and "pinings," and "minglings with the beauty of the universe," and "harmonies which dissolve the soul in a passionate sense of loveliness and divinity," the world has contrived to forget. The names of the books and of the writers are buried in as deep an oblivion as the name of the builder of Stonehenge. Some of the well puffed fashionable novels of eighteen hundred and twenty-nine hold the pastry of eighteen hundred and thirty; and others, which are now extolled in language almost too high-flown for the merits of Don Quixote, will, we have no doubt, line the trunks of eighteen hundred and thirty-one. But, though we have no apprehensions that puffing will ever confer permanent reputation on the undeserving, we still think its influence most pernicious. Men of real merit will, if they persevere, at last reach the station to which they are entitled, and intruders will be ejected with contempt and derision. But it is no small evil that the avenues to fame should be blocked up by a swarm of noisy, pushing, elbowing pretenders, who, though they will not ultimately be able to make good their own entrance, hinder, in the mean time, those who have a right to enter. All who will not disgrace themselves by joining in the unseemly scuffle must expect to be at first hustled and shouldered back. Some men of talents, accordingly, turn away in dejection from pursuits in which success appears to bear no proportion to desert. Others employ in self-defence the means by which competitors, far inferior to themselves, appear for a time to obtain a decided advantage. There are few who have sufficient confidence in their own powers and sufficient elevation of mind to wait with secure and contemptuous patience, while dunce after dunce presses before them. Those who will not stoop to the baseness of the modern fashion are too often discouraged. Those who stoop to it are always degraded.

We have of late observed with great pleasure some symptoms which lead us to hope that respectable literary men of all parties are beginning to be impatient of this insufferable nuisance. And we purpose to do what in us lies for the abating of it. We do not think that we can more usefully assist in this good work than by showing our honest countrymen what that sort of poetry is which puffing can drive through eleven editions, and how easy any bellman might, if a bellman would stoop to the necessary degree of meanness, become a "master-spirit of the age." We have no enmity to Mr. Robert Montgomery. We know nothing whatever about him, except what we have learned from his books, and from the portrait prefixed to one of them, in which he appears to be doing his very best to look like a man of genius and sensibility, though with less success than his strenuous exertions deserve. We select him, because his works have received more enthusiastic praise, and have deserved more unmixed contempt, than any which, as far as our knowledge extends, have appeared within the last three or four years. His writing bears the same relation to poetry which a Turkey carpet bears to a picture. There are colours in a Turkey carpet out of which a picture might be made. There are words in Mr. Montgomery's writing which, when disposed in certain orders and combinations, have made, and will again make, good poetry. But, as they now stand, they seem to be put together on principle in such a manner as to give no image of any thing "in the heavens above, or in the earth beneath, or in the waters under the earth."

The poem on the Omnipresence of the Deity commences with a description of the creation, in which we can find only one thought which has the least pretension to ingenuity, and that one thought is stolen from Dryden, and marred in the stealing;

> "Last, softly beautiful as music's close,
> Angelic woman into being rose."

The all-pervading influence of the Supreme Being is then described in a few tolerable lines borrowed from Pope, and a great many intolerable lines of Mr. Robert Montgomery's own. The following may stand as a specimen:

"But who could trace Thine unrestricted course,
Though Fancy follow'd with immortal force?
There's not a blossom fondled by the breeze,
There's not a fruit that beautifies the trees,
There's not a particle in sea or air,
But nature owns thy plastic influence there!
With fearful gaze, still be it mine to see
How all is fill'd and vivified by Thee;
Upon thy mirror, earth's majestic view,
To paint Thy Presence, and to feel it too."

The last two lines contain an excellent specimen of Mr. Robert Montgomery's Turkey-carpet style of writing. The majestic view of earth is the mirror of God's presence; and on this mirror Mr. Robert Montgomery paints God's presence. The use of a mirror, we submit, is not to be painted upon.

A few more lines, as bad as those which we have quoted, bring us to one of the most amusing instances of literary pilfering which we remember. It might be of use to plagiarists to know, as a general rule, that what they steal is, to employ a phrase common in advertisements, of no use to any but the right owner. We never fell in, however, with any plunderer who so little understood how to turn his booty to good account as Mr. Montgomery. Lord Byron, in a passage which every body knows by heart, has said, addressing the sea,

"Time writes no wrinkle on thine azure brow."

Mr. Robert Montgomery very coolly appropriates the image and reproduces the stolen goods in the following form:

"And thou, vast Ocean, on whose awful face
Time's iron feet can print no ruin-trace."

So may such ill got gains ever prosper!

The effect which the Ocean produces on Atheists is then described in the following lofty lines:

"Oh! never did the dark-soul'd ATHEIST stand,
And watch the breakers boiling on the strand,
And, while Creation stagger'd at his nod,
Mock the dread presence of the mighty God!
We hear Him in the wind-heaved ocean's roar,
Hurling her billowy crags upon the shore;
We hear Him in the riot of the blast,
And shake, while rush the raving whirlwinds past!"

If Mr. Robert Montgomery's genius were not far too free and aspiring to be shackled by the rules of syntax, we should suppose that it is at the nod of the Atheist that creation staggers. But Mr. Robert Montgomery's readers must take such grammar as they can get, and be thankful.

A few more lines bring us to another instance of unprofitable theft. Sir Walter Scott has these lines in the Lord of the Isles:

"The dew that on the violet lies,
Mocks the dark lustre of thine eyes."

This is pretty taken separately, and, as is always the case with the good things of good writers, much prettier in its place than can even be conceived by those who see it only detached from the context. Now for Mr. Montgomery:

"And the bright dew-bead on the bramble lies,
Like liquid rapture upon beauty's eyes."

The comparison of a violet, bright with the dew, to a woman's eyes, is as perfect as a comparison can be. Sir Walter's lines are part of a song addressed to a woman at daybreak, when the violets are bathed in dew; and the comparison is therefore peculiarly natural and graceful. Dew on a bramble is no more like a woman's eyes than dew anywhere else. There is a very pretty Eastern tale of which the fate of plagiarists often reminds us. The slave of a magician saw his master wave his wand, and heard him give orders to the spirits who arose at the summons. The slave stole the wand, and waved it himself in the air; but he had not observed that his master used the left hand for that purpose. The spirits thus irregularly summoned tore the thief to pieces instead of obeying his orders. There are very few who can safely venture to conjure with the rod of Sir Walter; and Mr. Robert Montgomery is not one of them.

Mr. Campbell, in one of his most pleasing pieces, has this line,

> "The sentinel stars set their watch in the sky."

The thought is good, and has a very striking propriety where Mr. Campbell has placed it, in the mouth of a soldier telling his dream. But, though Shakspeare assures us that "every true man's apparel fits your thief," it is by no means the case, as we have already seen, that every true poet's similitude fits your plagiarist. Let us see how Mr. Robert Montgomery uses the image:

> "Ye quenchless stars! so eloquently bright,
> Untroubled sentries of the shadowy night,
> While half the world is lapp'd in downy dreams,
> And round the lattice creep your midnight beams,
> How sweet to gaze upon your placid eyes,
> In lambent beauty looking from the skies."

Certainly the ideas of eloquence, of untroubled repose, of placid eyes, on the lambent beauty of which it is sweet to gaze, harmonize admirably with the idea of a sentry.

We would not be understood, however, to say, that Mr. Robert Montgomery cannot make similitudes for himself. A very few lines further on, we find one which has every mark of originality, and on which, we will be bound, none of the poets whom he has plundered will ever think of making reprisals :

> "The soul, aspiring, pants its source to mount,
> As streams meander level with their fount."

We take this to be, on the whole, the worst similitude in the world. In the first place, no stream meanders, or can possibly meander, level with its fount. In the next place, if streams did meander level with their founts, no two motions can be less like each other than that of meandering level and that of mounting upwards.

We have then an apostrophe to the Deity, couched in terms which, in any writer who dealt in meanings, we should call profane, but to which we suppose Mr. Robert Montgomery attaches no idea whatever.

> "Yes! pause and think, within one fleeting hour,
> How vast a universe obeys Thy power;
> Unseen, but felt, Thine interfused control
> Works in each atom, and pervades the whole;
> Expands the blossom, and erects the tree,
> Conducts each vapour, and commands each sea,
> Beams in each ray, bids whirlwinds be unfurl'd,
> Unrols the thunder, and upheaves a world!"

No field-preacher surely ever carried his irreverent familiarity so far as to bid the Supreme Being stop and think on the importance of the interests which are under his care. The grotesque indecency of such an address throws into shade the subordinate absurdities of the passage, the unfurling of whirlwinds, the unrolling of thunder, and the upheaving of worlds.

Then comes a curious specimen of our poet's English: —

> "Yet not alone created realms engage
> Thy faultless wisdom, grand, primeval sage!
> For all the thronging woes to life allied
> Thy mercy tempers, and Thy cares provide."

We should be glad to know what the word "For means here. If it is a preposition, it makes nonsense of the words, "Thy mercy tempers." If it is an adverb, it makes nonsense of the words, "Thy cares provide."

These beauties we have taken, almost at random, from the first part of the poem. The second part is a series of descriptions of various events, a battle, a murder, an execution, a marriage, a funeral, and so forth. Mr. Robert Montgomery terminates each of these descriptions by assuring us that the Deity was present at the battle, murder, execution, marriage, or funeral in question. And this proposition, which might be safely predicated of every event that ever happened or ever will happen, forms the only link which connects these descriptions with the subject or with each other.

How the descriptions are executed our readers are probably by this time able to conjecture. The battle is made up of the battles of all ages and nations: "red-mouthed cannons, uproaring to the clouds," and "hands grasping firm the glittering shield." The only military operations of which this part of the poem reminds us, are those which reduced the Abbey of Quedlinburgh to submission, the Templar with his cross, the Austrian and Prussian grenadiers in full uniform, and Curtius and Dentatus with their battering-ram. We ought not to pass unnoticed the slain war-horse, who will no more

"Roll his red eye, and rally for the fight;"

or the slain warrior who, while "lying on his bleeding breast," contrives to "stare ghastly and grimly on the skies." As to this last exploit, we can only say, as Dante did on a similar occasion,

"Forse per forza gia di' parlasia
Si stravolse così alcun del tutto:
Ma io nol vidi, nè credo che sia."

The tempest is thus described:

"But lo! around the marsh'lling clouds unite,
Like thick battalions halting for the fight;
The sun sinks back, the tempest spirits sweep
Fierce through the air, and flutter on the deep.
Till from their caverns rush the maniac blasts,
Tear the loose sails, and split the creaking masts,
And the lash'd billows, rolling in a train,
Rear their white heads, and race along the main!"

What, we should like to know, is the difference between the two operations which Mr. Robert Montgomery so accurately distinguishes from each other, the fierce sweeping of the tempest-spirits through the air, and the rushing of the maniac blasts from their caverns? And why does the former operation end exactly when the latter commences?

We cannot stop over each of Mr. Robert Montgomery's descriptions. We have a shipwrecked sailor, who "visions a viewless temple in the air;" a murderer who stands on a heath, "with ashy lips, in cold convulsion spread;" a pious man, to whom, as he lies in bed at night,

"The panorama of past life appears,
Warms his pure mind, and melts it into tears;"

a traveller, who loses his way, owing to the thickness of the "cloud-battalion," and the want of "heaven-lamps, to beam their holy light." We have a description of a convicted felon, stolen from that incomparable passage in Crabbe's Borough, which has made many a rough and cynical reader cry like a child. We can, however, conscientiously declare that persons of the most excitable sensibility may safely venture upon Mr.

Robert Montgomery's version. Then we have the "poor, mindless, pale-faced maniac boy," who

> "Rolls his vacant eye,
> To greet the glowing fancies of the sky."

What are the glowing fancies of the sky? And what is the meaning of the two lines which almost immediately follow?

> "A soulless thing, a spirit of the woods,
> He loves to commune with the fields and floods."

How can a soulless thing be a spirit? Then comes a panegyric on the Sunday. A baptism follows; after that a marriage: and we then proceed, in due course, to the visitation of the sick, and the burial of the dead.

Often as Death has been personified, Mr. Montgomery has found something new to say about him.

> "O Death! though dreadless vanquisher of earth,
> The Elements shrank blasted at thy birth!
> Careering round the world like tempest wind,
> Martyrs before, and victims strew'd behind;
> Ages on ages cannot grapple thee,
> Dragging the world into eternity!"

If there be any one line in this passage about which we are more in the dark than about the rest, it is the fourth. What the difference may be between the victims and the martyrs, and why the martyrs are to lie before Death, and the victims behind him, are to us great mysteries.

We now come to the third part, of which we may say with honest Cassio, "Why, this is a more excellent song than the other." Mr. Robert Montgomery is very severe on the infidels, and undertakes to prove, that, as he elegantly expresses it,

> "One great Enchanter helm'd the harmonious whole."

What an enchanter has to do with helming, or what a

helm has to do with harmony, he does not explain. He proceeds with his argument thus:

> "And dare men dream that dismal Chance has framed
> All that the eye perceives, or tongue has named;
> The spacious world, and all its wonders, born
> Designless, self-created, and forlorn;
> Like to the flashing bubbles on a stream,
> Fire from the cloud, or phantom in a dream?"

We should be sorry to stake our faith in a higher Power on Mr. Robert Montgomery's logic. He informs us that lightning is designless and self-created. If he can believe this, we cannot conceive why he may not believe that the whole universe is designless and self-created. A few lines before, he tells us that it is the Deity who bids "thunder rattle from the skiey deep." His theory is therefore this, that God made the thunder, but that the lightning made itself.

But Mr. Robert Montgomery's metaphysics are not at present our game. He proceeds to set forth the fearful effects of Atheism.

> "Then, blood-stain'd Murder, bare thy hideous arm,
> And thou, Rebellion, welter in thy storm:
> Awake, ye spirits of avenging crime;
> Burst from your bonds, and battle with the time!"

Mr. Robert Montgomery is fond of personification, and belongs, we need not say, to that school of poets who hold that nothing more is necessary to a personification in poetry than to begin a word with a capital letter. Murder may, without impropriety, bare her arm, as she did long ago, in Mr. Campbell's Pleasures of Hope. But what possible motive Rebellion can have for weltering in her storm, what avenging crime may be, who its spirits may be, why they should burst from their bonds, what their bonds may be, why they should battle with the time, what the time may be, and what a battle between the time and the spirits of avenging crime would resemble, we must confess ourselves quite unable to understand.

> "And here let Memory turn her tearful glance
> On the dark horrors of tumultuous France,
> When blood and blasphemy defiled her land,
> And fierce Rebellion shook her savage hand."

Whether Rebellion shakes her own hand, shakes the hand of Memory, or shakes the hand of France, or what any one of these three metaphors would mean, we know no more than we know what is the sense of the following passage:

> "Let the foul orgies of infuriate crime
> Picture the raging havoc of that time,
> When leagued Rebellion march'd to kindle man,
> Fright in her rear, and Murder in her van.
> And thou, sweet flower of Austria, slaughter'd Queen,
> Who dropp'd no tear upon the dreadful scene,
> When gush'd the life-blood from thine angel form,
> And martyr'd beauty perish'd in the storm,
> Once worshipp'd paragon of all who saw,
> Thy look obedience, and thy smile a law."

What is the distinction between the foul orgies and the raging havoc which the foul orgies are to picture? Why does Fright go behind Rebellion, and Murder before? Why should not Murder fall behind Fright? Or why should not all the three walk abreast? We have read of a hero who had

> "Amazement in his van, with flight combined,
> And Sorrow's faded form, and Solitude behind."

Gray, we suspect, could have given a reason for disposing the allegorical attendants of Edward thus. But to proceed, "Flower of Austria" is stolen from Byron. "Dropp'd" is false English. "Perish'd in the storm" means nothing at all; and "thy look obedience" means the very reverse of what Mr. Robert Montgomery intends to say.

Our poet then proceeds to demonstrate the immortality of the soul:

> "And shall the soul, the fount of reason, die,
> When dust and darkness round its temple lie?
> Did God breathe in it no ethereal fire,
> Dimless and quenchless, though the breath expire?"

The soul is a fountain; and therefore it is not to die, though dust and darkness lie round its temple, because an ethereal fire has been breathed into it, which cannot be quenched though its breath expire. Is it the fountain, or the temple, that breathes, and has fire breathed into it?

Mr. Montgomery apostrophizes the

> "Immortal beacons,—spirits of the just,"—

and describes their employments in another world, which are to be, it seems, bathing in light, hearing fiery streams flow, and riding on living cars of lightning. The deathbed of the sceptic is described with what we suppose is meant for energy. We then have the deathbed of a Christian made as ridiculous as false imagery and false English can make it. But this is not enough. The Day of Judgment is to be described, and a roaring cataract of nonsense is poured forth upon this tremendous subject. Earth, we are told, is dashed into Eternity. Furnace blazes wheel round the horizon, and burst into bright wizard phantoms. Racing hurricanes unroll and whirl quivering fire-clouds. The white waves gallop. Shadowy worlds career around. The red and raging eye of Imagination is then forbidden to pry further. But further Mr. Robert Montgomery persists in prying. The stars bound through the airy roar. The unbosomed deep yawns on the ruin. The billows of Eternity then begin to advance.

The world glares in fiery slumber. A car comes forward driven by living thunder.

> "Creation shudders with sublime dismay,
> And in a blazing tempest whirls away."

And this is fine poetry! This is what ranks its writer with the master-spirits of the age! This is what has been described, over and over again, in terms which would require some qualification if used respecting Paradise Lost! It is too much that this patchwork, made by stitching together old odds and ends of what, when new, was but tawdry frippery, is to be picked off the dunghill on which it ought to rot, and to be held up to admiration as an inestimable specimen of art. And what must we think of a system by means of which verses like those which we have quoted, verses fit only for the poet's corner of the Morning Post, can produce emolument and fame? The circulation of this writer's poetry has been greater than that of Southey's Roderick, and beyond all comparison greater than that of Cary's Dante or of the best works of Coleridge. Thus encouraged Mr. Robert Montgomery has favoured the public with volume after volume. We have given so much space to the examination of his first and most popular performance that we have none to spare for his Universal Prayer, and his smaller poems, which, as the puffing journals tell us, would alone constitute a sufficient title to literary immortality. We shall pass at once to his last publication, entitled Satan.

This poem was ushered into the world with the usual roar of acclamation. But the thing was now past a joke. Pretensions so unfounded, so impudent, and so successful, had aroused a spirit of resistance. In several magazines and reviews, accordingly, Satan has been handled somewhat roughly, and the arts of the puffers have been exposed with good sense and spirit. We shall, therefore, be very concise.

Of the two poems we rather prefer that on the Omnipresence of the Deity, for the same reason which induced Sir Thomas More to rank one bad book above another. "Marry, this is somewhat. This is rhyme. But the other is neither rhyme nor reason." Satan is a long soliloquy, which the Devil pronounces in five or six thousand lines of bad blank verse, concerning geography, politics, newspapers, fashionable society, theatrical amusements, Sir Walter Scott's novels, Lord Byron's poetry, and Mr. Martin's pictures. The new designs for Milton have, as was natural, particularly attracted the attention of a personage who occupies so conspicuous a place in them. Mr. Martin must be pleased to learn that, whatever may be thought of those performances on earth, they give full satisfaction in Pandæmonium, and that he is there thought to have hit off the likenesses of the various Thrones and Dominations very happily.

The motto to the poem of Satan is taken from the Book of Job: "Whence comest thou? From going to and fro in the earth, and walking up and down in it." And certainly Mr. Robert Montgomery has not failed to make his hero go to and fro, and walk up and down. With the exception, however, of this propensity to locomotion, Satan has not one Satanic quality. Mad Tom had told us that "the prince of darkness is a gentleman;" but we had yet to learn that he is a respectable and pious gentleman, whose principal fault is that he is something of a twaddle and far too liberal of his good advice. That happy change in his character which Origen anticipated, and of which Tillotson did not despair, seems to be rapidly taking place. Bad habits are not eradicated in a moment. It is not strange, therefore, that so old an offender should now and then relapse for a short time into wrong dispositions. But to give him his due, as the proverb recommends, we must say that he always returns, after two or three lines of impiety, to his preaching style. We would seriously advise Mr. Montgomery to omit or alter about a hundred lines in different parts of this large volume, and to republish it under the name of "Gabriel." The reflections of which it consists would come less absurdly, as far as there is a more and a less in extreme absurdity, from a good than from a bad angel.

We can afford room only for a single quotation. We give one taken at random, neither worse nor better, as far as we can perceive, than any other equal number of lines in the book. The Devil goes to the play, and moralises thereon as follows:

> "Music and Pomp their mingling spirits shed
> Around me; beauties in their cloud-like robes
> Shine forth, — a scenic paradise, it glares
> Intoxication through the reeling sense
> Of flush'd enjoyment. In the motley host
> Three prime gradations may be rank'd: the first,
> To mount upon the wings of Shakspeare's mind,
> And win a flash of his Promethean thought, —
> To smile and weep, to shudder, and achieve
> A round of passionate omnipotence,
> Attend: the second, are a sensual tribe,
> Convened to hear romantic harlots sing,
> On forms to banquet a lascivious gaze,
> While the bright perfidy of wanton eyes
> Through brain and spirit darts delicious fire:
> The last, a throng most pitiful! who seem,
> With their corroded figures, rayless glance,
> And death-like struggle of decaying age,
> Like painted skeletons in charnel pomp
> Set forth to satirize the human kind! —
> How fine a prospect for demoniac view!
> 'Creatures whose souls outbalance worlds awake!'
> Methinks I hear a pitying angel cry."

Here we conclude. If our remarks give pain to Mr. Robert Montgomery, we are sorry for it. But, at whatever cost of pain to individuals, literature must be purified from this taint. And, to show that we are not actuated by any feelings of personal enmity towards him, we hereby give notice that, as soon as any book shall, by means of puffing, reach a second edition, our intention is to do unto the writer of it as we have done unto Mr. Robert Montgomery.

SADLER'S LAW OF POPULATION.[1]

(*Edinburgh Review*, July 1830.)

We did not expect a good book from Mr. Sadler: and it is well that we did not; for he has given us a very bad one. The matter of his treatise is extraordinary; the manner more extraordinary still. His arrangement is confused, his repetitions endless, his style everything which it ought not to be. Instead of saying what he has to say with the perspicuity, the precision, and the simplicity in which consists the eloquence proper to scientific writing, he indulges without measure in vague, bombastic declamation, made up of those fine things which boys of fifteen admire, and which everybody, who is not destined to be a boy all his life, weeds vigorously out of his compositions after five-and-twenty. That portion of his two thick volumes which is not made up of statistical tables, consists principally of ejaculations, apostrophes, metaphors, similes, — all the worst of their respective kinds. His thoughts are dressed up in this shabby finery with so much profusion and so little discrimination, that they remind us of a company of wretched strolling players, who have huddled on suits of ragged and faded tinsel, taken from a common wardrobe, and fitting neither their persons

[1] *The Law of Population: a Treatise in Six Books, in Disproof of the Superfecundity of Human Beings, and developing the real Principle of their Increase.* By Michael Thomas Sadler, M. P. 2 vols. 8vo. London: 1830.

nor their parts; and who then exhibit themselves to the laughing and pitying spectators, in a state of strutting, ranting, painted, gilded beggary. "Oh, rare Daniels!" "Political economist, go and do thou likewise!" "Hear, ye political economists and anti-populationists!" "Population, if not proscribed and worried down by the Cerberean dogs of this wretched and cruel system, really does press against the level of the means of subsistence, and still elevating that level, it continues thus to urge society through advancing stages, till at length the strong and resistless hand of necessity presses the secret spring of human prosperity, and the portals of Providence fly open, and disclose to the enraptured gaze the promised land of contented and rewarded labour." These are specimens, taken at random, of Mr. Sadler's eloquence. We could easily multiply them; but our readers, we fear, are already inclined to cry for mercy.

Much blank verse and much rhyme is also scattered through these volumes, sometimes rightly quoted, sometimes wrongly, — sometimes good, sometimes insufferable, — sometimes taken from Shakspeare, and sometimes, for aught we know, Mr. Sadler's own. "Let man," cries the philosopher, "take heed how he rashly violates his trust;" and thereupon he breaks forth into singing as follows:

"What myriads wait in destiny's dark womb,
Doubtful of life or an eternal tomb!
'Tis his to blot them from the book of fate,
Or, like a second Deity, create:
To dry the stream of being in its source,
Or bid it, widening, win its restless course;
While, earth and heaven replenishing, the flood
Rolls to its Ocean fount, and rests in God."

If these lines are not Mr. Sadler's, we heartily beg

his pardon for our suspicion — a suspicion which, we acknowledge, ought not to be lightly entertained of any human being. We can only say that we never met with them before, and that we do not much care how long it may be before we meet with them, or with any others like them, again.

The spirit of this work is as bad as its style. We never met with a book which so strongly indicated that the writer was in a good humour with himself, and in a bad humour with everybody else; which contained so much of that kind of reproach which is vulgarly said to be no slander, and of that kind of praise which is vulgarly said to be no commendation. Mr. Malthus is attacked in language which it would be scarcely decent to employ respecting Titus Oates. "Atrocious," "execrable," "blasphemous," and other epithets of the same kind, are poured forth against that able, excellent, and honourable man, with a profusion which in the early part of the work excites indignation, but, after the first hundred pages, produces mere weariness and nausea. In the preface, Mr. Sadler excuses himself on the plea of haste. Two-thirds of his book, he tells us, were written in a few months. If any terms have escaped him which can be construed into personal disrespect, he shall deeply regret that he had not more time to revise them. We must inform him that the tone of his book required a very different apology; and that a quarter of a year, though it is a short time for a man to be engaged in writing a book, is a very long time for a man to be in a passion.

The imputation of being in a passion Mr. Sadler will not disclaim. His is a theme, he tells us, on which "it were impious to be calm;" and he boasts that, "instead of conforming to the candour of the present age, he has imitated the honesty of preceding ones, in expressing himself with the utmost plainness and freedom throughout." If Mr. Sadler really wishes that the controversy about his new principle of population should be carried on with all the license of the seventeenth century, we can have no personal objections. We are quite as little afraid of a contest in which quarter shall be neither given nor taken as he can be. But we would advise him seriously to consider, before he publishes the promised continuation of his work, whether he be not one of that class of writers who stand peculiarly in need of the candour which he insults, and who would have most to fear from that unsparing severity which he practises and recommends.

There is only one excuse for the extreme acrimony with which this book is written; and that excuse is but a bad one. Mr. Sadler imagines that the theory of Mr. Malthus is inconsistent with Christianity, and even with the purer forms of Deism. Now, even had this been the case, a greater degree of mildness and self-command than Mr. Sadler has shown would have been becoming in a writer who had undertaken to defend the religion of charity. But, in fact, the imputation which has been thrown on Mr. Malthus and his followers is so absurd as scarcely to deserve an answer. As it appears, however, in almost every page of Mr. Sadler's book, we will say a few words respecting it.

Mr. Sadler describes Mr. Malthus's principle in the following words: —

"It pronounces that there exists an evil in the principle of population; an evil, not accidental, but inherent; not of occasional occurrence, but in perpetual operation; not light, transient, or mitigated, but productive of miseries, compared with which all those inflicted by human institutions, that is to say, by the weakness and wickedness of man, however instigated, are 'light:' an evil, finally, for which there is no remedy save one, which had been long overlooked, and which is now enunciated in terms which evince anything rather than confidence. It is a principle, moreover, pre-eminently bold, as well as 'clear.' With a presumption, to call it by no fitter name, of which it may be doubted whether literature, heathen or Christian, furnishes a parallel, it professes to trace this supposed evil to its source, 'the laws of nature, which are those of God;' thereby implying, and indeed asserting, that the law by which the Deity multiplies his offspring, and that by which he makes provision for their sustentation, are different, and, indeed, irreconcilable."

"This theory," he adds, "in the plain apprehension of the many, lowers the character of the Deity in that attribute, which, as Rousseau has well observed, is the most essential to him, his goodness; or otherwise, impugns his wisdom."

Now nothing is more certain than that there is physical and moral evil in the world. Whoever, therefore, believes, as we do most firmly believe, in the goodness of God must believe that there is no incompatibility between the goodness of God and the existence of physical and moral evil. If, then, the goodness of God be not incompatible with the existence of physical and moral evil, on what grounds does Mr. Sadler maintain that the goodness of God is incompatible with the law of population laid down by Mr. Malthus?

Is there any difference between the particular form of evil which would be produced by over-population, and other forms of evil which we know to exist in the world? It is, says Mr. Sadler, not a light or transient evil, but a great and permanent evil. What then? The question of the origin of evil is a question of ay or no, — not a question of more or less. If any explanation can be found by which the slightest inconvenience ever sustained by any sentient being can be reconciled with the divine attribute of benevolence, that explanation will equally apply to the most dreadful and extensive calamities that can ever afflict the human race. The difficulty arises from an apparent contradiction in terms; and that difficulty is as complete in the case of a headache which lasts for an hour as in the case of a pestilence which unpeoples an empire, — in the case of the gust which makes us shiver for a moment as in the case of the hurricane in which an Armada is cast away.

It is, according to Mr. Sadler, an instance of presumption unparalleled in literature, heathen or Christian, to trace an evil to "the laws of nature, which are those of God," as its source. Is not hydrophobia an evil? And is it not a law of nature that hydrophobia should be communicated by the bite of a mad dog? Is not malaria an evil? And is it not a law of nature that in particular situations the human frame should be liable to malaria? We know that there is evil in the world. If it is not to be traced to the laws of nature, how did it come into the world? Is it supernatural? And, if we suppose it to be supernatural, is not the difficulty of reconciling it with the divine attributes as great as if we suppose it to be natural? Or, rather, what do the words natural and supernatural mean when applied to the operations of the Supreme Mind?

Mr. Sadler has attempted, in another part of his work, to meet these obvious arguments, by a distinction without a difference.

"The scourges of human existence, as necessary regulators of the numbers of mankind, it is also agreed by some, are not inconsistent with the wisdom or benevolence of the Governor of the universe; though such think that it is a mere after-concern to 'reconcile the undeniable state of the fact to the attributes we assign to the Deity.' 'The purpose of the earthquake,' say they, 'the hurricane, the drought, or the famine, by which thousands, and sometimes almost millions, of the human race, are at once overwhelmed, or left the victims of lingering want, is certainly inscrutable.' How singular is it that a sophism like this, so false, as a mere illustration, should pass for an argument, as it has long done! The principle of population is declared to be naturally productive of evils to mankind, and as having that constant and manifest tendency to increase their numbers beyond the means of their subsistence, which has produced the unhappy and disgusting consequences so often enumerated. This is, then, its universal tendency or rule. But is there in Nature the same constant tendency to these earthquakes, hurricanes, droughts, and famines, by which so many myriads, if not millions, are overwhelmed or reduced at once to ruin?, No; these awful events are strange exceptions to the ordinary course of things; their visitations are partial, and they occur at distant intervals of time. While Religion has assigned to them a very solemn office, Philosophy readily refers them to those great and benevolent principles of Nature by which the universe is regulated. But were there a constantly operating tendency to these calamitous occurrences; did we feel the earth beneath us tremulous, and giving ceaseless and certain tokens of the coming catastrophe of nature; were the hurricane heard mustering its devastating powers, and perpetually muttering around us; were the skies 'like brass,' without a cloud to produce one genial drop to refresh the thirsty earth, and famine, consequently, visibly on the approach; I say, would such a state of things, as resulting from the constant laws of Nature, be 'reconcilable with the attributes we assign to the Deity,' or with any attributes which in these inventive days could be assigned to him, so as to represent him as anything but the tormentor, rather than the kind benefactor, of his creatures? Life, in such a condition, would be like the unceasingly threatened and miserable existence of Damocles at the table of Dionysius, and the tyrant himself the worthy image of the Deity of the anti-populationists."

Surely this is wretched trifling. Is it on the number of bad harvests, or of volcanic eruptions, that this great question depends? Mr. Sadler's piety, it seems, would be proof against one rainy summer, but would be overcome by three or four in succession. On the coasts of the Mediterranean, where earthquakes are rare, he would be an optimist. South America would make him a sceptic, and Java a decided Manichean, To say that religion assigns a solemn office to these visitations is nothing to the purpose. Why was man so constituted as to need such warnings? It is equally unmeaning to say that philosophy refers these events to benevolent general laws of nature. In so far as the laws of nature produce evil, they are clearly not benevolent. They may produce much good. But why is this good mixed with evil? The most subtle and powerful intellects have been labouring for centuries to solve these difficulties. The true solution, we are inclined to think, is that which has been rather suggested, than developed, by Paley and Butler. But there it not one solution which will not apply quite as well to the evils of over population as to any other evil. Many excellent people think that it is presumptuous to meddle with such high questions at all, and that, though there doubtless is an explanation, our faculties are not sufficiently enlarged to comprehend that explanation. This mode of getting rid of the difficulty, again, will apply quite as well to the evils of over-population as to any other evils. We are sure that those who humbly confess their inability to expound the great enigma act more rationally and more decorously than Mr. Sadler, who tells us, with the utmost confidence, which are the means and which the ends, — which the exceptions and which the rules, in the government of the universe; — who consents to bear a little evil without denying the divine benevolence, but distinctly announces that a certain quantity of dry weather or stormy weather would force him to regard the Deity as the tyrant of his creatures.

The great discovery by which Mr. Sadler has, as he conceives, vindicated the ways of Providence is enounced with all the pomp of capital letters. We must particularly beg that our readers will peruse it with attention.

"No one fact relative to the human species is more clearly ascertained, whether by general observation or actual proof, than that their fecundity varies in different communities and countries. The principle which effects this variation, without the necessity of those cruel and unnatural expedients so frequently adverted to, constitutes what I presume to call THE LAW OF POPULATION; and that law may be thus briefly enunciated:—

"THE PROLIFICNESS OF HUMAN BEINGS, OTHERWISE SIMILARLY CIRCUMSTANCED, VARIES INVERSELY AS THEIR NUMBERS.

"The preceding definition may be thus amplified and explained. Premising, as a mere truism, that marriages under precisely similar circumstances will, on the average, be equally fruitful everywhere, I proceed to state, first, that the prolificness of a given number of marriages will, all other circumstances being the same, vary in proportion to the condensation of the population, so that that prolificness shall be greatest where the numbers on an equal space are the fewest, and, on the contrary, the smallest where those numbers are the largest."

Mr. Sadler, at setting out, abuses Mr. Malthus for enouncing his theory in terms taken from the exact sciences. "Applied to the mensuration of human fecundity," he tells us, "the most fallacious of all things is geometrical demonstration;" and he again informs us that those "act an irrational and irreverent part who affect to measure the mighty depth of God's mercies by their arithmetic, and to demonstrate, by their geometrical ratios, that it is inadequate to receive and contain the efflux of that fountain of life which is in Him."

It appears, however, that it is not to the use of mathematical words, but only to the use of those words in their right senses that Mr. Sadler objects. The law of inverse variation, or inverse proportion, is as much a part of mathematical science as the law of geometric progression. The only difference in this respect between Mr. Malthus and Mr. Sadler is, that Mr. Malthus knows what is meant by geometric progression, and that Mr. Sadler has not the faintest notion of what is meant by inverse variation. Had he understood the proposition which he has enounced with so much pomp, its ludicrous absurdity must at once have flashed on his mind.

Let it be supposed that there is a tract in the back settlements of America, or in New South Wales, equal in size to London, with only a single couple, a man and his wife, living upon it. The population of London, with its immediate suburbs, is now probably about a million and a half. The average fecundity of a marriage in London is, as Mr. Sadler tells us, 2·35. How many children will the woman in the back settlements bear according to Mr. Sadler's theory? The solution of the problem is easy. As the population in this tract in the back settlements is to the population of London, so will be the number of children born from a marriage in London to the number of children born from the marriage of this couple in the back settlements. That is to say —

2 : 1,500,000 : : 2·35 : 1,762,500.

The lady will have 1,762,500 children: a large "efflux of the fountain of life," to borrow Mr. Sadler's sonorous rhetoric, as the most philoprogenitive parent could possibly desire.

But let us, instead of putting cases of our own, look at some of those which Mr. Sadler has brought forward in support of his theory. The following table, he tells us, exhibits a striking proof of the truth of his main position. It seems to us to prove only that Mr. Sadler does not know what inverse proportion means.

Countries.	Inhabitants on a square mile, about	Children to a Marriage.
Cape of Good Hope - -	1	5·48
North America - - - -	4	5·22
Russia in Europe - - -	23	4·94
Denmark - - - - - - -	73	4·89
Prussia - - - - - - -	100	4·70
France - - - - - - -	140	4·22
England - - - - - - -	160	3·66

Is 1 to 160 as 3·66 to 5·48? If Mr. Sadler's principle were just, the number of children produced by a marriage at the Cape would be, not 5·48, but very near 600. Or take America and France. Is 4 to 140 as 4·22 to 5·22? The number of births to a marriage in North America ought, according to this proportion, to be about 150.

Mr. Sadler states the law of population in England thus: —

"Where the inhabitants are found to be on the square mile,
From 50 to 100 (2 counties) the births to 100 marriages are 420
— 100 to 150 (9 counties) 396
— 150 to 200 (16 counties) 390
— 200 to 250 (4 counties) 388
— 250 to 300 (5 counties) 378
— 300 to 350 (3 counties) 353
— 500 to 600 (2 counties) 331
— 4000 and upwards (1 county) 246

"Now, I think it quite reasonable to conclude, that, were there not another document in existence relative to this subject, the facts thus deduced from the census of England are fully sufficient to demonstrate the position, that the fecundity of human beings varies inversely as their numbers. How, I ask, can it be evaded?"

What, we ask, is there to evade? Is 246 to 420 as 50 to 4000? Is 331 to 396 as 100 to 500? If the law propounded by Mr. Sadler were correct, the births to a hundred marriages in the least populous part of England, would be, 246 × 4000 ÷ 50, that is 19,680, — nearly two hundred children to every mother. But we will not carry on these calculations. The absurdity of Mr. Sadler's proposition is so palpable that it is unnecessary to select particular instances. Let us see what are the extremes of population and fecundity in well-known countries. The space which Mr. Sadler generally takes is a square mile. The population at the Cape of Good Hope is, according to him, one to the square mile. That of London is two hundred thousand to the square mile. The number of children at the Cape, Mr. Sadler informs us, is 5·48 to a marriage. In London, he states it at 2·35 to a marriage. Now how can that of which all the variations lie between 2·35 and 5·48 vary, either directly or inversely, as that which admits of all the variations between one and two hundred thousand? Mr. Sadler evidently does not know the meaning of the word proportion. A million is a larger quantity than ten. A hundred is a larger quantity than five. Mr. Sadler thinks, therefore, that there is no impropriety in saying that a hundred is to five as a million is to ten, or in the inverse ratio of ten to a million. He proposes to prove that the fecundity of marriages varies in inverse proportion to the density of the population. But all that he attempts to prove is that, while the population increases from one to a hundred and sixty on the square mile, the fecundity will diminish from 5·48 to 3·66; and that again, while the population increases from one hundred and sixty to two hundred thousand on the square mile, the fecundity will diminish from 3·66 to 2·35.

The proposition which Mr. Sadler enounces, without understanding the words which he uses, would indeed, if it could be proved, set us at ease as to the dangers of over-population. But it is, as we have shown, a proposition so grossly absurd that it is difficult for any man to keep his countenance while he repeats it. The utmost that Mr. Sadler has ever attempted to prove is this, — that the fecundity of the human race diminishes as population becomes more condensed, — but that the diminution of fecundity bears a very small ratio to the increase of population, — so that, while the population on a square mile is multiplied two hundred-thousand-fold, the fecundity decreases by little more than one-half.

Does this principle vindicate the honour of God? Does it hold out any new hope or comfort to man? Not at all. We pledge ourselves to show, with the utmost strictness of reasoning, from Mr. Sadler's own principles, and from facts of the most notorious description, that every consequence which follows from the law of geometrical progression, laid down by Mr. Malthus, will follow from the law, miscalled a law of inverse variation, which has been laid down by Mr. Sadler.

London is the most thickly peopled spot of its size in the known world. Therefore the fecundity of the population of London must, according to Mr. Sadler, be less than the fecundity of human beings living on any other spot of equal size. Mr. Sadler tells us, that "the ratios of mortality are influenced by the different degrees in which the population is condensated; and that, other circumstances being similar, the relative number of deaths in a thinly-populated, or country district, is less than that which takes place in towns, and in towns of a moderate size less again than that which exists in large and populous cities." Therefore the mortality in London must, according to him, be greater than in other places. But, though, according to Mr. Sadler, the fecundity is less in London than elsewhere, and though the mortality is greater there than elsewhere, we find that even in London the number of births greatly exceeds the number of deaths. During the ten years which ended with 1820, there were fifty thousand more baptisms than burials within the bills of mortality. It follows, therefore, that, even within London itself, an increase of the population is taking place by internal propagation.

Now, if the population of a place in which the fecundity is less and the mortality greater than in other places still goes on increasing by propagation, it follows that in other places the population will increase, and increase still faster. There is clearly nothing in Mr. Sadler's boasted law of fecundity which will keep the population from multiplying till the whole earth is as thick with human beings as St. Giles's parish. If Mr. Sadler denies this, he must hold that, in places less thickly peopled than London, marriages may be less fruitful than in London, which is directly contrary to his own principles; or that in places less thickly peopled than London, and similarly situated, people will die faster than in London, which is again directly contrary to his own principles. Now, if it follows, as it clearly does follow, from Mr. Sadler's own doctrines, that the human race might be stowed together by three or four hundred to the acre, and might still, as far as the principle of propagation is concerned, go on increasing, what advantage, in a religious or moral point of view, has his theory over that of Mr. Malthus? The principle of Mr. Malthus, says Mr. Sadler, leads to consequences of the most frightful description. Be it so. But do not all these consequences spring equally from his own principle? Revealed religion condemns Mr. Malthus. Be it so. But Mr. Sadler must share in the reproach of heresy. The theory of Mr. Malthus represents the Deity as a Dionysius hanging the sword over the heads of his trembling slaves. Be it so. But under what rhetorical figure are we to represent the Deity of Mr. Sadler?

A man who wishes to serve the cause of religion ought to hesitate long before he stakes the truth of religion on the event of a controversy respecting facts in the physical world. For a time he may succeed in making a theory which he dislikes unpopular by persuading the public that it contradicts the Scriptures and is inconsistent with the attributes of the Deity. But, if at last an overwhelming force of evidence proves this maligned theory to be true, what is the effect of the arguments by which the objector has attempted to prove that it is irreconcilable with natural and revealed religion? Merely this, to make men infidels. Like the Israelites, in their battle with the Philistines, he has presumptuously and without warrant brought down the ark of God into the camp as a means of ensuring victory: — and the consequence of this profanation is that, when the battle is lost, the ark is taken.

In every age the Church has been cautioned against this fatal and impious rashness by its most illustrious members, — by the fervid Augustin, by the subtle Aquinas, by the all-accomplished Pascal. The warning has been given in vain. That close alliance which, under the disguise of the most deadly enmity, has always subsisted between fanaticism and atheism is still unbroken. At one time, the cry was, — "If you hold that the earth moves round the sun, you deny the truth of the Bible." Popes, conclaves, and religious orders, rose up against the Copernican heresy. But, as Pascal said, they could not prevent the earth from moving, or themselves from moving along with it. One thing, however, they could do, and they did. They could teach numbers to consider the Bible as a collection of old women's stories which the progress of civilisation and knowledge was refuting one by one. They had attempted to show that the Ptolemaic system was as much a part of Christianity as the resurrection of the dead. Was it strange, then, that, when the Ptolemaic system became an object of ridicule to every man of education in Catholic countries, the doctrine of the resurrection should be in peril? In the present generation, and in our own country, the prevailing system of geology has been, with equal folly, attacked on the ground that it is inconsistent with the Mosaic dates. And here we have Mr. Sadler, out of his especial zeal for religion, first proving that the doctrine of superfecundity is irreconcilable with the goodness of God, and then laying down principles, and stating facts, from which the doctrine of superfecundity necessarily follows. This blundering piety reminds us of the adventures of a certain missionary who went to convert the inhabitants of Madagascar. The good father had an audience of the king, and began to instruct his majesty in the history of the human race as given in the Scriptures. "Thus, sir," said he, "was woman made out of the rib of man, and ever since that time a woman has had one rib more than a man." "Surely, father, you must be mistaken there," said the king. "Mistaken!" said the missionary. "It is an indisputable fact. My faith upon it! My life upon it!" The good man had heard the fact asserted by his nurse when he was a child, — had always considered it as a strong confirmation of the Scriptures, and fully believed it without having ever thought of verifying it. The king ordered a man and woman, the leanest that could be found, to be brought before him, and desired his spiritual instructor to count their ribs. The father counted over and over, upward and downward, and still found the same number in both. He then cleared his throat, stammered, stuttered, and began to assure the king that, though he had committed a little error in saying that a woman had more ribs than a man, he was quite right in saying that the first woman was made out of the rib of the first man. "How can I tell that?" said the king. "You come to me with a strange story, which you say is revealed to you from heaven. I have already made you confess that one half of it is a lie: and how can you have the face to expect that I shall believe the other half?"

We have shown that Mr. Sadler's theory, if it be true, is as much a theory of superfecundity as that of Mr. Malthus. But it is not true. And from Mr. Sadler's own tables we will prove that it is not true.

The fecundity of the human race in England Mr. Sadler rates as follows: —

"Where the inhabitants are found to be on the square mile —

From 50 to 100 (2 counties) the births to 100 marriages are 420
— 100 to 150 (9 counties) 396
— 150 to 200 (16 counties) 390
— 200 to 250 (4 counties) 388
— 250 to 300 (5 counties) 378
— 300 to 350 (3 counties) 353
— 500 to 600 (2 counties) 331
— 4000 and upwards (1 county) . . . 246

Having given this table, he begins, as usual, to boast and triumph. "Were there not another document on the subject in existence," says he, "the facts thus deduced from the census of England are sufficient to demonstrate the position, that the fecundity of human beings varies inversely as their numbers." In no case would these facts demonstrate that the fecundity of human beings varies inversely as their numbers in the right sense of the words inverse variation. But certainly they would, "if there were no other document in existence," appear to indicate something like what Mr. Sadler means by inverse variation. Unhappily for him, however, there are other documents in existence; and he has himself furnished us with them. We will extract another of his tables: —

TABLE LXIV.

Showing the Operation of the Law of Population in the different Hundreds of the County of Lancaster.

Hundreds.	Population on each Square Mile.	Square Miles.	Population in 1821, exclusive of Towns of separate Jurisdiction.	Marriages from 1811 to 1821.	Baptisms from 1811 to 1821.	Baptisms to 100 Marriages.
Lonsdale .	96	441	42,486	3,651	16,129	442
Almondness	267	228	60,930	3,670	15,228	415
Leyland .	354	126	44,583	2,858	11,182	391
West Derby	409	377	154,040	24,182	86,407	357
Blackburn	513	286	146,608	10,814	31,463	291
Salford . .	869	373	322,592	40,143	114,941	286

Mr. Sadler rejoices much over this table. The results, he says, have surprised himself; and, indeed, as we shall show, they might well have done so.

The result of his inquiries with respect to France he presents in the following table: —

"The legitimate births are, in those departments where there are to each inhabitant —

From 4 to 5 hects.	(2 departs.)	to every 1000 marriages	5130
3 to 4	(3 do.)		4372
2 to 3	(30 do.)		4250
1 to 2	(44 do.)		4234
·06 to 1	(5 do.)		4146
and ·06	(1 do.)		2557

Then comes the shout of exultation as regularly as the *Gloria Patri* at the end of a Psalm. "Is there any possibility of gainsaying the conclusions these facts force upon us; namely that the fecundity of marriages is regulated by the density of the population, and inversely to it?"

Certainly these tables, taken separately, look well for Mr. Sadler's theory. He must be a bungling gamester who cannot win when he is suffered to pack the cards his own way. We must beg leave to shuffle them a little; and we will venture to promise our readers that some curious results will follow from the operation. In nine counties of England, says Mr. Sadler, in which the population is from 100 to 150 on the square mile, the births to 100 marriages are 396. He afterwards expresses some doubts as to the accuracy of the documents from which this estimate has been formed, and rates the number of births as high as 414. Let him take his choice. We will allow him every advantage.

In the table which we have quoted, numbered lxiv., he tells us that in Almondness, where the population is 267 to the square mile, there are 415 births to 100 marriages. The population of Almondness is twice as thick as the population of the nine counties referred to in the other table. Yet the number of births to a marriage is greater in Almondness than in those counties.

Once more, he tells us that in three counties, in which the population was from 300 to 350 on the square mile, the births to 100 marriages were 353. He afterwards rates them at 375. Again we say, let him take his choice. But from his table of the population of Lancashire it appears that, in the hundred of Leyland, where the population is 354 to the square mile, the number of births to 100 marriages is 391. Here again we have the marriages becoming more fruitful as the population becomes denser.

Let us now shuffle the censuses of England and France together. In two English counties which contain from fifty to 100 inhabitants on the square mile, the births to 100 marriages are, according to Mr. Sadler, 420. But in forty-four departments of France, in which there are from one to two hecatares to each inhabitant, that is to say, in which the population is from 125 to 250, or rather more, to the square mile, the number of births to 100 marriages is 423 and a fraction.

Again, in five departments of France in which there is less than one hecatare to each inhabitant, that is to say, in which the population is more than 250 to the square mile, the number of births to 100 marriages is 414 and a fraction. But, in the four counties of England in which the population is from 200 to 250 on the square mile, the number of births to 100 marriages is, according to one of Mr. Sadler's tables, only 388, and by his very highest estimate no more than 402.

Mr. Sadler gives us a long table of all the towns of England and Ireland, which, he tells us, irrefragably demonstrates his principle. We assert, and will prove, that these tables are alone sufficient to upset his whole theory.

It is very true that in the great towns the number of births to a marriage appears to be smaller than in the less populous towns. But we learn some other facts from these tables which we should be glad to know how Mr. Sadler will explain. We find that the fecundity in towns of fewer than 3,000 inhabitants is actually much greater than the average fecundity of the kingdom, and that the fecundity in towns of between 3,000 and 4,000 inhabitants is at least as great as the average fecundity of the kingdom. The average fecundity of a marriage in towns of fewer than 3,000 inhabitants is about four; in towns of between 3,000 and 4,000 inhabitants it is 3·60. Now the average fecundity of England, when it contained only 160 inhabitants to a square mile, and when, therefore, according to the new law of population, the fecundity must have been greater than it now is, was only, according to Mr. Sadler, 3·66 to a marriage. To proceed, — the fecundity of a marriage in the English towns of between 4,000 and 5,000 inhabitants is stated at 3·56. But, when we turn to Mr. Sadler's table of the counties, we find the fecundity of a marriage in Warwickshire and Staffordshire rated at only 3·48, and in Lancashire and Surrey at only 3·41.

These facts disprove Mr. Sadler's principle; and the fact on which he lays so much stress — that the fecundity is less in the great towns than in the small towns — does not tend in any degree to prove his principle. There is not the least reason to believe that the population is more dense, *on a given space*, in London or Manchester than in a town of 4,000 inhabitants. But it is quite certain that the population is more dense in a town of 4,000 inhabitants than in Warwickshire or Lancashire. That the fecundity of Manchester is less than the fecundity of Sandwich or Guildford is a circumstance which has nothing whatever to do with Mr. Sadler's theory. But that the fecundity of Sandwich is greater than the average fecundity of Kent, — that the fecundity of Guildford is greater than the average fecundity of Surrey, — as from his own tables appears to be the case, — these are facts utterly inconsistent with his theory.

We need not here examine why it is that the human race is less fruitful in great cities than in small towns or in the open country. The fact has long been notorious. We are inclined to attribute it to the same causes which tend to abridge human life in great cities, — to general sickliness and want of tone, produced by close air and sedentary employments. Thus far, and thus far only, we agree with Mr. Sadler, that, when population is crowded together in such masses that the general health and energy of the frame are impaired by the condensation, and by the habits attending on the condensation, then the fecundity of the race diminishes. But this is evidently a check of the same class with war, pestilence, and famine. It is a check for the operation of which Mr. Malthus has allowed.

That any condensation which does not affect the general health will affect fecundity, is not only not proved — it is disproved — by Mr. Sadler's own tables.

Mr. Sadler passes on to Prussia, and sums up his information respecting that country as follows: —

Inhabitants on a Square Mile, German.	Number of Provinces.	Births to 100 Marriages, 1754.	Births to 100 Marriages, 1784.	Births to 100 Marriages, Busching.
Under 1000	2	434	472	503
1000 to 2000	4	414	455	454
2000 to 3000	6	384	424	426
3000 to 4000	2	365	408	394

After the table comes the boast as usual:

"Thus is the law of population deduced from the registers of Prussia also; and were the argument to pause here, it is conclusive. The results obtained from the registers of this and the preceding countries exhibiting, as they do most clearly, the principle of human increase, it is utterly impossible should have been the work of chance; on the contrary, the regularity with which the facts class themselves in conformity with that principle, and the striking analogy which the whole of them bear to each other, demonstrate equally the design of Nature, and the certainty of its accomplishment."

We are sorry to disturb Mr. Sadler's complacency. But, in our opinion, this table completely disproves his whole principle. If we read the columns perpendicularly, indeed, they seem to be in his favour. But how stands the case if we read horizontally? Does Mr. Sadler believe that, during the thirty years which elapsed between 1754 and 1784, the population of Prussia had been diminishing? No fact in history is better ascertained than that, during the long peace which followed the seven years' war, it increased with great rapidity. Indeed, if the fecundity were what Mr. Sadler states it to have been, it must have increased with great rapidity. Yet, the ratio of births to marriages is greater in 1784 than in 1754, and that in every province. It is, therefore, perfectly clear that the fecundity does not diminish whenever the density of the population increases.

We will try another of Mr. Sadler's tables:

TABLE LXXXI.

Showing the Estimated Prolificness of Marriages in England at the close of the Seventeenth Century.

Places.	Number of Inhabitants.	One Annual Marriage, to	Number of Marriages.	Children to one Marriage.	Total Number of Births.
London	530,000	106	5,000	4·	20,000
Large Towns . .	870,000	128	6,800	4·5	30,000
Small Towns and Country Places	4,100,000	141	29,200	4·8	140,160
	5,500,000	134	41,000	4·65	190,760

Standing by itself, this table, like most of the others, seems to support Mr. Sadler's theory. But surely London, at the close of the seventeenth century, was far more thickly peopled than the kingdom of England now is. Yet the fecundity in London at the close of the seventeenth century was 4; and the average fecundity of the whole kingdom now is not more, according to Mr. Sadler, than 3½. Then, again, the large towns in 1700 were far more thickly peopled than Westmorland and the North Riding of Yorkshire now are. Yet the fecundity in those large towns was then 4·5. And Mr. Sadler tells us that it is now only 4·2 in Westmorland and the North Riding.

It is scarcely necessary to say any thing about the

censuses of the Netherlands, as Mr. Sadler himself confesses that there is some difficulty in reconciling them with his theory, and helps out his awkward explanation by supposing, quite gratuitously, as it seems to us, that the official documents are inaccurate. The argument which he has drawn from the United States will detain us but for a very short time. He has not told us, — perhaps he had not the means of telling us, — what proportion the number of births in the different parts of that country bears to the number of marriages. He shows that in the thinly-peopled states the number of children bears a greater proportion to the number of grown-up people than in the old states; and this, he conceives, is a sufficient proof that the condensation of the population is unfavourable to fecundity. We deny the inference altogether. Nothing can be more obvious than the explanation of the phenomenon. The back settlements are for the most part peopled by emigration from the old states; and emigrants are almost always breeders. They are almost always vigorous people in the prime of life. Mr. Sadler himself, in another part of his book, in which he tries very unsuccessfully to show that the rapid multiplication of the people of America is principally owing to emigration from Europe, states this fact in the plainest manner:

"Nothing is more certain, than that emigration is almost universally supplied by 'single persons in the beginning of mature life;' nor, secondly, that such persons, as Dr. Franklin long ago asserted, 'marry and raise families.'

"Nor is this all. It is not more true, that emigrants, generally speaking, consist of individuals in the prime of life, than that 'they are the most active and vigorous' of that age, as Dr. Seybert describes them to be. They are, as it respects the principle at issue, a select class, even compared with that of their own age generally considered. Their very object in leaving their native countries is to settle in life, a phrase that needs no explanation; and they do so. No equal number of human beings, therefore, have ever given so large or rapid an increase to a community as 'settlers' have invariably done."

It is perfectly clear that children are more numerous in the back settlements of America than in the maritime states, not because unoccupied land makes people prolific, but because the most prolific people go to the unoccupied land.

Mr. Sadler having, as he conceives, fully established his theory of population by statistical evidence, proceeds to prove, "that it is in unison, or rather required by the principles of physiology." The difference between himself and his opponents he states as follows: —

"In pursuing this part of my subject, I must begin by reminding the reader of the difference between those who hold the superfecundity of mankind and myself, in regard to those principles which will form the basis of the present argument. They contend, that production precedes population; I, on the contrary, maintain that population precedes, and is indeed the cause of, production. They teach that man breeds up to the capital, or in proportion to the abundance of the food, he possesses; I assert, that he is comparatively sterile when he is wealthy, and that he breeds in proportion to his poverty; not meaning, however, by that poverty, a state of privation approaching to actual starvation, any more than, I suppose, they would contend, that extreme and culpable excess is the grand patron of population. In a word, they hold that a state of ease and affluence is the great promoter of prolificness: I maintain that a considerable degree of labour, and even privation, is a more efficient cause of an increased degree of human fecundity."

To prove this point he quotes Aristotle, Hippocrates, Dr. Short, Dr. Gregory, Dr. Perceval, M. Villermi, Lord Bacon, and Rousseau. We will not dispute about it; for it seems quite clear to us that if he succeeds in establishing it he overturns his own theory. If men breed in proportion to their poverty, as he tells us here, — and at the same time breed in inverse proportion to their numbers, as he told us before, — it necessarily follows that the poverty of men must be in inverse proportion to their numbers. Inverse proportion, indeed, as we have shown, is not the phrase which expresses Mr. Sadler's meaning. To speak more correctly, it follows, from his own positions, that, if one population be thinner than another, it will also be poorer. Is this the fact? Mr. Sadler tells us, in one of those tables which we have already quoted, that in the United States the population is four to a square mile, and the fecundity 5·22 to a marriage, and that in Russia the population is twenty-three to a square mile, and the fecundity 4·94 to a marriage. Is the North American labourer poorer than the Russian boor? If not, what becomes of Mr. Sadler's argument?

The most decisive proof of Mr. Sadler's theory, according to him, is that which he has kept for the last. It is derived from the registers of the English Peerage. The Peers, he says, and says truly, are the class with respect to whom we possess the most accurate statistical information.

"Touching their *number*, this has been accurately known and recorded ever since the order has existed in the country. For several centuries past, the addition to it of a single individual has been a matter of public interest and notoriety: this hereditary honour conferring not personal dignity merely, but important privileges, and being almost always identified with great wealth and influence. The records relating to it are kept with the most scrupulous attention, not only by heirs and expectants, but they are appealed to by more distant connections, as conferring distinction on all who can claim such affinity. Hence there are few disputes concerning successions to this rank, but such as go back to very remote periods. In later times, the marriages, births, and deaths, of the nobility, have not only been registered by and known to those personally interested, but have been published periodically, and, consequently, subject to perpetual correction and revision; while many of the most powerful motives which can influence the human mind conspire to preserve these records from the slightest falsification. Compared with these, therefore, all other registers, or reports, whether of sworn searchers or others, are incorrectness itself."

Mr. Sadler goes on to tell us that the Peers are a marrying class, and that their general longevity proves them to be a healthy class. Still peerages often become extinct; — and from this fact he infers that they are a sterile class. So far, says he, from increasing in geometrical progression, they do not even keep up their numbers. "Nature interdicts their increase."

"Thus," says he, "in all ages of the world, and in every nation of it, have the highest ranks of the community been the most sterile, and the lowest the most prolific. As it respects our own country, from the lowest grade of society, the Irish peasant, to the highest, the British peer, this remains a conspicuous truth; and the regulation of the degree of fecundity conformably to this principle, through the intermediate gradations of society, constitutes one of the features of the system developed in these pages."

We take the issue which Mr. Sadler has himself offered. We agree with him, that the registers of the English Peerage are of far higher authority than any other statistical documents. We are content that by those registers his principles should be judged. And we meet him by positively denying his facts. We assert that the English nobles are not only not a sterile, but an eminently prolific, part of the community. Mr. Sadler concludes that they are sterile, merely because peerages often become extinct. Is this the proper way of ascertaining the point? Is it thus that he avails himself of those registers on the accuracy and fulness of which he descants so largely? Surely his right course would have been to count the marriages, and the number of births in the Peerage. This he has not done; — but we have done it. And what is the result?

It appears from the last edition of Debrett's *Peerage*, published in 1828, that there were at that time 287 peers of the United Kingdom, who had been married once or oftener. The whole number of marriages contracted by these 287 peers was 333. The number of children by these marriages was 1437, — more than five to a peer, — more than 4·3 to a marriage, — more, that is to say, than the average number in those counties of England in which, according to Mr. Sadler's own statement, the fecundity is the greatest.

But this is not all. These marriages had not, in 1828, produced their full effect. Some of them had been very lately contracted. In a very large proportion of them there was every probability of additional issue. To allow for this probability, we may safely add one to the average which we have already obtained, and rate the fecundity of a noble marriage in England at 5·3; — higher than the fecundity which Mr. Sadler assigns to the people of the United States. Even if we do not make this allowance, the average fecundity of the marriages of peers is higher by one-fifth than the average fecundity of marriages throughout the kingdom. And this is the sterile class! This is the class which "nature has interdicted from increasing!" The evidence to which Mr. Sadler has himself appealed proves that his principle is false, — utterly false, — wildly and extravagantly false. It proves that a class, living during half of every year in the most crowded population in the world, breeds faster than those whc live in the country; — that the class which enjoys the greatest degree of luxury and ease breeds faster than the class which undergoes labour and privation. To talk a little in Mr. Sadler's style, we must own that we are ourselves surprised at the results which our examination of the peerage has brought out. We certainly should have thought that the habits of fashionable life, and long residence even in the most airy parts of so great a city as London, would have been more unfavourable to the fecundity of the higher orders than they appear to be.

Peerages, it is true, often become extinct. But it is quite clear, from what we have stated, that this is not because peeresses are barren. There is no difficulty in discovering what the causes really are. In the first place, most of the titles of our nobles are limited to heirs male; so that, though the average fecundity of a noble marriage is upwards of five, yet, for the purpose of keeping up a peerage, it cannot be reckoned at much more than two and a half. Secondly, though the peers are, as Mr. Sadler says, a marrying class, the younger sons of peers are decidedly not a marrying class; so that a peer, though he has at least as great a chance of having a son as his neighbours, has less chance than they of having a collateral heir.

We have now disposed, we think, of Mr. Sadler's principle of population. Our readers must, by this time, be pretty well satisfied as to his qualifications for setting up theories of his own. We will, therefore, present them with a few instances of the skill and fairness which he shows when he undertakes to pull down the theories of other men. The doctrine of Mr. Malthus, that population, if not checked by want, by vice, by excessive mortality, or by the prudent self-denial of individuals, would increase in a geometric progression, is, in Mr. Sadler's opinion, at once false and atrocious.

"It may at once be denied," says he, "that human increase proceeds geometrically; and for this simple but decisive reason, that the existence of a geometrical ratio of increase in the works of nature, is neither true nor possible. It would fling into utter confusion all order, time, magnitude, and space."

This is as curious a specimen of reasoning as any that has been offered to the world since the days when theories were founded on the principle that nature abhors a vacuum. We proceed a few pages farther, however; and we then find that geometric progression is unnatural only in those cases in which Mr. Malthus conceives that it exists; and that, in all cases in which Mr. Malthus denies the existence of a geometric ratio, nature changes sides, and adopts that ratio as the rule of increase.

Mr. Malthus holds that subsistence will increase only in an arithmetical ratio. "As far as nature has to do with the question," says Mr. Sadler, "men might, for instance, plant twice the number of peas, and breed from a double number of the same animals, with equal prospect of their multiplication." Now, if Mr. Sadler thinks that, as far as nature is concerned, four sheep will double as fast as two, and eight as fast as four, how can he deny that the geometrical ratio of increase does exist in the works of nature? Or has he a definition of his own for geometrical progression, as well as for inverse proportion?

Mr. Malthus, and those who agree with him, have

generally referred to the United States, as a country in which the human race increases in a geometrical ratio, and have fixed on twenty-five years as the term in which the population of that country doubles itself. Mr. Sadler contends that it is physically impossible for a people to double in twenty-five years; nay, that thirty-five years is far too short a period, — that the Americans do not double by procreation in less than forty-seven years, — and that the rapid increase of their numbers is produced by emigration from Europe.

Emigration has certainly had some effect in increasing the population of the United States. But so great has the rate of that increase been that, after making full allowance for the effect of emigration, there will be a residue, attributable to procreation alone, amply sufficient to double the population in twenty-five years.

Mr. Sadler states the results of the four censuses as follows: —

> "There were, of white inhabitants, in the whole of the United States in 1790, 3,093,111; in 1800, 4,309,656; in 1810, 5,862,093; and in 1820, 7,861,710. The increase. in the first term, being 39 per cent.; that in the second, 36 per cent.; and that in the third and last, 33 per cent. It is superfluous to say, that it is utterly impossible to deduce the geometric theory of human increase, whatever be the period of duplication, from such terms as these."

Mr. Sadler is a bad arithmetician. The increase in the last term is not, as he states it, 33 per cent., but more than 34 per cent. Now, an increase of 32 per cent. in ten years, is more than sufficient to double the population in twenty-five years. And there is, we think, very strong reason to believe that the white population of the United States does increase by 32 per cent. every ten years.

Our reason is this. There is in the United States a class of persons whose numbers are not increased by emigration, — the negro slaves. During the interval which elapsed between the census of 1810 and the census of 1820, the change in their numbers must have been produced by procreation, and by procreation alone. Their situation, though much happier than that of the wretched beings who cultivate the sugar plantations of Trinidad and Demerara, cannot be supposed to be more favourable to health and fecundity than that of free labourers. In 1810, the slave trade had been but recently abolished; and there were in consequence many more male than female slaves, — a circumstance, of course, very unfavourable to procreation. Slaves are perpetually passing into the class of freemen; but no freeman ever descends into servitude; so that the census will not exhibit the whole effect of the procreation which really takes place.

We find, by the census of 1810, that the number of slaves in the Union was then 1,191,000. In 1820, they had increased to 1,538,000. That is to say, in ten years, they had increased 29 per cent. — within three per cent of that rate of increase which would double their numbers in twenty-five years. We may, we think, fairly calculate that, if the female slaves had been as numerous as the males, and if no manumissions had taken place, the census of the slave population would have exhibited an increase of 32 per cent. in ten years.

If we are right in fixing on 32 per cent. as the rate at which the white population of America increases by procreation in ten years, it will follow that, during the last ten years of the eighteenth century, nearly one-sixth of the increase was the effect of emigration; from

1800 to 1810, about one-ninth; and from 1810 to 1820, about one-seventeenth. This is what we should have expected; for it is clear that, unless the number of emigrants be constantly increasing, it must, as compared with the resident population, be relatively decreasing. The number of persons added to the population of the United States by emigration, between 1810 and 1820, would be nearly 120,000. From the data furnished by Mr. Sadler himself, we should be inclined to think that this would be a fair estimate.

"Dr. Seybert says, that the passengers to ten of the principal ports of the United States, in the year 1817, amounted to 22,235; of whom 11,977 were from Great Britain and Ireland; 4,164 from Germany and Holland; 1,245 from France; 58 from Italy; 2,901 from the British possessions in North America; 1,569 from the West Indies; and from all other countries, 321. These, however, we may conclude, with the editor of Styles's Register, were far short of the number that arrived."

We have not the honour of knowing either Dr. Seybert or the editor of Styles's Register. We cannot, therefore, decide on their respective claims to our confidence so peremptorily as Mr. Sadler thinks fit to do. Nor can we agree to what Mr. Sadler very gravely assigns as a reason for disbelieving Dr. Seybert's testimony. "Such accounts," he says, "if not wilfully exaggerated, must always fall short of the truth." It would be a curious question of casuistry to determine what a man ought to do in a case in which he cannot tell the truth except by being guilty of wilful exaggeration. We will, however, suppose, with Mr. Sadler, that Dr. Seybert, finding himself compelled to choose between two sins, preferred telling a falsehood to exaggerating; and that he has consequently underrated the number of emigrants. We will take it at double of the

Doctor's estimate, and suppose that, in 1817, 45,000 Europeans crossed to the United States. Now, it must be remembered that the year 1817 was a year of the severest and most general distress over all Europe, — a year of scarcity everywhere, and of cruel famine in some places. There can, therefore, be no doubt that the emigration of 1817 was very far above the average, probably more than three times that of an ordinary year. Till the year 1815, the war rendered it almost impossible to emigrate to the United States either from England or from the Continent. If we suppose the average emigration of the remaining years to have been 16,000, we shall probably not be much mistaken. In 1818 and 1819, the number was certainly much beyond that average; in 1815 and 1816, probably much below it. But, even if we were to suppose that, in every year from the peace to 1820, the number of emigrants had been as high as we have supposed it to be in 1817, the increase by procreation among the white inhabitants of the United States would still appear to be about 30 per cent. in ten years.

Mr. Sadler acknowledges that Cobbett exaggerates the number of emigrants when he states it at 150,000 a year. Yet even this estimate, absurdly great as it is, would not be sufficient to explain the increase of the population of the United States on Mr. Sadler's principles. He is, he tells us, "convinced that doubling in 35 years is a far more rapid duplication than ever has taken place in that country from procreation only." An increase of 20 per cent. in ten years, by procreation, would therefore be the very utmost that he would allow to be possible. We have already shown, by reference to the census of the slave population, that this doctrine is quite absurd. And, if we suppose it to be sound, we shall be driven to the conclusion that above eight hundred thousand people emigrated from Europe to the United States in a space of little more than five years. The whole increase of the white population from 1810 to 1820 was within a few hundreds of 2,000,000. If we are to attribute to procreation only 20 per cent. on the number returned by the census of 1810, we shall have about 830,000 persons to account for in some other way; — and to suppose that the emigrants who went to America between the peace of 1815 and the census of 1820, with the children who were born to them there, would make up that number, would be the height of absurdity.

We could say much more; but we think it quite unnecessary at present. We have shown that Mr. Sadler is careless in the collection of facts, — that he is incapable of reasoning on facts when he has collected them, — that he does not understand the simplest terms of science, — that he has enounced a proposition of which he does not know the meaning, — that the proposition which he means to enounce, and which he tries to prove, leads directly to all those consequences which he represents as impious and immoral, — and that, from the very documents to which he has himself appealed, it may be demonstrated that his theory is false. We may, perhaps, resume the subject when his next volume appears. Meanwhile, we hope that he will delay its publication until he has learned a little arithmetic, and unlearned a great deal of eloquence.

JOHN BUNYAN.[1]

(*Edinburgh Review*, December 1830.)

THIS is an eminently beautiful and splendid edition of a book which well deserves all that the printer and the engraver can do for it. The Life of Bunyan is, of course, not a performance which can add much to the literary reputation of such a writer as Mr. Southey. But it is written in excellent English, and, for the most part, in an excellent spirit. Mr. Southey propounds, we need not say, many opinions from which we altogether dissent; and his attempts to excuse the odious persecution to which Bunyan was subjected have sometimes moved our indignation. But we will avoid this topic. We are at present much more inclined to join in paying homage to the genius of a great man than to engage in a controversy concerning church-government and toleration.

We must not pass without notice the engravings with which this volume is decorated. Some of Mr. Heath's wood-cuts are admirably designed and executed. Mr. Martin's illustrations do not please us quite so well. His Valley of the Shadow of Death is not that Valley of the Shadow of Death which Bunyan imagined. At all events, it is not that dark and

[1] *The Pilgrim's Progress, with a Life of John Bunyan.* By ROBERT SOUTHEY, Esq., LL.D. Poet Laureate. Illustrated with Engravings. 8vo. London: 1830.

horrible glen which has from childhood been in our mind's eye. The valley is a cavern: the quagmire is a lake: the straight path runs zigzag: and Christian appears like a speck in the darkness of the immense vault. We miss, too, those hideous forms which make so striking a part of the description of Bunyan, and which Salvator Rosa would have loved to draw. It is with unfeigned diffidence that we pronounce judgment on any question relating to the art of painting. But it appears to us that Mr. Martin has not of late been fortunate in his choice of subjects. He should never have attempted to illustrate the Paradise Lost. There can be no two manners more directly opposed to each other than the manner of his painting and the manner of Milton's poetry. Those things which are mere accessories in the descriptions become the principal objects in the pictures; and those figures which are most prominent in the descriptions can be detected in the pictures only by a very close scrutiny. Mr. Martin has succeeded perfectly in representing the pillars and candelabra of Pandæmonium. But he has forgotten that Milton's Pandæmonium is merely the background to Satan. In the picture, the Archangel is scarcely visible amidst the endless colonnades of his infernal palace. Milton's Paradise, again, is merely the background to his Adam and Eve. But in Mr. Martin's picture the landscape is everything. Adam, Eve, and Raphael attract much less notice than the lake and the mountains, the gigantic flowers, and the giraffes which feed upon them. We read that James the Second sat to Varelst, the great flower-painter. When the performance was finished, his Majesty appeared in the midst of a bower of sun-flowers and tulips, which completely drew away all attention from the central figure.

All who looked at the portrait took it for a flower-piece. Mr. Martin, we think, introduces his immeasurable spaces, his innumerable multitudes, his gorgeous prodigies of architecture and landscape, almost as unseasonably as Varelst introduced his flower-pots and nosegays. If Mr. Martin were to paint Lear in the storm, we suspect that the blazing sky, the sheets of rain, the swollen torrents, and the tossing forest, would draw away all attention from the agonies of the insulted king and father. If he were to paint the death of Lear, the old man, asking the by-standers to undo his button, would be thrown into the shade by a vast blaze of pavilions, standards, armour, and heralds' coats. Mr. Martin would illustrate the Orlando Furioso well, the Orlando Innamorato still better, the Arabian Nights best of all. Fairy palaces and gardens, porticoes of agate, and groves flowering with emeralds and rubies, inhabited by people for whom nobody cares, these are his proper domain. He would succeed admirably in the enchanted ground of Alcina, or the mansion of Aladdin. But he should avoid Milton and Bunyan.

The characteristic peculiarity of the Pilgrim's Progress is that it is the only work of its kind which possesses a strong human interest. Other allegories only amuse the fancy. The allegory of Bunyan has been read by many thousands with tears. There are some good allegories in Johnson's works, and some of still higher merit by Addison. In these performances there is, perhaps, as much wit and ingenuity as in the Pilgrim's Progress. But the pleasure which is produced by the Vision of Mirza, the Vision of Theodore, the genealogy of Wit, or the contest between Rest and Labour, is exactly similar to the pleasure which we derive from one of Cowley's odes or from a canto of Hudibras. It is a pleasure which belongs wholly to the understanding, and in which the feelings have no part whatever. Nay, even Spenser himself, though assuredly one of the greatest poets that ever lived, could not succeed in the attempt to make allegory interesting. It was in vain that he lavished the riches of his mind on the House of Pride and the House of Temperance. One unpardonable fault, the fault of tediousness, pervades the whole of the Fairy Queen. We become sick of cardinal virtues and deadly sins, and long for the society of plain men and women. Of the persons who read the first canto, not one in ten reaches the end of the first book, and not one in a hundred perseveres to the end of the poem. Very few and very weary are those who are in at the death of the Blatant Beast. If the last six books, which are said to have been destroyed in Ireland, had been preserved, we doubt whether any heart less stout than that of a commentator would have held out to the end.

It is not so with the Pilgrim's Progress. That wonderful book, while it obtains admiration from the most fastidious critics, is loved by those who are too simple to admire it. Dr. Johnson, all whose studies were desultory, and who hated, as he said, to read books through, made an exception in favour of the Pilgrim's Progress. That work was one of the two or three works which he wished longer. It was by no common merit that the illiterate sectary extracted praise like this from the most pedantic of critics and the most bigoted of Tories. In the wildest parts of Scotland the Pilgrim's Progress is the delight of the peasantry. In every nursery the Pilgrim's Progress is a greater favourite than Jack the Giant-killer. Every reader knows the straight and narrow path as well as he knows a road in which he has gone backward and forward a hundred times. This is the highest miracle of genius, that things which are not should be as though they were, that the imaginations of one mind should become the personal recollections of another. And this miracle the tinker has wrought. There is no ascent, no declivity, no resting-place, no turn-stile, with which we are not perfectly acquainted. The wicket gate, and the desolate swamp which separates it from the City of Destruction, the long line of road, as straight as a rule can make it, the Interpreter's house and all its fair shows, the prisoner in the iron cage, the palace, at the doors of which armed men kept guard, and on the battlements of which walked persons clothed all in gold, the cross and the sepulchre, the steep hill and the pleasant arbour, the stately front of the House Beautiful by the wayside, the chained lions crouching in the porch, the low green valley of Humiliation, rich with grass and covered with flocks, all are as well known to us as the sights of our own street. Then we come to the narrow place where Apollyon strode right across the whole breadth of the way, to stop the journey of Christian, and where afterwards the pillar was set up to testify how bravely the pilgrim had fought the good fight. As we advance, the valley becomes deeper and deeper. The shade of the precipices on both sides falls blacker and blacker. The clouds gather overhead. Doleful voices, the clanking of chains, and the rushing of many feet to and fro, are heard through the darkness. The way, hardly discernible in gloom, runs close by the mouth of the burning pit, which sends forth its flames, its noisome smoke, and its hideous shapes, to terrify the adventurer. Thence he goes on, amidst the snares and pitfalls, with the mangled bodies of those who have perished lying in the ditch by his side. At the end of the long dark valley he passes the dens in which the old giants dwelt, amidst the bones of those whom they had slain.

Then the road passes straight on through a waste moor, till at length the towers of a distant city appear before the traveller; and soon he is in the midst of the innumerable multitudes of Vanity Fair. There are the jugglers and the apes, the shops and the puppet-shows. There are Italian Row, and French Row, and Spanish Row, and Britain Row, with their crowds of buyers, sellers, and loungers, jabbering all the languages of the earth.

Thence we go on by the little hill of the silver mine, and through the meadow of lilies, along the bank of that pleasant river which is bordered on both sides by fruit-trees. On the left branches off the path leading to the horrible castle, the court-yard of which is paved with the skulls of pilgrims; and right onward are the sheepfolds and orchards of the Delectable Mountains.

From the Delectable Mountains, the way lies through the fogs and briers of the Enchanted Ground, with here and there a bed of soft cushions spread under a green arbour. And beyond is the land of Beulah, where the flowers, the grapes, and the songs of birds never cease, and where the sun shines night and day. Thence are plainly seen the golden pavements and streets of pearl, on the other side of that black and cold river over which there is no bridge.

All the stages of the journey, all the forms which cross or overtake the pilgrims, giants, and hobgoblins, ill-favoured ones, and shining ones, the tall, comely, swarthy Madame Bubble, with her great purse by her side, and her fingers playing with the money, the black man in the bright vesture, Mr. Worldly Wiseman and my Lord Hategood, Mr. Talkative, and Mrs. Timorous, all are actually existing beings to us. We follow the travellers through their allegorical progress with interest not inferior to that with which we follow Elizabeth from Siberia to Moscow, or Jeanie Deans from Edinburgh to London. Bunyan is almost the only writer who ever gave to the abstract the interest of the concrete. In the works of many celebrated authors, men are mere personifications. We have not a jealous man, but jealousy; not a traitor, but perfidy; not a patriot, but patriotism. The mind of Bunyan, on the contrary, was so imaginative that personifications, when he dealt with them, became men. A dialogue between two qualities, in his dream, has more dramatic effect than a dialogue between two human beings in most plays. In this respect the genius of Bunyan bore a great resemblance to that of a man who had very little else in common with him, Percy Bysshe Shelley. The strong imagination of Shelley made him an idolater in his own despite. Out of the most indefinite terms of a hard, cold, dark, metaphysical system, he made a gorgeous Pantheon, full of beautiful, majestic, and life-like forms. He turned atheism itself into a mythology, rich with visions as glorious as the gods that live in the marble of Phidias, or the virgin saints that smile on us from the canvass of Murillo. The Spirit of Beauty, the Principle of Good, the Principle of Evil, when he treated of them, ceased to be abstractions. They took shape and colour. They were no longer mere words; but "intelligible forms;" "fair humanities;" objects of love, of adoration, or of fear. As there can be no stronger sign of a mind destitute of the poetical faculty than that tendency which was so common among the writers of the French school to turn images into abstractions, Venus, for example, into Love, Minerva into Wisdom, Mars into War, and Bacchus into Festivity, so there can be no stronger sign of a mind truly poetical than a disposition to reverse this abstracting process, and to make individuals out of generalities. Some of the metaphysical and ethical theories of Shelley were certainly most absurd and pernicious. But we doubt whether any modern poet has possessed in an equal degree some of the highest qualities of the great ancient masters. The words bard and inspiration, which seem so cold and affected when applied to other modern writers, have a perfect propriety when applied to him. He was not an author, but a bard. His poetry seems not to have been an art, but an inspiration. Had he lived to the full age of man, he might not improbably have given to the world some great work of the very highest rank in design and execution. But, alas !

ὁ Δάφνις ἔβα ῥόον· ἔκλυσε δίνα
τὸν Μώσαις φίλον ἄνδρα, τὸν οὐ Νύμφαισιν ἀπεχθῆ.

But we must return to Bunyan. The Pilgrim's Progress undoubtedly is not a perfect allegory. The types are often inconsistent with each other; and sometimes the allegorical disguise is altogether thrown off. The river, for example, is emblematic of death; and we are told that every human being must pass through the river. But Faithful does not pass through it. He is martyred, not in shadow, but in reality, at Vanity Fair. Hopeful talks to Christian about Esau's birthright and about his own convictions of sin as Bunyan might have talked with one of his own congregation. The damsels at the House Beautiful catechize Christiana's boys, as any good ladies might catechize any boys at a Sunday School. But we do not believe that any man, whatever might be his genius, and whatever his good luck, could long continue a figurative history without falling into many inconsistencies. We are sure that inconsistencies, scarcely less gross than the worst into which Bunyan has fallen, may be found in the shortest and most elaborate allegories of the Spectator and the Rambler. The Tale of a Tub and the History of John Bull swarm with similar errors, if the name of error can be properly applied to that which is unavoidable. It is not easy to make a simile go on all-fours. But we believe that no human ingenuity could produce such a centipede as a long allegory in which the correspondence between the outward sign and the thing signified should be exactly preserved. Certainly no writer, ancient or modern, has yet achieved the adventure. The best thing, on the whole, that an allegorist can do, is to present to his readers a succession of analogies, each of which may separately be striking and happy, without looking very nicely to see whether they harmonize with each other. This Bunyan has done; and, though a minute scrutiny may detect inconsistencies in every page of his Tale, the general effect which the Tale produces on all persons, learned and unlearned, proves that he has done well. The passages which it is most difficult to defend are those in which he altogether drops the allegory, and puts into the mouth of his pilgrims religious ejaculations and disquisitions, better suited to his own pulpit at Bedford or Reading than to the Enchanted Ground or to the Interpreter's Garden. Yet even these passages, though we will not undertake to defend them against the objections of critics, we feel that we could ill spare. We feel that the story owes much of its charm to these occasional glimpses of solemn and affecting subjects, which will not be hidden, which force themselves through the veil, and appear before us in their native aspect. The effect is not unlike that which is said to have been produced on the ancient stage, when the eyes of the actor were seen flaming through his mask, and giving life and expression to what would else have been an inanimate and uninteresting disguise.

It is very amusing and very instructive to compare the Pilgrim's Progress with the Grace Abounding. The latter work is indeed one of the most remarkable pieces of autobiography in the world. It is a full and open confession of the fancies which passed through the mind of an illiterate man, whose affections were warm, whose nerves were irritable, whose imagination was ungovernable, and who was under the influence of the strongest religious excitement. In whatever age Bunyan had lived, the history of his feelings would, in all probability, have been very curious. But the time in which his lot was cast was the time of a great stirring of the human mind. A tremendous burst of public feeling, produced by the tyranny of the hierarchy, menaced the old ecclesiastical institutions with destruction. To the gloomy regularity of one intolerant Church had succeeded the license of innumerable sects, drunk with the sweet and heady must of their new liberty. Fanaticism, engendered by persecution, and destined to engender persecution in turn, spread rapidly through society. Even the strongest and most commanding minds were not proof against this strange taint. Any time might have produced George Fox and James Naylor. But to one time alone belong the frantic delusions of such a statesman as Vane, and the hysterical tears of such a soldier as Cromwell.

The history of Bunyan is the history of a most excitable mind in an age of excitement. By most of his biographers he has been treated with gross injustice. They have understood in a popular sense all those strong terms of self-condemnation which he employed in a theological sense. They have, therefore, represented him as an abandoned wretch reclaimed by means almost miraculous, or, to use their favourite metaphor, "as a brand plucked from the burning." Mr. Ivimey calls him the depraved Bunyan and the wicked tinker of Elstow. Surely Mr. Ivimey ought to have been too familiar with the bitter accusations which the most pious people are in the habit of bringing against themselves, to understand literally all the strong expressions which are to be found in the Grace Abounding. It is quite clear, as Mr. Southey most justly remarks, that Bunyan never was a vicious man. He married very early; and he solemnly declares that he was strictly faithful to his wife. He does not appear to have been a drunkard. He owns, indeed, that, when a boy, he never spoke without an oath. But a single admonition cured him of this bad habit for life; and the cure must have been wrought early; for at eighteen he was in the army of the Parliament; and, if he had carried the vice of profaneness into that service, he would doubtless have received something more than an admonition from Serjeant Bind-their-kings-in-chains, or Captain Hew-Agag-in-pieces-before-the-Lord. Bell-ringing and playing at hockey on Sundays seem to have been the worst vices of this depraved tinker. They would have passed for virtues with Archbishop Laud. It is quite clear that, from a very early age, Bunyan was a man of a strict life and of a tender conscience. "He had been," says Mr. Southey, "a blackguard." Even this we think too hard a censure. Bunyan was not, we admit, so fine a gentleman as Lord Digby; but he was a blackguard no otherwise than as every labouring man that ever lived has been a blackguard. Indeed Mr. Southey acknowledges this. "Such he might have been expected to be by his birth, breeding, and vocation. Scarcely indeed, by possibility, could he have been otherwise." A man whose manners and sentiments are decidedly below those of his class deserves to be called a blackguard. But it is surely unfair to apply so strong a word of reproach to one who is only what the great mass of every community must inevitably be.

Those horrible internal conflicts which Bunyan has described with so much power of language prove, not that he was a worse man than his neighbours, but that his mind was constantly occupied by religious considerations, that his fervour exceeded his knowledge, and that his imagination exercised despotic power over his body and mind. He heard voices from heaven. He saw strange visions of distant hills, pleasant and sunny as his own Delectable Mountains. From those abodes he was shut out, and placed in a dark and horrible wilderness, where he wandered through ice and snow, striving to make his way into the happy region of light. At one time he was seized with an inclination to work miracles. At another time he thought himself actually possessed by the devil. He could distinguish the blasphemous whispers. He felt his infernal enemy pulling at his clothes behind him. He spurned with his feet and struck with his hands at the destroyer. Sometimes he was tempted to sell his part in the salvation of mankind. Sometimes a violent impulse urged him to start up from his food, to fall on his knees, and to break forth into prayer. At length he fancied that he had committed the unpardonable sin. His agony convulsed his robust frame. He was, he says, as if his breastbone would split; and this he took for a sign that he was destined to burst asunder like Judas. The agitation of his nerves made all his movements tremulous; and this trembling, he supposed, was a visible mark of his reprobation, like that which had been set on Cain. At one time, indeed, an encouraging voice seemed to rush in at the window, like the noise of wind, but very pleasant, and commanded, as he says, a great calm in his soul. At another time, a word of comfort "was spoke loud unto him; it showed a great word; it seemed to be writ in great letters." But these intervals of ease were short. His state, during two years and a half, was generally the most horrible that the human mind can imagine. "I walked," says he, with his own peculiar eloquence, "to a neighbouring town; and sat down upon a settle in the street, and fell into a very deep pause about the most fearful state my sin had brought me to; and, after long musing, I lifted up my head; but methought I saw as if the sun that shineth in the heavens did grudge to give me light; and as if the very stones in the street, and tiles upon the houses, did band themselves against me. Methought that they all combined together to banish me out of the world. I was abhorred of them, and unfit to dwell among them, because I had sinned against the Saviour. Oh, how happy now was every creature over I! for they stood fast, and kept their station. But I was gone and lost." Scarcely any madhouse could produce an instance of delusion so strong, or of misery so acute.

It was through this Valley of the Shadow of Death, overhung by darkness, peopled with devils, resounding with blasphemy and lamentation, and passing amidst quagmires, snares, and pitfalls, close by the very mouth of hell, that Bunyan journeyed to that bright and fruitful land of Beulah, in which he sojourned during the latter period of his pilgrimage. The only trace which his cruel sufferings and temptations seem to have left behind them was an affectionate compassion for those who were still in the state in which he had once been. Religion has scarcely ever worn a form so calm and soothing as in his allegory. The feeling which predominates through the whole book is a feeling of tenderness for weak, timid, and harassed minds. The character of Mr. Fearing, of Mr. Feeble-Mind, of Mr. Despondency and his daughter Miss Muchafraid, the account of poor Littlefaith who was robbed by the three thieves, of his spending money, the description of Christian's terror in the dungeons of Giant Despair and in his passage through the river, all clearly show how strong a sympathy Bunyan felt, after his own mind had become clear and cheerful, for persons afflicted with religious melancholy.

Mr. Southey, who has no love for the Calvinists, admits that, if Calvinism had never worn a blacker appearance than in Bunyan's works, it would never have become a term of reproach. In fact, those works of Bunyan with which we are acquainted are by no means more Calvinistic than the articles and homilies of the Church of England. The moderation of his opinions on the subject of predestination gave offence to some zealous persons. We have seen an absurd allegory, the heroine of which is named Hephzibah, written by some raving supralapsarian preacher who was dissatisfied with the mild theology of the Pilgrim's Progress. In this foolish book, if we recollect rightly, the Interpreter is called the Enlightener, and the House Beautiful is Castle Strength. Mr. Southey tells us that the Catholics had also their Pilgrim's Progress, without a Giant Pope, in which the Interpeter is the Director, and the House Beautiful Grace's Hall. It is surely a remarkable proof of the power of Bunyan's genius, that two religious parties, both of which regarded his opinions as heterodox, should have had recourse to him for assistance.

There are, we think, some characters and scenes in the Pilgrim's Progress, which can be fully comprehended and enjoyed only by persons familiar with the history of the times through which Bunyan lived. The character of Mr. Greatheart, the guide, is an example. His fighting is, of course, allegorical; but the allegory is not strictly preserved. He delivers a sermon on imputed righteousness to his companions; and, soon after, he gives battle to Giant Grim, who had taken upon him to back the lions. He expounds the fifty-third chapter of Isaiah to the household and guests of Gaius; and then he sallies out to attack Slaygood, who was of the nature of flesh-eaters, in his den. These are inconsistencies; but they are inconsistencies which add, we think, to the interest of the narrative. We have not the least doubt that Bunyan had in view some stout old Greatheart of Naseby and Worcester, who prayed with his men before he drilled them, who knew the spiritual state of every dragoon in his troop, and who, with the praises of God in his mouth, and a two-edged sword in his hand, had turned to flight, on many fields of battle, the swearing, drunken bravoes of Rupert and Lunsford.

Every age produces such men as By-ends. But the middle of the seventeenth century was eminently prolific of such men. Mr. Southey thinks that the satire was aimed at some particular individual; and this seems by no means improbable. At all events, Bunyan must have known many of those hypocrites who followed religion only when religion walked in silver slippers, when the sun shone, and when the people applauded. Indeed he might have easily found all the kindred of By-ends among the public men of his time. He might have found among the peers my Lord Turn-about, my Lord Time-server, and my Lord Fair-speech; in the House of Commons, Mr. Smooth-man, Mr. Anything, and Mr. Facing-both-ways; nor would "the parson of the parish, Mr. Two-tongues," have been wanting. The town of Bedford probably contained more than one politician who, after contriving to raise an estate by seeking the Lord during the reign of the saints, contrived to keep what he had got by persecuting the saints during the reign of the strumpets, and more than one priest who, during repeated changes in the discipline and doctrines of the church, had remained constant to nothing but his benefice.

One of the most remarkable passages in the Pilgrim's Progress is that in which the proceedings against Faithful are described. It is impossible to doubt that Bunyan intended to satirise the mode in which state trials were conducted under Charles the Second. The license given to the witnesses for the prosecution, the shameless partiality and ferocious insolence of the judge, the precipitancy and the blind rancour of the jury, remind us of those odious mummeries which, from the Restoration to the Revolution, were merely forms preliminary to hanging, drawing, and quartering. Lord Hategood performs the office of counsel for the prisoners as well as Scroggs himself could have performed it.

"JUDGE. Thou runagate, heretic, and traitor, hast thou heard what these honest gentlemen have witnessed against thee?

"FAITHFUL. May I speak a few words in my own defence?

"JUDGE. Sirrah, sirrah! thou deservest to live no longer, but to be slain immediately upon the place; yet, that all men may see our gentleness to thee, let us hear what thou, vile runagate, hast to say."

No person who knows the state trials can be at a loss for parallel cases. Indeed, write what Bunyan would, the baseness and cruelty of the lawyers of those times "sinned up to it still," and even went beyond it. The imaginary trial of Faithful, before a jury composed of personified vices, was just and merciful, when compared with the real trial of Alice Lisle before that tribunal where all the vices sat in the person of Jefferies.

The style of Bunyan is delightful to every reader, and invaluable as a study to every person who wishes to obtain a wide command over the English language. The vocabulary is the vocabulary of the common people. There is not an expression, if we except a few technical terms of theology, which would puzzle the rudest peasant. We have observed several pages which do not contain a single word of more than two syllables. Yet no writer has said more exactly what he meant to say. For magnificence, for pathos, for vehement exhortation, for subtle disquisition, for every purpose of the poet, the orator, and the divine, this homely dialect, the dialect of plain working men, was perfectly sufficient. There is no book in our literature on which we would so readily stake the fame of the old unpolluted English language, no book which shows so well how rich that language is in its own proper wealth, and how little it has been improved by all that it has borrowed.

Cowper said, forty or fifty years ago, that he dared not name John Bunyan in his verse, for fear of moving a sneer. To our refined forefathers, we suppose, Lord Roscommon's Essay on Translated Verse, and the Duke of Buckinghamshire's Essay on Poetry, appeared to be compositions infinitely superior to the allegory of the preaching tinker. We live in better times; and we are not afraid to say, that, though there were many clever men in England during the latter half of the seventeenth century, there were only two minds which possessed the imaginative faculty in a very eminent degree. One of those minds produced the Paradise Lost, the other the Pilgrim's Progress.

SADLER'S REFUTATION REFUTED.[1]

(*Edinburg Review*, January 1831.)

We have, in violation of our usual practice, transcribed Mr. Sadler's title-page from top to bottom, motto and all. The parallel implied between the Essay on the Human Understanding and the Essay on Superfecundity is exquisitely laughable. We can match it, however, with mottoes as ludicrous. We remember to have heard of a dramatic piece, entitled "News from Camperdown," written soon after Lord Duncan's victory, by a man once as much in his own good graces as Mr. Sadler is, and now as much forgotten as Mr. Sadler will soon be, Robert Heron. His piece was brought upon the stage, and damned, "as it is phrased," in the second act; but the author, thinking that it had been unfairly and unjustly "run down," published it, in order to put his critics to shame, with this motto from Swift:—"When a true genius appears in the

1 *A Refutation of an Article in the Edinburgh Review* (No. CII.) *entitled, "Sadler's Law of Population, and Disproof of Human Superfecundity;" containing also Additional Proofs of the Principle enunciated in that Treatise, founded on the Censuses of different Countries recently published.* By Michael Thomas Sadler, M.P. 8vo. London: 1830.

"Before anything came out against my Essay, I was told I must prepare myself for a storm coming against it, it being resolved by some men that it was necessary that book of mine should, as it is phrased, be run down."—John Locke.

world, you may know him by this mark — that the dunces are all in confederacy against him." We remember another anecdote, which may perhaps be acceptable to so zealous a churchman as Mr. Sadler. A certain Antinomian preacher, the oracle of a barn, in a county of which we do not think it proper to mention the name, finding that divinity was not by itself a sufficiently lucrative profession, resolved to combine with it that of dog-stealing. He was, by ill-fortune, detected in several offences of this description, and was in consequence brought before two justices, who, in virtue of the powers given them by an act of parliament, sentenced him to a whipping for each theft. The degrading punishment inflicted on the pastor naturally thinned the flock; and the poor man was in danger of wanting bread. He accordingly put forth a handbill, solemnly protesting his innocence, describing his sufferings, and appealing to the Christian charity of the public; and to his pathetic address he prefixed this most appropriate text: "Thrice was I beaten with rods. — *St. Paul's Epistle to the Corinthians.*" He did not perceive that, though St. Paul had been scourged, no number of whippings, however severe, will of themselves entitle a man to be considered as an apostle. Mr. Sadler seems to us to have fallen into a somewhat similar error. He should remember that, though Locke may have been laughed at, so has Sir Claudius Hunter; and that it takes something more than the laughter of all the world to make a Locke.

The body of this pamphlet by no means justifies the parallel so modestly insinuated on the title-page. Yet we must own that, though Mr. Sadler has not risen to the level of Locke, he has done what was almost as difficult, if not as honourable — he has fallen below his own. He is at best a bad writer. His arrangement is an elaborate confusion. His style has been constructed, with great care, in such a manner as to produce the least possible effect by means of the greatest possible number of words. Aspiring to the exalted character of a Christian philosopher, he can never preserve through a single paragraph either the calmness of a philosopher or the meekness of a Christian. His ill-nature would make a very little wit formidable. But, happily, his efforts to wound resemble those of a juggler's snake. The bags of poison are full, but the fang is wanting. In this foolish pamphlet, all the unpleasant peculiarities of his style and temper are brought out in the strongest manner. He is from the beginning to the end in a paroxysm of rage, and would certainly do us some mischief if he knew how. We will give a single instance for the present. Others will present themselves as we proceed. We laughed at some doggerel verses which he cited, and which we, never having seen them before, suspected to be his own. We are now sure that, if the principle on which Solomon decided a famous case of filiation were correct, there can be no doubt as to the justice of our suspicion. Mr. Sadler, who, whatever elements of the poetical character he may lack, possesses the poetical irritability in an abundance which might have sufficed for Homer himself, resolved to retaliate on the person, who, as he supposed, had reviewed him. He has, accordingly, ransacked some collection of college verses, in the hope of finding, among the performances of his supposed antagonist, something as bad as his own. And we must in fairness admit that he has succeeded pretty well. We must admit that the gentleman in question sometimes put into his exercises, at seventeen, almost as great nonsense as Mr. Sadler is in the habit of putting into his books at sixty.

Mr. Sadler complains that we have devoted whole pages to mere abuse of him. We deny the charge. We have, indeed, characterised, in terms of just reprehension, that spirit which shows itself in every part of his prolix work. Those terms of reprehension we are by no means inclined to retract; and we conceive that we might have used much stronger expressions, without the least offence either to truth or to decorum. There is a limit prescribed to us by our sense of what is due to ourselves. But we think that no indulgence is due to Mr. Sadler. A writer who distinctly announces that he has not conformed to the candour of the age — who makes it his boast that he expresses himself throughout with the greatest plainness and freedom — and whose constant practice proves that by plainness and freedom he means coarseness and rancour — has no right to expect that others shall remember courtesies which he has forgotten, or shall respect one who has ceased to respect himself.

Mr. Sadler declares that he has never vilified Mr. Malthus personally, and has confined himself to attacking the doctrines which that gentleman maintains. We should wish to leave that point to the decision of all who have read Mr. Sadler's book, or any twenty pages of it. To quote particular instances of a temper which penetrates and inspires the whole work, is to weaken our charge. Yet, that we may not be suspected of flinching, we will give two specimens, — the two first which occur to our recollection. "Whose minister is it that speaks thus?" says Mr. Sadler, after misrepresenting in a most extraordinary manner, though, we are willing to believe, unintentionally, one of the positions of Mr. Malthus. "Whose minister is it that speaks thus? That of the lover and avenger of little children?" Again, Mr. Malthus recommends, erroneously perhaps, but assuredly from humane motives, that alms, when given, should be given very sparingly. Mr. Sadler quotes the recommendation, and adds the following courteous comment: — "The tender mercies of the wicked are cruel." We cannot think that a writer who indulges in these indecent and unjust attacks on professional and personal character has any right to complain of our sarcasms on his metaphors and rhymes.

We will now proceed to examine the reply which Mr. Sadler has thought fit to make to our arguments. He begins by attacking our remarks on the origin of evil. They are, says he, too profound for common apprehension; and he hopes that they are too profound for our own. That they seem profound to him we can well believe. Profundity, in its secondary as in its primary sense, is a relative term. When Grildrig was nearly drowned in the Brobdignagian cream-jug he doubtless thought it very deep. But to common apprehension our reasoning would, we are persuaded, appear perfectly simple.

The theory of Mr. Malthus, says Mr. Sadler, cannot be true, because it asserts the existence of a great and terrible evil, and is therefore inconsistent with the goodness of God. We answer thus. We know that there are in the world great and terrible evils. In spite of these evils, we believe in the goodness of God. Why may we not then continue to believe in his goodness, though another evil should be added to the list?

How does Mr. Sadler answer this? Merely by telling us that we are too wicked to be reasoned with. He completely shrinks from the question; a question, be it remembered, not raised by us — a question which we should have felt strong objections to raising unnecessarily — a question put forward by himself, as intimately connected with the subject of his two ponderous volumes. He attempts to carp at detached parts of our reasoning on the subject. With what success he carries on this guerilla war after declining a general action with the main body of our argument our readers shall see.

"The reviewer sends me to Paley, who is, I confess, rather more intelligible on the subject, and who, fortunately, has decided the very point in dispute. I will first give the words of the reviewer, who, when speaking of my general argument regarding the magnitude of the evils, moral and physical, implied in the theory I oppose, sums up his ideas thus: — 'Mr. Sadler says, that it is not a light or transient evil, but a great and permanent evil. What then? The question of the origin of evil is a question of ay or no, — *not a question of* MORE *or* LESS.' But what says Paley? His express rule is this, that 'when we cannot resolve all appearances into benevolence of design, *we make the* FEW *give place to the* MANY, *the* LITTLE *to the* GREAT; *that we take our judgment from a large and decided preponderancy.*' Now in weighing these two authorities, directly at issue on this point, I think there will be little trouble in determining which we shall make 'to give place;' or, if we 'look to a large and decided preponderancy' of either talent, learning, or benevolence, from whom we shall 'take our judgment.' The effrontery, or, to speak more charitably, the ignorance of a reference to Paley on this subject, and in this instance is really marvellous."

Now, does not Mr. Sadler see that the very words which he quotes from Paley contain in themselves a refutation of his whole argument? Paley says, indeed, as every man in his senses would say, that in a certain case, which he has specified, the more and the less come into question. But in what case? "When we *cannot* resolve all appearances into the benevolence of design." It is better that there should be a little evil than a great deal of evil. This is self-evident. But it is also self-evident that no evil is better than a little evil. Why, then, is there any evil? It is a mystery which we cannot solve. It is a mystery which Paley, by the very words which Mr. Sadler has quoted, acknowledges himself unable to solve; and it is because he cannot solve that mystery that he proceeds to take into consideration the more and the less. Believing in the divine goodness, we must necessarily believe that the evils which exist are necessary to avert greater evils. But what those greater evils are we do not know. How the happiness of any part of the sentient creation would be in any respect diminished if, for example, children cut their teeth without pain, we cannot understand. The case is exactly the same with the principle of Mr. Malthus. If superfecundity exists, it exists, no doubt, because it is a less evil than some other evil which otherwise would exist. Can Mr. Sadler prove that this is an impossibility?

One single expression which Mr. Sadler employs on this subject is sufficient to show how utterly incompetent he is to discuss it. "On the Christian hypothesis," says he, "no doubt exists as to the origin of evil." He does not, we think, understand what is meant by the origin of evil. The Christian Scriptures profess to give no solution of that mystery. They relate facts; but they leave the metaphysical question undetermined. They tell us that man fell; but why he was not so constituted as to be incapable of falling, or why the Supreme Being has not mitigated the consequences of the Fall more than they actually have been mitigated, the

Scriptures did not tell us, and, it may without presumption be said, could not tell us, unless we had been creatures different from what we are. There is something, either in the nature of our faculties or in the nature of the machinery employed by us for the purpose of reasoning, which condemns us, on this and similar subjects, to hopeless ignorance. Man can understand these high matters only by ceasing to be man, just as a fly can understand a lemma of Newton only by ceasing to be a fly. To make it an objection to the Christian system that it gives us no solution of these difficulties, is to make it an objection to the Christian system that it is a system formed for human beings. Of the puzzles of the Academy, there is not one which does not apply as strongly to Deism as to Christianity, and to Atheism as to Deism. There are difficulties in everything. Yet we are sure that something must be true.

If revelation speaks on the subject of the origin of evil it speaks only to discourage dogmatism and temerity. In the most ancient, the most beautiful, and the most profound of all works on the subject, the Book of Job, both the sufferer who complains of the divine government, and the injudicious advisers who attempt to defend it on wrong principles, are silenced by the voice of supreme wisdom, and reminded that the question is beyond the reach of the human intellect. St. Paul silences the supposed objector, who strives to force him into controversy, in the same manner. The church has been, ever since the apostolic times, agitated by this question, and by a question which is inseparable from it, the question of fate and free-will. The greatest theologians and philosophers have acknowledged that these things were too high for them, and have contented themselves with hinting at what seemed to be the most probable solution. What says Johnson? "All our effort ends in belief that for the evils of life there is some good reason, and in confession that the reason cannot be found." What says Paley? "Of the origin of evil no universal solution has been discovered. I mean no solution which reaches to all cases of complaint. — The consideration of general laws, although it may concern the question of the origin of evil very nearly, which I think it does, rests in views disproportionate to our faculties, and in a knowledge which we do not possess. It serves rather to account for the obscurity of the subject, than to supply us with distinct answers to our difficulties." What says presumptuous ignorance? "No doubt whatever exists as to the origin of evil." It is remarkable that Mr. Sadler does not tell us what his solution is. The world, we suspect, will lose little by his silence.

He falls on the reviewer again.

> "Though I have shown," says he, "and on authorities from which none can lightly differ, not only the cruelty and immorality which this system necessarily involves, but its most revolting feature, its gross partiality, he has wholly suppressed this, the most important part of my argument; as even the bare notice of it would have instantly exposed the sophistry to which he has had recourse. If, however, he would fairly meet the whole question, let him show me that 'hydrophobia,' which he gives as an example of the laws of God and nature, is a calamity to which the poor alone are liable; or that 'malaria,' which, with singular infelicity, he has chosen as an illustration of the fancied evils of population, is a respecter of persons."

We said nothing about this argument, as Mr. Sadler calls it, merely because we did not think it worth while; and we are half ashamed to say anything about it now. But, since Mr. Sadler is so urgent for an answer, he shall have one. If there is evil, it must be either partial or universal. Which is the better of the two? Hydrophobia, says this great philosopher, is no argument against the divine goodness, because mad dogs bite rich and poor alike; but, if the rich were exempted, and only nine people suffered for ten who suffer now, hydrophobia would forthwith, simply because it would produce less evil than at present, become an argument against the divine goodness! To state such a proposition, is to refute it. And is not the malaria a respecter of persons? It infests Rome. Does it infest London? There are complaints peculiar to the tropical countries. There are others which are found only in mountainous districts; others which are confined to marshy regions; others again which run in particular families. Is not this partiality? Why is it more inconsistent with the divine goodness that poor men should suffer an evil from which rich men are exempt, than that a particular portion of the community should inherit gout, scrofula, insanity, and other maladies? And are there no miseries under which, in fact, the poor alone are suffering? Mr. Sadler himself acknowledges, in this very paragraph, that there are such; but he tells us that these calamities are the effects of misgovernment, and that this misgovernment is the effect of political economy. Be it so. But does he not see that he is only removing the difficulty one step farther? Why does Providence suffer men, whose minds are filled with false and pernicious notions, to have power in the state? For good ends, we doubt not, if the fact be so; but for ends inscrutable to us, who see only a small part of the vast scheme, and who see that small part only for a short period. Does Mr. Sadler doubt that the Supreme Being has power as absolute over the revolutions of political as over the organisation of natural bodies? Surely not: and, if not, we do not see that he vindicates the ways of Providence by attributing the distresses, which the poor, as he confesses, endure, to an error in legislation rather than to a law of physiology. Turn the question as we may, disguise it as we may, we shall find that it at last resolves itself into the same great enigma, — the origin of physical and moral evil: an enigma which the highest human intellects have given up in despair, but which Mr. Sadler thinks himself perfectly able to solve.

He next accuses us of having paused long on verbal criticism. We certainly did object to his improper use of the words, "inverse variation." Mr. Sadler complains of this with his usual bitterness.

"Now what is the Reviewer's quarrel with me on this occasion? That he does not understand the meaning of my terms? No. He acknowledges the contrary. That I have not fully explained the sense in which I have used them? No. An explanation, he knows, is immediately subjoined, though he has carefully suppressed it. That I have varied the sense in which I have applied them? No. I challenge him to show it. But he nevertheless goes on for many pages together in arguing against what he knows, and, in fact, acknowledges, I did not mean; and then turns round and argues again, though much more feebly, indeed, against what he says I did mean! Now, even had I been in error as to the use of a word, I appeal to the reader whether such an unworthy and disingenuous course would not, if generally pursued, make controversy on all subjects, however important, that into which, in such hands, it always degenerates — a dispute about words."

The best way to avoid controversies about words is to use words in their proper senses. Mr. Sadler may think our objection captious; but how he can think it disingenuous we do not well understand. If we had represented him as meaning what we knew that he did not mean, we should have acted in a disgraceful manner. But we did not represent him, and he allows that we did not represent him, as meaning what he did not mean. We blamed him, and with perfect justice and propriety, for saying what he did not mean. Every man has in one sense a right to define his own terms; that is to say, if he chooses to call one two, and two seven, it would be absurd to charge him with false arithmetic for saying that seven is the double of one. But it would be perfectly fair to blame him for changing the established sense of words. The words, "inverse variation," in matters not purely scientific, have often been used in the loose way in which Mr. Sadler has used them. But we shall be surprised if he can find a single instance of their having been so used in a matter of pure arithmetic.

We will illustrate our meaning thus. Lord Thurlow, in one of his speeches about Indian affairs, said that one Hastings was worth twenty Macartneys. He might, with equal propriety, have said ten Macartneys, or a hundred Macartneys. Nor would there have been the least inconsistency in his using all the three expressions in one speech. But would this be an excuse for a financier who, in a matter of account, should reason as if ten, twenty, and a hundred were the same number?

Mr. Sadler tells us that he purposely avoided the use of the word proportion in stating his principle. He seems, therefore, to allow that the word proportion would have been improper. Yet he did in fact employ it in explaining his principle, accompanied with an awkward explanation intended to signify that, though he said proportion, he meant something quite different from proportion. We should not have said so much on this subject, either in our former article, or at present, but that there is in all Mr. Sadler's writings an air of scientific pedantry, which renders his errors fair game. We will now let the matter rest; and, instead of assailing Mr. Sadler with our verbal criticism, proceed to defend ourselves against his literal criticism.

"The Reviewer promised his readers that some curious results should follow from his shuffling. We will enable him to keep his word.

"'In two English counties,' says he, 'which contain from 50 to 100 inhabitants on the square mile, the births to 100 marriages are, according to Mr. Sadler, 420; but in 44 departments of France, in which there are from one to two hecatares [*hectares*] to each inhabitant, that is to say, in which the population is from 125 to 250, or rather more, to the square mile, the number of births to one hundred marriages is 423 and a fraction.'

"The first curious result is, that our Reviewer is ignorant, not only of the name, but of the extent, of a French hectare; otherwise he is guilty of a practice which, even if transferred to the gambling-table, would, I presume, prevent him from being allowed ever to shuffle, even there, again. He was most ready to pronounce upon a mistake of one per cent. in a calculation of mine, the difference in no wise affecting the argument in hand; but here I must inform him, that his error, whether wilfully or ignorantly put forth, involves his entire argument.

"The French hectare I had calculated to contain $107708\frac{67}{100}$ English square feet, or $2\frac{47265}{100000}$ acres; Dr. Kelly takes it, on authority which he gives, at $107644\frac{143923}{1000000}$ English square feet, or $2\frac{471169}{1000000}$ acres. The last French *Annuaires*, however, state it, I perceive, as being equal to $2\frac{473914}{1000000}$ acres. The difference is very trifling, and will not in the slightest degree cover our critic's error. The first calculation gives about $258\frac{83}{100}$ hectares to an English square mile; the second, $258\frac{73}{100}$; the last. or French calculation, $258\frac{98}{100}$. When, therefore, the Reviewer calculates the population of the departments of France thus: 'from one to two hectares to each inhabitant, that is to say, in which the population is from 125 to 250, or rather more, to the square mile;' his '*that is to say*' is that which he ought not to have said—no rare case with him, as we shall show throughout."

We must inform Mr. Sadler, in the first place, that we inserted the vowel which amuses him so much, not from ignorance or from carelessness, but advisedly, and in conformity with the practice of several respectable writers. He will find the word hecatare in Rees's Cyclopædia. He will find it also in Dr. Young. We prefer the form which we have employed, because it is etymologically correct. Mr. Sadler seems not to know that a hecatare is so called, because it contains a hundred *ares*.

We were perfectly acquainted with the extent as well as with the name of a hecatare. Is it at all strange that we should use the words "250, or rather more," in speaking of 258 and a fraction? Do not people constantly employ round numbers with still greater looseness, in translating foreign distances and foreign money? If indeed, as Mr. Sadler says, the difference which he chooses to call an error involved the entire argument, or any part of the argument, we should have been guilty of gross unfairness. But it is not so. The difference between 258 and 250, as even Mr. Sadler would see if he were not blind with fury, was a difference to his advantage. Our point was this. The fecundity of a dense population in certain departments of France is greater than that of a thinly scattered population in certain counties of England. The more dense, therefore, the population in those departments of France, the stronger was our case. By putting 250, instead of 258, we understated our case. Mr. Sadler's correction of our orthography leads us to suspect that he knows very little of Greek; and his correction of our calculation quite satisfies us that he knows very little of logic.

But, to come to the gist of the controversy. Our argument, drawn from Mr. Sadler's own Tables, remains absolutely untouched. He makes excuses indeed; for an excuse is the last thing that Mr. Sadler will ever want. There is something half laughable and half provoking in the facility with which he asserts and retracts, says and unsays, exactly as suits his argument. Sometimes the register of baptisms is imperfect, and sometimes the register of burials. Then again these registers become all at once exact almost to an unit. He brings forward a census of Prussia in proof of his theory. We show that it directly confutes his theory; and it forthwith becomes "notoriously and grossly defective." The census of the Netherlands is not to be easily dealt with; and the census of the Netherlands is therefore pronounced inaccurate. In his book on the Law of Population, he tells us that "in the slave-holding States of America, the male slaves constitute a decided majority of that unfortunate class." This fact we turned against him; and, forgetting that he had himself stated it, he tells that "it is as erroneous as many other ideas which we entertain," and that "he will venture to assert that the female slaves were, at the nubile age, as numerous as the males." The increase of the negroes in the United States puzzles him; and he creates a vast slave trade to solve it. He confounds together things perfectly different; the slave-trade carried on under the American flag, and the slave-trade carried on for the supply of the American soil, — the slave-trade with Africa, and the internal slave-trade between the different States. He exaggerates a few occasional acts of smuggling into an immense and regular importation, and makes his escape as well as he can under cover of this hubbub of words. Documents are authentic and facts true precisely in proportion to the support which they afford to his theory. This is one way, undoubtedly, of making books: but we question much whether it be the way to make discoveries.

As to the inconsistencies which we pointed out between his theory and his own tables, he finds no difficulty in explaining them away or facing them out. In one case there would have been no contradiction if, instead of taking one of his tables, we had multiplied the number of three tables together, and taken the average. Another would never have existed if there had not been a great migration of people into Lancashire. Another is not to be got over by any device. But then it is very small, and of no consequence to the argument.

Here, indeed, he is perhaps right. The inconsistencies which we noticed were, in themselves, of little moment. We gave them as samples, — as mere hints, to caution those of our readers who might also happen to be readers of Mr. Sadler against being deceived by his packing. He complains of the word packing. We repeat it; and, since he has defied us to the proof, we will go fully into the question which, in our last article, we only glanced at, and prove, in such a manner as shall not leave even to Mr. Sadler any shadow of excuse, that his theory owes its speciousness to packing, and to packing alone.

That our readers may fully understand our reasoning, we will again state what Mr. Sadler's proposition is. He asserts that, on a given space, the number of children to a marriage becomes less and less as the population becomes more and more numerous.

We will begin with the censuses of France given by Mr. Sadler. By joining the departments together in combinations which suit his purpose, he has contrived to produce three tables, which he presents as decisive proofs of his theory.

The first is as follows: —

"The legitimate births are, in those departments where there are to each inhabitant —

From 4 to 5 hects.	(2 departs.) to every 1000 marriages	5130
3 to 4 ..	(3 do.)	4372
2 to 3 ..	(30 do.)	4250
1 to 2 ..	(44 do.)	4234
·06 to 1 ..	(5 do.)	4146
and ·06 ..	(1 do.)	2657

The two other computations he has given in one table. We subjoin it.

Hect. to each Inhabitant.	Number of Departments.	Legit. Births to 100 Marriages.	Legit. Births to 100 Mar. (1826.)
4 to 5	2	497	397
3 to 4	3	439	389
2 to 3	30	424	379
1 to 2	44	420	375
under 1	5	415	372
and ·06	1	263	253

These tables, as we said in our former article, certainly look well for Mr. Sadler's theory. "Do they?" says he. "Assuredly they do; and in admitting this, the Reviewer has admitted the theory to be proved." We cannot absolutely agree to this. A theory is not proved, we must tell Mr. Sadler, merely because the evidence in its favour looks well at first sight. There is an old proverb, very homely in expression, but well deserving to be had in constant remembrance by all men, engaged either in action or in speculation — "One story is good till another is told!"

We affirm, then, that the results which these tables present, and which seem so favourable to Mr. Sadler's theory, are produced by packing, and by packing alone.

In the first place, if we look at the departments singly, the whole is in disorder. About the department in which Paris is situated there is no dispute: Mr. Malthus distinctly admits that great cities prevent propagation. There remain eighty-four departments; and of these there is not, we believe, a single one in the place which, according to Mr. Sadler's principle, it ought to occupy.

That which ought to be highest in fecundity is tenth in one table, fourteenth in another, and only thirty-first according to the third. That which ought to be third is twenty-second by the table, which places it highest. That which ought to be fourth is fortieth by the table, which places it highest. That which ought to be eighth is fiftieth or sixtieth. That which ought to be tenth from the top is at about the same distance from the bottom. On the other hand, that which, according to Mr. Sadler's principle, ought to be last but two of all the eighty-four is third in two of the tables, and seventh in that which places it lowest; and that which ought to be last is, in one of Mr. Sadler's tables, above that which ought to be first, in two of them, above that which ought to be third, and, in all of them, above that which ought to be fourth.

By dividing the departments in a particular manner,

Mr. Sadler has produced results which he contemplates with great satisfaction. But, if we draw the lines a little higher up or a little lower down, we shall find that all his calculations are thrown into utter confusion; and that the phenomena, if they indicate any thing, indicate a law the very reverse of that which he has propounded.

Let us take, for example, the thirty-two departments, as they stand in Mr. Sadler's table, from Lozére to Meuse inclusive, and divide them into two sets of sixteen departments each. The set from Lozére and Loiret inclusive consists of those departments in which the space to each inhabitant is from 3·8 hecatares to 2·42. The set from Cantal to Meuse inclusive consists of those departments in which the space to each inhabitant is from 2·42 hecatares to 2·07. That is to say, in the former set the inhabitants are from 68 to 107 on the square mile, or thereabouts. In the latter they are from 107 to 125. Therefore, on Mr. Sadler's principle, the fecundity ought to be smaller in the latter set than in the former. It is, however, greater, and that in every one of Mr. Sadler's three tables.

Let us now go a little lower down, and take another set of sixteen departments — those which lie together in Mr. Sadler's tables, from Hérault to Jura inclusive. Here the population is still thicker than in the second of those sets which we before compared. The fecundity, therefore, ought, on Mr. Sadler's principle, to be less than in that set. But it is again greater, and that in all Mr. Sadler's three tables. We have a regularly ascending series, where, if his theory had any truth in it, we ought to have a regularly descending series. We will give the results of our calculation.

The number of children to 1000 marriages is —

	First Table.	Second Table.	Third Table.
In the sixteen departments where there are from 68 to 107 people on a square mile	4188	4226	3780
In the sixteen departments where there are from 107 to 125 people on a square mile	4374	4332	3855
In the sixteen departments where there are from 134 to 125 people on a square mile	4484	4416	3914

We will give another instance, if possible still more decisive. We will take the three departments of France which ought, on Mr. Sadler's principle, to be the lowest in fecundity of all the eighty-five, saving only that in which Paris stands; and we will compare them with the three departments in which the fecundity ought, according to him, to be greater than in any other department of France, two only excepted. We will compare Bas Rhin, Rhone, and Nord, with Lozére, Landes, and Indre. In Lozére, Landes, and Indre, the population is from 68 to 84 on the square mile, or nearly so. In Bas Rhin, Rhone, and Nord, it is from 300 to 417 on the square mile. There cannot be a more overwhelming answer to Mr. Sadler's theory than the table which we subjoin:

The number of births to 1000 marriages is —

	First Table.	Second Table.	Third Table.
In the three departments in which there are from 68 to 84 people on the square mile	4372	4390	3890
In the three departments in which there are from 300 to 417 people on the square mile	4457	4510	4060

These are strong cases. But we have a still stronger case. Take the whole of the third, fourth, and fifth divisions into which Mr. Sadler has portioned out the French departments. These three divisions make up almost the whole kingdom of France. They contain seventy-nine out of the eighty-five departments. Mr. Sadler has contrived to divide them in such a manner that, to a person who looks merely at his averages, the fecundity seems to diminish as the population thickens. We will separate them into two parts instead of three. We will draw the line between the department of Gironde and that of Hérault. On the one side are the thirty-two departments from Cher to Gironde inclusive. On the other side are the forty-six departments from Hérault to Nord inclusive. In all the departments of the former set, the population is under 132 on the square mile. In all the departments of the latter set, it is above 132 on the square mile. It is clear that, if there be one word of truth in Mr. Sadler's theory, the fecundity in the latter of these divisions must be very decidedly smaller than in the former. Is it so? It is, on the contrary, greater in all the three tables. We give the result.

The number of births to 1000 marriages is —

	First Table.	Second Table.	Third Table.
In the thirty-two departments in which there are from 86 to 132 people on the square mile	4210	4199	3760
In the forty-seven departments in which there are from 132 to 417 people on the square mile	4250	4224	3766

This fact is alone enough to decide the question. Yet it is only one of a crowd of similar facts. If the line between Mr. Sadler's second and third divisions be drawn six departments lower down, the third and fourth divisions will, in all the tables, be above the second. If the line between the third and fourth divisions be drawn two departments lower down, the fourth division will be above the third in all the tables. If the line between the fourth and fifth divisions be drawn two departments lower down, the fifth will, in all the tables, be above the fourth, above the third, and even above the second. How then has Mr. Sadler obtained his results? By packing solely. By placing in one compartment a district no larger than the Isle of Wight; in another, a district somewhat less than Yorkshire; in a third, a territory much larger than the island of Great Britain.

By the same artifice it is that he has obtained from the census of England those delusive averages which he brings forward with the utmost ostentation in proof of his principle. We will examine the facts relating to England, as we have examined those relating to France.

If we look at the counties one by one, Mr. Sadler's principle utterly fails. Hertfordshire with 251 on the square mile; Worcestershire with 258; and Kent with 282, exhibit a far greater fecundity than the East-Riding of York, which has 151 on the square mile; Monmouthshire, which has 145; or Northumberland, which has 108. The fecundity of Staffordshire, which has more than 300 on the square mile, is as high as the average fecundity of the counties which have from 150 to 200 on the square mile. But, instead of confining ourselves to particular instances, we will try masses.

Take the eight counties of England which stand together in Mr. Sadler's list, from Cumberland to Dorset inclusive. In these the population is from 107 to 150 on the square mile. Compare with these the eight counties from Berks to Durham inclusive, in which the population is from 175 to 200 on the square mile. Is the fecundity in the latter counties smaller than in the former? On the contrary, the result stands thus:

The number of children to 100 marriages is—

In the eight counties of England, in which there are from 107 to 146 people on the square mile 388

In the eight counties of England, in which there are from 175 to 200 people on the square mile 402

Take the six districts from the East-Riding of York to the County of Norfolk inclusive. Here the population is from 150 to 170 on the square mile. To these oppose the six counties from Derby to Worcester inclusive. The population is from 200 to 260. Here again we find that a law, directly the reverse of that which Mr. Sadler has laid down, appears to regulate the fecundity of the inhabitants.

The number of children to 100 marriages is—

In the six counties in which there are from 150 to 170 people on the square mile . . . 392

In the six counties in which there are from 200 to 260 people on the square mile . . . 399

But we will make another experiment on Mr. Sadler's tables, if possible more decisive than any of those which we have hitherto made. We will take the four largest divisions into which he has distributed the English counties, and which follow each other in regular order. That our readers may fully comprehend the nature of that packing by which his theory is supported, we will set before them this part of his table.

COUNTIES.	Population on a Square Mile.	Population in 1821.	Square Miles in each County.	Number of Marriages from 1810 to 1820.	Number of Baptisms from 1810 to 1820.	Proportion of Births to 100 Marriages.
Lincoln	105	288,800	2748	20,892	87,620	
Cumberland	107	159,300	1478	10,299	45,085	
Northumberland	108	203,000	1871	12,997	45,871	
Hereford	122	105,300	860	6,202	27,909	
Rutland	127	18,900	149	1,286	5,125	
Huntingdon	134	49,800	370	3,766	13,633	
Cambridge	145	124,400	858	9,894	37,491	
Monmouth	145	72,300	498	4,586	13,411	
Dorset	146	147,400	1005	9,554	39,060	
From 100 *to* 150.				79,476	315,205	396
York, East Riding	151	194,300	1280	15,313	55,606	
Salop	156	210,300	1341	13,613	58,542	
Sussex	162	237,700	1463	15,779	68,700	
Northampton	163	165,800	1017	12,346	42,336	
Wilts	164	226,600	1379	15,654	58,845	
Norfolk	168	351 300	2092	25,752	102,259	
Devon	173	447,900	2579	35,264	130,758	
Southampton	177	289,000	1628	24,561	88,170	
Berks	178	134,700	756	9,301	38,841	
Suffolk	182	276,000	1512	19,885	76,327	
Bedford	184	85,400	463	6.536	22,871	
Buckingham	185	136,800	740	9,505	37,518	
Oxford	186	139,800	752	9,131	39,633	
Essex	193	295,300	1532	19,726	79,792	
Cornwall	198	262,600	1327	17,363	74,611	
Durham	199	211,900	1061	14,787	58,222	
From 150 *to* 200.				264,516	1,033,039	390
Derby	212	217,600	1026	14,226	58,804	
Somerset	220	362,500	1642	24,356	95,802	
Leicester	221	178,100	804	13,366	47,013	
Nottingham	228	190,700	837	14,296	55,517	
From 200 *to* 250.				66,244	257,136	388
Hertford	251	132,400	528	7,386	35,741	
Worcester	258	188,200	729	13,178	53,838	
Chester	262	275,500	1052	20,305	75,012	
Gloucester	272	342,600	1256	28,884	90,671	
Kent	282	434,600	1537	33,502	135,060	
From 250 *to* 300.				103,255	390,322	378

These averages look well, undoubtedly, for Mr. Sadler's theory. The numbers 396, 390, 388, 378, follow each other very speciously in a descending order. But let our readers divide these thirty-four counties into two equal sets of seventeen counties each, and try whether the principle will then hold good. We have made this calculation, and we present them with the following result.

The number of children to 100 marriages is—

In the seventeen counties of England in which there are from 100 to 177 people on the square mile 387

In the seventeen counties in which there are from 177 to 282 people on the square mile . 389

The difference is small, but not smaller than differences which Mr. Sadler has brought forward as proofs of his theory. We say, that these English tables no more prove that fecundity increases with the population than that it diminishes with the population. The thirty-four counties which we have taken make up, at least, four-fifths of the kingdom: and we see that, through those thirty-four counties, the phenomena are directly opposed to Mr. Sadler's principle. That in the capital, and in great manufacturing towns, marriages are less prolific than in the open country, we admit, and Mr. Malthus admits. But that any condensation of the population, short of that which injures all physical energies, will diminish the prolific powers of man, is, from these very tables of Mr. Sadler, completely disproved.

It is scarcely worth while to proceed with instances, after proofs so overwhelming as those which we have given. Yet we will show that Mr. Sadler has formed his averages on the census of Prussia by an artifice exactly similar to that which we have already exposed.

Demonstrating the Law of Population from the Censuses of Prussia, at two several Periods.

PROVINCES.	Inhabitants on a Square League.	Births to each Marriage. 1756.	Average.	Births to each Marriage. 1784.	Average.
West Prussia	832		4·34	4·75	4·72
Pomerania . .	928	4·3		4·69	
East Prussia .	1175	5·07	4·14	5·10	4·45
New Mark . .	1190	4·22		4·43	
Mark of Brandenburg .	1790	3·88		4·60	
East Friesland	1909	3·39		3·66	
Guelderland . .	2083	4·33	3·84	3·74	4·24
Silesia and Glatz	2314			4·84	
Cleves . . .	2375	3·80		4·03	
Minden and Ravensburg	2549	3·67		4·31	
Magdeburg . .	2692	4·03		4·57	
Neufchatel, &c.	2700	3·39		3·98	
Halberstadt . .	3142	3·71	3·65	4·48	4·08
Ticklingburg and Lingen	3461	3·59		3·69	

Of the census of 1756 we will say nothing, as Mr. Sadler, finding himself hard pressed by the argument which we drew from it, now declares it to be grossly defective. We confine ourselves to the census of 1784: and we will draw our lines at points somewhat different from those at which Mr. Sadler has drawn his. Let the first compartment remain as it stands. Let East Prussia, which contains a much larger population than his last compartment, stand alone in the second division. Let the third consist of the New Mark, the Mark of Brandenburg, East Friesland and Guelderland, and the fourth of the remaining provinces. Our readers will find that, on this arrangement, the division which, on Mr. Sadler's principle, ought to be second in fecundity stands higher than that which ought to be first; and that the division which ought to be fourth stands higher than that which ought to be third. We will give the result in one view.

The number of births to a marriage is—

In those provinces of Prussia where there are fewer than 1000 people on the square league	4·72
In the province in which there are 1175 people on the square league	5·10
In the provinces in which there are from 1190 to 2083 people on the square mile	4.10
In the provinces in which there are from 2314 to 3461 people on the square league	4·27

We will go no farther with this examination. In fact, we have nothing more to examine. The tables which we have scrutinised constitute the whole strength of Mr. Sadler's case; and we confidently leave it to our readers to say, whether we have not shown that the strength of his case is weakness.

Be it remembered too that we are reasoning on data furnished by Mr. Sadler himself. We have not made collections of facts to set against his, as we easily might have done. It is on his own showing, it is out of his own mouth, that his theory stands condemned.

That packing which we have exposed is not the only sort of packing which Mr. Sadler has practised. We mentioned in our review some facts relating to the towns of England, which appear from Mr. Sadler's tables, and which it seems impossible to explain if his principles be sound. The average fecundity of a marriage in towns of fewer than 3000 inhabitants is greater than the average fecundity of the kingdom. The average fecundity in towns of from 4000 to 5000 inhabitants is greater than the average fecundity of Warwickshire, Lancashire, or Surrey. How is it, we asked, if Mr. Sadler's principle be correct, that the fecundity of Guildford should be greater than the average fecundity of the county in which it stands?

Mr. Sadler, in reply, talks about "the absurdity of comparing the fecundity in the small towns alluded to with that in the counties of Warwick and Stafford, or those of Lancaster and Surrey." He proceeds thus—

"In Warwickshire, far above half the population is comprised in large towns, including, of course, the immense metropolis of one great branch of our manufactures, Birmingham. In the county of Stafford, besides the large and populous towns in its iron districts, situated so close together as almost to form, for considerable distances, a continuous street; there is, in its potteries, a great population, recently accumulated, not included, indeed, in the towns distinctly enumerated in the censuses, but vastly exceeding in its condensation that found in the places to which the Reviewer alludes. In Lancashire again, to which he also appeals, one-fourth of the entire population is made up of the inhabitants of two only of the towns of that county; far above half of it is contained in towns, compared with which those he refers to are villages; even the hamlets of the manufacturing parts of Lancashire are often far more populous than the places he mentions. But he presents us with a climax of absurdity in appealing lastly to the population of Surrey as quite rural compared with that of the twelve towns, having less than 5000 inhabitants in their respective jurisdictions, such as Saffron-Walden, Monmouth, &c. Now, in the last census, Surrey numbered 398,658 inhabitants, and, to say not a word about the other towns of the county, much above two hundred thousands of these are *within the Bills of Mortality!* 'We should, therefore, be glad to know' how it is utterly inconsistent with my principle that the fecundity of Guildford, which numbers about 3000 inhabitants, should be greater than the average fecundity of Surrey, made up, as the bulk of the population of Surrey is, of the inhabitants of some of the worst parts of the metropolis? Or why the fecundity of a given number of marriages in the eleven little rural towns he alludes to, being somewhat higher than that of an equal number, half taken for instance, from the heart of Birmingham or Manchester, and half from the populous districts by which they are surrounded, is inconsistent with my theory?

> "Had the Reviewer's object, in this instance, been to discover the truth, or had he known how to pursue it, it is perfectly clear, at first sight, that he would not have instituted a comparison between the prolificness which exists in the small towns he has alluded to, and that in certain districts, the population of which is made up, partly of rural inhabitants and partly of accumulations of people in immense masses, the prolificness of which, if he will allow me still the use of the phrase, is inversely as their magnitude; but he would have compared these small towns with the country places properly so called, and then again the different classes of towns with each other; this method would have led him to certain conclusions on the subject."

Now, this reply shows that Mr. Sadler does not in the least understand the principle which he has himself laid down. What is that principle? It is this, that the fecundity of human beings *on given spaces*, varies inversely as their numbers. We know what he means by inverse variation. But we must suppose that he uses the words, "given spaces" in the proper sense. Given spaces are equal spaces. Is there any reason to believe, that in those parts of Surrey which lie within the bills of mortality there is any space, equal in area to the space on which Guildford stands, which is more thickly peopled than the space on which Guildford stands? We do not know that there is any such. We are sure that there are not many. Why, therefore, on Mr. Sadler's principle, should the people of Guildford be more prolific than the people who live within the bills of mortality? And, if the people of Guildford ought, as on Mr. Sadler's principle they unquestionably ought, to stand as low in the scale of fecundity as the people of Southwark itself, it follows, most clearly, that they ought to stand far lower than the average obtained by taking all the people of Surrey together.

The same remark applies to the case of Birmingham, and to all the other cases which Mr. Sadler mentions. Towns of 5000 inhabitants may be, and often are, as thickly peopled, "on a given space," as Birmingham. They are, in other words, as thickly peopled as a portion of Birmingham, equal to them in area. If so, on Mr. Sadler's principle, they ought to be as low in the scale of fecundity as Birmingham. But they are not so. On the contrary, they stand higher than the average obtained by taking the fecundity of Birmingham in combination with the fecundity of the rural districts of Warwickshire.

The plain fact is, that Mr. Sadler has confounded the population of a city with its population "on a given space," — a mistake which, in a gentleman who assures us that mathematical science was one of his early and favourite studies, is somewhat curious. It is as absurd, on his principle, to say that the fecundity of London ought to be less than the fecundity of Edinburgh, because London has a greater population than Edinburgh, as to say that the fecundity of Russia ought to be greater than that of England, because Russia has a greater population than England. He cannot say that the spaces on which towns stand are too small to exemplify the truth of his principle. For he has himself brought forward the scale of fecundity in towns, as a proof of his principle. And, in the very passage which we quoted above, he tells us that, if we knew how to pursue truth, or wished to find it, we "should have compared these small towns with country places, and the different classes of towns with each other." That is to say, we ought to compare together such unequal spaces as give results favourable to his theory, and never to compare such equal spaces as give results opposed to it. Does he mean any thing by "a given space?" Or does he mean merely such a space as suits his argument? It is perfectly clear that, if he is allowed to take this course, he may prove any thing. No fact can come amiss to him. Suppose, for example, that the fecundity of New York should prove to be smaller than the fecundity of Liverpool. "That," says Mr. Sadler, "makes for my theory. For there are more people within two miles of the Broadway of New York, than within two miles of the Exchange of Liverpool." Suppose, on the other hand, that the fecundity of New York should be greater than the fecundity of Liverpool. "This," says Mr. Sadler again, "is an unanswerable proof of my theory. For there are many more people within forty miles of Liverpool than within forty miles of New York." In order to obtain his numbers, he takes spaces in any combinations which may suit him. In order to obtain his averages, he takes numbers in any combinations which may suit him. And then he tells us that, because his tables, at the first glance, look well for his theory, his theory is irrefragably proved.

We will add a few words respecting the argument which we drew from the peerage. Mr. Sadler asserted that the Peers were a class condemned by nature to sterility. We denied this, and showed, from the last edition of Debrett, that the Peers of the United Kingdom have considerably more than the average number of children to a marriage. Mr. Sadler's answer has amused us much. He denies the accuracy of our counting, and, by reckoning all the Scotch and Irish Peers as Peers of the United Kingdom, certainly makes very different numbers from those which we gave. A member of the Parliament of the United Kingdom might have been expected, we think, to know better what a Peer of the United Kingdom is.

By taking the Scotch and Irish Peers, Mr. Sadler has altered the average. But it is considerably higher than the average fecundity of England, and still, therefore, constitutes an unanswerable argument against his theory.

The shifts to which, in this difficulty, he has recourse, are exceedingly diverting. "The average fecundity of the marriages of Peers," said we, "is higher by one-fifth than the average fecundity of marriages throughout the kingdom."

"Where, or by whom did the Reviewer find it supposed," answers Mr. Sadler, "that the registered baptisms expressed the full fecundity of the marriages of England?"

Assuredly, if the registers of England are so defective as to explain the difference which, on our calculation, exists between the fecundity of the peers and the fecundity of the people, no argument against Mr. Sadler's theory can be drawn from that difference. But what becomes of all the other arguments which Mr. Sadler has founded on these very registers? Above all, what becomes of his comparison between the censuses of England and France? In the pamphlet before us, he dwells with great complacency on a coincidence which seems to him to support his theory, and which to us seems, of itself, sufficient to overthrow it.

"In my table of the population of France, in the forty-four departments in which there are from one to two hectares to each inhabitant, the fecundity of 100 marriages, calculated on the average of the results of the three computations relating to different periods given in my table, is $406\frac{7}{10}$. In the twenty-two counties of England, in which there is from one to two hectares to each inhabitant, or from 129 to 259 on the square mile, — beginning, therefore, with Huntingdonshire, and ending with Worcestershire, — the whole number of marriages during ten years will be found to amount to 379,624, and the whole number of the births during the same term to 1,545,549 — or 407$\frac{1}{10}$ births to 100 marriages! A difference of one in one thousand only, compared with the French proportion!"

Does not Mr. Sadler see that, if the registers of England, which are notoriously very defective, give a result exactly corresponding almost to an unit with that obtained from the registers of France, which are notoriously very full and accurate, this proves the very reverse of what he employs it to prove? The correspondence of the registers proves that there is no correspondence in the facts. In order to raise the average fecundity of England even to the level of the average fecundity of the peers of the three kingdoms, which is 3·81 to a marriage, it is necessary to add nearly six per cent. to the number of births given in the English registers. But, if this addition be made, we shall have, in the counties of England, from Huntingdonshire to Worcestershire inclusive, 4·30 births to a marriage or thereabouts; and the boasted coincidence between the phenomena of propagation in France and England disappears at once. This is a curious specimen of Mr. Sadler's proficiency in the art of making excuses. In the same pamphlet he reasons as if the same registers were accurate to one in a thousand, and as if they were wrong at the very least by one in eighteen.

He tries to show that we have not taken a fair criterion of the fecundity of the peers. We are not quite sure that we understand his reasoning on this subject. The order of his observations is more than usually confused, and the cloud of words more than usually thick. We will give the argument on which he seems to lay most stress in his own words :

> " But I shall first notice a far more obvious and important blunder into which the Reviewer has fallen ; or into which, I rather fear, he knowingly wishes to precipitate his readers, since I have distinctly pointed out what ought to have preserved him from it in the very chapter he is criticising and contradicting. It is this :— he has entirely omitted " counting " the sterile marriages of all those peerages which have become extinct during the very period his counting embraces. He counts, for instance, Earl Fitzwilliam, his marriages, and heir ; but has he not omitted to enumerate the marriages of those branches of the same noble house, which have become extinct since that venerable individual possessed his title ? He talks of my having appealed merely to the extinction of peerages in my argument ; .but, on his plan of computation, extinctions are perpetually and wholly lost sight of. In computing the average prolificness of the marriages of the nobles, he positively counts from a select class of them only, one from which the unprolific are constantly weeded, and regularly disappear ; and he thus comes to the conclusion, that the peers are 'an eminently prolific class !' Just as though a farmer should compute the rate of increase, not from the quantity of seed sown, but from that part of it only which comes to perfection, entirely omitting all which had failed to spring up or come to maturity. Upon this principle the most scanty crop ever obtained, in which the husbandman should fail to receive 'seed again,' as the phrase is, might be so 'counted' as to appear 'eminently prolific' indeed."

If we understand this passage rightly, it decisively proves that Mr. Sadler is incompetent to perform even the lowest offices of statistical research. What shadow of reason is there to believe that the peers who were alive in the year 1828 differed as to their prolificness from any other equally numerous set of peers taken at random ? In what sense were the peers who were alive in 1828 analogous to that part of the seed which comes to perfection ? Did we entirely omit all that failed ? On the contrary, we counted the sterile as well as the fruitful marriages of all the peers of the United Kingdom living at one time. In what way were the peers who were alive in 1828 a select class? In what way were the sterile weeded from among them? Did every peer who had been married without having issue die in 1827? What shadow of reason is there to suppose that there was not the ordinary proportion of barren marriages among the marriages contracted by the noblemen whose names are in Debrett's last edition? But we ought, says Mr. Sadler, to have counted all the sterile marriages of all the peers "whose titles had become extinct during the period which our counting embraced;" that is to say, since the earliest marriage contracted by any peer living in 1828. Was such a proposition ever heard of before? Surely we were bound to do no such thing, unless at the same time we had counted also the children born from all the fruitful marriages contracted by peers during the same period. Mr. Sadler would have us divide the number of children born to peers living in 1828, not by the number of marriages which those peers contracted, but by the number of marriages which those peers contracted added to a crowd of marriages selected, on account of their sterility, from among the noble marriages which have taken place during the last fifty years. Is this the way to obtain fair averages? We might as well require that all the noble marriages which during the last fifty years have produced ten children apiece should be added to those of the peers living in 1828. The proper way to ascertain whether a set of people be prolific or sterile is, not to take marriages selected from the mass either on account of their fruitfulness or on account of their sterility, but to take a collection of marriages which there is no reason to think either more or less fruitful than others. What reason is there to think that the marriages contracted by the peers who were alive in 1828 were more fruitful than those contracted by the peers who were alive in 1800 or in 1750?

We will add another passage from Mr. Sadler's pamphlet on this subject. We attributed the extinction of peerages partly to the fact that those honours are for the most part limited to heirs male.

> "This is a discovery indeed! Peeresses, 'eminently prolific,' do not, as Macbeth conjured his spouse, 'bring forth men-children only;' they actually produce daughters as well as sons!! Why, does not the Reviewer see, that so long as the rule of nature, which proportions the sexes so accurately to each other, continues to exist, a tendency to a diminution in one sex proves, as certainly as the demonstration of any mathematical problem, a tendency to a diminution in both; but to talk of 'eminently prolific' peeresses, and still maintain that the rapid extinction in peerages is owing to their not bearing male children exclusively, is arrant nonsense."

Now, if there be any proposition on the face of the earth which we should not have expected to hear characterised as arrant nonsense, it is this, — that an honour limited to males alone is more likely to become extinct than an honour which, like the crown of England, descends indifferently to sons and daughters. We have heard, nay, we actually know families, in which, much as Mr. Sadler may marvel at it, there are daughters and no sons. Nay, we know many such families. We are as much inclined as Mr. Sadler to trace the benevolent and wise arrangements of Providence in the physical world, when once we are satisfied as to the facts on which we proceed. And we have always considered it as an arrangement deserving of the highest admiration, that, though in families the number of males and females differs widely, yet in great collections of human beings the disparity almost disappears. The chance undoubtedly is, that in a thousand marriages the number of daughters will not very much exceed the number of sons. But the chance also is, that several of those marriages will produce daughters, and daughters only. In every generation of the peerage there are several such cases. When a peer whose title is limited to male heirs dies, leaving only daughters, his peerage must expire, unless he have, not only a collateral heir, but a collateral heir descended through an uninterrupted line of males from the first possessor of the honour. If the deceased peer was the first nobleman of his family, then, by the supposition, his peerage will become extinct. If he was the second, it will become extinct, unless he leaves a brother or a brother's son. If the second peer had a brother, the first peer must have had at least two sons; and this is more than the average number of sons to a marriage in England. When, therefore, it is considered how many peerages are in the first and second generation, it will not appear strange that extinctions should frequently take place. There are peerages which descend to females as well as males. But, in such cases, if a peer dies, leaving only daughters, the very fecundity of the marriage is a cause of the extinction of the peerage. If there were only one daughter, the honour would descend. If there are several, it falls into abeyance.

But it is needless to multiply words in a case so clear; and indeed it is needless to say anything more about Mr. Sadler's book. We have, if we do not deceive ourselves, completely exposed the calculations on which his theory rests; and we do not think that we should either amuse our readers or serve the cause of science if we were to rebut in succession a series of futile charges brought in the most angry spirit against ourselves; ignorant imputations of ignorance, and unfair complaints of unfairness, — conveyed in long, dreary, declamations, so prolix that we cannot find space to quote them, and so confused that we cannot venture to abridge them.

There is much indeed in this foolish pamphlet to laugh at, from the motto in the first page down to some wisdom about cows in the last. One part of it indeed is solemn enough, we mean a certain *jeu d'esprit* of Mr. Sadler's touching a tract of Dr. Arbuthnot's. This is indeed "very tragical mirth," as Peter Quince's playbill has it; and we would not advise any person who reads for amusement to venture on it as long as he can procure a volume of the Statutes at Large. This, however, to do Mr. Sadler justice, is an exception. His witticisms, and his tables of figures, constitute the only parts of his work which can be perused with perfect gravity. His blunders are diverting, his excuses exquisitely comic. But his anger is the most grotesque exhibition that we ever saw. He foams at the mouth with the love of truth, and vindicates the Divine benevolence with a most edifying heartiness of hatred. On this subject we will give him one word of parting advice. If he raves in this way to ease his mind, or because he thinks that he does himself credit by it, or from a sense of religious duty, far be it from us to interfere. His peace, his reputation, and his religion are his own concern; and he, like the nobleman to whom his treatise is dedicated, has a right to do what he will with his own. But, if he has adopted his abusive style from a notion that it would hurt our feelings, we must inform him that he is altogether mistaken; and that he would do well in future to give us his arguments, if he has any, and to keep his anger for those who fear it.

CIVIL DISABILITIES OF THE JEWS.[1]

(*Edinburgh Review*, January 1831.)

THE distinguished member of the House of Commons who, towards the close of the late Parliament, brought forward a proposition for the relief of the Jews, has given notice of his intention to renew it. The force of reason, in the last session, carried the measure through one stage, in spite of the opposition of power. Reason and power are now on the same side; and we have little doubt that they will conjointly achieve a decisive victory. In order to contribute our share to the success of just principles, we propose to pass in review, as rapidly as possible, some of the arguments, or phrases claiming to be arguments, which have been employed to vindicate a system full of absurdity and injustice.

The constitution, it is said, is essentially Christian; and therefore to admit Jews to office is to destroy the constitution. Nor is the Jew injured by being excluded from political power. For no man has any right to power. A man has a right to his property; a man has a right to be protected from personal injury. These rights the law allows to the Jew; and with these rights it would be atrocious to interfere. But it is a mere matter of favour to admit any man to political

[1] *Statement of the Civil Disabilities and Privations affecting Jews in England.* 8vo. London: 1829.

power; and no man can justly complain that he is shut out from it.

We cannot but admire the ingenuity of this contrivance for shifting the burden of the proof from those to whom it properly belongs, and who would, we suspect, find it rather cumbersome. Surely no Christian can deny that every human being has a right to be allowed every gratification which produces no harm to others, and to be spared every mortification which produces no good to others. Is it not a source of mortification to a class of men that they are excluded from political power? If it be, they have, on Christian principles, a right to be freed from that mortification, unless it can be shown that their exclusion is necessary for the averting of some greater evil. The presumption is evidently in favour of toleration. It is for the prosecutor to make out his case.

The strange argument which we are considering would prove too much even for those who advance it. If no man has a right to political power, then neither Jew nor Gentile has such a right. The whole foundation of government is taken away. But if government be taken away, the property and the persons of men are insecure; and it is acknowledged that men have a right to their property and to personal security. If it be right that the property of men should be protected, and if this can only be done by means of government, then it must be right that government should exist. Now there cannot be government unless some person or persons possess political power. Therefore it is right that some person or persons should possess political power. That is to say, some person or persons must have a right to political power.

It is because men are not in the habit of considering

what the end of government is, that Catholic disabilities and Jewish disabilities have been suffered to exist so long. We hear of essentially Protestant governments and essentially Christian governments, words which mean just as much as essentially Protestant cookery, or essentially Christian horsemanship. Government exists for the purpose of keeping the peace, for the purpose of compelling us to settle our disputes by arbitration instead of settling them by blows, for the purpose of compelling us to supply our wants by industry instead of supplying them by rapine. This is the only operation for which the machinery of government is peculiarly adapted, the only operation which wise governments ever propose to themselves as their chief object. If there is any class of people who are not interested, or who do not think themselves interested, in the security of property and the maintenance of order, that class ought to have no share of the powers which exist for the purpose of securing property and maintaining order. But why a man should be less fit to exercise those powers because he wears a beard, because he does not eat ham, because he goes to the synagogue on Saturdays instead of going to the church on Sundays, we cannot conceive.

The points of difference between Christianity and Judaism have very much to do with a man's fitness to be a bishop or a rabbi. But they have no more to do with his fitness to be a magistrate, a legislator, or a minister of finance, than with his fitness to be a cobbler. Nobody has ever thought of compelling cobblers to make any declaration on the true faith of a Christian. Any man would rather have his shoes mended by a heretical cobbler than by a person who had subscribed all the thirty-nine articles, but had never handled an awl. Men act thus, not because they are indifferent to religion, but because they do not see what religion has to do with the mending of their shoes. Yet religion has as much to do with the mending of shoes as with the budget and the army estimates. We have surely had several signal proofs within the last twenty years that a very good Christian may be a very bad Chancellor of the Exchequer.

But it would be monstrous, say the persecutors, that Jews should legislate for a Christian community. This is a palpable misrepresentation. What is proposed is, not that the Jews should legislate for a Christian community, but that a legislature composed of Christians and Jews should legislate for a community composed of Christians and Jews. On nine hundred and ninety-nine questions out of a thousand, on all questions of police, of finance, of civil and criminal law, of foreign policy, the Jew, as a Jew, has no interest hostile to that of the Christian, or even to that of the Churchman. On questions relating to the ecclesiastical establishment, the Jew and the Churchman may differ. But they cannot differ more widely than the Catholic and the Churchman, or the Independent and the Churchman. The principle that Churchmen ought to monopolize the whole power of the state would at least have an intelligible meaning. The principle that Christians ought to monopolize it has no meaning at all. For no question connected with the ecclesiastical institutions of the country can possibly come before Parliament, with respect to which there will not be as wide a difference between Christians as there can be between any Christian and any Jew.

In fact, the Jews are not now excluded from political power. They possess it; and as long as they are allowed to accumulate large fortunes, they must possess it. The distinction which is sometimes made between civil privileges and political power is a distinction without a difference. Privileges are power. Civil and political are synonymous words, the one derived from the Latin, the other from the Greek. Nor is this mere verbal quibbling. If we look for a moment at the facts of the case, we shall see that the things are inseparable, or rather identical.

That a Jew should be a judge in a Christian country would be most shocking. But he may be a juryman. He may try issues of fact; and no harm is done. But if he should be suffered to try issues of law, there is an end of the constitution. He may sit in a box plainly dressed, and return verdicts. But that he should sit on the bench in a black gown and white wig, and grant new trials, would be an abomination not to be thought of among baptized people. The distinction is certainly most philosophical.

What power in civilised society is so great as that of the creditor over the debtor? If we take this away from the Jew, we take away from him the security of his property. If we leave it to him, we leave to him a power more despotic by far than that of the king and all his cabinet.

It would be impious to let a Jew sit in Parliament. But a Jew may make money; and money may make members of Parliament. Gattan and Old Sarum may be the property of a Hebrew. An elector of Penryn will take ten pounds from Shylock rather than nine pounds nineteen shillings and eleven pence three farthings from Antonio. To this no objection is made. That a Jew should possess the substance of legislative power, that he should command eight votes on every division as if he were the great Duke of Newcastle himself, is exactly as it should be. But that he should pass the bar and sit down on those mysterious cushions of green leather, that he should cry "hear" and "order," and talk about being on his legs, and being, for one, free to say this and to say that, would be a profanation sufficient to bring ruin on the country.

That a Jew should be privy-councillor to a Christian king would be an eternal disgrace to the nation. But the Jew may govern the money-market, and the money-market may govern the world. The minister may be in doubt as to his scheme of finance till he has been closeted with the Jew. A congress of sovereigns may be forced to summon the Jew to their assistance. The scrawl of the Jew on the back of a piece of paper may be worth more than the royal word of three kings, or the national faith of three new American republics. But that he should put Right Honourable before his name would be the most frightful of national calamities.

It was in this way that some of our politicians reasoned about the Irish Catholics. The Catholics ought to have no political power. The sun of England is set for ever if the Catholics exercise political power. Give the Catholics every thing else; but keep political power from them. These wise men did not see that, when every thing else had been given, political power had been given. They continued to repeat their cuckoo song, when it was no longer a question whether Catholics should have political power or not, when a Catholic Association bearded the Parliament, when a Catholic agitator exercised infinitely more authority than the Lord Lieutenant.

If it is our duty as Christians to exclude the Jews

from political power, it must be our duty to treat them as our ancestors treated them, to murder them, and banish them, and rob them. For in that way, and in that way alone, can we really deprive them of political power. If we do not adopt this course, we may take away the shadow, but we must leave them the substance. We may do enough to pain and irritate them; but we shall not do enough to secure ourselves from danger, if danger really exists. Where wealth is, there power must inevitably be.

The English Jews, we are told, are not Englishmen. They are a separate people, living locally in this island, but living morally and politically in communion with their brethren who are scattered over all the world. An English Jew looks on a Dutch or a Portuguese Jew as his countryman, and on an English Christian as a stranger. This want of patriotic feeling, it is said, renders a Jew unfit to exercise political functions.

The argument has in it something plausible; but a close examination shows it to be quite unsound. Even if the alleged facts are admitted, still the Jews are not the only people who have preferred their sect to their country. The feeling of patriotism, when society is in a healthful state, springs up, by a natural and inevitable association, in the minds of citizens who know that they owe all their comforts and pleasures to the bond which unites them in one community. But, under a partial and oppressive government, these associations cannot acquire that strength which they have in a better state of things. Men are compelled to seek from their party that protection which they ought to receive from their country, and they, by a natural consequence, transfer to their party that affection which they would otherwise have felt for their country. The

Huguenots of France called in the help of England against their Catholic kings. The Catholics of France called in the help of Spain against a Huguenot king. Would it be fair to infer, that at present the French Protestants would wish to see their religion made dominant by the help of a Prussian or English army? Surely not. And why is it that they are not willing, as they formerly were willing, to sacrifice the interests of their country to the interests of their religious persuasion? The reason is obvious: they were persecuted then, and are not persecuted now. The English Puritans, under Charles the First, prevailed on the Scotch to invade England. Do the Protestant Dissenters of our time wish to see the Church put down by an invasion of foreign Calvinists? If not, to what cause are we to attribute the change? Surely to this, that the Protestant Dissenters are far better treated now than in the seventeenth century. Some of the most illustrious public men that England ever produced were inclined to take refuge from the tyranny of Laud in North America. Was this because Presbyterians and Independents are incapable of loving their country? But it is idle to multiply instances. Nothing is so offensive to a man who knows any thing of history or of human nature as to hear those who exercise the powers of government accuse any sect of foreign attachments. If there be any proposition universally true in politics it is this, that foreign attachments are the fruit of domestic misrule. It has always been the trick of bigots to make their subjects miserable at home, and then to complain that they look for relief abroad; to divide society, and to wonder that it is not united; to govern as if a section of the state were the whole, and to censure the other sections of the state for their want of patriotic spirit. If the Jews have not felt towards England like children, it is because she has treated them like a step-mother. There is no feeling which more certainly developes itself in the minds of men living under tolerably good government than the feeling of patriotism. Since the beginning of the world, there never was any nation, or any large portion of any nation, not cruelly oppressed, which was wholly destitute of that feeling. To make it therefore ground of accusation against a class of men, that they are not patriotic, is the most vulgar legerdemain of sophistry. It is the logic which the wolf employs against the lamb. It is to accuse the mouth of the stream of poisoning the source.

If the English Jews really felt a deadly hatred to England, if the weekly prayer of their synagogues were that all the curses denounced by Ezekiel on Tyre and Egypt might fall on London, if, in their solemn feasts, they called down blessings on those who should dash our children to pieces on the stones, still, we say, their hatred to their countrymen would not be more intense than that which sects of Christians have often borne to each other. But in fact the feeling of the Jews is not such. It is precisely what, in the situation in which they are placed, we should expect it to be. They are treated far better than the French Protestants were treated in the sixteenth and seventeenth centuries, or than our Puritans were treated in the time of Laud. They, therefore, have no rancour against the government or against their countrymen. It will not be denied that they are far better affected to the state than the followers of Coligni or Vane. But they are not so well treated as the dissenting sects of Christians are now treated in England; and on this account, and, we firmly believe, on this account alone, they have a more exclusive spirit. Till we have carried the experiment farther, we are not entitled to conclude that they cannot be made Englishmen altogether. The statesman who treats them as aliens, and then abuses them for not entertaining all the feelings of natives, is as unreasonable as the tyrant who punished their fathers for not making bricks without straw.

Rulers must not be suffered thus to absolve themselves of their solemn responsibility. It does not lie in their mouths to say that a sect is not patriotic. It is their business to make it patriotic. History and reason clearly indicate the means. The English Jews are, as far as we can see, precisely what our government has made them. They are precisely what any sect, what any class of men, treated as they have been treated, would have been. If all the red-haired people in Europe had, during centuries, been outraged and oppressed, banished from this place, imprisoned in that, deprived of their money, deprived of their teeth, convicted of the most improbable crimes on the feeblest evidence, dragged at horses' tails, hanged, tortured, burned alive, if, when manners became milder, they had still been subject to debasing restrictions and exposed to vulgar insults, locked up in particular streets in some countries, pelted and ducked by the rabble in others, excluded every where from magistracies and honours, what would be the patriotism of gentlemen with red hair? And if, under such circumstances, a proposition were made for admitting red-haired men to office, how striking a speech might an eloquent admirer of our old institutions deliver against so revolutionary a measure! "These men," he might say, "scarcely consider themselves as Englishmen. They think a red-haired Frenchman or a red-haired German more closely connected with them than a man with brown hair born in their own parish. If a foreign sovereign patronises red hair, they love him better than their own native king. They are not Englishmen: they cannot be Englishmen: nature has forbidden it: experience proves it to be impossible. Right to political power they have none; for no man has a right to political power. Let them enjoy personal security; let their property be under the protection of the law. But if they ask for leave to exercise power over a community of which they are only half members, a community the constitution of which is essentially dark-haired, let us answer them in the words of our wise ancestors, *Nolumus leges Angliæ mutari.*

But, it is said, the Scriptures declare that the Jews are to be restored to their own country; and the whole nation looks forward to that restoration. They are, therefore, not so deeply interested as others in the prosperity of England. It is not their home, but merely the place of their sojourn, the house of their bondage. This argument, which first appeared in the Times newspaper, and which has attracted a degree of attention proportioned not so much to its own intrinsic force as to the general talent with which that journal is conducted, belongs to a class of sophisms by which the most hateful persecutions may easily be justified. To charge men with practical consequences which they themselves deny is disingenuous in controversy; it is atrocious in government. The doctrine of predestination, in the opinion of many people, tends to make those who hold it utterly immoral. And certainly it would seem that a man who believes his eternal destiny to be already irrevocably fixed is likely to indulge his passions without restraint and to neglect his religious duties. If he is an heir of wrath, his exertions must be unavailing. If he is preordained to life, they must be superfluous. But would it be wise to punish every man who holds the higher doctrines of Calvinism, as if he had actually committed all those crimes which we know some Antinomians to have committed? Assuredly not. The fact notoriously is that there are many Calvinists as moral in their conduct as any Arminian, and many Arminians as loose as any Calvinist.

It is altogether impossible to reason from the opinions which a man professes to his feelings and his actions; and in fact no person is ever such a fool as to reason thus, except when he wants a pretext for persecuting his neighbours. A Christian is commanded, under the strongest sanctions, to be just in all his dealings. Yet to how many of the twenty-four millions of professing Christians in these islands would any man in his senses lend a thousand pounds without security? A man who should act, for one day, on the supposition that all the people about him were influenced by the religion which they professed, would find himself ruined before night; and no man ever does act on that supposition in any of the ordinary concerns of life, in borrowing, in lending, in buying, or in selling. But when any of our fellow-creatures are to be oppressed, the case is different. Then we represent those motives which we know to be so feeble for good as omnipotent for evil. Then we lay to the charge of our victims all the vices and follies to which their doctrines, however remotely, seem to tend. We forget that the same weakness, the same laxity, the same disposition to prefer the present to the future, which make men worse than a good religion, make them better than a bad one.

It was in this way that our ancestors reasoned, and that some people in our own time still reason, about the Catholics. A Papist believes himself bound to obey the pope. The pope has issued a bull deposing Queen Elizabeth. Therefore every Papist will treat her grace as an usurper. Therefore every Papist is a traitor. Therefore every Papist ought to be hanged, drawn, and quartered. To this logic we owe some of the most hateful laws that ever disgraced our history. Surely the answer lies on the surface. The Church of Rome may have commanded these men to treat the queen as an usurper. But she has commanded them to do many other things which they have never done. She enjoins her priests to observe strict purity. You are always taunting them with their licentiousness. She commands all her followers to fast often, to be charitable to the poor, to take no interest for money, to fight no duels, to see no plays. Do they obey these injunctions? If it be the fact that very few of them strictly observe her precepts, when her precepts are opposed to their passions and interests, may not loyalty, may not humanity, may not the love of ease, may not the fear of death, be sufficient to prevent them from executing those wicked orders which she has issued against the sovereign of England? When we know that many of these people do not care enough for their religion to go without beef on a Friday for it, why should we think that they will run the risk of being racked and hanged for it?

People are now reasoning about the Jews as our fathers reasoned about the Papists. The law which is inscribed on the walls of the synagogues prohibits covetousness. But if we were to say that a Jew mortgagee would not foreclose because God had commanded him not to covet his neighbour's house, every body would think us out of our wits. Yet it passes for an argument to say that a Jew will take no interest in the prosperity of the country in which he lives, that he will not care how bad its laws and police may be, how heavily it may be taxed, how often it may be conquered and given up to spoil, because God has promised that, by some unknown means, and at some undetermined time, perhaps ten thousand years hence, the Jews shall migrate to Palestine. Is not this the most profound ignorance of human nature? Do we not know that what is remote and indefinite affects men far less than what is near and certain? The argument too applies to Christians as strongly as to Jews. The Christian believes as well as the Jew, that at some future period the present order of things will come to an end. Nay, many Christians believe that the Messiah will shortly establish a kingdom on the earth, and reign visibly over all its inhabitants. Whether this doctrine be orthodox or not we shall not here inquire. The number of people who hold it is very much greater than the number of Jews residing in England. Many of those who hold it are distinguished by rank, wealth, and ability. It is preached from pulpits, both of the Scottish and of the English church. Noblemen and members of Parliament have written in defence of it. Now wherein does this doctrine differ, as far as its political tendency is concerned, from the doctrine of the Jews? If a Jew is unfit to legislate for us because he believes that he or his remote descendants will be removed to Palestine, can we safely open the House of Commons to a fifth-monarchy man, who expects that before this generation shall pass away, all the kingdoms of the earth will be swallowed up in one divine empire?

Does a Jew engage less eagerly than a Christian in any competition which the law leaves open to him? Is he less active and regular in his business than his neighbours? Does he furnish his house meanly, because he is a pilgrim and sojourner in the land? Does the expectation of being restored to the country of his fathers make him insensible to the fluctuations of the stock-exchange? Does he, in arranging his private affairs, ever take into the account the chance of his migrating to Palestine? If not, why are we to suppose that feelings which never influence his dealings as a merchant, or his dispositions as a testator, will acquire a boundless influence over him as soon as he becomes a magistrate or a legislator?

There is another argument which we would not willingly treat with levity, and which yet we scarcely know how to treat seriously. Scripture, it is said, is full of terrible denunciations against the Jews. It is foretold that they are to be wanderers. Is it then right to give them a home? It is foretold that they are to be oppressed. Can we with propriety suffer them to be rulers? To admit them to the rights of citizens is manifestly to insult the Divine oracles.

We allow that to falsify a prophecy inspired by Divine Wisdom would be a most atrocious crime. It is, therefore, a happy circumstance for our frail species, that it is a crime which no man can possibly commit. If we admit the Jews to seats in Parliament, we shall, by so doing, prove that the prophecies in question, whatever they may mean, do not mean that the Jews shall be excluded from Parliament.

In fact it is already clear that the prophecies do not bear the meaning put upon them by the respectable persons whom we are now answering. In France and in the United States the Jews are already admitted to all the rights of citizens. A prophecy, therefore, which should mean that the Jews would never, during the course of their wanderings, be admitted to all the rights of citizens in the places of their sojourn, would be a false prophecy. This, therefore, is not the meaning of the prophecies of Scripture.

But we protest altogether against the practice of confounding prophecy with precept, of setting up predictions which are often obscure against a morality which is always clear. If actions are to be considered as just and good merely because they have been predicted, what action was ever more laudable than that crime which our bigots are now, at the end of eighteen centuries, urging us to avenge on the Jews, that crime which made the earth shake and blotted out the sun from heaven? The same reasoning which is now employed to vindicate the disabilities imposed on our Hebrew countrymen will equally vindicate the kiss of Judas and the judgment of Pilate. "The Son of man goeth, as it is written of him; but woe to that man by whom the Son of man is betrayed." And woe to those who in any age or in any country, disobey his benevolent commands under pretence of accomplishing his predictions. If this argument justifies the laws now existing against the Jews, it justifies equally all the cruelties which have ever been committed against them, the sweeping edicts of banishment and confiscation, the dungeon, the rack, and the slow fire. How can we excuse ourselves for leaving property to people who are to "serve their enemies in hunger, and in thirst, and in nakedness, and in want of all things;" for giving protection to the persons of those who are to "fear day and night, and to have none assurance of their life;" for not seizing on the children of a race whose "sons and daughters are to be given unto another people?"

We have not so learned the doctrines of Him who commanded us to love our neighbour as ourselves, and who, when he was called upon to explain what He meant by a neighbour, selected as an example a heretic and an alien. Last year, we remember, it was represented by a pious writer in the John Bull newspaper, and by some other equally fervid Christians, as a monstrous indecency, that the measure for the relief of the Jews should be brought forward in Passion week. One of these humorists ironically recommended that it should be read a second time on Good Friday. We should have had no objection; nor do we believe that the day could be commemorated in a more worthy manner. We know of no day fitter for terminating long hostilities, and repairing cruel wrongs, than the day on which the religion of mercy was founded. We know of no day fitter for blotting out from the statute-book the last traces of intolerance than the day on which the spirit of intolerance produced the foulest of all judicial murders, the day on which the list of the victims of intolerance, that noble list wherein Socrates and More are enrolled, was glorified by a yet greater and holier name.

MOORE'S LIFE OF LORD BYRON.[1]

(*Edinburgh Review*, June 1831.)

WE have read this book with the greatest pleasure. Considered merely as a composition, it deserves to be classed among the best specimens of English prose which our age has produced. It contains, indeed, no single passage equal to two or three which we could select from the Life of Sheridan. But, as a whole, it is immeasurably superior to that work. The style is agreeable, clear, and manly, and when it rises into eloquence, rises without effort or ostentation. Nor is the matter inferior to the manner. It would be difficult to name a book which exhibits more kindness, fairness, and modesty. It has evidently been written, not for the purpose of showing, what, however, it often shows, how well its author can write, but for the purpose of vindicating, as far as truth will permit, the memory of a celebrated man who can no longer vindicate himself. Mr. Moore never thrusts himself between Lord Byron and the public. With the strongest temptations to egotism, he has said no more about himself than the subject absolutely required.

A great part, indeed the greater part, of these volumes, consists of extracts from the Letters and Jour-

[1] *Letters and Journals of Lord Byron; with Notices of his Life.* By THOMAS MOORE, Esq. 2 vols. 4to. London: 1830.

nals of Lord Byron; and it is difficult to speak too highly of the skill which has been shown in the selection and arrangement. We will not say that we have not occasionally remarked in these two large quartos an anecdote which should have been omitted, a letter which should have been suppressed, a name which should have been concealed by asterisks, or asterisks which do not answer the purpose of concealing the name. But it is impossible, on a general survey, to deny that the task has been executed with great judgment and great humanity. When we consider the life which Lord Byron had led, his petulance, his irritability, and his communicativeness, we cannot but admire the dexterity with which Mr. Moore has contrived to exhibit so much of the character and opinions of his friend, with so little pain to the feelings of the living.

The extracts from the journals and correspondence of Lord Byron are in the highest degree valuable, not merely on account of the information which they contain respecting the distinguished man by whom they were written, but on account also of their rare merit as compositions. The Letters, at least those which were sent from Italy, are among the best in our language. They are less affected than those of Pope and Walpole; they have more matter in them than those of Cowper. Knowing that many of them were not written merely for the person to whom they were directed, but were general epistles, meant to be read by a large circle, we expected to find them clever and spirited, but deficient in ease. We looked with vigilance for instances of stiffness in the language and awkwardness in the transitions. We have been agreeably disappointed; and we must confess that, if the epistolary style of Lord Byron was artificial, it was a rare and admirable instance of that highest art which cannot be distinguished from nature.

Of the deep and painful interest which this book excites no abstract can give a just notion. So sad and dark a story is scarcely to be found in any work of fiction; and we are little disposed to envy the moralist who can read it without being softened.

The pretty fable by which the Duchess of Orleans illustrated the character of her son the Regent might, with little change, be applied to Byron. All the fairies, save one, had been bidden to his cradle. All the gossips had been profuse of their gifts. One had bestowed nobility, another genius, a third beauty. The malignant elf who had been uninvited came last, and, unable to reverse what her sisters had done for their favourite, had mixed up a curse with every blessing. In the rank of Lord Byron, in his understanding, in his character, in his very person, there was a strange union of opposite extremes. He was born to all that men covet and admire. But in every one of those eminent advantages which he possessed over others was mingled something of misery and debasement. He was sprung from a house, ancient indeed and noble, but degraded and impoverished by a series of crimes and follies which had attained a scandalous publicity. The kinsman whom he succeeded had died poor, and, but for merciful judges, would have died upon the gallows. The young peer had great intellectual powers; yet there was an unsound part in his mind. He had naturally a generous and feeling heart: but his temper was wayward and irritable. He had a head which statuaries loved to copy, and a foot the deformity of which the beggars in the streets mimicked. Distinguished at once by the strength and by the weakness of his intellect, affectionate yet perverse, a poor lord, and a handsome cripple, he required, if ever man required, the firmest and the most judicious training. But, capriciously as nature had dealt with him, the parent to whom the office of forming his character was intrusted was more capricious still. She passed from paroxysms of rage to paroxysms of tenderness. At one time she stifled him with her caresses: at another time she insulted his deformity. He came into the world; and the world treated him as his mother had treated him, sometimes with fondness, sometimes with cruelty, never with justice. It indulged him without discrimination, and punished him without discrimination. He was truly a spoiled child, not merely the spoiled child of his parent, but the spoiled child of nature, the spoiled child of fortune, the spoiled child of fame, the spoiled child of society. His first poems were received with a contempt which, feeble as they were, they did not absolutely deserve. The poem which he published on his return from his travels was, on the other hand, extolled far above its merit. At twenty-four he found himself on the highest pinnacle of literary fame, with Scott, Wordsworth, Southey, and a crowd of other distinguished writers beneath his feet. There is scarcely an instance in history of so sudden a rise to so dizzy an eminence.

Every thing that could stimulate, and every thing that could gratify the strongest propensities of our nature, the gaze of a hundred drawing-rooms, the acclamations of the whole nation, the applause of applauded men, the love of lovely women, all this world and all the glory of it were at once offered to a youth to whom nature had given violent passions, and to whom education had never taught to control them. He lived as many men live who have no similar excuse to plead for their faults. But his countrymen and his countrywomen would love him and admire him. They were resolved to see in his excesses only the flash and outbreak of that same fiery mind which glowed in his poetry. He attacked religion; yet in religious circles his name was mentioned with fondness, and in many religious publications his works were censured with singular tenderness. He lampooned the Prince Regent; yet he could not alienate the Tories. Every thing, it seemed, was to be forgiven to youth, rank, and genius.

Then came the reaction. Society, capricious in its indignation as it had been capricious in its fondness, flew into a rage with its froward and petted darling. He had been worshipped with an irrational idolatry. He was persecuted with an irrational fury. Much has been written about those unhappy domestic occurrences which decided the fate of his life. Yet nothing is, nothing ever was, positively known to the public, but this, that he quarrelled with his lady, and that she refused to live with him. There have been hints in abundance, and shrugs and shakings of the head, and "Well, well, we know," and "We could an if we would," and "If we list to speak," and "There be that might an they list." But we are not aware that there is before the world substantiated by credible, or even by tangible evidence, a single fact indicating that Lord Byron was more to blame than any other man who is on bad terms with his wife. The professional men whom Lady Byron consulted were undoubtedly of opinion that she ought not to live with her husband. But it is to be remembered that they formed that opinion without hearing both sides. We do not say, we do not mean to insinuate, that Lady Byron was in any respect to blame. We think that those who condemn her on the evidence which is now before the public are as rash as those who condemn her husband. We will not pronounce any judgment, we cannot, even in our own minds, form any judgment, on a transaction which is so imperfectly known to us. It would have been well if, at the time of the separation, all those who knew as little about the matter then as we know about it now had shown that forbearance which, under such circumstances, is but common justice.

We know no spectacle so ridiculous as the British public in one of its periodical fits of morality. In general, elopements, divorces, and family quarrels, pass with little notice. We read the scandal, talk about it for a day, and forget it. But once in six or seven years our virtue becomes outrageous. We cannot suffer the laws of religion and decency to be violated. We must make a stand against vice. We must teach libertines that the English people appreciate the importance of domestic ties. Accordingly some unfortunate man, in no respect more depraved than hundreds whose offences have been treated with lenity, is singled out as an expiatory sacrifice. If he has children, they are to be taken from him. If he has a profession, he is to be driven from it. He is cut by the higher orders, and hissed by the lower. He is, in truth, a sort of whipping-boy, by whose vicarious agonies all the other transgressors of the same class are, it is supposed, sufficiently chastised. We reflect very complacently on our own severity, and compare with great pride the high standard of morals established in England with the Parisian laxity. At length our anger is satiated. Our victim is ruined and heart-broken. And our virtue goes quietly to sleep for seven years more.

It is clear that those vices which destroy domestic happiness ought to be as much as possible repressed. It is equally clear that they cannot be repressed by penal legislation. It is therefore right and desirable that public opinion should be directed against them. But it should be directed against them uniformly, steadily, and temperately, not by sudden fits and starts. There should be one weight and one measure. Decimation is always an objectionable mode of punishment. It is the resource of judges too indolent and hasty to investigate facts and to discriminate nicely between shades of guilt. It is an irrational practice, even when adopted by military tribunals. When adopted by the tribunal of public opinion, it is infinitely more irrational. It is good that a certain portion of disgrace should constantly attend on certain bad actions. But it is not good that the offenders should merely have to stand the risks of a lottery of infamy, that ninety-nine out of every hundred should escape, and that the hundredth, perhaps the most innocent of the hundred, should pay for all. We remember to have seen a mob assembled in Lincoln's Inn to hoot a gentleman against whom the most oppressive proceeding known to the English law was then in progress. He was hooted because he had been an unfaithful husband, as if some of the most popular men of the age, Lord Nelson for example, had not been unfaithful husbands. We remember a still stronger case. Will posterity believe that, in an age in which men whose gallantries were universally known, and had been legally proved, filled some of the highest offices in the state and in the army, presided at the meetings of religious and benevolent institutions, were the delight of every society, and the favourites of the multitude, a crowd of moralists went to the theatre, in order to pelt a poor actor for disturbing the conjugal felicity of an alderman? What there was in the circumstances either of the offender or of the sufferer to vindicate the zeal of the audience, we could never conceive. It has never been supposed that the situation of an actor is peculiarly favourable to the rigid virtues, or that an alderman enjoys any special immunity from injuries such as that which on this occasion roused the anger of the public. But such is the justice of mankind.

In these cases the punishment was excessive; but the offence was known and proved. The case of Lord Byron was harder. True Jedwood justice was dealt out to him. First came the execution, then the investigation, and last of all, or rather not at all, the accusation. The public, without knowing any thing whatever about the transactions in his family, flew into a violent passion with him, and proceeded to invent stories which might justify its anger. Ten or twenty different accounts of the separation, inconsistent with each other, with themselves, and with common sense, circulated at the same time. What evidence there might be for any one of these, the virtuous people who repeated them neither knew nor cared. For in fact these stories were not the causes, but the effects of the public indignation. They resembled those loathsome slanders which Lewis Goldsmith, and other abject libellers of the same class, were in the habit of publishing about Bonaparte; such as that he poisoned a girl with arsenic when he was at the military school, that he hired a grenadier to shoot Dessaix at Marengo, that he filled St. Cloud with all the pollutions of Capreæ. There was a time when anecdotes like these obtained some credence from persons who, hating the French emperor without knowing why, were eager to believe any thing which might justify their hatred. Lord Byron fared in the same way. His countrymen were in a bad humour with him. His writings and his character had lost the charm of novelty. He had been guilty of the offence which, of all offences, is punished most severely; he had been over-praised; he had excited too warm an interest; and the public, with its usual justice, chastised him for its own folly. The attachments of the multitude bear no small resemblance to those of the wanton enchantress in the Arabian Tales, who, when the forty days of her fondness were over, was not content with dismissing her lovers, but condemned them to expiate, in loathsome shapes, and under cruel penances, the crime of having once pleased her too well.

The obloquy which Byron had to endure was such as might well have shaken a more constant mind. The newspapers were filled with lampoons. The theatres shook with execrations. He was excluded from circles where he had lately been the observed of all observers. All those creeping things that riot in the decay of nobler natures hastened to their repast; and they were right; they did after their kind. It is not every day that the savage envy of aspiring dunces is gratified by the agonies of such a spirit, and the degradation of such a name.

The unhappy man left his country for ever. The howl of contumely followed him across the sea, up the Rhine, over the Alps; it gradually waxed fainter; it died away; those who had raised it began to ask each other, what, after all, was the matter about which they had been so clamorous, and wished to invite back the criminal whom they had just chased from them. His poetry became more popular than it had ever been; and his complaints were read with tears by thousands and tens of thousands who had never seen his face.

He had fixed his home on the shores of the Adriatic, in the most picturesque and interesting of cities, beneath the brightest of skies, and by the brightest of seas. Censoriousness was not the vice of the neighbours whom he had chosen. They were a race corrupted by a bad government and a bad religion, long renowned for skill in the arts of voluptuousness, and tolerant of all the caprices of sensuality. From the public opinion of the country of his adoption, he had nothing to dread. With the public opinion of the country of his birth, he was at open war. He plunged into wild and desperate excesses, ennobled by no generous or tender sentiment. From his Venetian harem he sent forth volume after volume, full of eloquence, of wit, of pathos, of ribaldry, and of bitter disdain. His health sank under the effects of his intemperance. His hair turned grey. His food ceased to nourish him. A hectic fever withered him up. It seemed that his body and mind were about to perish together.

From this wretched degradation he was in some measure rescued by a connection, culpable indeed, yet such as, if it were judged by the standard of morality established in the country where he lived, might be called virtuous. But an imagination polluted by vice, a temper embittered by misfortune, and a frame habituated to the fatal excitement of intoxication, prevented him from fully enjoying the happiness which he might have derived from the purest and most tranquil of his many attachments. Midnight draughts of ardent spirits and Rhenish wines had begun to work the ruin of his fine intellect. His verse lost much of the energy and condensation which had distinguished it. But he would not resign, without a struggle, the empire which he had exercised over the men of his generation. A new dream of ambition arose before him; to be the chief of a literary party; to be the great mover of an intellectual revolution; to guide the public mind of England from his Italian retreat, as Voltaire had guided the public mind of France from the villa of Ferney. With this hope, as it should seem, he established the Liberal. But, powerfully as he had affected the imaginations of his contemporaries, he mistook his own powers if he hoped to direct their opinions; and he still more grossly mistook his own disposition, if he thought that he could long act in concert with other men of letters. The plan failed, and failed ignominiously. Angry with himself, angry with his coadjutors, he relinquished it, and turned to another project, the last and noblest of his life.

A nation, once the first among the nations, preeminent in knowledge, preëminent in military glory, the cradle of philosophy, of eloquence, and of the fine arts, had been for ages bowed down under a cruel yoke. All the vices which oppression generates, the abject vices which it generates in those who submit to it, the ferocious vices which it generates in those who struggle against it, had deformed the character of that miserable race. The valour which had won the great battle of human civilisation, which had saved Europe, which had subjugated Asia, lingered only among pirates and robbers. The ingenuity, once so conspicuously displayed in every department of physical and moral science, had been depraved into a timid and servile cunning. On a sudden this degraded people had risen on their oppressors. Discountenanced or betrayed by the surrounding potentates, they had found in themselves something of that which might well supply the place of all foreign assistance, something of the energy of their fathers.

As a man of letters, Lord Byron could not but be interested in the event of this contest. His political opinions, though, like all his opinions, unsettled, leaned strongly towards the side of liberty. He had assisted the Italian insurgents with his purse, and, if their struggle against the Austrian government had been prolonged, would probably have assisted them with his sword. But to Greece he was attached by peculiar ties. He had when young resided in that country. Much of his most splendid and popular poetry had been inspired by its scenery and by its history. Sick of inaction, degraded in his own eyes by his private vices and by his literary failures, pining for untried excitement and honourable distinction, he carried his exhausted body and his wounded spirit to the Grecian camp.

His conduct in his new situation showed so much vigour and good sense as to justify us in believing that, if his life had been prolonged, he might have distinguished himself as a soldier and a politician. But pleasure and sorrow had done the work of seventy years upon his delicate frame. The hand of death was upon him: he knew it; and the only wish which he uttered was that he might die sword in hand.

This was denied to him. Anxiety, exertion, exposure, and those fatal stimulants which had become indispensable to him, soon stretched him on a sick bed, in a strange land, amidst strange faces, without one human being that he loved near him. There, at thirty-six, the most celebrated Englishman of the nineteenth century closed his brilliant and miserable career.

We cannot even now retrace those events without feeling something of what was felt by the nation, when it was first known that the grave had closed over so much sorrow and so much glory; something of what was felt by those who saw the hearse, with its long train of coaches, turn slowly northward, leaving behind it that cemetery which had been consecrated by the dust of so many great poets, but of which the doors were closed against all that remained of Byron. We well remember that on that day, rigid moralists could not refrain from weeping for one so young, so illustrious, so unhappy, gifted with such rare gifts, and tried by such strong temptations. It is unnecessary to make any reflections. The history carries its moral with it. Our age has indeed been fruitful of warnings to the eminent, and of consolations to the obscure. Two men have died within our recollection, who, at a time of life at which many people have hardly completed their education, had raised themselves, each in his own department, to the height of glory. One of them died at Longwood; the other at Missolonghi.

It is always difficult to separate the literary character of a man who lives in our own time from his personal character. It is peculiarly difficult to make this separation in the case of Lord Byron. For it is scarcely too much to say, that Lord Byron never wrote without some reference, direct or indirect, to himself. The interest excited by the events of his life mingles itself in our minds, and probably in the minds of almost all our readers, with the interest which properly belongs to his works. A generation must pass away before it will be possible to form a fair judgment of his books, considered merely as books. At present they are not only books, but relics. We will however venture, though with unfeigned diffidence, to offer some desultory remarks on his poetry.

His lot was cast in the time of a great literary revolution. That poetical dynasty which had dethroned the successors of Shakspeare and Spenser was, in its turn, dethroned by a race who represented themselves as heirs of the ancient line, so long dispossessed by usurpers. The real nature of this revolution has not, we think, been comprehended by the great majority of those who concurred in it.

Wherein especially does the poetry of our times differ from that of the last century? Ninety-nine persons out of a hundred would answer that the poetry of the last century was correct, but cold and mechanical, and that the poetry of our time, though wild and irregular, presented far more vivid images, and excited the passions far more strongly than that of Parnell, of Addison, or of Pope. In the same manner we constantly hear it said, that the poets of the age of Elizabeth had far more genius, but far less correctness, than those of the age of Anne. It seems to be taken for granted, that there is some incompatibility, some antithesis between correctness and creative power. We rather suspect that this notion arises merely from an abuse of words, and that it has been the parent of many of the fallacies which perplex the science of criticism.

What is meant by correctness in poetry? If by correctness be meant the conforming to rules which have their foundation in truth and in the principles of human nature, then correctness is only another name for excellence. If by correctness be meant the conforming to rules purely arbitrary, correctness may be another name for dulness and absurdity.

A writer who describes visible objects falsely and violates the propriety of character, a writer who makes the mountains "nod their drowsy heads" at night, or a dying man take leave of the world with a rant like that of Maximin, may be said in the high and just sense of the phrase, to write incorrectly. He violates the first great law of his art. His imitation is altogether unlike the thing imitated. The four poets who are most eminently free from incorrectness of this description are Homer, Dante, Shakspeare, and Milton. They are, therefore, in one sense, and that the best sense, the most correct of poets.

When it is said that Virgil, though he had less genius than Homer, was a more correct writer, what sense is attached to the word correctness? Is it meant that the story of the Æneid is developed more skilfully than that of the Odyssey? that the Roman describes the face of the external world, or the emotions of the mind, more accurately than the Greek? that the characters of Achates and Mnestheus are more nicely discriminated, and more consistently supported, than those of Achilles, of Nestor, and of Ulysses? The fact incontestably is that, for every violation of the fundamental laws of poetry which can be found in Homer, it would be easy to find twenty in Virgil.

Troilus and Cressida is perhaps of all the plays of Shakspeare that which is commonly considered as the most incorrect. Yet it seems to us infinitely more correct, in the sound sense of the term, than what are called the most correct plays of the most correct dramatists. Compare it, for example, with the Iphigénie of Racine. We are sure that the Greeks of Shakspeare bear a far greater resemblance than the Greeks of Racine to the real Greeks who besieged Troy; and for this reason, that the Greeks of Shakspeare are human beings, and the Greeks of Racine mere names, mere words printed in capitals at the head of paragraphs of declamation. Racine, it is true, would have shuddered at the thought of making a warrior at the siege of Troy quote Aristotle. But of what use is it to avoid a single anachronism, when the whole play is one anachronism, the sentiments and phrases of Versailles in the camp of Aulis?

In the sense in which we are now using the word correctness, we think that Sir Walter Scott, Mr. Wordsworth, Mr. Coleridge, are far more correct poets than those who are commonly extolled as the models of correctness, Pope, for example, and Addison. The single description of a moonlight night in Pope's Iliad contains more inaccuracies than can be found in all the Excursion. There is not a single scene in Cato, in which all that conduces to poetical illusion, all the propriety of character, of language, of situation, is not more grossly violated than in any part of the Lay of the last Minstrel. No man can possibly think that the Romans of Addison resemble the real Romans so closely as the moss-troopers of Scott resemble the real moss-troopers. Wat Tinlinn and William of Deloraine are not, it is true, persons of so much dignity as Cato. But the dignity of the persons represented has as little to do with the correctness of poetry as with the correctness of painting. We prefer a gipsy by Reynolds to his Majesty's head on a sign-post, and a Borderer by Scott to a Senator by Addison.

In what sense, then, is the word correctness used

by those who say, with the author of the Pursuits of Literature, that Pope was the most correct of English Poets, and that next to Pope came the late Mr. Gifford? What is the nature and value of that correctness, the praise of which is denied to Macbeth, to Lear, and to Othello, and given to Hoole's translations and to all the Seatonian prize-poems? We can discover no eternal rule, no rule founded in reason and in the nature of things, which Shakspeare does not observe much more strictly than Pope. But if by correctness be meant the conforming to a narrow legislation which, while lenient to the *mala in se*, multiplies, without the shadow of a reason, the *mala prohibita*, if by correctness be meant a strict attention to certain ceremonious observances, which are no more essential to poetry than etiquette to good government, or than the washings of a Pharisee to devotion, then, assuredly, Pope may be a more correct poet than Shakspeare; and, if the code were a little altered, Colley Cibber might be a more correct poet than Pope. But it may well be doubted whether this kind of correctness be a merit, nay, whether it be not an absolute fault.

It would be amusing to make a digest of the irrational laws which bad critics have framed for the government of poets. First in celebrity and in absurdity stand the dramatic unities of place and time. No human being has ever been able to find any thing that could, even by courtesy, be called an argument for these unities, except that they have been deduced from the general practice of the Greeks. It requires no very profound examination to discover that the Greek dramas, often admirable as compositions, are, as exhibitions of human character and human life, far inferior to the English plays of the age of Elizabeth.

Every scholar knows that the dramatic part of the Athenian tragedies was at first subordinate to the lyrical part. It would, therefore, have been little less than a miracle if the laws of the Athenian stage had been found to suit plays in which there was no chorus. All the greatest masterpieces of the dramatic art have been composed in direct violation of the unities, and could never have been composed if the unities had not been violated. It is clear, for example, that such a character as that of Hamlet could never have been developed within the limits to which Alfieri confined himself. Yet such was the reverence of literary men during the last century for these unities that Johnson who, much to his honour, took the opposite side, was, as he says, "frightened at his own temerity," and "afraid to stand against the authorities which might be produced against him."

There are other rules of the same kind without end. "Shakspeare," says Rymer, "ought not to have made Othello black; for the hero of a tragedy ought always to be white." "Milton," says another critic, "ought not to have taken Adam for his hero; for the hero of an epic poem ought always to be victorious." "Milton," says another, "ought not to have put so many similes into his first book; for the first book of an epic poem ought always to be the most unadorned. There are no similes in the first book of the Iliad." "Milton," says another, "ought not to have placed in an epic poem such lines as these:—

"'While thus I called, and strayed I knew not whither.'"

And why not? The critic is ready with a reason, a lady's reason. "Such lines," says he, "are not, it must be allowed, unpleasing to the ear; but the redundant syllable ought to be confined to the drama, and not admitted into epic poetry." As to the redundant syllable in heroic rhyme on serious subjects, it has been, from the time of Pope downward, proscribed by the general consent of all the correct school. No magazine would have admitted so incorrect a couplet as that of Drayton;

> "As when we lived untouch'd with these disgraces,
> When as our kingdom was our dear embraces."

Another law of heroic rhyme, which, fifty years ago, was considered as fundamental, was, that there should be a pause, a comma at least, at the end of every couplet. It was also provided that there should never be a full stop except at the end of a line. Well do we remember to have heard a most correct judge of poetry revile Mr. Rogers for the incorrectness of that most sweet and graceful passage,

> "Such grief was ours, — it seems but yesterday, —
> When in thy prime, wishing so much to stay,
> 'Twas thine, Maria, thine without a sigh
> At midnight in a sister's arms to die.
> Oh thou wert lovely; lovely was thy frame,
> And pure thy spirit as from heaven it came:
> And when recalled to join the blest above
> Thou diedst a victim to exceeding love,
> Nursing the young to health. In happier hours,
> When idle Fancy wove luxuriant flowers,
> Once in thy mirth thou badst me write on thee;
> And now I write what thou shalt never see."

Sir Roger Newdigate is fairly entitled, we think, to be ranked among the great critics of this school. He made a law that none of the poems written for the prize which he established at Oxford should exceed fifty lines. This law seems to us to have at least as much foundation in reason as any of those which we have mentioned; nay, much more, for the world, we believe, is pretty well agreed in thinking that the shorter a prize-poem is, the better.

We do not see why we should not make a few more rules of the same kind; why we should not enact that the number of scenes in every act shall be three or some multiple of three, that the number of lines in every scene shall be an exact square, that the *dramatis personæ* shall never be more or fewer than sixteen, and that, in heroic rhymes, every thirty-sixth line shall have twelve syllables. If we were to lay down these canons, and to call Pope, Goldsmith, and Addison incorrect writers for not having complied with our whims, we should act precisely as those critics act who find incorrectness in the magnificent imagery and the varied music of Coleridge and Shelley.

The correctness which the last century prized so much resembles the correctness of those pictures of the garden of Eden which we see in old Bibles. We have an exact square, enclosed by the rivers Pison, Gihon, Hiddekel, and Euphrates, each with a convenient bridge in the centre, rectangular beds of flowers, a long canal, neatly bricked and railed in, the tree of knowledge, clipped like one of the limes behind the Tuilleries, standing in the centre of the grand alley, the snake twined round it, the man on the right hand, the woman on the left, and the beasts drawn up in an exact circle round them. In one sense the picture is correct enough. That is to say, the squares are correct; the circles are correct; the man and the woman are in a most correct line with the tree; and the snake forms a most correct spiral.

But if there were a painter so gifted that he could place on the canvass that glorious paradise, seen by the interior eye of him whose outward sight had failed with long watching and labouring for liberty and truth, if there were a painter who could set before us the mazes of the sapphire brook, the lake with its fringe of myrtles, the flowery meadows, the grottoes overhung by vines, the forests shining with Hesperian fruit and with the plumage of gorgeous birds, the massy shade of that nuptial bower which showered down roses on the sleeping lovers, what should we think of a connoisseur who should tell us that this painting, though finer than the absurd picture in the old Bible, was not so correct? Surely we should answer, It is both finer and more correct; and it is finer because it is more correct. It is not made up of correctly drawn diagrams; but it is a correct painting, a worthy representation of that which it is intended to represent.

It is not in the fine arts alone that this false correctness is prized by narrow-minded men, by men who cannot distinguish means from ends, or what is accidental from what is essential. M. Jourdain admired correctness in fencing. "You had no business to hit me then. You must never thrust in quart till you have thrust in tierce." M. Tomès liked correctness in medical practice. "I stand up for Artemius. That he killed his patient is plain enough. But still he acted quite according to rule. A man dead is a man dead; and there is an end of the matter. But if rules are to be broken, there is no saying what consequences may follow." We have heard of an old German officer, who was a great admirer of correctness in military operations. He used to revile Bonaparte for spoiling the science of war, which had been carried to such exquisite perfection by Marshal

Daun. "In my youth we used to march and countermarch all the summer without gaining or losing a square league, and then we went into winter quarters. And now comes an ignorant, hot-headed young man, who flies about from Bologne to Ulm, and from Ulm to the middle of Moravia, and fights battles in December. The whole system of his tactics is monstrously incorrect." The world is of opinion, in spite of critics like these, that the end of fencing is to hit, that the end of medicine is to cure, that the end of war is to conquer, and that those means are the most correct which best accomplish the ends.

And has poetry no end, no eternal and immutable principles? Is poetry, like heraldry, mere matter of arbitrary regulation? The heralds tell us that certain scutcheons and bearings denote certain conditions, and that to put colours on colours, or metals on metals, is false blazonry. If all this were reversed, if every coat of arms in Europe were new fashioned, if it were decreed that or should never be placed but on argent, or argent but on or, that illegitimacy should be denoted by a lozenge, and widowhood by a bend, the new science would be just as good as the old science, because both the new and the old would be good for nothing. The mummery of Portcullis and Rouge Dragon, as it has no other value than that which caprice has assigned to it, may well submit to any laws which caprice may impose on it. But it is not so with that great imitative art, to the power of which all ages, the rudest and the most enlightened, bear witness. Since its first great masterpieces were produced, every thing that is changeable in this world has been changed. Civilisation has been gained, lost, gained again. Religions, and languages, and forms of government, and usages of private life, and modes of thinking, all have undergone a succession of revolutions. Every thing has passed away but the great features of nature, and the heart of man, and the miracles of that art of which it is the office to reflect back the heart of man and the features of nature. Those two strange old poems, the wonder of ninety generations, still retain all their freshness. They still command the veneration of minds enriched by the literature of many nations and ages. They are still, even in wretched translations, the delight of schoolboys. Having survived ten thousand capricious fashions, having seen successive codes of criticism become obsolete, they still remain to us, immortal with the immortality of truth, the same when perused in the study of an English scholar, as when they were first chanted at the banquets of the Ionian princes.

Poetry is, as was said more than two thousand years ago, imitation. It is an art analogous in many respects to the art of painting, sculpture, and acting. The imitations of the painter, the sculptor, and the actor, are indeed, within certain limits, more perfect than those of the poet. The machinery which the poet employs consists merely of words; and words cannot, even when employed by such an artist as Homer or Dante, present to the mind images of visible objects quite so lively and exact as those which we carry away from looking on the works of the brush and the chisel. But, on the other hand, the range of poetry is infinitely wider than that of any other imitative art, or than that of all the other imitative arts together. The sculptor can imitate only form; the painter only form and colour; the actor, until the poet supplies him with words, only form, colour, and motion. Poetry holds the outer world in common with the other arts. The heart of man is the province of poetry, and of poetry alone. The painter, the sculptor, and the actor can exhibit no more of human passion and character than that small portion which overflows into the gesture and the face, always an imperfect, often a deceitful, sign of that which is within. The deeper and more complex parts of human nature can be exhibited by means of words alone. Thus the objects of the imitation of poetry are the whole external and the whole internal universe, the face of nature, the vicissitudes of fortune, man as he is in himself, man as he appears in society, all things which really exist, all things of which we can form an image in our minds by combining together parts of things which really exist. The domain of this imperial art is commensurate with the imaginative faculty.

An art essentially imitative ought not surely to be subjected to rules which tend to make its imitations less perfect than they otherwise would be; and those who obey such rules ought to be called, not correct, but incorrect artists. The true way to judge of the rules by which English poetry was governed during the last century is to look at the effects which they produced.

It was in 1780 that Johnson completed his Lives of the Poets. He tells us in that work that, since the time of Dryden, English poetry had shown no tendency to relapse into its original savageness, that its language had been refined, its numbers tuned, and its sentiments improved. It may perhaps be doubted whether the nation had any great reason to exult in the refinements and improvements which gave it Douglas for Othello, and the Triumphs of Temper for the Fairy Queen.

It was during the thirty years which preceded the

appearance of Johnson's Lives that the diction and versification of English poetry were, in the sense in which the word is commonly used, most correct. Those thirty years are, as respects poetry, the most deplorable part of our literary history. They have indeed bequeathed to us scarcely any poetry which deserves to be remembered. Two or three hundred lines of Gray, twice as many of Goldsmith, a few stanzas of Beattie and Collins, a few strophes of Mason, and a few clever prologues and satires, were the masterpieces of this age of consummate excellence. They may all be printed in one volume, and that volume would be by no means a volume of extraordinary merit. It would contain no poetry of the very highest class, and little which could be placed very high in the second class. The Paradise Regained or Comus would outweigh it all.

At last, when poetry had fallen into such utter decay that Mr. Hayley was thought a great poet, it began to appear that the excess of the evil was about to work the cure. Men became tired of an insipid conformity to a standard which derived no authority from nature or reason. A shallow criticism had taught them to ascribe a superstitious value to the spurious correctness of poetasters. A deeper criticism brought them back to the true correctness of the first great masters. The eternal laws of poetry regained their power, and the temporary fashions which had superseded those laws went after the wig of Lovelace and the hoop of Clarissa.

It was in a cold and barren season that the seeds of that rich harvest which we have reaped were first sown. While poetry was every year becoming more feeble and more mechanical, while the monotonous versification which Pope had introduced, no longer redeemed by his brilliant wit and his compactness of expression, palled on the ear of the public, the great works of the old masters were every day attracting more and more of the admiration which they deserved. The plays of Shakspeare were better acted, better edited, and better known than they had ever been. Our fine ancient ballads were again read with pleasure, and it became a fashion to imitate them. Many of the imitations were altogether contemptible. But they showed that men had at least begun to admire the excellence which they could not rival. A literary revolution was evidently at hand. There was a ferment in the minds of men, a vague craving for something new, a disposition to hail with delight any thing which might at first sight wear the appearance of originality. A reforming age is always fertile of impostors. The same excited state of public feeling which produced the great separation from the see of Rome produced also the excesses of the Anabaptists. The same stir in the public mind of Europe which overthrew the abuses of the old French government, produced the Jacobins and Theophilanthropists. Macpherson and Della Crusca were to the true reformers of English poetry what Knipperdoling was to Luther, or Clootz to Turgot. The success of Chatterton's forgeries and of the far more contemptible forgeries of Ireland showed that people had begun to love the old poetry well, though not wisely. The public was never more disposed to believe stories without evidence, and to admire books without merit. Any thing which could break the dull monotony of the correct school was acceptable.

The forerunner of the great restoration of our literature was Cowper. His literary career began and ended at nearly the same time with that of Alfieri. A comparison between Alfieri and Cowper may, at first sight, appear as strange as that which a loyal Presbyterian minister is said to have made in 1745 between George the Second and Enoch. It may seem that the gentle, shy, melancholy Calvinist, whose spirit had been broken by fagging at school, who had not courage to earn a livelihood by reading the titles of bills in the House of Lords, and whose favourite associates were a blind old lady and an evangelical divine, could have nothing in common with the haughty, ardent, and voluptuous nobleman, the horse-jockey, the libertine, who fought Lord Ligonier in Hyde Park, and robbed the Pretender of his queen. But though the private lives of these remarkable men present scarcely any points of resemblance, their literary lives bear a close analogy to each other. They both found poetry in its lowest state of degradation, feeble, artificial, and altogether nerveless. They both possessed precisely the talents which fitted them for the task of raising it from that deep abasement. They cannot, in strictness, be called great poets. They had not in any very high degree the creative power,

> "The vision and the faculty divine;"

but they had great vigour of thought, great warmth of feeling, and what, in their circumstances, was above all things important, a manliness of taste which approached to roughness. They did not deal in mechanical versification and conventional phrases. They wrote concerning things the thought of which set their hearts on fire; and thus what they wrote, even when it wanted every other grace, had that inimitable grace which sincerity and strong passion impart to the rudest and most homely compositions. Each of them sought for inspiration in a noble and affecting subject, fertile of images which had not yet been hackneyed. Liberty was the muse of Alfieri, Religion was the muse of Cowper. The same truth is found in their lighter pieces. They were not among those who deprecated the severity, or deplored the absence, of an unreal mistress in melodious commonplaces. Instead of raving about imaginary Chloes and Sylvias, Cowper wrote of Mrs. Unwin's knitting-needles. The only love-verses of Alfieri were addressed to one whom he truly and passionately loved. "Tutte le rime amorose che seguono," says he, "tutte sono per essa, e ben sue, e di lei solamente; poichè mai d' altra donna per certo non canterò."

These great men were not free from affectation. But their affectation was directly opposed to the affectation which generally prevailed. Each of them expressed, in strong and bitter language, the contempt which he felt for the effeminate poetasters who were in fashion both in England and in Italy. Cowper complains that

> "Manner is all in all, whate'er is writ,
> The substitute for genius, taste, and wit."

He praised Pope; yet he regretted that Pope had

> "Made poetry a mere mechanic art,
> And every warbler had his tune by heart."

Alfieri speaks with similar scorn of the tragedies of his predecessors. "Mi cadevano dalle mani per la languidezza, trivialità e prolissità dei modi e del verso, senza parlare poi della snervatezza dei pensieri. Or perchè mai questa nostra divina lingua, sì maschia anco, ed energica, e feroce, in bocca di Dante, dovra, ella farsi così sbiadata ed eunuca nel dialogo tragico?"

To men thus sick of the languid manner of their

contemporaries ruggedness seemed a venial fault, oı rather a positive merit. In their hatred of meretricious ornament, and of what Cowper calls "creamy smoothness," they erred on the opposite side. Their style was too austere, their versification too harsh. It is not easy, however, to overrate the service which they rendered to literature. The intrinsic value of their poems is considerable. But the example which they set of mutiny against an absurd system was invaluable. The part which they performed was rather that of Moses than that of Joshua. They opened the house of bondage; but they did not enter the promised land.

During the twenty years which followed the death of Cowper, the revolution in English poetry was fully consummated. None of the writers of this period, not even Sir Walter Scott, contributed so much to the consummation as Lord Byron. Yet Lord Byron contributed to it unwillingly, and with constant self-reproach and shame. All his tastes and inclinations led him to take part with the school of poetry which was going out against the school which was coming in. Of Pope himself he spoke with extravagant admiration. He did not venture directly to say that the little man of Twickenham was a greater poet than Shakspeare or Milton; but he hinted pretty clearly that he thought so. Of his contemporaries, scarcely any had so much of his admiration as Mr. Gifford, who, considered as a poet, was merely Pope, without Pope's wit and fancy, and whose satires are decidedly inferior in vigour and poignancy to the very imperfect juvenile performance of Lord Byron himself. He now and then praised Mr. Wordsworth and Mr. Coleridge, but ungraciously and without cordiality. When he attacked them, he brought his whole soul to the work.

Of the most elaborate of Mr. Wordsworth's poems he could find nothing to say, but that it was "clumsy, and frowsy, and his aversion." Peter Bell excited his spleen to such a degree that he evoked the shades of Pope and Dryden, and demanded of them whether it were possible that such trash could evade contempt? In his heart he thought his own Pilgrimage of Harold inferior to his Imitation of Horace's Art of Poetry, a feeble echo of Pope and Johnson. This insipid performance he repeatedly designed to publish, and was withheld only by the solicitations of his friends. He has distinctly declared his approbation of the unities, the most absurd laws by which genius was ever held in servitude. In one of his works, we think in his letter to Mr. Bowles, he compares the poetry of the eighteenth century to the Parthenon, and that of the nineteenth to a Turkish mosque, and boasts that, though he had assisted his contemporaries in building their grotesque and barbarous edifice, he had never joined them in defacing the remains of a chaster and more graceful architecture. In another letter he compares the change which had recently passed on English poetry to the decay of Latin poetry after the Augustan age. In the time of Pope, he tells his friend, it was all Horace with us. It is all Claudian now.

For the great old masters of the art he had no very enthusiastic veneration. In his letter to Mr. Bowles he uses expressions which clearly indicate that he preferred Pope's Iliad to the original. Mr. Moore confesses that his friend was no very fervent admirer of Shakspeare. Of all the poets of the first class, Lord Byron seems to have admired Dante and Milton most. Yet in the fourth canto of Childe Harold, he places Tasso, a writer not merely inferior to them, but of quite a different order of mind, on at least a footing of equality with them. Mr. Hunt is, we suspect, quite correct in saying that Lord Byron could see little or no merit in Spenser.

But Byron the critic and Byron the poet were two very different men. The effects of the noble writer's theory may indeed often be traced in his practice. But his disposition led him to accommodate himself to the literary taste of the age in which he lived; and his talents would have enabled him to accommodate himself to the taste of any age. Though he said much of his contempt for mankind, and though he boasted that amidst the inconstancy of fortune and of fame he was all-sufficient to himself, his literary career indicated nothing of that lonely and unsocial pride which he affected. We cannot conceive him, like Milton or Wordsworth, defying the criticism of his contemporaries, retorting their scorn, and labouring on a poem in the full assurance that it would be unpopular, and in the full assurance that it would be immortal. He has said, by the mouth of one of his heroes, in speaking of political greatness, that "he must serve who fain would sway;" and this he assigns as a reason for not entering into political life. He did not consider that the sway which he had exercised in literature had been purchased by servitude, by the sacrifice of his own taste to the taste of the public.

He was the creature of his age; and whenever he had lived he would have been the creature of his age. Under Charles the First Byron would have been more quaint than Donne. Under Charles the Second the rants of Byron's rhyming plays would have pitted it, boxed it, and galleried it, with those of any Bays or Bilboa. Under George the First the monotonous smoothness of Byron's versification and the terseness of his expression would have made Pope himself envious.

As it was, he was the man of the last thirteen years of the eighteenth century, and of the first twenty-three years of the nineteenth century. He belonged half to the old, and half to the new school of poetry. His personal taste led him to the former; his thirst of praise to the latter; his talents were equally suited to both. His fame was a common ground on which the zealots of both sides, Gifford, for example, and Shelley, might meet. He was the representative, not of either literary party, but of both at once, and of their conflict, and of the victory by which that conflict was terminated. His poetry fills and measures the whole of the vast interval through which our literature has moved since the time of Johnson. It touches the Essay on Man at the one extremity, and the Excursion at the other.

There are several parallel instances in literary history. Voltaire, for example, was the connecting link between the France of Lewis the Fourteenth and the France of Lewis the Sixteenth, between Racine and Boileau on the one side, and Condorcet and Beaumarchais on the other. He, like Lord Byron, put himself at the head of an intellectual revolution, dreading it all the time, murmuring at it, sneering at it, yet choosing rather to move before his age in any direction than to be left behind and forgotten. Dryden was the connecting link between the literature of the age of James the First, and the literature of the age of Anne. Oromasdes and Arimanes fought for him. Arimanes carried him off. But his heart was to the last with Oromasdes. Lord Byron was, in the same manner, the mediator between two generations, between two hostile poetical sects. Though always sneering at Mr. Wordsworth, he was yet, though perhaps unconsciously, the interpreter between Mr. Wordsworth and the multitude. In the Lyrical Ballads and the Excursion Mr. Wordsworth appeared as the high priest of a worship, of which nature was the idol. No poems have ever indicated a more exquisite perception of the beauty of the outer world, or a more passionate love and reverence for that beauty. Yet they were not popular; and it is not likely that they ever will be popular as the poetry of Sir Walter Scott is popular. The feeling which pervaded them was too deep for general sympathy. Their style was often too mysterious for general comprehension. They made a few esoteric disciples, and many scoffers. Lord Byron founded what may be called an exoteric Lake school; and all the readers of verse in England, we might say in Europe, hastened to sit at his feet. What Mr. Wordsworth had said like a recluse, Lord Byron said like a man of the world, with less profound feeling, but with more perspicuity, energy, and conciseness. We would refer our readers to the last two cantos of Childe Harold and to Manfred, in proof of these observations.

Lord Byron, like Mr. Wordsworth, had nothing dramatic in his genius. He was indeed the reverse of a great dramatist, the very antithesis to a great dramatist. All his characters, Harold looking on the sky, from which his country and the sun are disappearing together, the Giaour, standing apart in the gloom of the side aisle, and casting a haggard scowl from under his long hood at the crucifix and the censer, Conrad leaning on his sword by the watch-tower, Lara smiling on the dancers, Alp gazing steadily on the fatal cloud as it passes before the moon, Manfred wandering among the precipices of Berne, Azzo on the judgment-seat, Ugo at the bar, Lambro frowning on the siesta of his daughter and Juan, Cain presenting his unacceptable offering, are essentially the same. The varieties are varieties merely of age, situation, and outward show. If ever Lord Byron attempted to exhibit men of a different kind, he always made them either insipid or unnatural. Selim is nothing. Bonnivart is nothing. Don Juan, in the first and best cantos, is a feeble copy of the Page in the Marriage of Figaro. Johnson, the man whom Juan meets in the slave-market, is a most striking failure. How differently would Sir Walter Scott have drawn a bluff, fearless Englishman, in such a situation! The portrait would have seemed to walk out of the canvass.

Sardanapalus is more coarsely drawn than any dramatic personage that we can remember. His heroism and his effeminacy, his contempt of death and his dread of a weighty helmet, his kingly resolution to be seen in the foremost ranks, and the anxiety with which he calls for a looking-glass, that he may be seen to advantage, are contrasted, it is true, with all the point of Juvenal. Indeed the hint of the character seems to have been taken from what Juvenal says of Otho:

> "Speculum civilis sarcina belli.
> Nimirum summi ducis est occidere Galbam,
> Et curare cutem summi constantia civis,
> Bedriaci in campo spolium affectare Palati,
> Et pressum in faciem digitis extendere panem."

These are excellent lines in a satire. But it is not the business of the dramatist to exhibit characters in this sharp antithetical way. It is not thus that Shakspeare makes Prince Hal rise from the rake of Eastcheap into the hero of Shrewsbury, and sink again into the rake of Eastcheap. It is not thus that Shakspeare has exhibited the union of effeminacy and valour in Antony. A dramatist cannot commit a greater error than that of following those pointed descriptions of character in which satirists and historians indulge so much. It is by rejecting what is natural that satirists and historians produce these striking characters. Their great object generally is to ascribe to every man as many contradictory qualities as possible: and this is an object easily attained. By judicious selection and judicious exaggeration, the intellect and the disposition of any human being might be described as being made up of nothing but startling contrasts. If the dramatist attempts to create a being answering to one of these descriptions, he fails, because he reverses an imperfect analytical process. He produces, not a man, but a personified epigram. Very eminent writers have fallen into this snare. Ben Jonson has given us a Hermogenes, taken from the lively lines of Horace; but the inconsistency which is so amusing in the satire appears unnatural and disgusts us in the play. Sir Walter Scott has committed a far more glaring error of the same kind in the novel of Peveril. Admiring, as every judicious reader must admire, the keen and vigorous lines in which Dryden satirised the Duke of Buckingham, Sir Walter attempted to make a Duke of Buckingham to suit them, a real living Zimri; and he made, not a man, but the most grotesque of all monsters. A writer who should attempt to introduce into a play or a novel such a Wharton as the Wharton of Pope, or a Lord Hervey answering to Sporus, would fail in the same manner.

But to return to Lord Byron; his women, like his

men, are all of one breed. Haidee is a half-savage and girlish Julia; Julia is a civilised and matronly Haidee. Leila is a wedded Zuleika, Zuleika a virgin Leila. Gulnare and Medora appear to have been intentionally opposed to each other. Yet the difference is a difference of situation only. A slight change of circumstances would, it should seem, have sent Gulnare to the lute of Medora, and armed Medora with the dagger of Gulnare.

It is hardly too much to say, that Lord Byron could exhibit only one man and only one woman, a man proud, moody, cynical, with defiance on his brow, and misery in his heart, a scorner of his kind, implacable in revenge, yet capable of deep and strong affection: a woman all softness and gentleness, loving to caress and to be caressed, but capable of being transformed by passion into a tigress.

Even these two characters, his only two characters, he could not exhibit dramatically. He exhibited them in the manner, not of Shakspeare, but of Clarendon. He analysed them; he made them analyse themselves; but he did not make them show themselves. We are told, for example, in many lines of great force and spirit, that the speech of Lara was bitterly sarcastic, that he talked little of his travels, that if he was much questioned about them, his answers became short, and his brow gloomy. But we have none of Lara's sarcastic speeches or short answers. It is not thus that the great masters of human nature have portrayed human beings. Homer never tells us that Nestor loved to relate long stories about his youth. Shakspeare never tells us that in the mind of Iago every thing that is beautiful and endearing was associated with some filthy and debasing idea.

It is curious to observe the tendency which the dialogue of Lord Byron always has to lose its character of a dialogue, and to become soliloquy. The scenes between Manfred and the Chamois-hunter, between Manfred and the Witch of the Alps, between Manfred and the Abbot, are instances of this tendency. Manfred, after a few unimportant speeches, has all the talk to himself. The other interlocutors are nothing more than good listeners. They drop an occasional question or ejaculation which sets Manfred off again on the inexhaustible topic of his personal feelings. If we examine the fine passages in Lord Byron's dramas, the description of Rome, for example, in Manfred, the description of a Venetian revel in Marino Faliero, the concluding invective which the old doge pronounces against Venice, we shall find that there is nothing dramatic in these speeches, that they derive none of their effect from the character or situation of the speaker, and that they would have been as fine, or finer, if they had been published as fragments of blank verse by Lord Byron. There is scarcely a speech in Shakspeare of which the same could be said. No skilful reader of the plays of Shakspeare can endure to see what are called the fine things taken out, under the name of "Beauties" or of "Elegant Extracts," or to hear any single passage, "To be or not to be," for example, quoted as a sample of the great poet. "To be or not to be" has merit undoubtedly as a composition. It would have merit if put into the mouth of a chorus. But its merit as a composition vanishes when compared with its merit as belonging to Hamlet. It is not too much to say that the great plays of Shakspeare would lose less by being deprived of all the passages which are commonly called the fine passages, than those passages lose by being read separately from the play. This is perhaps the highest praise which can be given to a dramatist.

On the other hand, it may be doubted whether there is, in all Lord Byron's plays, a single remarkable passage which owes any portion of its interest or effect to its connection with the characters or the action. He has written only one scene, as far as we can recollect, which is dramatic even in manner, the scene between Lucifer and Cain. The conference is animated, and each of the interlocutors has a fair share of it. But this scene, when examined, will be found to be a confirmation of our remarks. It is a dialogue only in form. It is a soliloquy in essence. It is in reality a debate carried on within one single unquiet and sceptical mind. The questions and the answers, the objections and the solutions, all belong to the same character.

A writer who showed so little dramatic skill in works professedly dramatic was not likely to write narrative with dramatic effect. Nothing could indeed be more rude and careless than the structure of his narrative poems. He seems to have thought, with the hero of the Rehearsal, that the plot was good for nothing but to bring in fine things. His two longest works, Childe Harold and Don Juan, have no plan whatever. Either of them might have been extended to any length, or cut short at any point. The state in which the Giaour appears illustrates the manner in which all Byron's poems were constructed. They are all, like the Giaour, collections of fragments; and, though there may be no empty spaces marked by asterisks, it is still easy to perceive, by the clumsiness of the joining, where the parts for the sake of which the whole was composed end and begin.

It was in description and meditation that Byron excelled. "Description," as he said in Don Juan, "was his forte." His manner is indeed peculiar, and is almost unequalled; rapid, sketchy, full of vigour; the selection happy; the strokes few and bold. In spite of the reverence which we feel for the genius of Mr. Wordsworth we cannot but think that the minuteness of his descriptions often diminishes their effect, He has accustomed himself to gaze on nature with the eye of a lover, to dwell on every feature, and to mark every change of aspect. Those beauties which strike the most negligent observer, and those which only a close attention discovers, are equally familiar to him and are equally prominent in his poetry. The proverb of old Hesiod, that half is often more than the whole, is eminently applicable to description. The policy of the Dutch who cut down most of the precious trees in the Spice Islands, in order to raise the value of what remained, was a policy which poets would do well to imitate. It was a policy which no poet understood better than Lord Byron. Whatever his faults might be, he was never, while his mind retained its vigour, accused of prolixity.

His descriptions, great as was their intrinsic merit, derived their principal interest from the feeling which always mingled with them. He was himself the beginning, the middle, and the end, of all his own poetry, the hero of every tale, the chief object in every landscape. Harold, Lara, Manfred, and a crowd of other characters, were universally considered merely as loose incognitos of Byron; and there is every reason to believe that he meant them to be so considered. The wonders of the outer world, the Tagus, with the mighty fleets of England riding on its bosom, the towers of

Cintra everhanging the shaggy forest of cork-trees and willows, the glaring marble of Pentelicus, the banks of the Rhine, the glaciers of Clarens, the sweet Lake of Leman, the dell of Egeria with its summer-birds and rustling lizards, the shapeless ruins of Rome overgrown with ivy and wall-flowers, the stars, the sea, the mountains, all were mere accessaries, the background to one dark and melancholy figure.

Never had any writer so vast a command of the whole eloquence of scorn, misanthropy and despair. That Marah was never dry. No art could sweeten, no draughts could exhaust, its perennial waters of bitterness. Never was there such variety in monotony as that of Byron. From maniac laughter to piercing lamentation, there was not a single note of human anguish of which he was not master. Year after year, and month after month, he continued to repeat that to be wretched is the destiny of all; that to be eminently wretched is the destiny of the eminent; that all the desires by which we are cursed lead alike to misery, if they are not gratified, to the misery of disappointment, if they are gratified, to the misery of satiety. His heroes are men who have arrived by different roads at the same goal of despair, who are sick of life, who are at war with society, who are supported in their anguish only by an unconquerable pride resembling that of Prometheus on the rock or of Satan in the burning marl, who can master their agonies by the force of their will, and who, to the last, defy the whole power of earth and heaven. He always described himself as a man of the same kind with his favourite creations, as a man whose heart had been withered, whose capacity for happiness was gone and could not be restored, but whose invincible spirit dared the worst that could befall him here or hereafter.

How much of this morbid feeling sprang from an original disease of the mind, how much from real misfortune, how much from the nervousness of dissipation, how much was fanciful, how much was merely affected, it is impossible for us, and would probably have been impossible for the most intimate friends of Lord Byron, to decide. Whether there ever existed, or can ever exist, a person answering to the description which he gave of himself may be doubted; but that he was not such a person is beyond all doubt. It is ridiculous to imagine that a man whose mind was really imbued with scorn of his fellow-creatures would have published three or four books every year in order to tell them so; or that a man who could say with truth that he neither sought sympathy nor needed it would have admitted all Europe to hear his farewell to his wife, and his blessings on his child. In the second canto of Childe Harold, he tells us that he is insensible to fame and obloquy:

> "Ill may such contest now the spirit move,
> Which heeds nor keen reproof nor partial praise."

Yet we know on the best evidence that, a day or two before he published these lines, he was greatly, indeed childishly, elated by the compliments paid to his maiden speech in the House of Lords.

We are far, however, from thinking that his sadness was altogether feigned. He was naturally a man of great sensibility; he had been ill educated; his feelings had been early exposed to sharp trials; he had been crossed in his boyish love; he had been mortified by the failure of his first literary efforts; he was straitened in pecuniary circumstances; he was unfortunate in his domestic relations; the public treated him with cruel injustice; his health and spirits suffered from his dissipated habits of life; he was, on the whole, an unhappy man. He early discovered that, by parading his unhappiness before the multitude, he produced an immense sensation. The world gave him every encouragement to talk about his mental sufferings. The interest which his first confessions excited induced him to affect much that he did not feel; and the affectation probably reacted on his feelings. How far the character in which he exhibited himself was genuine, and how far theatrical, it would probably have puzzled himself to say.

There can be no doubt that this remarkable man owed the vast influence which he exercised over his contemporaries at least as much to his gloomy egotism as to the real power of his poetry. We never could very clearly understand how it is that egotism, so unpopular in conversation, should be so popular in writing; or how it is that men who affect in their compositions qualities and feelings which they have not, impose so much more easily on their contemporaries than on posterity. The interest which the loves of Petrarch excited in his own time, and the pitying fondness with which half Europe looked upon Rousseau, are well known. To readers of our age, the love of Petrarch seems to have been love of that kind which breaks no hearts, and the sufferings of Rousseau to have deserved laughter rather than pity, to have been partly counterfeited, and partly the consequences of his own perverseness and vanity.

What our grandchildren may think of the character of Lord Byron, as exhibited in his poetry, we will not pretend to guess. It is certain, that the interest which he excited during his life is without a parallel in literary history. The feeling with which young readers of poetry regarded him can be conceived only by those who have experienced it. To people who are unacquainted with real calamity, "nothing is so dainty sweet as lovely melancholy." This faint image of sorrow has in all ages been considered by young gentlemen as an agreeable excitement. Old gentlemen and middle-aged gentlemen have so many real causes of sadness that they are rarely inclined "to be as sad as night only for wantonness." Indeed they want the power almost as much as the inclination. We know very few persons engaged in active life who, even if they were to procure stools to be melancholy upon, and were to sit down with all the premeditation of Master Stephen, would be able to enjoy much of what somebody calls the "ecstasy of woe."

Among that large class of young persons whose reading is almost entirely confined to works of imagination, the popularity of Lord Byron was unbounded. They bought pictures of him; they treasured up the smallest relics of him; they learned his poems by heart, and did their best to write like him, and to look like him. Many of them practised at the glass in the hope of catching the curl of the upper lip, and the scowl of the brow, which appear in some of his portraits. A few discarded their neckcloths in imitation of their great leader. For some years the Minerva press sent forth no novel without a mysterious, unhappy, Lara-like peer. The number of hopeful under-graduates and medical students who became things of dark imaginings, on whom the freshness of the heart ceased to fall like dew, whose passions had consumed themselves to dust, and to whom the relief of tears was denied, passes all calculation. This was not the worst. There was created in the minds of many of these enthusiasts a pernicious and absurd association between intellectual power and moral depravity. From the poetry of Lord Byron they drew a system of ethics, compounded of misanthropy and voluptuousness, a system in which the two great commandments were, to hate your neighbour, and to love your neighbour's wife.

This affectation has passed away; and a few more years will destroy whatever yet remains of that magical potency which once belonged to the name of Byron. To us he is still a man, young, noble, and unhappy. To our children he will be merely a writer; and their impartial judgment will appoint his place among writers, without regard to his rank or to his private history. That his poetry will undergo a severe sifting, that much of what has been admired by his contemporaries will be rejected as worthless, we have little doubt. But we have as little doubt, that, after the closest scrutiny, there will still remain much that can only perish with the English language.

SAMUEL JOHNSON.[1]

(*Edinburgh Review*, September 1831.)

THIS work has greatly disappointed us. Whatever faults we may have been prepared to find in it, we fully expected that it would be a valuable addition to English literature; that it would contain many curious facts, and many judicious remarks; that the style of the notes would be neat, clear, and precise; and that the typographical execution would be, as in new editions of classical works it ought to be, almost faultless. We are sorry to be obliged to say that the merits of Mr. Croker's performance are on a par with those of a certain leg of mutton on which Dr. Johnson dined, while travelling from London to Oxford, and which he, with characteristic energy, pronounced to be "as bad as bad could be, ill fed, ill killed, ill kept, and ill dressed." This edition is ill compiled, ill arranged, ill written, and ill printed.

Nothing in the work has astonished us so much as the ignorance or carelessness of Mr. Croker with respect to facts and dates. Many of his blunders are such as we should be surprised to hear any well edu-

[1] *The Life of Samuel Johnson, LL.D. Including a Journal of a Tour to the Hebrides, by James Boswell, Esq. A new Edition, with numerous Additions and Notes.* By JOHN WILSON CROKER, LL.D. F.R.S. Five volumes 8vo. London: 1831.

cated gentleman commit, even in conversation. The notes absolutely swarm with misstatements into which the editor never would have fallen, if he had taken the slightest pains to investigate the truth of his assertions, or if he had even been well acquainted with the book on which he undertook to comment. We will give a few instances.

Mr. Croker tells us in a note that Derrick, who was master of the ceremonies at Bath, died very poor in 1760.[1] We read on; and, a few pages later, we find Dr. Johnson and Boswell talking of this same Derrick as still living and reigning, as having retrieved his character, as possessing so much power over his subjects at Bath, that his opposition might be fatal to Sheridan's lectures on oratory.[2] And all this is in 1763. The fact is, that Derrick died in 1769.

In one note we read, that Sir Herbert Croft, the author of that pompous and foolish account of Young, which appears among the Lives of the Poets, died in 1805.[3] Another note in the same volume states, that this same Sir Herbert Croft died at Paris, after residing abroad for fifteen years, on the 27th of April 1816.[4]

Mr. Croker informs us, that Sir William Forbes of Pitsligo, the author of the Life of Beattie, died in 1816.[5] A Sir William Forbes undoubtedly died in that year, but not the Sir William Forbes in question, whose death took place in 1806. It is notorious, indeed, that the biographer of Beattie lived just long enough to complete the history of his friend. Eight or nine years before the date which Mr. Croker has assigned for Sir William's death, Sir Walter Scott

[1] I. 394. [2] I. 404. [3] IV. 321
[4] IV. 428. [5] II. 262.

lamented that event in the introduction to the fourth canto of Marmion. Every school-girl knows the lines:

> "Scarce had lamented Forbes paid
> The tribute to his Minstrel's shade;
> The tale of friendship scarce was told,
> Ere the narrator's heart was cold:
> Far may we search before we find
> A heart so manly and so kind!"

In one place, we are told, that Allan Ramsay, the painter, was born in 1709, and died in 1784;[1] in another, that he died in 1784, in the seventy-first year of his age.[2]

In one place, Mr. Croker says, that at the commencement of the intimacy between Dr. Johnson and Mrs. Thrale, in 1765, the lady was twenty-five years old.[3] In other places he says, that Mrs. Thrale's thirty-fifth year coincided with Johnson's seventieth.[4] Johnson was born in 1709. If, therefore, Mrs. Thrale's thirty-fifth year coincided with Johnson's seventieth, she could have been only twenty-one years old in 1765. This is not all. Mr. Croker, in another place, assigns the year 1777 as the date of the complimentary lines which Johnson made on Mrs. Thrale's thirty-fifth birth-day.[5] If this date be correct, Mrs. Thrale must have been born in 1742, and could have been only twenty-three when her acquaintance with Johnson commenced. Mr. Croker therefore gives us three different statements as to her age. Two of the three must be incorrect. We will not decide between them; we will only say, that the reasons which Mr. Croker gives for thinking that Mrs. Thrale was exactly thirty-five years old when Johnson was seventy, appear to us utterly frivolous.

[1] IV. 105. [2] V. 281. [3] I. 510. [4] IV. 271. 322. [5] III. 463.

Again, Mr. Croker informs his readers that "Lord Mansfield survived Johnson full ten years."[1] Lord Mansfield survived Dr. Johnson just eight years and a quarter.

Johnson found in the Library of a French lady, whom he visited during his short visit to Paris, some works which he regarded with great disdain. "I looked," says he, "into the books in the lady's closet, and, in contempt, showed them to Mr. Thrale. Prince Titi, Bibliothèque des Fées, and other books."[2] "The History of Prince Titi," observes Mr. Croker, "was said to be the autobiography of Frederick Prince of Wales, but was probably written by Ralph his secretary." A more absurd note never was penned. The history of Prince Titi, to which Mr. Croker refers, whether written by Prince Frederick or by Ralph, was certainly never published. If Mr. Croker had taken the trouble to read with attention that very passage in Park's Royal and Noble Authors which he cites as his authority, he would have seen that the manuscript was given up to the government. Even if this memoir had been printed, it is not very likely to find its way into a French lady's bookcase. And would any man in his senses speak contemptuously of a French lady, for having in her possession an English work, so curious and interesting as a Life of Prince Frederick, whether written by himself or by a confidential secretary, must have been? The history at which Johnson laughed was a very proper companion to the Bibliothèque des Fées, a fairy tale about good Prince Titi and naughty Prince Violent. Mr. Croker may find it in the Magasin des Enfans, the first French book which the little girls of England read to their governesses.

[1] II. 151. [2] III. 271.

Mr. Croker states that Mr. Henry Bate, who afterwards assumed the name of Dudley, was proprietor of the Morning Herald, and fought a duel with George Robinson Stoney, in consequence of some attacks on Lady Strathmore which appeared in that paper.[1] Now Mr. Bate was then connected, not with the Morning Herald, but with the Morning Post; and the dispute took place before the Morning Herald was in existence. The duel was fought in January, 1777. The Chronicle of the Annual Register for that year contains an account of the transaction, and distinctly states that Mr. Bate was editor of the Morning Post. The Morning Herald, as any person may see by looking at any number of it, was not established till some years after this affair. For this blunder there is, we must acknowledge, some excuse: for it certainly seems almost incredible to a person living in our time that any human being should ever have stooped to fight with a writer in the Morning Post.

"James de Duglas," says Mr. Croker, "was requested by King Robert Bruce, in his last hours, to repair, with his heart to Jerusalem, and humbly to deposit it at the sepulchre of our Lord, which he did in 1329.[2] Now, it is well known that he did no such thing, and for a very sufficient reason, because he was killed by the way. Nor was it in 1329 that he set out. Robert Bruce died in 1329, and the expedition of Douglas took place in the following year, "Quand le printems vint et la saison," says Froissart, in June, 1330, says Lord Hailes, whom Mr. Croker cites as the authority for his statement.

Mr. Croker tells us that the great Marquis of Montrose was beheaded at Edinburgh in 1650.[3] There is not

[1] V. 196. [2] IV. 29. [3] II. 526.

a forward boy at any school in England who does not know that the marquis was hanged. The account of the execution is one of the finest passages in Lord Clarendon's History. We can scarcely suppose that Mr. Croker has never read that passage; and yet we can scarcely suppose that any person who has ever perused so noble and pathetic a story can have utterly forgotten all its most striking circumstances.

"Lord Townshend," says Mr. Croker, "was not secretary of state till 1720."[1] Can Mr. Croker possibly be ignorant that Lord Townshend was made secretary of state at the accession of George I. in 1714, that he continued to be secretary of state till he was displaced by the intrigues of Sunderland and Stanhope at the close of 1716, and that he returned to the office of secretary of state, not in 1720, but in 1721?

Mr. Croker, indeed, is generally unfortunate in his statements respecting the Townshend family. He tells us that Charles Townshend, the chancellor of the exchequer, was "nephew of the prime minister, and son of a peer who was secretary of state, and leader of the House of Lords."[2] Charles Townshend was not nephew, but grandnephew, of the Duke of Newcastle, not son, but grandson, of the Lord Townshend who was secretary of state, and leader of the House of Lords.

"General Burgoyne surrendered at Saratoga," says Mr. Croker, "in March, 1778."[3] General Burgoyne surrendered on the 17th of October, 1777.

"Nothing," says Mr. Croker, "can be more unfounded than the assertion that Byng fell a martyr *to political party*. By a strange coincidence of circumstances, it happened that there was a total change of administration between his condemnation and his death:

[1] III. 52. [2] III. 368. [3] IV. 222.

so that one party presided at his trial, and another at his execution: there can be no stronger proof that he was *not* a political martyr."[1] Now what will our readers think of this writer, when we assure them that this statement, so confidently made, respecting events so notorious, is absolutely untrue? One and the same administration was in office when the court-martial on Byng commenced its sittings, through the whole trial, at the condemnation, and at the execution. In the month of November, 1756, the Duke of Newcastle and Lord Hardwicke resigned; the Duke of Devonshire became first lord of the treasury, and Mr. Pitt, secretary of state. This administration lasted till the month of April, 1757. Byng's court-martial began to sit on the 28th of December, 1756. He was shot on the 14th of March, 1757. There is something at once diverting and provoking in the cool and authoritative manner in which Mr. Croker makes these random assertions. We do not suspect him of intentionally falsifying history. But of this high literary misdemeanour we do without hesitation accuse him, that he has no adequate sense of the obligation which a writer, who professes to relate facts, owes to the public. We accuse him of a negligence and an ignorance analogous to that *crassa negligentia*, and that *crassa ignorantia*, on which the law animadverts in magistrates and surgeons, even when malice and corruption are not imputed. We accuse him of having undertaken a work which, if not performed with strict accuracy, must be very much worse than useless, and of having performed it as if the difference between an accurate and an inaccurate statement was not worth the trouble of looking into the most common book of reference.

[1] I. 298.

But we must proceed. These volumes contain mistakes more gross, if possible, than any that we have yet mentioned. Boswell has recorded some observations made by Johnson on the changes which had taken place in Gibbon's religious opinions. That Gibbon when a lad at Oxford turned Catholic is well known. "It is said," cried Johnson, laughing, "that he has been a Mahommedan." "This sarcasm," says the editor, "probably alludes to the tenderness with which Gibbon's malevolence to Christianity induced him to treat Mahommedanism in his history." Now the sarcasm was uttered in 1776; and that part of the History of the Decline and Fall of the Roman Empire which relates to Mahommedanism was not published till 1788, twelve years after the date of this conversation, and near four years after the death of Johnson.[1]

"It was in the year 1761," says Mr. Croker, "that Goldsmith published his Vicar of Wakefield. This

[1] A defence of this blunder was attempted. That the celebrated chapters in which Gibbon has traced the progress of Mahommedanism were not written in 1776 could not be denied. But it was confidently asserted that his partiality to Mahommedanism appeared in his first volume. This assertion is untrue. No passage which can by any art be construed into the faintest indication of the faintest partiality for Mahommedanism has ever been quoted or ever will be quoted from the first volume of the History of the Decline and Fall of the Roman Empire.

To what then, it has been asked, could Johnson allude? Possibly to some anecdote or some conversation of which all trace is lost. One conjecture may be offered, though with diffidence. Gibbon tells us in his memoirs, that at Oxford he took a fancy for studying Arabic, and was prevented from doing so by the remonstrances of his tutor. Soon after this, the young man fell in with Bossuet's controversial writings, and was speedily converted by them to the Roman Catholic faith. The apostasy of a gentleman commoner would of course be for a time the chief subject of conversation in the common room of Magdalene. His whim about Arabic learning would naturally be mentioned, and would give occasion to some jokes about the probability of his turning Mussulman. If such jokes were made, Johnson, who frequently visited Oxford, was very likely to hear of them.

leads the editor to observe a more serious inaccuracy of Mrs. Piozzi, than Mr. Boswell notices, when he says Johnson left her table to go and sell the Vicar of Wakefield for Goldsmith. Now Dr. Johnson was not acquainted with the Thrales till 1765, four years after the book had been published."[1] Mr. Croker, in reprehending the fancied inaccuracy of Mrs. Thrale, has himself shown a degree of inaccuracy, or, to speak more properly, a degree of ignorance, hardly credible. In the first place, Johnson became acquainted with the Thrales, not in 1765, but in 1764, and during the last weeks of 1764 dined with them every Thursday, as is written in Mrs. Piozzi's anecdotes. In the second place, Goldsmith published the Vicar of Wakefield, not in 1761, but in 1766. Mrs. Thrale does not pretend to remember the precise date of the summons which called Johnson from her table to the help of his friend. She says only that it was near the beginning of her acquaintance with Johnson, and certainly not later than 1766. Her accuracy is therefore completely vindicated. It was probably after one of her Thursday dinners in 1764 that the celebrated scene of the landlady, the sheriff's officer, and the bottle of Madeira, took place.[2]

The very page which contains this monstrous blunder, contains another blunder, if possible, more monstrous still. Sir Joseph Mawbey, a foolish member of Parliament, at whose speeches and whose pig-styes the wits of Brookes's were, fifty years ago, in the habit of laughing most unmercifully, stated, on the authority of Garrick, that Johnson, while sitting in a coffee-house

[1] V. 409.

[2] This paragraph has been altered; and a slight inaccuracy immaterial to the argument, has been removed.

at Oxford, about the time of his doctor's degree, used some contemptuous expressions respecting Home's play and Macpherson's Ossian. "Many men," he said, "many women, and many children, might have written Douglas." Mr. Croker conceives that he has detected an inaccuracy, and glories over poor Sir Joseph in a most characteristic manner. "I have quoted this anecdote solely with the view of showing to how little credit hearsay anecdotes are in general entitled. Here is a story published by Sir Joseph Mawbey, a member of the House of Commons, and a person every way worthy of credit, who says he had it from Garrick. Now mark: Johnson's visit to Oxford, about the time of his doctor's degree, was in 1754, the first time he had been there since he left the university. But Douglas was not acted till 1756, and Ossian not published till 1760. All, therefore, that is new in Sir Joseph Mawbey's story is false."[1] Assuredly we need not go far to find ample proof that a member of the House of Commons may commit a very gross error. Now mark, say we, in the language of Mr. Croker. The fact is, that Johnson took his Master's degree in 1754[2] and his Doctor's degree in 1775.[3] In the spring of 1776,[4] he paid a visit to Oxford, and at this visit a conversation respecting the works of Home and Macpherson might have taken place, and, in all probability, did take place. The only real objection to the story Mr. Croker has missed. Boswell states, apparently on the best authority, that as early at least as the year 1763, Johnson, in conversation with Blair, used the same expressions respecting Ossian, which Sir Joseph represents him as having used respecting Douglas.[5] Sir Joseph, or Garrick, con-

[1] V. 409. [2] I. 262. [3] III. 205. [4] III. 326. [5] I. 405.

founded, we suspect, the two stories. But their error is venial, compared with that of Mr. Croker.

We will not multiply instances of this scandalous inaccuracy. It is clear that a writer who, even when warned by the text on which he is commenting, falls into such mistakes as these, is entitled to no confidence whatever. Mr. Croker has committed an error of five years with respect to the publication of Goldsmith's novel, an error of twelve years with respect to the publication of part of Gibbon's History, an error of twenty-one years with respect to an event in Johnson's life so important as the taking of the doctoral degree. Two of these three errors he has committed, while ostentatiously displaying his own accuracy, and correcting what he represents as the loose assertions of others. How can his readers take on trust his statements concerning the births, marriages, divorces, and deaths of a crowd of people, whose names are scarcely known to this generation? It is not likely that a person who is ignorant of what almost every body knows can know that of which almost every body is ignorant. We did not open this book with any wish to find blemishes in it. We have made no curious researches. The work itself, and a very common knowledge of literary and political history, have enabled us to detect the mistakes which we have pointed out, and many other mistakes of the same kind. We must say, and we say it with regret, that we do not consider the authority of Mr. Croker, unsupported by other evidence, as sufficient to justify any writer who may follow him in relating a single anecdote or in assigning a date to a single event.

Mr. Croker shows almost as much ignorance and heedlessness in his criticisms as in his statements concerning facts. Dr. Johnson said, very reasonably as it appears to us, that some of the satires of Juvenal are too gross for imitation. Mr. Croker, who, by the way, is angry with Johnson for defending Prior's tales against the charge of indecency, resents this aspersion on Juvenal, and indeed refuses to believe that the doctor can have said any thing so absurd. "He probably said — some *passages* of them — for there are none of Juvenal's satires to which the same objection may be made as to one of Horace's, that it is *altogether* gross and licentious.[1] Surely Mr. Croker can never have read the second and ninth satires of Juvenal.

Indeed the decisions of this editor on points of classical learning, though pronounced in a very authoritative tone, are generally such that, if a schoolboy under our care were to utter them, our soul assuredly should not spare for his crying. It is no disgrace to a gentleman who has been engaged during near thirty years in political life that he has forgotten his Greek and Latin. But he becomes justly ridiculous if, when no longer able to construe a plain sentence, he affects to sit in judgment on the most delicate questions of style and metre. From one blunder, a blunder which no good scholar would have made, Mr. Croker was saved, as he informs us, by Sir Robert Peel, who quoted a passage exactly in point from Horace. We heartily wish that Sir Robert, whose classical attainments are well known, had been more frequently consulted. Unhappily he was not always at his friend's elbow; and we have therefore a rich abundance of the strangest errors. Boswell has preserved a poor epigram by Johnson, inscribed "Ad Lauram parituram." Mr. Croker censures the poet for applying the word puella to a lady in

[1] I. 167.

Laura's situation, and for talking of the beauty of Lucina. "Lucina," he says, "was never famed for her beauty."[1] If Sir Robert Peel had seen this note, he probably would have again refuted Mr. Croker's criticisms by an appeal to Horace. In the secular ode, Lucina is used as one of the names of Diana, and the beauty of Diana is extolled by all the most orthodox doctors of the ancient mythology, from Homer in his Odyssey, to Claudian in his Rape of Proserpine. In another ode, Horace describes Diana as the goddess who assists the "laborantes utero puellas." But we are ashamed to detain our readers with this fourth-form learning.

Boswell found, in his tour to the Hebrides, an inscription written by a Scotch minister. It runs thus: "Joannes Macleod, &c., gentis suæ Philarchus, &c., Floræ Macdonald matrimoniali vinculo conjugatus turrem hanc Beganodunensem proævorum habitaculum longe vetustissimum, diu penitus labefactatam, anno æræ vulgaris MDCLXXXVI. instauravit." — "The minister," says Mr. Croker, "seems to have been no contemptible Latinist. Is not Philarchus a very happy term to express the paternal and kindly authority of the head of a clan?"[2] The composition of this eminent Latinist, short as it is, contains several words that are just as much Coptic as Latin, to say nothing of the incorrect structure of the sentence. The word Philarchus, even if it were a happy term expressing a paternal and kindly authority, would prove nothing for the minister's Latin, whatever it might prove for his Greek. But it is clear that the word Philarchus means, not a man who rules by love, but a man who loves rule. The Attic writers of the best age used

[1] I. 133. [2] II. 458.

the word φίλαρχος in the sense which we assign to it. Would Mr. Croker translate φιλόσοφος, a man who acquires wisdom by means of love, or φιλοκερδής, a man who makes money by means of love? In fact, it requires no Bentley or Casaubon to perceive, that Philarchus is merely a false spelling for Phylarchus, the chief of a tribe.

Mr. Croker has favoured us with some Greek of his own. "At the altar," says Dr. Johnson, "I recommended my ϑ φ." "These letters," says the editor, "(which Dr. Strahan seems not to have understood) probably mean ϑνητοι φιλοι, *departed friends*."[1] Johnson was not a first-rate Greek scholar; but he knew more Greek than most boys when they leave school; and no schoolboy could venture to use the word ϑνητοι in the sense which Mr. Croker ascribes to it without imminent danger of a flogging.

Mr. Croker has also given us a specimen of his skill in translating Latin. Johnson wrote a note in which he consulted his friend Dr. Lawrence, on the propriety of losing some blood. The note contains these words: — "Si per te licet, imperatur nuncio Holderum ad me deducere." Johnson should rather have written "imperatum est." But the meaning of the words is perfectly clear. "If you say yes, the messenger has orders to bring Holder to me." Mr. Croker translates the words as follows: "If you consent, pray tell the

[1] IV. 251. An attempt was made to vindicate this blunder by quoting a grossly corrupt passage from the Ἱκέτιδες of Euripides:

> *βᾶϑι καὶ ἀντίασον γονάτων, ἔπι χεῖρα βαλοῦσα,*
> *τέκνων τε ϑνατῶν κομίσαι δέμας.*

The true reading, as every scholar knows, is, *τέκνων τεϑνεώτων κομίσαι δέμας*. Indeed without this emendation it would not be easy to construe the words, even if *ϑνατῶν* could bear the meaning which Mr. Croker assigns to it.

messenger to bring Holder to me."[1] If Mr. Croker is resolved to write on points of classical learning, we would advise him to begin by giving an hour every morning to our old friend Corderius.

Indeed we cannot open any volume of this work in any place, and turn it over for two minutes in any direction, without lighting on a blunder. Johnson, in his Life of Tickell, stated that the poem entitled The Royal Progress, which appears in the last volume of the Spectator, was written on the accession of George I. The word "arrival" was afterwards substituted for "accession." "The reader will observe," says Mr. Croker, "that the Whig term *accession*, which might imply legality, was altered into a statement of the simple fact of King George's *arrival*."[2] Now Johnson, though a bigoted Tory, was not quite such a fool as Mr. Croker here represents him to be. In the Life of Granville, Lord Lansdowne, which stands a very few pages from the Life of Tickell, mention is made of the accession of Anne, and of the accession of George I. The word arrival was used in the Life of Tickell for the simplest of all reasons. It was used because the subject of the poem called The Royal Progress was the arrival of the king, and not his accession, which took place near two months before his arrival.

The editor's want of perspicacity is indeed very amusing. He is perpetually telling us that he cannot understand something in the text which is as plain as language can make it. "Mattaire," said Dr. Johnson, "wrote Latin verses from time to time, and published a set in his old age, which he called *Senilia*, in which he shows so little learning or taste in writing, as to make Carteret a dactyl."[3] Hereupon we have this

[1] V. 17. [2] IV. 425. [3] IV. 335.

note: "The editor does not understand this objection, nor the following observation." The following observation, which Mr. Croker cannot understand, is simply this: "In matters of genealogy," says Johnson, "it is necessary to give the bare names as they are. But in poetry and in prose of any elegance in the writing, they require to have inflection given to them." If Mr. Croker had told Johnson that this was unintelligible, the doctor would probably have replied, as he replied on another occasion, "I have found you a reason, sir; I am not bound to find you an understanding." Every body who knows any thing of Latinity knows that, in genealogical tables, Joannes Baro de Carteret, or Vicecomes de Carteret, may be tolerated, but that in compositions which pretend to elegance, Carteretus, or some other form which admits of inflection, ought to be used.

All our readers have doubtless seen the two distichs of Sir William Jones, respecting the division of the time of a lawyer. One of the distichs is translated from some old Latin lines; the other is original. The former runs thus:

"Six hours to sleep, to law's grave study six,
Four spend in prayer, the rest on nature fix."

"Rather," says Sir William Jones,

"Six hours to law, to soothing slumbers seven,
Ten to the world allot, and all to heaven."

The second couplet puzzles Mr. Croker strangely. "Sir William," says he, "has shortened his day to twenty-three hours, and the general advice of 'all to heaven,' destroys the peculiar appropriation of a certain period to religious exercises."[1] Now, we did

[1] V. 233.

not think that it was in human dulness to miss the meaning of the lines so completely. Sir William distributes twenty-three hours among various employments. One hour is thus left for devotion. The reader expects that the verse will end with "and one to heaven." The whole point of the lines consists in the unexpected substitution of "all" for "one." The conceit is wretched enough; but it is perfectly intelligible, and never, we will venture to say, perplexed man, woman, or child before.

Poor Tom Davies, after failing in business, tried to live by his pen. Johnson called him "an author generated by the corruption of a bookseller." This is a very obvious, and even a commonplace allusion to the famous dogma of the old physiologists. Dryden made a similar allusion to that dogma before Johnson was born. Mr. Croker, however, is unable to understand what the doctor meant. "The expression," he says, "seems not quite clear." And he proceeds to talk about the generation of insects, about bursting into gaudier life, and Heaven knows what.[1]

There is still a stranger instance of the editor's talent for finding out difficulty in what is perfectly plain. "No man," said Johnson, "can now be made a bishop for his learning and piety." "From this too just observation," says Boswell, "there are some eminent exceptions." Mr. Croker is puzzled by Boswell's very natural and simple language. "That a general observation should be pronounced *too just*, by the very person who admits that it is not universally just, is not a little odd."[2]

A very large proportion of the two thousand five hundred notes which the editor boasts of having added

[1] IV. 323.   [2] III. 228.

to those of Boswell and Malone consists of the flattest and poorest reflections, reflections such as the least intelligent reader is quite competent to make for himself, and such as no intelligent reader would think it worth while to utter aloud. They remind us of nothing so much as of those profound and interesting annotations which are penciled by sempstresses and apothecaries' boys on the dog-eared margins of novels borrowed from circulating libraries; "How beautiful!" "Cursed prosy!" "I don't like Sir Reginald Malcolm at all." "I think Pelham is a sad dandy." Mr. Croker is perpetually stopping us in our progress through the most delightful narrative in the language, to observe that really Dr. Johnson was very rude, that he talked more for victory than for truth, that his taste for port wine with capillaire in it was very odd, that Boswell was impertinent, that it was foolish in Mrs. Thrale to marry the music-master; and so forth.

We cannot speak more favourably of the manner in which the notes are written than of the matter of which they consist. We find in every page words used in wrong senses, and constructions which violate the plainest rules of grammar. We have the vulgarism of "mutual friend," for "common friend." We have "fallacy" used as synonymous with "falsehood." We have many such inextricable labyrinths of pronouns as that which follows: "Lord Erskine was fond of this anecdote; he told it to the editor the first time that he had the honour of being in his company." Lastly, we have a plentiful supply of sentences resembling those which we subjoin. "Markland, *who*, with Jortin and Thirlby, Johnson calls three contemporaries of great eminence."[1] "Warburton himself did not feel, as Mr.

[1] IV. 377.

Boswell was disposed to think he did, kindly or gratefully *of Johnson*."[1] "It was *him* that Horace Walpole called a man who never made a bad figure but as an author."[2] One or two of these solecisms should perhaps be attributed to the printer, who has certainly done his best to fill both the text and the notes with all sorts of blunders. In truth, he and the editor have between them made the book so bad, that we do not well see how it could have been worse.

When we turn from the commentary of Mr. Croker to the work of our old friend Boswell, we find it not only worse printed than in any other edition with which we are acquainted, but mangled in the most wanton manner. Much that Boswell inserted in his narrative is, without the shadow of a reason, degraded to the appendix. The editor has also taken upon himself to alter or omit passages which he considers as indecorous. This prudery is quite unintelligible to us. There is nothing immoral in Boswell's book, nothing which tends to inflame the passions. He sometimes uses plain words. But if this be a taint which requires expurgation, it would be desirable to begin by expurgating the morning and evening lessons. The delicate office which Mr. Croker has undertaken he has performed in the most capricious manner. One strong, old-fashioned, English word, familiar to all who read their Bibles, is changed for a softer synonyme in some passages, and suffered to stand unaltered in others. In one place a faint allusion made by Johnson to an indelicate subject, an allusion so faint that, till Mr. Croker's note pointed it out to us, we had never noticed it, and of which we are quite sure that the meaning would never be discovered by any of those

[1] IV. 415. [2] II. 461.

for whose sake books are expurgated, is altogether omitted. In another place, a coarse and stupid jest of Dr. Taylor on the same subject, expressed in the broadest language, almost the only passage, as far as we remember, in all Boswell's book, which we should have been inclined to leave out, is suffered to remain.

We complain, however, much more of the additions than of the omissions. We have half of Mrs. Thrale's book, scraps of Mr. Tyers, scraps of Mr. Murphy, scraps of Mr. Cradock, long prosings of Sir John Hawkins, and connecting observations by Mr. Croker himself, inserted into the midst of Boswell's text. To this practice we most decidedly object. An editor might as well publish Thucydides with extracts from Diodorus interspersed, or incorporate the Lives of Suetonius with the History and Annals of Tacitus. Mr. Croker tells us, indeed, that he has done only what Boswell wished to do, and was prevented from doing by the law of copyright. We doubt this greatly. Boswell has studiously abstained from availing himself of the information given by his rivals, on many occasions on which he might have cited them without subjecting himself to the charge of piracy. Mr. Croker has himself, on one occasion, remarked very justly that Boswell was unwilling to owe any obligation to Hawkins. But, be this as it may, if Boswell had quoted from Sir John and from Mrs. Thrale, he would have been guided by his own taste and judgment in selecting his quotations. On what Boswell quoted he would have commented with perfect freedom ; and the borrowed passages, so selected, and accompanied by such comments, would have become original. They would have dove-tailed into the work. No hitch, no crease, would have been discernible. The whole would appear one and indivisible,

> "Ut per læve severos
> Effundat junctura ungues."

This is not the case with Mr. Croker's insertions. They are not chosen as Boswell would have chosen them. They are not introduced as Boswell would have introduced them. They differ from the quotations scattered through the original Life of Johnson, as a withered bough stuck in the ground differs from a tree skilfully transplanted with all its life about it.

Not only do these anecdotes disfigure Boswell's book; they are themselves disfigured by being inserted in his book. The charm of Mrs. Thrale's little volume is utterly destroyed. The feminine quickness of observation, the feminine softness of heart, the colloquial incorrectness and vivacity of style, the little amusing airs of a half-learned lady, the delightful garrulity, the "dear Doctor Johnson," the "it was so comical," all disappear in Mr. Croker's quotations. The lady ceases to speak in the first person; and her anecdotes, in the process of transfusion, become as flat as Champagne in decanters, or Herodotus in Beloe's version. Sir John Hawkins, it is true, loses nothing; and for the best of reasons. Sir John had nothing to lose.

The course which Mr. Croker ought to have taken is quite clear. He should have reprinted Boswell's narrative precisely as Boswell wrote it; and in the notes or the appendix he should have placed any anecdotes which he might have thought it advisable to quote from other writers. This would have been a much more convenient course for the reader, who has now constantly to keep his eye on the margin in order to see whether he is perusing Boswell, Mrs. Thrale, Murphy, Hawkins, Tyers, Cradock, or Mr. Croker. We greatly doubt whether even the Tour to the Hebrides ought to have been inserted in the midst of the Life. There is one marked distinction between the two works. Most of the Tour was seen by Johnson in manuscript. It does not appear that he ever saw any part of the Life.

We love, we own, to read the great productions of the human mind as they were written. We have this feeling even about scientific treatises; though we know that the sciences are always in a state of progression, and that the alterations made by a modern editor in an old book on any branch of natural or political philosophy are likely to be improvements. Some errors have been detected by writers of this generation in the speculations of Adam Smith. A short cut has been made to much knowledge at which Sir Isaac Newton arrived through arduous and circuitous paths. Yet we still look with peculiar veneration on the Wealth of Nations and on the Principia, and should regret to see either of those great works garbled even by the ablest hands. But in works which owe much of their interest to the character and situation of the writers the case is infinitely stronger. What man of taste and feeling can endure *rifacimenti*, harmonies, abridgments, expurgated editions? Who ever reads a stage-copy of a play when he can procure the original? Who ever cut open Mrs. Siddons's Milton? Who ever got through ten pages of Mr. Gilpin's translation of John Bunyan's Pilgrim into modern English? Who would lose, in the confusion of a Diatessaron, the peculiar charm which belongs to the narrative of the disciple whom Jesus loved? The feeling of a reader who has become intimate with any great original work is that which Adam expressed towards his bride:

> "Should God create another Eve, and I
> Another rib afford, yet loss of thee
> Would never from my heart."

No substitute, however exquisitely formed, will fill the void left by the original. The second beauty may be equal or superior to the first; but still it is not she.

The reasons which Mr. Croker has given for incorporating passages from Sir John Hawkins and Mrs. Thrale with the narrative of Boswell would vindicate the adulteration of half the classical works in the language. If Pepys's Diary and Mrs. Hutchinson's Memoirs had been published a hundred years ago, no human being can doubt that Mr. Hume would have made great use of those books in his History of England. But would it, on that account, be judicious in a writer of our times to publish an edition of Hume's History of England, in which large extracts from Pepys and Mrs. Hutchinson should be incorporated with the original text? Surely not. Hume's history, be its faults what they may, is now one great entire work, the production of one vigorous mind, working on such materials as were within its reach. Additions made by another hand may supply a particular deficiency, but would grievously injure the general effect. With Boswell's book the case is stronger. There is scarcely, in the whole compass of literature, a book which bears interpolation so ill. We know no production of the human mind which has so much of what may be called the race, so much of the peculiar flavour of the soil from which it sprang. The work could never have been written if the writer had not been precisely what he was. His character is displayed in every page, and this display of character gives a delightful interest to many passages which have no other interest.

The Life of Johnson is assuredly a great, a very great work. Homer is not more decidedly the first of heroic poets, Shakspeare is not more decidedly the first of dramatists, Demosthenes is not more decidedly the first of orators, than Boswell is the first of biographers. He has no second. He has distanced all his competitors so decidedly that it is not worth while to place them. Eclipse is first, and the rest nowhere.

We are not sure that there is in the whole history of the human intellect so strange a phænomenon as this book. Many of the greatest men that ever lived have written biography. Boswell was one of the smallest men that ever lived, and he has beaten them all. He was, if we are to give any credit to his own account or to the united testimony of all who knew him, a man of the meanest and feeblest intellect. Johnson described him as a fellow who had missed his only chance of immortality by not having been alive when the Dunciad was written. Beauclerk used his name as a proverbial expression for a bore. He was the laughing-stock of the whole of that brilliant society which has owed to him the greater part of its fame. He was always laying himself at the feet of some eminent man, and begging to be spit upon and trampled upon. He was always earning some ridiculous nickname, and then "binding it as a crown unto him," not merely in metaphor, but literally. He exhibited himself, at the Shakspeare Jubilee, to all the crowd which filled Stratford-on-Avon, with a placard round his hat bearing the inscription of Corsica Boswell. In his Tour, he proclaimed to all the world that at Edinburgh he was known by the appellation of

Paoli Boswell. Servile and impertinent, shallow and pedantic, a bigot and a sot, bloated with family pride, and eternally blustering about the dignity of a born gentleman, yet stooping to be a talebearer, an eavesdropper, a common butt in the taverns of London, so curious to know every body who was talked about, that, Tory and high Churchman as he was, he manœuvred, we have been told, for an introduction to Tom Paine, so vain of the most childish distinctions, that when he had been to court, he drove to the office where his book was printing without changing his clothes, and summoned all the printer's devils to admire his new ruffles and sword; such was this man, and such he was content and proud to be. Every thing which another man would have hidden, every thing the publication of which would have made another man hang himself, was matter of gay and clamorous exultation to his weak and diseased mind. What silly things he said, what bitter retorts he provoked, how at one place he was troubled with evil presentiments which came to nothing, how at another place, on waking from a drunken doze, he read the prayerbook and took a hair of the dog that had bitten him, how he went to see men hanged and came away maudlin, how he added five hundred pounds to the fortune of one of his babies because she was not scared at Johnson's ugly face, how he was frightened out of his wits at sea, and how the sailors quieted him as they would have quieted a child, how tipsy he was at Lady Cork's one evening and how much his merriment annoyed the ladies, how impertinent he was to the Duchess of Argyle and with what stately contempt she put down his impertinence, how Colonel Macleod sneered to his face at his impudent obtrusiveness, how his father and the very wife of his bosom laughed and fretted at his fooleries; all these things he proclaimed to all the world, as if they had been subjects for pride and ostentatious rejoicing. All the caprices of his temper, all the illusions of his vanity, all his hypochondriac whimsies, all his castles in the air, he displayed with a cool self-complacency, a perfect unconsciousness that he was making a fool of himself, to which it is impossible to find a parallel in the whole history of mankind. He has used many people ill; but assuredly he has used nobody so ill as himself.

That such a man should have written one of the best books in the world is strange enough. But this is not all. Many persons who have conducted themselves foolishly in active life, and whose conversation has indicated no superior powers of mind, have left us valuable works. Goldsmith was very justly described by one of his contemporaries as an inspired idiot, and by another as a being

> "Who wrote like an angel, and talked like poor Poll."

La Fontaine was in society a mere simpleton. His blunders would not come in amiss among the stories of Hierocles. But these men attained literary eminence in spite of their weaknesses. Boswell attained it by reason of his weaknesses. [If he had not been a great fool, he would never have been a great writer.] Without all the qualities which made him the jest and the torment of those among whom he lived, without the officiousness, the inquisitiveness, the effrontery, the toad-eating, the insensibility to all reproof, he never could have produced so excellent a book. He was a slave, proud of his servitude, a Paul Pry, convinced that his own curiosity and garrulity were virtues, an unsafe companion who never scrupled to repay the most liberal hospitality by the basest violation of confidence, a man without delicacy, without shame, without sense enough to know when he was hurting the feelings of others or when he was exposing himself to derision; and because he was all this, he has, in an important department of literature, immeasurably surpassed such writers as Tacitus, Clarendon, Alfieri, and his own idol Johnson.

Of the talents which ordinarily raise men to eminence as writers, Boswell had absolutely none. There is not in all his books a single remark of his own on literature, politics, religion, or society, which is not either commonplace or absurd. His dissertations on hereditary gentility, on the slave-trade, and on the entailing of landed estates, may serve as examples. To say that these passages are sophistical would be to pay them an extravagant compliment. They have no pretence to argument, or even to meaning. He has reported innumerable observations made by himself in the course of conversation. Of those observations we do not remember one which is above the intellectual capacity of a boy of fifteen. He has printed many of his own letters, and in these letters he is always ranting or twaddling. Logic, eloquence, wit, taste, all those things which are generally considered as making a book valuable, were utterly wanting to him. He had, indeed, a quick observation and a retentive memory. These qualities, if he had been a man of sense and virtue, would scarcely of themselves have sufficed to make him conspicuous; but, because he was a dunce, a parasite, and a coxcomb, they have made him immortal.

Those parts of his book which, considered abstractedly, are most utterly worthless, are delightful when we read them as illustrations of the character of the writer. Bad in themselves, they are good dramatically, like the nonsense of Justice Shallow, the clipped English of Dr. Cains, or the misplaced consonants of Fluellen. Of all confessors, Boswell is the most candid. Other men who have pretended to lay open their own hearts, Rousseau, for example, and Lord Byron, have evidently written with a constant view to effect, and are to be then most distrusted when they seem to be most sincere. There is scarcely any man who would not rather accuse himself of great crimes and of dark and tempestuous passions than proclaim all his little vanities and wild fancies. It would be easier to find a person who would avow actions like those of Cæsar Borgia or Danton, than one who would publish a daydream like those of Alnaschar and Malvolio. Those weaknesses which most men keep covered up in the most secret places of the mind, not to be disclosed to the eye of friendship or of love, were precisely the weaknesses which Boswell paraded before all the world. He was perfectly frank, because the weakness of his understanding and the tumult of his spirits prevented him from knowing when he made himself ridiculous. His book resembles nothing so much as the conversation of the inmates of the Palace of Truth.

His fame is great; and it will, we have no doubt, be lasting; but it is fame of a peculiar kind, and indeed marvellously resembles infamy. We remember no other case in which the world has made so great a distinction between a book and its author. In general, the book and the author are considered as one. To admire the book is to admire the author. The case of Boswell is an exception, we think the only exception, to this rule. His work is universally allowed to be interesting, instructive, eminently original: yet it has brought him nothing but contempt. All the world reads it: all the world delights in it: yet we do not remember ever to have read or ever to have heard any expression of respect and admiration for the man to whom we owe so much instruction and amusement. While edition after edition of his book was coming forth, his son, as Mr. Croker tells us, was ashamed of it, and hated to hear it mentioned. This feeling was natural and reasonable. Sir Alexander saw that, in proportion to the celebrity of the work, was the degradation of the author. The very editors of this unfortunate gentleman's books have forgotten their allegiance, and, like those Puritan casuists who took arms by the authority of the king against his person, have attacked the writer while doing homage to the writings. Mr. Croker, for example, has published two thousand five hundred notes on the life of Johnson, and yet scarcely ever mentions the biographer whose performance he has taken such pains to illustrate without some expression of contempt.

An ill-natured man Boswell certainly was not. Yet the malignity of the most malignant satirist could scarcely cut deeper than his thoughtless loquacity. Having himself no sensibility to derision and contempt, he took it for granted that all others were equally callous. He was not ashamed to exhibit himself to the whole world as a common spy, a common tattler, a humble companion without the excuse of poverty, and to tell a hundred stories of his own pertness and folly, and of the insults which his pertness and folly brought upon him. It was natural that he should show little discretion in cases in which the feelings or the honour of others might be concerned. No man, surely, ever published such stories respecting persons whom he professed to love and revere. He would infallibly have made his hero as contemptible as he has made himself, had not his hero really possessed some moral and intellectual qualities of a very high order. The best proof that Johnson was really an extraordinary man is that his character, instead of being degraded, has, on the whole, been decidedly raised by a work in which all his vices and weaknesses are exposed more unsparingly than they ever were exposed by Churchill or by Kenrick.

Johnson grown old, Johnson in the fulness of his fame and in the enjoyment of a competent fortune, is better known to us than any other man in history. Every thing about him, his coat, his wig, his figure, his face, his scrofula, his St. Vitus's dance, his rolling walk, his blinking eye, the outward signs which too clearly marked his approbation of his dinner, his insatiable appetite for fish-sauce and veal-pie with plums, his inextinguishable thirst for tea, his trick of touching the posts as he walked, his mysterious practice of treasuring up scraps of orange-peel, his morning slumbers, his midnight disputations, his contortions, his mutterings, his gruntings, his puffings, his vigorous, acute, and ready eloquence, his sarcastic wit, his vehemence, his insolence, his fits of tempestuous rage, his queer inmates, old Mr. Levett and blind Mrs. Williams, the cat Hodge and the negro Frank, all are as familiar to us as the objects by which we have been surrounded from childhood. But we have no minute information respecting those years of Johnson's life during which his character and his manners became immutably fixed. We know him, not as he was known to the men of his own generation, but as he was known to men whose father he might have been. That celebrated club of which he was the most distinguished member contained few persons who could remember a time when his fame was not fully established and his habits completely formed. He had made himself a name in literature while Reynolds and the Wartons were still boys. He was about twenty years older than Burke, Goldsmith, and Gerard Hamilton, about thirty years older than Gibbon, Beauclerk, and Langton, and about forty years older than Lord Stowell, Sir William Jones, and Windham. Boswell and Mrs. Thrale, the two writers from whom we derive most of our knowledge respecting him, never saw him till long after he was fifty years old, till most of his great works had become classical, and till the pension bestowed on him by the Crown had placed him above poverty. Of those eminent men who were his most intimate associates towards the close of his life, the only one, as far as we remember, who knew him during the first ten or twelve years of his residence in the capital, was David Garrick; and it does not appear that, during those years, David Garrick saw much of his fellow-townsman.

Johnson came up to London precisely at the time when the condition of a man of letters was most miserable and degraded. It was a dark night between two sunny days. The age of patronage had passed away. The age of general curiosity and intelligence had not arrived. The number of readers is at present so great that a popular author may subsist in comfort and opulence on the profits of his works. In the reigns of William the Third, of Anne, and of George the First, even such men as Congreve and Addison would scarcely have been able to live like gentlemen by the mere sale of their writings. But the deficiency of the natural demand for literature was, at the close of the seventeenth and at the beginning of the eighteenth century, more than made up by artificial encouragement, by a vast system of bounties and premiums. There was, perhaps, never a time at which the rewards of literary merit were so splendid, at which men who could write well found such easy admittance into the most distinguished society, and to the highest honours of the state. The chiefs of both the great parties into which the kingdom was divided patronised literature with emulous munificence. Congreve, when he had scarcely attained his majority, was rewarded for his first comedy with places which made him independent for life. Smith, though his Hippolytus and Phædra failed, would have been consoled with three hundred a year but for his own folly. Rowe was not only Poet Laureate, but also land-surveyor of the customs in the port of London, clerk of the council to the Prince of Wales, and secretary of the Presentations to the Lord Chancellor. Hughes was secretary to the Commissions of the Peace. Ambrose Philips was judge of the Prerogative Court in Ireland. Locke was Commissioner of Appeals and of the Board of Trade. Newton was Master of the Mint. Stepney and Prior were employed in embassies of high dignity and importance. Gay, who commenced life as apprentice to a silk mercer, became a secretary of legation at five-and-twenty. It was to a poem on the Death of Charles the Second, and to the City and Country Mouse, that Montague owed his introduction into public life, his earldom, his garter, and his Auditorship of the Exchequer. Swift, but for the unconquerable prejudice of the queen, would have been a bishop. Oxford, with his white staff in his hand, passed through the crowd of his suitors to welcome Parnell, when that ingenious writer deserted the Whigs. Steele was a commissioner of stamps and a member of Parliament. Arthur Mainwaring was a commissioner of the customs, and auditor of the imprest. Tickell was secretary to the Lords Justices of Ireland. Addison was secretary of state.

This liberal patronage was brought into fashion, as it seems, by the magnificent Dorset, almost the only noble versifier in the court of Charles the Second who possessed talents for composition which were independent of the aid of a coronet. Montague owed his elevation to the favour of Dorset, and imitated through the whole course of his life the liberality to which he was himself so greatly indebted. The Tory leaders, Harley and Bolingbroke in particular, vied with the chiefs of the Whig party in zeal for the encouragement of letters. But soon after the accession of the house of Hanover a change took place. The supreme power passed to a man who cared little for poetry or eloquence. The importance of the House of Commons was constantly on the increase. The government was under the necessity of bartering for Parliamentary support much of that patronage which had been employed in fostering literary merit; and Walpole was by no means inclined to divert any part of the fund of corruption to purposes which he considered as idle. He had eminent talents for government and for debate. But he had paid little attention to books, and felt little respect for authors. One of the coarse jokes of his friend, Sir Charles Hanbury Williams, was far more pleasing to him than Thomson's Seasons or Richardson's Pamela. He had observed that some of the distinguished writers whom the favour of Halifax had turned into statesmen had been mere encumbrances to their party, dawdlers in office, and mutes in Parliament. During the whole course of his administration, therefore, he scarcely befriended a single man of genius. The best writers of the age gave all their support to the opposition, and contributed to excite that discontent which, after plunging the nation into a foolish and unjust war, overthrew the minister to make room for men less able and equally immoral. The opposition could reward its eulogists with little more than promises and caresses. St. James's would give nothing: Leicester house had nothing to give.

Thus, at the time when Johnson commenced his literary career, a writer had little to hope from the patronage of powerful individuals. The patronage of the public did not yet furnish the means of comfortable subsistence. The prices paid by booksellers to authors were so low that a man of considerable talents and unremitting industry could do little more than provide for the day which was passing over him. The lean kine had eaten up the fat kine. The thin and withered ears had devoured the good ears. The season of rich harvests was over, and the period of famine had begun. All that is squalid and miserable might now be summed up in the word Poet. That word denoted a creature dressed like a scarecrow, familiar with compters and spunging-houses, and perfectly qualified to decide on the comparative merits of the Common Side in the King's Bench prison and of Mount Scoundrel in the Fleet. Even the poorest pitied him; and they well might pity him. For if their condition was equally abject, their aspirings were not equally high, nor their sense of insult equally acute. To lodge in a garret up four pair of stairs, to dine in a cellar among footmen out of place, to translate ten hours a day for the wages of a ditcher, to be hunted by bailiffs from one haunt of beggary and pestilence to another, from Grub Street to St. George's Fields, and from St. George's Fields to the alleys behind St. Martin's church, to sleep on a bulk in June and amidst the ashes of a glass-house in December, to die in an hospital and to be buried in a parish vault, was the fate of more than one writer who, if he had lived thirty years earlier, would have been admitted to the sittings of the Kitcat or the Scriblerus club, would have sat in Parliament, and would have been entrusted with embassies to the High Allies; who, if he had lived in our time, would have found encouragement scarcely less munificent in Albemarle Street or in Paternoster Row.

As every climate has its peculiar diseases, so every walk of life has its peculiar temptations. The literary character, assuredly, has always had its share of faults, vanity, jealousy, morbid sensibility. To these faults were now superadded the faults which are commonly found in men whose livelihood is precarious, and whose principles are exposed to the trial of severe distress. All the vices of the gambler and of the beggar were blended with those of the author. The prizes in the wretched lottery of book-making were scarcely less ruinous than the blanks. If good fortune came, it came in such a manner that it was almost certain to be abused. After months of starvation and despair, a full third night or a well-received dedication filled the pocket of the lean, ragged, unwashed poet with guineas. He hastened to enjoy those luxuries with the images of which his mind had been haunted while he was sleeping amidst the cinders and eating potatoes at the Irish ordinary in Shoe Lane. A week of taverns soon qualified him for another year of night-cellars. Such was the life of Savage, of Boyse, and of a crowd of others. Sometimes blazing in gold-laced hats and waistcoats; sometimes lying in bed because their coats had gone to pieces, or wearing paper cravats because their linen was in pawn; sometimes drinking Champagne and Tokay with Betty Careless; sometimes standing at the window of an eating-house in Porridge island, to snuff up the scent of what they could not afford to taste; they knew luxury; they knew beggary; but they never knew comfort. These men were irreclaimable. They looked on a regular and frugal life with the same aversion which an old gipsy or a Mohawk hunter feels for a stationary abode, and for the restraints and securities of civilised communities. They were as untameable, as much wedded to their desolate freedom, as the wild ass. They could no more be broken into the offices of social man than the unicorn could be trained to serve and abide by the crib. It was well if they did not, like beasts of a still fiercer race, tear the hands which ministered to their necessities. To assist them was impossible; and the most benevolent of mankind at length became weary of giving relief which was dissipated with the wildest profusion as soon as it had been received. If a sum was bestowed on the wretched adventurer, such as, properly husbanded, might have supplied him for six months, it was instantly spent in strange freaks of sensuality, and, before forty-eight hours had elapsed, the poet was again pestering all his acquaintance for twopence to get a plate of shin of beef at a subterraneous cook-shop. If his friends gave him an asylum in their houses, those houses were forthwith turned into bagnios and taverns. All order was destroyed; all business was suspended. The most good-natured host began to repent of his eagerness to serve a man of genius in distress when he heard his guest roaring for fresh punch at five o'clock in the morning.

A few eminent writers were more fortunate. Pope had been raised above poverty by the active patronage which, in his youth, both the great political parties had extended to his Homer. Young had received the only pension ever bestowed, to the best of our recollection, by Sir Robert Walpole, as the reward of mere literary merit. One or two of the many poets who attached themselves to the opposition, Thomson in particular and Mallet, obtained, after much severe suffering, the means of subsistence from their political friends. Richardson, like a man of sense, kept his shop; and his shop kept him, which his novels, admirable as they are, would scarcely have done. But nothing could be more deplorable than the state even of the ablest men, who at that time depended for subsistence on their writings. Johnson, Collins, Fielding, and Thomson, were certainly four of the most distinguished persons that England produced during the eighteenth century. It is well known that they were all four arrested for debt.

Into calamities and difficulties such as these Johnson plunged in his twenty-eighth year. From that time till he was three or four and fifty, we have little information respecting him; little, we mean, compared with the full and accurate information which we possess respecting his proceedings and habits towards the close of his life. He emerged at length from cock-lofts and sixpenny ordinaries into the society of the polished and the opulent. His fame was established. A pension sufficient for his wants had been conferred on him: and he came forth to astonish a generation with which he had almost as little in common as with Frenchmen or Spaniards.

In his early years he had occasionally seen the great; but he had seen them as a beggar. He now came among them as a companion. The demand for amusement and instruction had, during the course of twenty years, been gradually increasing. The price of literary labour had risen; and those rising men of letters with whom Johnson was henceforth to associate were for the most part persons widely different from those who had walked about with him all night in the streets for want of a lodging. Burke, Robertson, the Wartons, Gray, Mason, Gibbon, Adam Smith, Beattie, Sir William Jones, Goldsmith, and Churchill, were the most distinguished writers of what may be called the second generation of the Johnsonian age. Of these men Churchill was the only one in whom we can trace the stronger lineaments of that character which, when Johnson first came up to London, was common among authors. Of the rest, scarcely any had felt the pressure of severe poverty. Almost all had been early admitted into the most respectable society on an equal footing. They were men of quite a different species from the dependents of Curll and Osborne.

Johnson came among them the solitary specimen of a past age, the last survivor of the genuine race of Grub Street hacks; the last of that generation of authors whose abject misery and whose dissolute manners had furnished inexhaustible matter to the satirical genius of Pope. From nature, he had received an uncouth figure, a diseased constitution, and an irritable temper. The manner in which the earlier years of his manhood had been passed had given to his demeanour, and even to his moral character, some peculiarities appalling to the civilised beings who were the companions of his old age. The perverse irregularity of his hours, the slovenliness of his person, his fits of strenuous exertion, interrupted by long intervals of sluggishness, his strange abstinence, and his equally strange voracity, his active benevolence, contrasted with the constant rudeness and the occasional ferocity of his manners in society, made him, in the opinion of those with whom he lived during the last twenty years of his life, a complete original. An original he was, undoubtedly, in some respects. But if we possessed full information concerning those who shared his early hardships, we should probably find that what we call his singularities of manner were, for the most part, failings which he had in common with the class to which he belonged. He ate at Streatham Park as he had been used to eat behind the screen at St. John's Gate, when he was ashamed to show his ragged clothes. He ate as it was natural that a man should eat, who, during a great part of his life, had passed the morning in doubt whether he should have food for the afternoon. The habits of his early life had accustomed him to bear privation with fortitude, but not to taste pleasure with moderation. He could fast; but, when he did not fast, he tore his dinner like a famished wolf, with the veins swelling on his forehead, and the perspiration running down his cheeks. He scarcely ever took wine. But when he drank it, he drank it greedily and in large tumblers. These were, in fact, mitigated symptoms of that same moral disease which raged with such deadly malignity in his friends Savage and Boyse. The roughness and violence which he showed in society were to be expected from a man whose temper, not naturally gentle, had been long tried by the bitterest calamities, by the want of meat, of fire, and of clothes, by the importunity of creditors, by the insolence of booksellers, by the derision of fools, by the insincerity of patrons, by that bread which is the bitterest of all food, by those stairs which are the most toilsome of all paths, by that deferred hope which makes the heart sick. Through all these things the ill-dressed, coarse, ungainly pedant had struggled manfully up to eminence and command. It was natural that, in the exercise of his power, he should be "eo immitior, quia toleraverat," that, though his heart was undoubtedly generous and humane, his demeanour in society should be harsh and despotic. For severe distress he had sympathy, and not only sympathy, but munificent relief. But for the suffering which a harsh world inflicts upon a delicate mind he had no pity; for it was a kind of suffering which he could scarcely conceive. He would carry home on his shoulders a sick and starving girl from the streets. He turned his house into a place of refuge for a crowd of wretched old creatures who could find no other asylum; nor could all their peevishness and ingratitude weary out his benevolence. But the pangs of wounded vanity seemed to him ridiculous; and he scarcely felt sufficient compassion even for the pangs of wounded affection. He had seen and felt so much of sharp misery, that he was not affected by paltry vexations; and he seemed to think that every body ought to be as much hardened to those vexations as himself. He was angry with Boswell for complaining of a headache, with Mrs. Thrale for grumbling about the dust on the road, or the smell of the kitchen. These were, in his phrase, "foppish lamentations," which people ought to be ashamed to utter in a world so full of sin and sorrow. Goldsmith crying because the Good-natured

Man had failed, inspired him with no pity. Though his own health was not good, he detested and despised valetudinarians. Pecuniary losses, unless they reduced the loser absolutely to beggary, moved him very little. People whose hearts had been softened by prosperity might weep, he said, for such events; but all that could be expected of a plain man was not to laugh. He was not much moved even by the spectacle of Lady Tavistock dying of a broken heart for the loss of her lord. Such grief he considered as a luxury reserved for the idle and the wealthy. A washerwoman, left a widow with nine small children, would not have sobbed herself to death.

A person who troubled himself so little about small or sentimental grievances was not likely to be very attentive to the feelings of others in the ordinary intercourse of society. He could not understand how a sarcasm or a reprimand could make any man really unhappy. "My dear doctor," said he to Goldsmith, "what harm does it do to a man to call him Holofernes?" "Pooh, ma'am," he exclaimed to Mrs. Carter, "who is the worse for being talked of uncharitably?" Politeness has been well defined as benevolence in small things. Johnson was impolite, not because he wanted benevolence, but because small things appeared smaller to him than to people who had never known what it was to live for fourpence halfpenny a day.

The characteristic peculiarity of his intellect was the union of great powers with low prejudices. If we judged of him by the best parts of his mind, we should place him almost as high as he was placed by the idolatry of Boswell; if by the worst parts of his mind, we should place him even below Boswell himself. Where he was not under the influence of some strange scruple, or some domineering passion, which prevented him from boldly and fairly investigating a subject, he was a wary and acute reasoner, a little too much inclined to scepticism, and a little too fond of paradox. No man was less likely to be imposed upon by fallacies in argument or by exaggerated statements of fact. But if, while he was beating down sophisms and exposing false testimony, some childish prejudices, such as would excite laughter in a well managed nursery, came across him, he was smitten as if by enchantment. His mind dwindled away under the spell from gigantic elevation to dwarfish littleness. Those who had lately been admiring its amplitude and its force were now as much astonished at its strange narrowness and feebleness as the fisherman in the Arabian tale, when he saw the Genie, whose stature had overshadowed the whole sea-coast, and whose might seemed equal to a contest with armies, contract himself to the dimensions of his small prison, and lie there the helpless slave of the charm of Solomon.

Johnson was in the habit of sifting with extreme severity the evidence for all stories which were merely odd. But when they were not only odd but miraculous, his severity relaxed. He began to be credulous precisely at the point where the most credulous people begin to be sceptical. It is curious to observe, both in his writings and in his conversation, the contrast between the disdainful manner in which he rejects unauthenticated anecdotes, even when they are consistent with the general laws of nature, and the respectful manner in which he mentions the wildest stories relating to the invisible world. A man who told him of a water-spout or a meteoric stone generally had the lie direct given him for his pains. A man who told him of a prediction or a dream wonderfully accomplished was sure of a courteous hearing. "Johnson," observed Hogarth, "like King David, says in his haste that all men are liars." "His incredulity," says Mrs. Thrale, "amounted almost to disease." She tells us how he browbeat a gentleman, who gave him an account of a hurricane in the West Indies, and a poor quaker who related some strange circumstance about the red-hot balls fired at the siege of Gibraltar. "It is not so. It cannot be true. Don't tell that story again. You cannot think how poor a figure you make in telling it." He once said, half jestingly we suppose, that for six months he refused to credit the fact of the earthquake at Lisbon, and that he still believed the extent of the calamity to be greatly exaggerated. Yet he related with a grave face how old Mr. Cave of St. John's Gate saw a ghost, and how this ghost was something of a shadowy being. He went himself on a ghost-hunt to Cock Lane, and was angry with John Wesley for not following up another scent of the same kind with proper spirit and perseverance. He rejects the Celtic genealogies and poems without the least hesitation; yet he declares himself willing to believe the stories of the second sight. If he had examined the claims of the Highland seers with half the severity with which he sifted the evidence for the genuineness of Fingal, he would, we suspect, have come away from Scotland with a mind fully made up. In his Lives of the Poets, we find that he is unwilling to give credit to the accounts of Lord Roscommon's early proficiency in his studies; but he tells with great solemnity an absurd romance about some intelligence preternaturally impressed on the mind of that nobleman. He avows himself to be in great doubt about the truth of the story, and ends by warning his readers not wholly to slight such impressions.

Many of his sentiments on religious subjects are worthy of a liberal and enlarged mind. He could discern clearly enough the folly and meanness of all bigotry except his own. When he spoke of the scruples of the Puritans, he spoke like a person who had really obtained an insight into the divine philosophy of the New Testament, and who considered Christianity as a noble scheme of government, tending to promote the happiness and to elevate the moral nature of man. The horror which the sectaries felt for cards, Christmas ale, plum-porridge, mince-pies, and dancing bears, excited his contempt. To the arguments urged by some very worthy people against showy dress he replied with admirable sense and spirit, "Let us not be found, when our Master calls us, stripping the lace off our waistcoats, but the spirit of contention from our souls and tongues. Alas! sir, a man who cannot get to heaven in a green coat will not find his way thither the sooner in a grey one." Yet he was himself under the tyranny of scruples as unreasonable as those of Hudibras or Ralpho, and carried his zeal for ceremonies and for ecclesiastical dignities to lengths altogether inconsistent with reason or with Christian charity. He has gravely noted down in his diary that he once committed the sin of drinking coffee on Good Friday. In Scotland, he thought it his duty to pass several months without joining in public worship, solely because the ministers of the kirk had not been ordained by bishops. His mode of estimating the piety of his neighbours was somewhat singular. "Campbell," said he, "is a good man, a pious man. I am afraid he has not been in the inside of a church for many years; but he never passes a church without pulling off his hat: this shows he has good principles." Spain and Sicily must surely contain many pious robbers and well-principled assassins. Johnson could easily see that a Roundhead who named all his children after Solomon's singers, and talked in the House of Commons about seeking the Lord, might be an unprincipled villain whose religious mummeries only aggravated his guilt. But a man who took off his hat when he passed a church episcopally consecrated must be a good man, a pious man, a man of good principles. Johnson could easily see that those persons who looked on a dance or a laced waistcoat as sinful, deemed most ignobly of the attributes of God and of the ends of revelation. But with what a storm of invective he would have overwhelmed any man who had blamed him for celebrating the redemption of mankind with sugarless tea and butterless buns.

Nobody spoke more contemptuously of the cant of patriotism. Nobody saw more clearly the error of those who regarded liberty, not as a means, but as an end, and who proposed to themselves, as the object of their pursuit, the prosperity of the state as distinct from the prosperity of the individuals who compose the state. His calm and settled opinion seems to have been that forms of government have little or no influence on the happiness of society. This opinion, erroneous as it is, ought at least to have preserved him from all intemperance on political questions. It did not, however, preserve him from the lowest, fiercest, and most absurd extravagances of party-spirit, from rants which, in every thing but the diction, resembled those of Squire

Western. He was, as a politician, half ice and half fire. On the side of his intellect he was a mere Pococurante, far too apathetic about public affairs, far too sceptical as to the good or evil tendency of any form of polity. His passions, on the contrary, were violent even to slaying against all who leaned to Whiggish principles. The well-known lines which he inserted in Goldsmith's Traveller express what seems to have been his deliberate judgment:

> "How small, of all that human hearts endure,
> That part which kings or laws can cause or cure!"

He had previously put expressions very similar into the mouth of Rasselas. It is amusing to contrast these passages with the torrents of raving abuse which he poured forth against the Long Parliament and the American Congress. In one of the conversations reported by Boswell this inconsistency displays itself in the most ludicrous manner.

"Sir Adam Ferguson," says Boswell, "suggested that luxury corrupts a people, and destroys the spirit of liberty. Johnson: 'Sir, that is all visionary. I would not give half a guinea to live under one form of government rather than another. It is of no moment to the happiness of an individual. Sir, the danger of the abuse of power is nothing to a private man. What Frenchman is prevented passing his life as he pleases?' Sir Adam: 'But, sir, in the British constitution it is surely of importance to keep up a spirit in the people, so as to preserve a balance against the crown.' Johnson: 'Sir, I perceive you are a vile Whig. Why all this childish jealousy of the power of the crown? The crown has not power enough.'"

One of the old philosophers, Lord Bacon tells us, used to say that life and death were just the same to him. "Why then," said an objector, "do you not kill yourself?" The philosopher answered, "Because it is just the same." If the difference between two forms of government be not worth half a guinea, it is not easy to see how Whiggism can be viler than Toryism, or how the crown can have too little power. If the happiness of individuals is not affected by political abuses, zeal for liberty is doubtless ridiculous. But zeal for monarchy must be equally so. No person would have been more quick-sighted than Johnson to such a contradiction as this in the logic of an antagonist.

The judgments which Johnson passed on books were, in his own time, regarded with superstitious veneration, and, in our time, are generally treated with indiscriminate contempt. They are the judgments of a strong but enslaved understanding. The mind of the critic was hedged round by an uninterrupted fence of prejudices and superstitions. Within his narrow limits, he displayed a vigour and an activity which ought to have enabled him to clear the barrier that confined him.

How it chanced that a man who reasoned on his premises so ably, should assume his premises so foolishly, is one of the great mysteries of human nature. The same inconsistency may be observed in the schoolmen of the middle ages. Those writers show so much acuteness and force of mind in arguing on their wretched data, that a modern reader is perpetually at a loss to comprehend how such minds came by such data. Not a flaw in the superstructure of the theory which they are rearing escapes their vigilance. Yet they are blind to the obvious unsoundness of the foundation. It is the same with some eminent lawyers.

Their legal arguments are intellectual prodigies, abounding with the happiest analogies and the most refined distinctions. The principles of their arbitrary science being once admitted, the statute-book and the reports being once assumed as the foundations of reasoning, these men must be allowed to be perfect masters of logic. But if a question arises as to the postulates on which their whole system rests, if they are called upon to vindicate the fundamental maxims of that system which they have passed their lives in studying, these very men often talk the language of savages or of children. Those who have listened to a man of this class in his own court, and who have witnessed the skill with which he analyses and digests a vast mass of evidence, or reconciles a crowd of precedents which at first sight seem contradictory, scarcely know him again when, a few hours later, they hear him speaking on the other side of Westminster Hall in his capacity of legislator. They can scarcely believe that the paltry quirks which are faintly heard through a storm of coughing, and which do not impose on the plainest country gentleman, can proceed from the same sharp and vigorous intellect which had excited their admiration under the same roof, and on the same day.

Johnson decided literary questions like a lawyer, not like a legislator. He never examined foundations where a point was already ruled. His whole code of criticism rested on pure assumption, for which he sometimes quoted a precedent or an authority, but rarely troubled himself to give a reason drawn from the nature of things. He took it for granted that the kind of poetry which flourished in his own time, which he had been accustomed to hear praised from his childhood, and which he had himself written with success, was the best kind of poetry. In his biographical work he has repeatedly laid it down as an undeniable proposition that during the latter part of the seventeenth century, and the earlier part of the eighteenth, English poetry had been in a constant progress of improvement. Waller, Denham, Dryden, and Pope, had been, according to him, the great reformers. He judged of all works of the imagination by the standard established among his own contemporaries. Though he allowed Homer to have been a greater man than Virgil, he seems to have thought the Æneid a greater poem than the Iliad. Indeed he well might have thought so; for he preferred Pope's Iliad to Homer's. He pronounced that, after Hoole's translation of Tasso, Fairfax's would hardly be reprinted. He could see no merit in our fine old English ballads, and always spoke with the most provoking contempt of Percy's fondness for them. Of the great original works of imagination which appeared during his time, Richardson's novels alone excited his admiration. He could see little or no merit in Tom Jones, in Gulliver's Travels, or in Tristram Shandy. To Thomson's Castle of Indolence, he vouchsafed only a line of cold commendation, of commendation much colder than what he has bestowed on the Creation of that portentous bore, Sir Richard Blackmore. Gray was, in his dialect, a barren rascal. Churchill was a blockhead. The contempt which he felt for the trash of Macpherson was indeed just; but it was, we suspect, just by chance. He despised the Fingal for the very reason which led many men of genius to admire it. He despised it, not because it was essentially common-place, but because it had a superficial air of originality.

He was undoubtedly an excellent judge of compositions fashioned on his own principles. But when a deeper philosophy was required, when he undertook to pronounce judgment on the works of those great minds which "yield homage only to eternal laws," his failure was ignominious. He criticized Pope's Epitaphs excellently. But his observations on Shakspeare's plays and Milton's poems seem to us for the most part as wretched as if they had been written by Rymer himself, whom we take to have been the worst critic that ever lived.

Some of Johnson's whims on literary subjects can be compared only to that strange nervous feeling which made him uneasy if he had not touched every post between the Mitre tavern and his own lodgings. His preference of Latin epitaphs to English epitaphs is an instance. An English epitaph, he said, would disgrace Smollett. He declared that he would not pollute the walls of Westminster Abbey with an English epitaph on Goldsmith. What reason there can be for celebrating a British writer in Latin, which there was not for covering the Roman arches of triumph with Greek inscriptions, or for commemorating the deeds of the heroes of Thermopylæ in Egyptian hieroglyphics, we are utterly unable to imagine.

On men and manners, at least on the men and manners of a particular place and a particular age, Johnson had certainly looked with a most observant and discriminating eye. His remarks on the education of children, on marriage, on the economy of families, on the rules of society, are always striking, and generally sound. In his writings, indeed, the knowledge of life which he possessed in an eminent degree is very imperfectly exhibited. Like those unfortunate chiefs of the middle ages who were suffocated by their own chain-mail and cloth of gold, his maxims perish under that load of words which was designed for their defence and their ornament. But it is clear from the remains of his conversation, that he had more of that homely wisdom which nothing but experience and observation can give than any writer since the time of Swift. If he had been content to write as he talked, he might have left books on the practical art of living superior to the Directions to Servants.

Yet even his remarks on society, like his remarks on literature, indicate a mind at least as remarkable for narrowness as for strength. He was no master of the great science of human nature. He had studied, not the genus man, but the species Londoner. Nobody was ever so thoroughly conversant with all the forms of life and all the shades of moral and intellectual character which were to be seen from Islington to the Thames, and from Hyde-Park corner to Mile-end green. But his philosophy stopped at the first turnpike-gate. Of the rural life of England he knew nothing; and he took it for granted that every body who lived in the country was either stupid or miserable. "Country gentlemen," said he, "must be unhappy; for they have not enough to keep their lives in motion;" as if all those peculiar habits and associations which made Fleet Street and Charing Cross the finest views in the world to himself had been essential parts of human nature. Of remote countries and past times he talked with wild and ignorant presumption. "The Athenians of the age of Demosthenes," he said to Mrs. Thrale, "were a people of brutes, a barbarous people." In conversation with Sir Adam Ferguson he used similar language. "The boasted Athenians," he said, "were barbarians. The mass of every people must be barbarous where there is no printing." The fact was this: he saw that a Londoner who could not read was a very stupid and brutal fellow: he saw that great refinement of taste and activity of intellect were rarely found in a Londoner who had not read much; and, because it was by means of books that people acquired almost all their knowledge in the society with which he was acquainted, he concluded, in defiance of the strongest and clearest evidence, that the human mind can be cultivated by means of books alone. An Athenian citizen might possess very few volumes; and the largest library to which he had access might be much less valuable than Johnson's bookcase in Bolt Court. But the Athenian might pass every morning in conversation with Socrates, and might hear Pericles speak four or five times every month. He saw the plays of Sophocles and Aristophanes: he walked amidst the friezes of Phidias and the paintings of Zeuxis: he knew by heart the choruses of Æschylus: he heard the rhapsodist at the corner of the street reciting the shield of Achilles or the Death of Argus: he was a legislator, conversant with high questions of alliance, revenue, and war: he was a soldier, trained under a liberal and generous discipline: he was a judge, compelled every day to weigh the effect of opposite arguments. These things were in themselves an education, an education eminently fitted, not, indeed, to form exact or profound thinkers, but to give quickness to the perceptions, delicacy to the taste, fluency to the expression, and politeness to the manners. All this was overlooked. An Athenian who did not improve his mind by reading was, in Johnson's opinion, much such a person as a Cockney who made his mark, much such a person as black Frank before he went to school, and far inferior to a parish clerk or a printer's devil.

Johnson's friends have allowed that he carried to a ridiculous extreme his unjust contempt for foreigners. He pronounced the French to be a very silly people, much behind us, stupid, ignorant creatures. And this judgment he formed after having been at Paris about a month, during which he would not talk French, for fear of giving the natives an advantage over him in conversation. He pronounced them, also, to be an indelicate people, because a French footman touched the sugar with his fingers. That ingenious and amusing traveller, M. Simond, has defended his countrymen very successfully against Johnson's accusation, and has pointed out some English practices which, to an impartial spectator, would seem at least as inconsistent with physical cleanliness and social decorum as those which Johnson so bitterly reprehended. To the sage, as Boswell loves to call him, it never occurred to doubt that there must be something eternally and immutably good in the usages to which he had been accustomed. In fact, Johnson's remarks on society beyond the bills of mortality, are generally of much the same kind with those of honest Tom Dawson, the English footman in Dr. Moore's Zeluco. "Suppose the king of France has no sons, but only a daughter, then, when the king dies, this here daughter, according to that there law, cannot be made queen, but the next near relative, provided he is a man, is made king, and not the last king's daughter, which, to be sure, is very unjust. The French footguards are dressed in blue, and all the marching regiments in white, which has a very foolish appearance for soldiers; and as for blue regimentals, it is only fit for the blue horse or the artillery."

Johnson's visit to the Hebrides introduced him to a state of society completely new to him; and a salutary suspicion of his own deficiencies seems on that occasion to have crossed his mind for the first time. He confessed, in the last paragraph of his Journey, that his thoughts on national manners were the thoughts of one who had seen but little, of one who had passed his time almost wholly in cities. This feeling, however, soon passed away. It is remarkable that to the last he entertained a fixed contempt for all those modes of life and those studies which tend to emancipate the mind from the prejudices of a particular age or a particular nation. Of foreign travel and of history he spoke with the fierce and boisterous contempt of ignorance. "What does a man learn by travelling? Is Beauclerk the better for travelling? What did Lord Charlemont learn in his travels, except that there was a snake in one of the pyramids of Egypt?" History was, in his opinion, to use the fine expression of Lord Plunkett, an old almanack: historians could, as he conceived, claim no higher dignity than that of almanack-makers; and his favourite historians were those who, like Lord Hailes, aspired to no higher dignity. He always spoke with contempt of Robertson. Hume he would not even read. He affronted one of his friends for talking to him about Catiline's conspiracy, and declared that he never desired to hear of the Punic war again as long as he lived.

Assuredly one fact which does not directly affect our own interests, considered in itself, is no better worth knowing than another fact. The fact that there is a snake in a pyramid, or the fact that Hannibal crossed the Alps, are in themselves as unprofitable to us as the fact that there is a green blind in a particular house in Threadneedle Street, or the fact that a Mr. Smith comes into the city every morning on the top of one of the Blackwall stages. But it is certain that those who will not crack the shell of history will never get at the kernel. Johnson, with hasty arrogance, pronounced the kernel worthless, because he saw no value in the shell. The real use of travelling to distant countries and of studying the annals of past times is to preserve men from the contraction of mind which those can hardly escape whose whole communion is with one generation and one neighbourhood, who arrive at conclusions by means of an induction not sufficiently copious, and who therefore constantly confound exceptions with rules, and accidents with essential properties. In short, the real use of travelling and of studying history is to keep men from being what Tom Dawson was in fiction, and Samuel Johnson in reality.

Johnson, as Mr. Burke most justly observed, appears far greater in Boswell's books than in his own. His conversation appears to have been quite equal to his writings in matter, and far superior to them in manner. When he talked, he clothed his wit and his sense in forcible and natural expressions. As soon as he took his pen in his hand to write for the public, his style became systematically vicious. All his books are written in a learned language, in a language which nobody hears from his mother or his nurse, in a language in which nobody ever quarrels, or drives bargains, or makes love, in a language in which nobody ever thinks. It is clear that Johnson himself did not think in the dialect in which he wrote. The expressions which came first to his tongue were simple, energetic, and picturesque. When he wrote for publication, he did his sentences out of English into

Johnsonese. His letters from the Hebrides to Mrs. Thrale are the original of that work of which the Journey to the Hebrides is the translation; and it is amusing to compare the two versions. "When we were taken up stairs," says he in one of his letters, "a dirty fellow bounced out of the bed on which one of us was to lie." This incident is recorded in the Journey as follows: "Out of one of the beds on which we were to repose started up, at our entrance, a man black as a Cyclops from the forge." Sometimes Johnson translated aloud. "The Rehearsal," he said, very unjustly, "has not wit enough to keep it sweet;" then, after a pause, "it has not vitality enough to preserve it from putrefaction."

Mannerism is pardonable, and is sometimes even agreeable, when the manner, though vicious, is natural. Few readers, for example, would be willing to part with the mannerism of Milton or of Burke. But a mannerism which does not sit easy on the mannerist, which has been adopted on principle, and which can be sustained only by constant effort, is always offensive. And such is the mannerism of Johnson.

The characteristic faults of his style are so familiar to all our readers, and have been so often burlesqued, that it is almost superfluous to point them out. It is well known that he made less use than any other eminent writer of those strong plain words, Anglo-Saxon or Norman-French, of which the roots lie in the inmost depths of our language; and that he felt a vicious partiality for terms which, long after our own speech had been fixed, were borrowed from the Greek and Latin, and which, therefore, even when lawfully naturalised, must be considered as born aliens, not entitled to rank with the king's English. His constant practice of padding out a sentence with useless epithets, till it became as stiff as the bust of an exquisite, his antithetical forms of expression, constantly employed even where there is no opposition in the ideas expressed, his big words wasted on little things, his harsh inversions, so widely different from those graceful and easy inversions which give variety, spirit, and sweetness to the expression of our great old writers, all these peculiarities have been imitated by his admirers and parodied by his assailants, till the public has become sick of the subject.

Goldsmith said to him, very wittily and very justly, "If you were to write a fable about little fishes, doctor, you would make the little fishes talk like whales." No man surely ever had so little talent for personation as Johnson. Whether he wrote in the character of a disappointed legacy-hunter or an empty town fop, of a crazy virtuoso or a flippant coquette, he wrote in the same pompous and unbending style. His speech, like Sir Piercy Shafton's Euphuistic eloquence, bewrayed him under every disguise. Euphelia and Rhodoclea talk as finely as Imlac the poet, or Seged, Emperor of Ethiopia. The gay Cornelia describes her reception at the country-house of her relations, in such terms as these: "I was surprised, after the civilities of my first reception, to find, instead of the leisure and tranquillity which a rural life always promises, and, if well conducted, might always afford, a confused wildness of care, and a tumultuous hurry of diligence, by which every face was clouded, and every motion agitated." The gentle Tranquilla informs us, that she "had not passed the earlier part of life without the flattery of courtship, and the joys of triumph; but had danced the round of gaiety amidst the murmurs of envy and the gratulations of applause, had been attended from pleasure to pleasure by the great, the sprightly, and the vain, and had seen her regard solicited by the obsequiousness of gallantry, the gaiety of wit, and the timidity of love." Surely Sir John Falstaff himself did not wear his petticoats with a worse grace. The reader may well cry out, with honest Sir Hugh Evans, "I like not when a 'oman has a great peard: I spy a great peard under her muffler." [1]

We had something more to say. But our article is already too long; and we must close it. We would fain part in good humour from the hero, from the biographer, and even from the editor, who, ill as he has performed his task, has at least this claim to our gratitude, that he has induced us to read Boswell's book again. As we close it, the club-room is before us, and the table on which stands the omelet for Nugent, and the lemons for Johnson. There are assembled those heads which live for ever on the canvass of Reynolds. There are the spectacles of Burke and the tall thin form of Langton, the courtly sneer of Beauclerk and the beaming smile of Garrick, Gibbon tapping his snuff-box and Sir Joshua with his trumpet in his ear. In the foreground is that strange figure which is as familiar to us as the figures of those among whom we have been brought up, the gigantic body, the huge massy face, seamed with the scars of disease, the brown coat, the black worsted stockings, the grey wig with the scorched foretop, the dirty hands, the nails bitten and pared to the quick. We see the eyes and mouth moving with convulsive twitches; we see the heavy

[1] It is proper to observe that this passage bears a very close resemblance to a passage in the Rambler (No. 20). The resemblance may possibly be the effect of unconscious plagiarism.

form rolling; we hear it puffing; and then comes the "Why, sir!" and the "What then, sir?" and the "No, sir!" and the "You don't see your way through the question, sir!"

What a singular destiny has been that of this remarkable man! To be regarded in his own age as a classic, and in ours as a companion. To receive from his contemporaries that full homage which men of genius have in general received only from posterity! To be more intimately known to posterity than other men are known to their contemporaries! That kind of fame which is commonly the most transient is, in his case, the most durable. The reputation of those writings, which he probably expected to be immortal, is every day fading; while those peculiarities of manner and that careless table-talk the memory of which, he probably thought, would die with him, are likely to be remembered as long as the English language is spoken in any quarter of the globe.

JOHN HAMPDEN.[1]

(*Edinburgh Review*, December 1831.)

We have read this book with great pleasure, though not exactly with that kind of pleasure which we had expected. We had hoped that Lord Nugent would have been able to collect, from family papers and local traditions, much new and interesting information respecting the life and character of the renowned leader of the Long Parliament, the first of those great English commoners whose plain addition of Mister has, to our ears, a more majestic sound than the proudest of the feudal titles. In this hope we have been disappointed; but assuredly not from any want of zeal or diligence on the part of the noble biographer. Even at Hampden, there are, it seems, no important papers relating to the most illustrious proprietor of that ancient domain. The most valuable memorials of him which still exist, belong to the family of his friend, Sir John Eliot. Lord Eliot has furnished the portrait which is engraved for this work, together with some very interesting letters. The portrait is undoubtedly an original, and probably the only original now in existence. The intellectual forehead, the mild penetration of the eye, and the inflexible resolution expressed by the

[1] *Some Memorials of John Hampden, his Party, and his Times.* By Lord Nugent. 2 vols. 8vo. London: 1831.

lines of the mouth, sufficiently guarantee the likeness. We shall probably make some extracts from the letters. They contain almost all the new information that Lord Nugent has been able to procure respecting the private pursuits of the great man whose memory he worships with an enthusiastic, but not extravagant, veneration.

The public life of Hampden is surrounded by no obscurity. His history, more particularly from the year 1640 to his death, is the history of England. These Memoirs must be considered as Memoirs of the history of England; and, as such, they well deserve to be attentively perused. They contain some curious facts which, to us at least, are new, much spirited narrative, many judicious remarks, and much eloquent declamation.

We are not sure that even the want of information respecting the private character of Hampden is not in itself a circumstance as strikingly characteristic as any which the most minute chronicler, O'Meara, Mrs. Thrale, or Boswell himself, ever recorded concerning their heroes. The celebrated Puritan leader is an almost solitary instance of a great man who neither sought nor shunned greatness, who found glory only because glory lay in the plain path of duty. During more than forty years he was known to his country neighbours as a gentleman of cultivated mind, of high principles, of polished address, happy in his family, and active in the discharge of local duties; and to political men, as an honest, industrious, and sensible member of Parliament, not eager to display his talents, stanch to his party, and attentive to the interests of his constituents. A great and terrible crisis came. A direct attack was made by an arbitrary government on a sacred right of Englishmen, on a right which was the chief security for all their other rights. The nation looked round for a defender. Calmly and unostentatiously the plain Buckinghamshire Esquire placed himself at the head of his countrymen, and right before the face and across the path of tyranny. The times grew darker and more troubled. Public service, perilous, arduous, delicate, was required; and to every service the intellect and the courage of this wonderful man were found fully equal. He became a debater of the first order, a most dexterous manager of the House of Commons, a negotiator, a soldier. He governed a fierce and turbulent assembly, abounding in able men, as easily as he had governed his family. He showed himself as competent to direct a campaign as to conduct the business of the petty sessions. We can scarcely express the admiration which we feel for a mind so great, and, at the same time, so healthful and so well proportioned, so willingly contracting itself to the humblest duties, so easily expanding itself to the highest, so contented in repose, so powerful in action. Almost every part of this virtuous and blameless life which is not hidden from us in modest privacy is a precious and splendid portion of our national history. Had the private conduct of Hampden afforded the slightest pretence for censure, he would have been assailed by the same blind malevolence which, in defiance of the clearest proofs, still continues to call Sir John Eliot an assassin. Had there been even any weak part in the character of Hampden, had his manners been in any respect open to ridicule, we may be sure that no mercy would have been shown to him by the writers of Charles's faction. Those writers have carefully preserved every little circumstance which could tend to make their opponents odious or contemptible.

They have made themselves merry with the cant of injudicious zealots. They have told us that Pym broke down in a speech, that Ireton had his nose pulled by Hollis, that the Earl of Northumberland cudgelled Henry Marten, that St. John's manners were sullen, that Vane had an ugly face, that Cromwell had a red nose. But neither the artful Clarendon nor the scurrilous Denham could venture to throw the slightest imputation on the morals or the manners of Hampden. What was the opinion entertained respecting him by the best men of his time, we learn from Baxter. That eminent person, eminent not only for his piety and his fervid devotional eloquence, but for his moderation, his knowledge of political affairs, and his skill in judging of characters, declared in the Saint's Rest that one of the pleasures which he hoped to enjoy in heaven was the society of Hampden. In the editions printed after the Restoration, the name of Hampden was omitted. "But I must tell the reader," says Baxter, "that I did blot it out, not as changing my opinion of the person. . . . Mr. John Hampden was one that friends and enemies acknowledged to be most eminent for prudence, piety, and peaceable counsels, having the most universal praise of any gentleman that I remember of that age. I remember a moderate, prudent, aged gentleman, far from him, but acquainted with him, whom I have heard saying, that if he might choose what person he would be then in the world, he would be John Hampden." We cannot but regret that we have not fuller memorials of a man who, after passing through the most severe temptations by which human virtue can be tried, after acting a most conspicuous part in a revolution and a civil war, could yet deserve such praise as this from such authority.

Yet the want of memorials is surely the best proof that hatred itself could find no blemish on his memory.

The story of his early life is soon told. He was the head of a family which had been settled in Buckinghamshire before the Conquest. Part of the estate which he inherited had been bestowed by Edward the Confessor on Baldwyn de Hampden, whose name seems to indicate that he was one of the Norman favourites of the last Saxon king. During the contest between the houses of York and Lancaster, the Hampdens adhered to the party of the Red Rose, and were, consequently, persecuted by Edward the Fourth, and favoured by Henry the Seventh. Under the Tudors, the family was great and flourishing. Griffith Hampden, high sheriff of Buckinghamshire, entertained Elizabeth with great magnificence at his seat. His son, William Hampden, sate in the Parliament which that Queen summoned in the year 1593. William married Elizabeth Cromwell, aunt of the celebrated man who afterwards governed the British islands with more than regal power; and from this marriage sprang John Hampden.

He was born in 1594. In 1597 his father died, and left him heir to a very large estate. After passing some years at the grammar school of Thame, young Hampden was sent, at fifteen, to Magdalene College, in the University of Oxford. At nineteen, he was admitted a student of the Inner Temple, where he made himself master of the principles of the English law. In 1619, he married Elizabeth Symeon, a lady to whom he appears to have been fondly attached. In the following year he was returned to parliament by a borough which has in our time obtained a miserable celebrity, the borough of Grampound.

Of his private life during his early years little is known beyond what Clarendon has told us. "In his entrance into the world," says that great historian, "he indulged himself in all the license in sports, and exercises, and company, which were used by men of the most jolly conversation." A remarkable change, however, passed on his character. "On a sudden," says Clarendon, "from a life of great pleasure and license, he retired to extraordinary sobriety and strictness, to a more reserved and melancholy society." It is probable that this change took place when Hampden was about twenty-five years old. At that age he was united to a woman whom he loved and esteemed. At that age he entered into political life. A mind so happily constituted as his would naturally, under such circumstances, relinquish the pleasures of dissipation for domestic enjoyments and public duties.

His enemies have allowed that he was a man in whom virtue showed itself in its mildest and least austere form. With the morals of a Puritan, he had the manners of an accomplished courtier. Even after the change in his habits, "he preserved," says Clarendon, "his own natural cheerfulness and vivacity, and, above all, a flowing courtesy to all men." These qualities distinguished him from most of the members of his sect and his party, and, in the great crisis in which he afterwards took a principal part, were of scarcely less service to the country than his keen sagacity and his dauntless courage.

In January, 1621, Hampden took his seat in the House of Commons. His mother was exceedingly desirous that her son should obtain a peerage. His family, his possessions, and his personal accomplishments were such, as would, in any age, have justified him in pretending to that honour. But in the reign of James the First there was one short cut to the House of Lords. It was but to ask, to pay, and to have. The sale of titles was carried on as openly as the sale of boroughs in our times. Hampden turned away with contempt from the degrading honours with which his family desired to see him invested, and attached himself to the party which was in opposition to the court.

It was about this time, as Lord Nugent has justly remarked, that parliamentary opposition began to take a regular form. From a very early age, the English had enjoyed a far larger share of liberty than had fallen to the lot of any neighbouring people. How it chanced that a country conquered and enslaved by invaders, a country of which the soil had been portioned out among foreign adventurers and of which the laws were written in a foreign tongue, a country given over to that worst tyranny, the tyranny of caste over caste, should have become the seat of civil liberty, the object of the admiration and envy of surrounding states, is one of the most obscure problems in the philosophy of history. But the fact is certain. Within a century and a half after the Norman conquest, the Great Charter was conceded. Within two centuries after the Conquest, the first House of Commons met. Froissart tells us, what indeed his whole narrative sufficiently proves, that, of all the nations of the fourteenth century, the English were the least disposed to endure oppression. "C'est le plus périlleux peuple qui soit au monde, et plus outrageux et orgueilleux." The good canon probably did not perceive that all the prosperity and internal peace which this dangerous people enjoyed were the fruits of the spirit which he designates as proud and outrageous. He has, however, borne ample testimony to the effect, though he was not sagacious enough to trace it to its cause. "En le royaume d'Angleterre," says he, "toutes gens, laboureurs et marchands, ont appris de vivre en paix, et à mener leurs marchandises paisiblement, et les laboureurs labourer." In the fifteenth century, though England was convulsed by the struggle between the two branches of the royal family, the physical and moral condition of the people continued to improve. Villenage almost wholly disappeared. The calamities of war were little felt, except by those who bore arms. The oppressions of the government were little felt, except by the aristocracy. The institutions of the country, when compared with the institutions of the neighbouring kingdoms, seem to have been not undeserving of the praises of Fortescue. The government of Edward the Fourth, though we call it cruel and arbitrary, was humane and liberal when compared with that of Lewis the Eleventh, or that of Charles the Bold. Comines, who had lived amidst the wealthy cities of Flanders, and who had visited Florence and Venice, had never seen a people so well governed as the English. "Or selon mon advis," says he, "entre toutes les seigneuries du monde, dont j'ay connoissance, ou la chose publique est mieulx traitée, et ou regne moins de violence sur le peuple, et ou il n'y an uls édifices abbatus ny demolis pour guerre, c'est Angleterre ; et tombe le sort et le malheur sur ceulx qui font la guerre."

About the close of the fifteenth and the commencement of the sixteenth century, a great portion of the influence which the aristocracy had possessed passed to the crown. No English king has ever enjoyed such absolute power as Henry the Eighth. But while the royal prerogatives were acquiring strength at the expense of the nobility, two great revolutions took place, destined to be the parents of many revolutions, the invention of Printing, and the reformation of the Church.

The immediate effect of the Reformation in England was by no means favourable to political liberty. The authority which had been exercised by the Popes was transferred almost entire to the King. Two formidable powers which had often served to check each other were united in a single despot. If the system on which the founders of the Church of England acted could have been permanent, the Reformation would have been, in a political sense, the greatest curse that ever fell on our country. But that system carried within it the seeds of its own death. It was possible to transfer the name of Head of the Church from Clement to Henry; but it was impossible to transfer to the new establishment the veneration which the old establishment had inspired. Mankind had not broken one yoke in pieces only in order to put on another. The supremacy of the Bishop of Rome had been for ages considered as a fundamental principle of Christianity. It had for it every thing that could make a prejudice deep and strong, venerable antiquity, high authority, general consent. It had been taught in the first lessons of the nurse. It was taken for granted in all the exhortations of the priest. To remove it was to break innumerable associations, and to give a great and perilous shock to the principles. Yet this prejudice, strong as it was, could not stand in the great day of the deliverance of the human reason. And it was not to be expected that the public mind, just after freeing itself by an unexampled effort, from a bondage which it had endured for ages, would patiently submit to a tyranny which could plead no ancient title. Rome had at least prescription on its side. But Protestant intolerance, despotism in an upstart sect, infallibility claimed by guides who acknowledged that they had passed the greater part of their lives in error, restraints imposed on the liberty of private judgment at the pleasure of rulers who could vindicate their own proceedings only by asserting the liberty of private judgment, these things could not long be borne. Those who had pulled down the crucifix could not long continue to persecute for the surplice. It required no great sagacity to perceive the inconsistency and dishonesty of men who, dissenting from almost all Christendom, would suffer none to dissent from themselves, who demanded freedom of conscience, yet refused to grant it, who execrated persecution, yet persecuted, who urged reason against the authority of one opponent, and authority against the reasons of another. Bonner acted at least in accordance with his own principles. Cranmer could vindicate himself from the charge of being a heretic only by arguments which made him out to be a murderer.

Thus the system on which the English Princes acted with respect to ecclesiastical affairs for some time after the Reformation was a system too obviously unreasonable to be lasting. The public mind moved while the government moved, but would not stop where the government stopped. The same impulse which had carried millions away from the Church of Rome continued to carry them forward in the same direction. As Catholics had become Protestants, Protestants became Puritans; and the Tudors and Stuarts were as unable to avert the latter change as the Popes had been to avert the former. The dissenting party increased and became strong under every kind of discouragement and oppression. They were a sect. The government persecuted them; and they became an opposition. The old constitution of England furnished to them the means of resisting the sovereign without breaking the law. They were the majority of the House of Commons. They had the power of giving or withholding supplies; and, by a judicious exercise of this power, they might hope to take from the Church its usurped authority over the consciences of men, and from the Crown some part of the vast prerogative which it had recently acquired at the expense of the nobles and of the Pope.

The faint beginnings of this memorable contest may be discerned early in the reign of Elizabeth. The conduct of her last Parliament made it clear that one of those great revolutions which policy may guide but cannot stop was in progress. It was on the question of monopolies that the House of Commons gained its first great victory over the Throne. The conduct of the extraordinary woman who then governed England is an admirable study for politicians who live in unquiet times. It shows how thoroughly she understood the people whom she ruled, and the crisis in which she was called to act. What she held she held firmly. What she gave she gave graciously. She saw that it was necessary to make a concession to the nation; and she made it, not grudgingly, not tardily, not as a matter of bargain and sale, not, in a word, as Charles the First would have made it, but promptly and cordially. Before a bill could be framed or an address presented, she applied a remedy to the evil of which the nation complained. She expressed in the warmest terms her gratitude to her faithful Commons for detecting abuses which interested persons had concealed from her. If her successors had inherited her wisdom with her crown, Charles the First might have died of old age, and James the Second would never have seen St. Germain's.

She died; and the kingdom passed to one who was, in his own opinion, the greatest master of king-craft that ever lived, but who was, in truth, one of those kings whom God seems to send for the express purpose of hastening revolutions. Of all the enemies of liberty whom Britain has produced, he was at once the most harmless and the most provoking. His office resembled that of the man who, in a Spanish bull-fight, goads the torpid savage to fury, by shaking a red rag in the air, and by now and then throwing a dart, sharp enough to sting, but too small to injure. The policy of wise tyrants has always been to cover their violent acts with popular forms. James was always obtruding his despotic theories on his subjects without the slightest necessity. His foolish talk exasperated them infinitely more than forced loans or benevolences would have done. Yet, in practice, no king ever held his prerogatives less tenaciously. He neither gave way gracefully to the advancing spirit of liberty nor took vigorous measures to stop it, but retreated before it with ludicrous haste, blustering and insulting as he retreated. The English people had been governed during near a hundred and fifty years by Princes who, whatever might be their frailties or their vices, had all possessed great force of character, and who, whether beloved or hated, had always been feared. Now, at length, for the first time since the day when the sceptre of Henry the Fourth dropped from the hand of his lethargic grandson, England had a king whom she despised.

The follies and vices of the man increased the contempt which was produced by the feeble policy of the sovereign. The indecorous gallantries of the Court, the habits of gross intoxication in which even the ladies indulged, were alone sufficient to disgust a people whose manners were beginning to be strongly tinctured with austerity. But these were trifles. Crimes of the most frightful kind had been discovered; others were suspected. The strange story of the Gowries was not forgotten. The ignominious fondness of the King for his minions, the perjuries, the sorceries, the poisonings, which his chief favourites had planned within the walls of his palace, the pardon which, in direct violation of his duty and of his word, he had granted to the mysterious threats of a murderer, made him an object of loathing to many of his subjects. What opinion grave and moral persons residing at a distance from the Court entertained respecting him, we learn from Mrs. Hutchinson's Memoirs. England was no place, the seventeenth century no time, for Sporus and Locusta.

This was not all. The most ridiculous weaknesses seemed to meet in the wretched Solomon of Whitehall, pedantry, buffoonery, garrulity, low curiosity, the most contemptible personal cowardice. Nature and education had done their best to produce a finished specimen of all that a king ought not to be. His awkward figure, his rolling eye, his rickety walk, his nervous tremblings, his slobbering mouth, his broad Scotch accent, were imperfections which might have been found in the best and greatest man. Their effect, however, was to make James and his office objects of contempt, and to dissolve those associations which had been created by the noble bearing of preceding monarchs, and which were in themselves no inconsiderable fence to royalty.

The sovereign whom James most resembled was, we think, Claudius Cæsar. Both had the same feeble vacillating temper, the same childishness, the same coarseness, the same poltroonery. Both were men of learning; both wrote and spoke, not, indeed, well, but still in a manner in which it seems almost incredible that men so foolish should have written or spoken. The follies and indecencies of James are well described in the words which Suetonius uses respecting Claudius: "Multa talia, etiam privatis deformia, nedum principi, neque infacundo, neque indocto, immo etiam pertinaciter liberalibus studiis dedito." The description given by Suetonius of the manner in which the Roman prince transacted business exactly suits the Briton. "In cognoscendo ac decernendo mira varietate animi fuit, modo circumspectus et sagax, modo inconsultus ac præceps, nonnunquam frivolus amentique similis." Claudius was ruled successively by two bad women: James successively by two bad men. Even the description of the person of Claudius, which we find in the ancient memoirs, might, in many points, serve for that of James. "Ceterum et ingredientem destituebant poplites minus firmi, et remisse quid vel serio agentem multa dehonestabant, risus indecens, ira turpior, spumante rictu, præterea linguæ titubantia."

The Parliament which James had called soon after his accession had been refractory. His second Parliament, called in the spring of 1614, had been more refractory still. It had been dissolved after a session of two months; and during six years the King had governed without having recourse to the legislature.

During those six years, melancholy and disgraceful events, at home and abroad, had followed one another in rapid succession; the divorce of Lady Essex, the murder of Overbury, the elevation of Villiers, the pardon of Somerset, the disgrace of Coke, the execution of Raleigh, the battle of Prague, the invasion of the Palatinate by Spinola, the ignominious flight of the son-in-law of the English king, the depression of the Protestant interest all over the continent. All the extraordinary modes by which James could venture to raise money had been tried. His necessities were greater than ever; and he was compelled to summon the Parliament in which Hampden first appeared as a public man.

This Parliament lasted about twelve months. During that time it visited with deserved punishment several of those who, during the preceding six years, had enriched themselves by peculation and monopoly. Michell, one of the grasping patentees who had purchased of the favourite the power of robbing the nation, was fined and imprisoned for life. Mompesson, the original, it is said, of Massinger's Overreach, was outlawed and deprived of his ill gotten wealth. Even Sir Edward Villiers, the brother of Buckingham, found it convenient to leave England. A greater name is to be added to the ignominious list. By this Parliament was brought to justice that illustrious philosopher whose memory genius has half redeemed from the infamy due to servility, to ingratitude, and to corruption.

After redressing internal grievances, the Commons proceeded to take into consideration the state of Europe. The King flew into a rage with them for meddling with such matters, and, with characteristic judgment, drew them into a controversy about the origin of their House and of its privileges. When he found that he could not convince them, he dissolved them in a passion, and sent some of the leaders of the Opposition to ruminate on his logic in prison.

During the time which elapsed between this dissolution and the meeting of the next Parliament, took place the celebrated negotiation respecting the Infanta. The would-be despot was unmercifully browbeaten. The would-be Solomon was ridiculously overreached. Steenie, in spite of the begging and sobbing of his dear dad and gossip, carried off baby Charles in triumph to Madrid. The sweet lads, as James called them, came back safe, but without their errand. The great master of king-craft, in looking for a Spanish match, had found a Spanish war. In February, 1624, a Parliament met, during the whole sitting of which, James was a mere puppet in the hands of his baby, and of his poor slave and dog. The Commons were disposed to support the King in the vigorous policy which his favourite urged him to adopt. But they were not disposed to place any confidence in their feeble sovereign and his dissolute courtiers, or to relax in their efforts to remove public grievances. They therefore lodged the money which they voted for the war in the hands of Parliamentary Commissioners. They impeached the treasurer, Lord Middlesex, for corruption, and they passed a bill by which patents of monopoly were declared illegal.

Hampden did not, during the reign of James, take any prominent part in public affairs. It is certain, however, that he paid great attention to the details of Parliamentary business, and to the local interests of his own country. It was in a great measure owing to his exertions that Wendover and some other boroughs on which the popular party could depend recovered the elective franchise, in spite of the opposition of the Court.

The health of the King had for some time been declining. On the twenty-seventh of March, 1625, he expired. Under his weak rule, the spirit of liberty had grown strong, and had become equal to a great contest. The contest was brought on by the policy of his successor. Charles bore no resemblance to his father. He was not a driveller, or a pedant, or a buffoon, or a coward. It would be absurd to deny that he was a scholar and a gentleman, a man of exquisite taste in the fine arts, a man of strict morals in private life. His talents for business were respectable; his demeanour was kingly. But he was false, imperious, obstinate, narrow-minded, ignorant of the temper of his people, unobservant of the signs of his times. The whole principle of his government was resistance to public opinion; nor did he make any real concession to that opinion till it mattered not whether he resisted or conceded, till the nation, which had long ceased to love him or to trust him, had at last ceased to fear him.

His first Parliament met in June, 1625. Hampden sat in it as burgess for Wendover. The King wished for money. The commons wished for the redress of grievances. The war, however, could not be carried on without funds. The plan of the Opposition was, it should seem, to dole out supplies by small sums, in order to prevent a speedy dissolution. They gave the King two subsidies only, and proceeded to complain that his ships had been employed against the Huguenots in France, and to petition in behalf of the Puritans who were persecuted in England. The King dissolved them, and raised money by Letters under his Privy Seal. The supply fell far short of what he needed; and, in the spring of 1626, he called together another Parliament. In this Parliament, Hampden again sat for Wendover.

The Commons resolved to grant a very liberal supply, but to defer the final passing of the act for that purpose till the grievances of the nation should be redressed. The struggle which followed far exceeded in violence any that had yet taken place. The Commons impeached Buckingham. The King threw the managers of the impeachment into prison. The Commons denied the right of the King to levy tonnage and poundage without their consent. The King dissolved them. They put forth a remonstrance. The King circulated a declaration vindicating his measures, and committed some of the most distinguished members of the Opposition to close custody. Money was raised by a forced loan, which was apportioned among the people according to the rate at which they had been respectively assessed to the last subsidy. On this occasion it was, that Hampden made his first stand for the fundamental principle of the English constitution. He positively refused to lend a farthing. He was required to give his reasons. He answered, "that he could be content to lend as well as others, but feared to draw upon himself that curse in Magna Charta which should be read twice a year against those who infringe it." For this spirited answer, the Privy Council committed him close prisoner to the Gate House. After some time, he was again brought up; but he persisted in his refusal, and was sent to a place of confinement in Hampshire.

The government went on, oppressing at home, and blundering in all its measures abroad. A war was foolishly undertaken against France, and more foolishly conducted. Buckingham led an expedition against Rhé, and failed ignominiously. In the mean time soldiers were billeted on the people. Crimes of which ordinary justice should have taken cognisance were punished by martial law. Near eighty gentlemen were imprisoned for refusing to contribute to the forced loan. The lower people who showed any signs of insubordination were dressed into the fleet, or compelled to serve in the army. Money, however, came in slowly; and the King was compelled to summon another Parliament. In the hope of conciliating his subjects, he set at liberty the persons who had been imprisoned for refusing to comply with his unlawful demands. Hampden regained his freedom, and was immediately reelected burgess for Wendover.

Early in 1628 the Parliament met. During its first session, the Commons prevailed on the King, after many delays and much equivocation, to give, in return for five subsidies, his full and solemn assent to that celebrated instrument, the second great charter of the liberties of England, known by the name of the Petition of Right. By agreeing to this act, the King bound himself to raise no taxes without the consent of Parliament, to imprison no man except by legal process, to billet no more soldiers on the people, and to leave the cognisance of offences to the ordinary tribunals.

In the summer, this memorable Parliament was prorogued. It met again in January, 1629. Buckingham was no more. That weak, violent, and dissolute adventurer, who, with no talents or acquirements but those of a mere courtier, had, in a great crisis of foreign and domestic politics, ventured on the part of prime minister, had fallen, during the recess of Parliament, by the hand of an assassin. Both before and after his death the war had been feebly and unsuccessfully conducted. The King had continued, in direct violation of the Petition of Right, to raise tonnage and poundage without the consent of Parliament. The troops had again been billeted on the people; and it was clear to the Commons that the five subsidies which they had given as the price of the national liberties had been given in vain.

They met accordingly in no complying humour. They took into their most serious consideration the measures of the government concerning tonnage and poundage. They summoned the officers of the custom-house to their bar. They interrogated the barons of the exchequer. They committed one of the sheriffs of London. Sir John Eliot, a distinguished member of the Opposition, and an intimate friend of Hampden, proposed a resolution condemning the unconstitutional imposition. The Speaker said that the King had commanded him to put no such question to the vote. This decision produced the most violent burst of feeling ever seen within the walls of Parliament. Hayman remonstrated vehemently against the disgraceful language which had been heard from the chair. Eliot dashed the paper which contained his resolution on the floor of the House. Valentine and Hollis held the Speaker down in his seat by main force, and read the motion amidst the loudest shouts. The door was locked. The key was laid on the table. Black Rod knocked for admittance in vain. After passing several strong resolutions, the House adjourned. On the day appointed for its meeting it was dissolved by the King, and several of its most eminent members, among whom were Hollis and Sir John Eliot, were committed to prison.

Though Hampden had as yet taken little part in the debates of the House, he had been a member of many very important committees, and had read and written much concerning the law of Parliament. A manuscript volume of Parliamentary cases, which is still in existence, contains many extracts from his notes.

He now retired to the duties and pleasures of a rural life. During the eleven years which followed the dissolution of the Parliament of 1628, he resided at his seat in one of the most beautiful parts of the county of Buckingham. The house, which has since his time been greatly altered, and which is now, we believe, almost entirely neglected, was an old English mansion, built in the days of the Plantagenets and the Tudors. It stood on the brow of a hill which overlooks a narrow valley. The extensive woods which surround it were pierced by long avenues. One of those avenues the grandfather of the great statesman had cut for the approach of Elizabeth; and the opening, which is still visible for many miles, retains the name of the Queen's Gap. In this delightful retreat, Hampden passed several years, performing with great activity all the duties of a landed gentleman and a magistrate, and amusing himself with books and with field sports.

He was not in his retirement unmindful of his persecuted friends. In particular, he kept up a close correspondence with Sir John Eliot, who was confined in the Tower. Lord Nugent has published several of the Letters. We may perhaps be fanciful; but it seems to us that every one of them is an admirable illustration of some part of the character of Hampden which Clarendon has drawn.

Part of the correspondence relates to the two sons of Sir John Eliot. These young men were wild and unsteady; and their father, who was now separated from them, was naturally anxious about their conduct. He at length resolved to send one of them to France, and the other to serve a campaign in the Low Countries. The letter which we subjoin shows that Hampden, though rigorous towards himself, was not uncharitable towards others, and that his puritanism was perfectly compatible with the sentiments and the tastes of an accomplished gentleman. It also illustrates admirably what has been said of him by Clarendon: "He was of that rare affability and temper in debate, and of that seeming humility and submission of judgment, as if he brought no opinion of his own with him, but a desire of information and instruction. Yet he had so subtle a way of interrogating, and, under cover of doubts, insinuating his objections, that he infused his own opinions into those from whom he pretended to learn and receive them."

The letter runs thus: "I am so perfectly acquainted with your clear insight into the dispositions of men, and ability to fit them with courses suitable, that, had you bestowed sons of mine as you have done your own, my judgment durst hardly have called it into question, especially when, in laying the design, you have prevented the objections to be made against it. For if Mr. Richard Eliot will, in the intermissions of action, add study to practice, and adorn that lively spirit with flowers of contemplation, he will raise our expectations of another Sir Edward Vere, that had this character — all summer in the field, all winter in his study —

in whose fall fame makes this kingdom a great loser; and, having taken this resolution from counsel with the highest wisdom, as I doubt not you have, I hope and pray that the same power will crown it with a blessing answerable to our wish. The way you take with my other friend shows you to be none of the Bishop of Exeter's converts;[1] of whose mind neither am I superstitiously. But had my opinion been asked, I should, as vulgar conceits use to do, have showed my power rather to raise objections than to answer them. A temper between France and Oxford, might have taken away his scruples, with more advantage to his years. . . . . For although he be one of those that, if his age were looked for in no other book but that of the mind, would be found no ward if you should die to-morrow, yet it is a great hazard, methinks, to see so sweet a disposition guarded with no more, amongst a people whereof many make it their religion to be superstitious in impiety, and their behaviour to be affected in ill manners. But God, who only knoweth the periods of life and opportunities to come, hath designed him, I hope, for his own service betime, and stirred up your providence to husband him so early for great affairs. Then shall he be sure to find Him in France that Abraham did in Sechem and Joseph in Egypt, under whose wing alone is perfect safety."

Sir John Eliot employed himself, during his imprisonment, in writing a treatise on government, which he transmitted to his friend. Hampden's criticisms are strikingly characteristic. They are written with all that "flowing courtesy" which is ascribed to him by Clarendon. The objections are insinuated with so

[1] Hall, Bishop of Exeter, had written strongly, both in verse and in prose, against the fashion of sending young men of quality to travel.

much delicacy that they could scarcely gall the most irritable author. We see too how highly Hampden valued in the writings of others that conciseness which was one of the most striking peculiarities of his own eloquence. Sir John Eliot's style was, it seems, too diffuse, and it is impossible not to admire the skill with which this is suggested. "The piece," says Hampden, "is as complete an image of the pattern as can be drawn by lines, a lively character of a large mind, the subject, method, and expression, excellent and homogeneal, and, to say truth, sweetheart, somewhat exceeding my commendations. My words cannot render them to the life. Yet, to show my ingenuity rather than wit, would not a less model have given a full representation of that subject, not by diminution but by contraction of parts? I desire to learn. I dare not say. The variations upon each particular seem many; all, I confess, excellent. The fountain was full, the channel narrow; that may be the cause; or that the author resembled Virgil, who made more verses by many than he intended to write. To extract a just number, had I seen all his, I could easily have bid him make fewer; but if he had bade me tell him which he should have spared, I had been posed."

This is evidently the writing not only of a man of good sense and natural good taste, but of a man of literary habits. Of the studies of Hampden little is known. But, as it was at one time in contemplation to give him the charge of the education of the Prince of Wales, it cannot be doubted that his acquirements were considerable. Davila, it is said, was one of his favourite writers. The moderation of Davila's opinions and the perspicuity and manliness of his style could not but recommend him to so judicious a reader.

It is not improbable that the parallel between France and England, the Huguenots and the Puritans, had struck the mind of Hampden, and that he already found within himself powers not unequal to the lofty part of Coligni.

While he was engaged in these pursuits, a heavy domestic calamity fell on him. His wife, who had borne him nine children, died in the summer of 1634. She lies in the parish church of Hampden, close to the manor-house. The tender and energetic language of her epitaph still attests the bitterness of her husband's sorrow, and the consolation which he found in a hope full of immortality.

In the mean time, the aspect of public affairs grew darker and darker. The health of Eliot had sunk under an unlawful imprisonment of several years. The brave sufferer refused to purchase liberty, though liberty would to him have been life, by recognising the authority which had confined him. In consequence of the representations of his physicians, the severity of restraint was somewhat relaxed. But it was in vain. He languished and expired a martyr to that good cause for which his friend Hampden was destined to meet a more brilliant, but not a more honourable death.

All the promises of the King were violated without scruple or shame. The Petition of Right, to which he had, in consideration of monies duly numbered, given a solemn assent, was set at nought. Taxes were raised by the royal authority. Patents of monopoly were granted. The old usages of feudal times were made pretexts for harassing the people with exactions unknown during many years. The Puritans were persecuted with cruelty worthy of the Holy Office. They were forced to fly from the country. They were imprisoned. They were whipped. Their ears were cut off. Their noses were slit. Their cheeks were branded with red-hot iron. But the cruelty of the oppressor could not tire out the fortitude of the victims. The mutilated defenders of liberty again defied the vengeance of the Star Chamber, came back with undiminished resolution to the place of their glorious infamy, and manfully presented the stumps of their ears to be grubbed out by the hangman's knife. The hardy sect grew up and flourished in spite of every thing that seemed likely to stunt it, struck its roots deep into a barren soil, and spread its branches wide to an inclement sky. The multitude thronged round Prynne in the pillory with more respect than they paid to Mainwaring in the pulpit, and treasured up the rags which the blood of Burton had soaked, with a veneration such as mitres and surplices had ceased to inspire.

For the misgovernment of this disastrous period Charles himself is principally responsible. After the death of Buckingham, he seems to have been his own prime minister. He had, however, two counsellors who seconded him, or went beyond him, in intolerance and lawless violence, the one a superstitious driveller, as honest as a vile temper would suffer him to be, the other a man of great valour and capacity, but licentious, faithless, corrupt, and cruel.

Never were faces more strikingly characteristic of the individuals to whom they belonged, than those of Laud and Strafford, as they still remain portrayed by the most skilful hand of that age. The mean forehead, the pinched features, the peering eyes, of the prelate, suit admirably with his disposition. They mark him out as a lower kind of Saint Dominic, differing from the fierce and gloomy enthusiast who founded the Inquisition, as we might imagine the familiar imp of a spiteful witch to differ from an archangel of darkness. When we read His Grace's judgments, when we read the report which he drew up, setting forth that he had sent some separatists to prison, and imploring the royal aid against others, we feel a movement of indignation. We turn to his Diary, and we are at once as cool as contempt can make us. There we learn how his picture fell down, and how fearful he was lest the fall should be an omen; how he dreamed that the Duke of Buckingham came to bed to him, that King James walked past him, that he saw Thomas Flaxney in green garments, and the Bishop of Worcester with his shoulders wrapped in linen. In the early part of 1627, the sleep of this great ornament of the church seems to have been much disturbed. On the fifth of January, he saw a merry old man with a wrinkled countenance, named Grove, lying on the ground. On the fourteenth of the same memorable month, he saw the Bishop of Lincoln jump on a horse and ride away. A day or two after this he dreamed that he gave the King drink in a silver cup, and that the King refused it, and called for glass. Then he dreamed that he had turned Papist; of all his dreams the only one, we suspect, which came through the gate of horn. But of these visions our favourite is that which, as he has recorded, he enjoyed on the night of Friday, the ninth of February, 1627. "I dreamed," says he, "that I had the scurvy; and that forthwith all my teeth became loose. There was one in especial in my lower jaw, which I could scarcely keep in with my finger till I had called for help." Here was a man to have the superintendence of the opinions of a great nation!

But Wentworth, — who ever names him without thinking of those harsh dark features, ennobled by their expression into more than the majesty of an antique Jupiter; of that brow, that eye, that cheek, that lip, wherein, as in a chronicle, are written the events of many stormy and disastrous years, high enterprise accomplished, frightful dangers braved, power unsparingly exercised, suffering unshrinkingly borne; of that fixed look, so full of severity, of mournful anxiety, of deep thought, of dauntless resolution, which seems at once to forebode and to defy a terrible fate, as it lowers on us from the living canvass of Vandyke? Even at this day the haughty earl overawes posterity as he overawed his contemporaries, and excites the same interest when arraigned before the tribunal of history which he excited at the bar of the House of Lords. In spite of ourselves, we sometimes feel towards his memory a certain relenting similar to that relenting which his defence, as Sir John Denham tells us, produced in Westminster Hall.

This great, brave, bad man entered the House of Commons at the same time with Hampden, and took the same side with Hampden. Both were among the richest and most powerful commoners in the kingdom. Both were equally distinguished by force of character, and by personal courage. Hampden had more judgment and sagacity than Wentworth. But no orator of that time equalled Wentworth in force and brilliancy of expression. In 1626 both these eminent men were committed to prison by the King, Wentworth, who was among the leaders of the Opposition, on account of his parliamentary conduct, Hampden, who had not as yet taken a prominent part in debate, for refusing to pay taxes illegally imposed.

Here their path separated. After the death of

Buckingham, the King attempted to seduce some of the chiefs of the Opposition from their party; and Wentworth was among those who yielded to the seduction. He abandoned his associates, and hated them ever after with the deadly hatred of a renegade. High titles and great employments were heaped upon him. He became Earl of Strafford, Lord Lieutenant of Ireland, President of the Council of the North; and he employed all his power for the purpose of crushing those liberties of which he had been the most distinguished champion. His counsels respecting public affairs were fierce and arbitrary. His correspondence with Laud abundantly proves that government without parliaments, government by the sword, was his favourite scheme. He was angry even that the course of justice between man and man should be unrestrained by the royal prerogative. He grudged to the Courts of King's Bench and Common Pleas even that measure of liberty which the most absolute of the Bourbons allowed to the Parliaments of France. In Ireland, where he stood in the place of the King, his practice was in strict accordance with his theory. He set up the authority of the executive government over that of the courts of law. He permitted no person to leave the island without his licence. He established vast monopolies for his own private benefit. He imposed taxes arbitrarily. He levied them by military force. Some of his acts are described even by the partial Clarendon as powerful acts, acts which marked a nature excessively imperious, acts which caused dislike and terror in sober and dispassionate persons, high acts of oppression. Upon a most frivolous charge, he obtained a capital sentence from a court-martial against a man of high rank who had given him offence. He debauched the daughter-in-law of the Lord Chancellor of Ireland, and then commanded that nobleman to settle his estate according to the wishes of the lady. The Chancellor refused. The Lord Lieutenant turned him out of office, and threw him into prison. When the violent acts of the Long Parliament are blamed, let it not be forgotten from what a tyranny they rescued the nation.

Among the humbler tools of Charles were Chief-Justice Finch and Noy the Attorney-General. Noy had, like Wentworth, supported the cause of liberty in Parliament, and had, like Wentworth, abandoned that cause for the sake of office. He devised, in conjunction with Finch, a scheme of exaction which made the alienation of the people from the throne complete. A writ was issued by the King, commanding the city of London to equip and man ships of war for his service. Similar writs were sent to the towns along the coast. These measures, though they were direct violations of the Petition of Right, had at least some show of precedent in their favour. But, after a time, the government took a step for which no precedent could be pleaded, and sent writs of ship-money to the inland counties. This was a stretch of power on which Elizabeth herself had not ventured, even at a time when all laws might with propriety have been made to bend to that highest law, the safety of the state. The inland counties had not been required to furnish ships, or money in the room of ships, even when the Armada was approaching our shores. It seemed intolerable that a prince who, by assenting to the Petition of Right, had relinquished the power of levying ship-money even in the out-ports, should be the first to levy it on parts of the kingdom where it had been unknown under the most absolute of his predecessors.

Clarendon distinctly admits that this tax was intended, not only for the support of the navy, but "for a spring and magazine that should have no bottom, and for an everlasting supply of all occasions." The nation well understood this; and from one end of England to the other the public mind was strongly excited.

Buckinghamshire was assessed at a ship of four hundred and fifty tons, or a sum of four thousand five hundred pounds. The share of the tax which fell to Hampden was very small; so small, indeed, that the sheriff was blamed for setting so wealthy a man at so low a rate. But, though the sum demanded was a trifle, the principle involved was fearfully important. Hampden, after consulting the most eminent constitutional lawyers of the time, refused to pay the few shillings at which he was assessed, and determined to incur all the certain expense, and the probable danger, of bringing to a solemn hearing this great controversy between the people and the Crown. "Till this time," says Clarendon, "he was rather of reputation in his own country than of public discourse or fame in the kingdom; but then he grew the argument of all tongues, every man inquiring who and what he was that durst, at his own charge, support the liberty and prosperity of the kingdom."

Towards the close of the year 1636, this great cause came on in the Exchequer Chamber before all the judges of England. The leading counsel against the writ was the celebrated Oliver St. John, a man whose temper was melancholy, whose manners were reserved, and who was as yet little known in Westminster Hall, but whose great talents had not escaped the penetrating eye of Hampden. The Attorney-General and Solicitor-General appeared for the Crown.

The arguments of the counsel occupied many days; and the Exchequer Chamber took a considerable time for deliberation. The opinion of the bench was divided. So clearly was the law in favour of Hampden that, though the judges held their situations only during the royal pleasure, the majority against him was the least possible. Five of the twelve pronounced in his favour. The remaining seven gave their voices for the writ.

The only effect of this decision was to make the public indignation stronger and deeper. "The judgment," says Clarendon, "proved of more advantage and credit to the gentleman condemned than to the King's service." The courage which Hampden had shown on this occasion, as the same historian tells us, "raised his reputation to a great height generally throughout the kingdom." Even courtiers and crown-lawyers spoke respectfully of him. "His carriage," says Clarendon, "throughout that agitation, was with that rare temper and modesty, that they who watched him narrowly to find some advantage against his person, to make him less resolute in his cause, were compelled to give him a just testimony." But his demeanour, though it impressed Lord Falkland with the deepest respect, though it drew forth the praises of Solicitor-General Herbert, only kindled into a fiercer flame the ever-burning hatred of Strafford. That minister, in his letters to Laud, murmured against the lenity with which Hampden was treated. "In good faith," he wrote, "were such men rightly served, they should be whipped into their right wits." Again he says, "I still wish Mr. Hampden, and others to his likeness, were well whipped into their right senses. And if the rod be so used that it smart not, I am the more sorry."

The person of Hampden was now scarcely safe. His prudence and moderation had hitherto disappointed those who would gladly have had a pretence for sending him to the prison of Eliot. But he knew that the eye of a tyrant was on him. In the year 1637 misgovernment had reached its height. Eight years had passed without a Parliament. The decision of the Exchequer Chamber had placed at the disposal of the Crown the whole property of the English people. About the time at which that decision was pronounced, Prynne, Bastwick, and Burton were mutilated by the sentence of the Star Chamber, and sent to rot in remote dungeons. The estate and the person of every man who had opposed the court were at its mercy.

Hampden determined to leave England. Beyond the Atlantic Ocean, a few of the persecuted Puritans had formed, in the wilderness of Connecticut, a settlement which has since become a prosperous commonwealth, and which, in spite of the lapse of time and of the change of government, still retains something of the character given to it by its first founders. Lord Saye and Lord Brooke were the original projectors of this scheme of emigration. Hampden had been early consulted respecting it. He was now, it appears, desirous to withdraw himself beyond the reach of oppressors who, as he probably suspected, and as we know, were bent on punishing his manful resistance to their tyranny. He was accompanied by his kinsman, Oliver Cromwell, over whom he possessed great influence, and in whom he alone had discovered, under an exterior appearance of coarseness and extravagance, those great and commanding talents which were afterwards the admiration and the dread of Europe.

The cousins took their passage in a vessel which lay

in the Thames, and which was bound for North America. They were actually on board, when an order of council appeared, by which the ship was prohibited from sailing. Seven other ships, filled with emigrants, were stopped at the same time.

Hampden and Cromwell remained; and with them remained the Evil Genius of the House of Stuart. The tide of public affairs was even now on the turn. The King had resolved to change the ecclesiastical constitution of Scotland, and to introduce into the public worship of that kingdom ceremonies which the great body of the Scots regarded as popish. This absurd attempt produced, first discontents, then riots, and at length open rebellion. A provisional government was established at Edinburgh, and its authority was obeyed throughout the kingdom. This government raised an army, appointed a general, and summoned an Assembly of the Kirk. The famous instrument called the Covenant was put forth at this time, and was eagerly subscribed by the people.

The beginnings of this formidable insurrection were strangely neglected by the King and his advisers. But towards the close of the year 1638 the danger became pressing. An army was raised; and early in the following spring Charles marched northward at the head of a force sufficient, as it seemed, to reduce the Covenanters to submission.

But Charles acted at this conjuncture as he acted at every important conjuncture throughout his life. After oppressing, threatening, and blustering, he hesitated and failed. He was bold in the wrong place, and timid in the wrong place. He would have shown his wisdom by being afraid before the liturgy was read in St. Giles's church. He put off his fear till he had reached the Scottish border with his troops. Then, after a feeble campaign, he concluded a treaty with the insurgents, and withdrew his army. But the terms of the pacification were not observed. Each party charged the other with foul play. The Scots refused to disarm. The King found great difficulty in re-assembling his forces. His late expedition had drained his treasury. The revenues of the next year had been anticipated. At another time, he might have attempted to make up the deficiency by illegal expedients; but such a course would clearly have been dangerous when part of the island was in rebellion. It was necessary to call a Parliament. After eleven years of suffering, the voice of the nation was to be heard once more.

In April, 1640, the Parliament met; and the King had another chance of conciliating his people. The new House of Commons was, beyond all comparison, the least refractory House of Commons that had been known for many years. Indeed, we have never been able to understand how, after so long a period of misgovernment, the representatives of the nation should have shown so moderate and so loyal a disposition. Clarendon speaks with admiration of their dutiful temper. "The House, generally," says he, "was exceedingly disposed to please the King, and to do him service." "It could never be hoped," he observes elsewhere, "that more sober or dispassionate men would ever meet together in that place, or fewer who brought ill purposes with them."

In this Parliament Hampden took his seat as member for Buckinghamshire, and thenceforward, till the day of his death, gave himself up, with scarcely any intermission, to public affairs. He took lodgings in

Gray's Inn Lane, near the house occupied by Pym, with whom he lived in habits of the closest intimacy. He was now decidedly the most popular man in England. The Opposition looked to him as their leader, and the servants of the King treated him with marked respect.

Charles requested the Parliament to vote an immediate supply, and pledged his word that, if they would gratify him in this request, he would afterwards give them time to represent their grievances to him. The grievances under which the nation suffered were so serious, and the royal word had been so shamefully violated, that the Commons could hardly be expected to comply with this request. During the first week of the session, the minutes of the proceedings against Hampden were laid on the table by Oliver St. John, and a committee reported that the case was matter of grievance. The King sent a message to the Commons, offering, if they would vote him twelve subsidies, to give up the prerogative of ship-money. Many years before, he had received five subsidies in consideration of his assent to the Petition of Right. By assenting to that petition, he had given up the right of levying ship-money, if he ever possessed it. How he had observed the promises made to his third Parliament, all England knew; and it was not strange that the Commons should be somewhat unwilling to buy from him, over and over again, their own ancient and undoubted inheritance.

His message, however, was not unfavourably received. The Commons were ready to give a large supply; but they were not disposed to give it in exchange for a prerogative of which they altogether denied the existence. If they acceded to the proposal of the King, they recognised the legality of the writs of ship-money.

Hampden, who was a greater master of parliamentary tactics than any man of his time, saw that this was the prevailing feeling, and availed himself of it with great dexterity. He moved that the question should be put, "Whether the House would consent to the proposition made by the King, as contained in the message." Hyde interfered, and proposed that the question should be divided; that the sense of the House should be taken merely on the point whether there should be a supply or no supply; and that the manner and the amount should be left for subsequent consideration.

The majority of the House was for granting a supply, but against granting it in the manner proposed by the King. If the House had divided on Hampden's question, the court would have sustained a defeat; if on Hyde's, the court would have gained an apparent victory. Some members called for Hyde's motion, others for Hampden's. In the midst of the uproar, the secretary of state, Sir Harry Vane, rose and stated that the supply would not be accepted unless it were voted according to the tenor of the message. Vane was supported by Herbert, the Solicitor-General. Hyde's motion was therefore no further pressed, and the debate on the general question was adjourned till the next day.

On the next day the King came down to the House of Lords, and dissolved the Parliament with an angry speech. His conduct on this occasion has never been defended by any of his apologists. Clarendon condemns it severely. "No man," says he, "could imagine what offence the Commons had given." The offence which they had given is plain. They had, indeed, behaved most temperately and most respectfully. But they had shown a disposition to redress wrongs and to vindicate the laws; and this was enough to make them hateful to a king whom no law could bind, and whose whole government was one system of wrong.

The nation received the intelligence of the dissolution with sorrow and indignation. The only persons to whom this event gave pleasure were those few discerning men who thought that the maladies of the state were beyond the reach of gentle remedies. Oliver St. John's joy was too great for concealment. It lighted up his dark and melancholy features, and made him, for the first time, indiscreetly communicative. He told Hyde that things must be worse before they could be better, and that the dissolved Parliament would never have done all that was necessary. St. John, we think, was in the right. No good could then have been done by any Parliament which did not fully understand that no confidence could safely be placed in the King, and that, while he enjoyed more than the shadow of power, the nation would never enjoy more than the shadow of liberty.

As soon as Charles had dismissed the Parliament, he threw several members of the House of Commons into prison. Ship-money was exacted more rigorously than ever; and the Mayor and Sheriffs of London were prosecuted before the Star Chamber for slackness in levying it. Wentworth, it is said, observed, with characteristic insolence and cruelty, that things would never go right till the Aldermen were hanged. Large sums were raised by force on those counties in which the troops were quartered. All the wretched shifts of a beggared exchequer were tried. Forced loans were raised. Great quantities of goods were bought on long credit and sold for ready-money. A scheme for debasing the currency was under consideration. At length, in August, the King again marched northward.

The Scots advanced into England to meet him. It is by no means improbable that this bold step was taken by the advice of Hampden, and of those with whom he acted; and this has been made matter of grave accusation against the English Opposition. It is said that to call in the aid of foreigners in a domestic quarrel is the worst of treasons, and that the Puritan leaders, by taking this course, showed that they were regardless of the honour and independence of the nation, and anxious only for the success of their own faction. We are utterly unable to see any distinction between the case of the Scotch invasion in 1640, and the case of the Dutch invasion in 1688; or rather, we see distinctions which are to the advantage of Hampden and his friends. We believe Charles to have been a worse and more dangerous king than his son. The Dutch were strangers to us, the Scots a kindred people speaking the same language, subjects of the same prince, not aliens in the eye of the law. If, indeed, it had been possible that a Scotch army or a Dutch army could have enslaved England, those who persuaded Leslie to cross the Tweed, and those who signed the invitation to the Prince of Orange, would have been traitors to their country. But such a result was out of the question. All that either a Scotch or a Dutch invasion could do was to give the public feeling of England an opportunity to show itself. Both expeditions would have ended in complete and ludicrous discomfiture, had Charles and James been supported by their soldiers and their people. In neither case, therefore, was the independence of England endangered; in both cases her liberties were preserved.

The second campaign of Charles against the Scots was short and ignominious. His soldiers, as soon as they saw the enemy, ran away as English soldiers have never run either before or since. It can scarcely be doubted that their flight was the effect, not of cowardice, but of disaffection. The four northern counties of England were occupied by the Scotch army, and the King retired to York.

The game of tyranny was now up. Charles had risked and lost his last stake. It is not easy to retrace the mortifications and humiliations which the tyrant now had to endure, without a feeling of vindictive pleasure. His army was mutinous; his treasury was empty; his people clamoured for a Parliament; addresses and petitions against the government were presented. Strafford was for shooting the petitioners by martial law; but the King could not trust the soldiers. A great council of Peers was called at York; but the King could not trust even the Peers. He struggled, evaded, hesitated, tried every shift, rather than again face the representatives of his injured people. At length no shift was left. He made a truce with the Scots, and summoned a Parliament.

The leaders of the popular party had, after the late dissolution, remained in London for the purpose of organizing a scheme of opposition to the court. They now exerted themselves to the utmost. Hampden, in particular, rode from county to county, exhorting the electors to give their votes to men worthy of their confidence. The great majority of the returns was on the side of the Opposition. Hampden was himself chosen member both for Wendover and Buckinghamshire. He made his election to serve for the county.

On the third of November, 1640, a day to be long remembered, met that great Parliament, destined to every extreme of fortune, to empire and to servitude, to glory and to contempt; at one time the sovereign of its sovereign, at another time the servant of its servants. From the first day of meeting the attendance was great; and the aspect of the members was that of men not disposed to do the work negligently. The dissolution of the late Parliament had convinced most of them that half measures would no longer suffice. Clarendon tells us, that "the same men who, six months before, were observed to be of very moderate tempers, and to wish that gentle remedies might be applied, talked now in another dialect both of kings and persons; and said that they must now be of another temper than they were the last Parliament." The debt of vengeance was swollen by all the usury which had been accumulating during many years; and payment was made to the full.

This memorable crisis called forth parliamentary abilities such as England had never before seen. Among the most distinguished members of the House of Commons were Falkland, Hyde, Digby, young Harry Vane, Oliver St. John, Denzil Hollis, Nathaniel Fiennes. But two men exercised a paramount influence over the legislature and the country, Pym and Hampden; and, by the universal consent of friends and enemies, the first place belonged to Hampden.

On occasions which required set speeches Pym generally took the lead. Hampden very seldom rose till late in a debate. His speaking was of that kind which has, in every age, been held in the highest estimation by English Parliaments, ready, weighty, perspicuous, condensed. His perception of the feelings of the House was exquisite, his temper unalterably placid, his manner eminently courteous and gentlemanlike. "Even with those," says Clarendon, "who are able to preserve themselves from his infusions, and who discerned those opinions to be fixed in him with which they could not comply, he always left the character of an ingenious and conscientious person." His talents for business were as remarkable as his talents for debate. "He was," says Clarendon, "of an industry and vigilance not to be tired out or wearied by the most laborious, and of parts not to be imposed upon by the most subtle and sharp." Yet it was rather to his moral than to his intellectual qualities that he was indebted for the vast influence which he possessed. "When this parliament began," — we again quote Clarendon, — "the eyes of all men were fixed upon him, as their *patriæ pater*, and the pilot that must steer the vessel through the tempests and rocks which threatened it. And I am persuaded his power and interest at that time were greater to do good or hurt than any man's in the kingdom, or than any man of his rank hath had in any time; for his reputation of honesty was universal, and his affections seemed so publicly guided, that no corrupt or private ends could bias them. . . . He was indeed a very wise man, and of great parts, and possessed with the most absolute spirit of popularity, and the most absolute faculties to govern the people, of any man I ever knew."

It is sufficient to recapitulate shortly the acts of the Long Parliament during its first session. Strafford and Laud were impeached and imprisoned. Strafford was afterwards attainted by Bill, and executed. Lord Keeper Finch fled to Holland, Secretary Windebank to France. All those whom the King had, during the last twelve years, employed for the oppression of his people, from the servile judges who had pronounced in favour of the crown against Hampden, down to the sheriffs who had distrained for ship-money, and the custom-house officers who had levied tonnage and poundage, were summoned to answer for their conduct. The Star Chamber, the High Commission Court, the Council of York, were abolished. Those unfortunate victims of Laud who, after undergoing ignominious exposure and cruel manglings, had been sent to languish in distant prisons, were set at liberty, and conducted through London in triumphant procession. The King was compelled to give the judges patents for life or during good behaviour. He was deprived of those oppressive powers which were the last relics of the old feudal tenures. The Forest Courts and the Stannary Courts were reformed. It was provided that the Parliament then sitting should not be prorogued or dissolved without its own consent, and that a Parliament should be held at least once every three years.

Many of these measures Lord Clarendon allows to have been most salutary; and few persons will, in our times, deny that, in the laws passed during this session, the good greatly preponderated over the evil. The abolition of those three hateful courts, the Northern Council, the Star Chamber, and the High Commission, would alone entitle the Long Parliament to the lasting gratitude of Englishmen.

The proceeding against Strafford undoubtedly seems hard to people living in our days. It would probably have seemed merciful and moderate to people living in the sixteenth century. It is curious to compare the trial of Charles's minister with the trial, if it can be so called, of Lord Seymour of Sudeley, in the blessed reign of Edward the Sixth. None of the great reformers of our Church doubted the propriety of passing an act of Parliament for cutting off Lord Seymour's head without a legal conviction. The pious Cranmer voted for that act; the pious Latimer preached for it; the pious Edward returned thanks for it; and all the pious Lords of the council together exhorted their victim to what they were pleased facetiously to call "the quiet and patient suffering of justice."

But it is not necessary to defend the proceedings against Strafford by any such comparison. They are justified, in our opinion, by that which alone justifies capital punishment or any punishment, by that which alone justifies war, by the public danger. That there is a certain amount of public danger which will justify a legislature in sentencing a man to death by retrospective law, few people, we suppose, will deny. Few people, for example, will deny that the French Convention was perfectly justified in placing Robespierre, St. Just, and Couthon under the ban of the law, without a trial. This proceeding differed from the proceeding against Strafford only in being much more rapid and violent. Strafford was fully heard. Robespierre was not suffered to defend himself. Was there, then, in the case of Strafford, a danger sufficient to justify an act of attainder? We believe that there was. We believe that the contest in which the Parliament was engaged against the King was a contest for the security of our property, for the liberty of our persons, for every thing which makes us to differ from the subjects of Don Miguel. We believe that the cause of the

Commons was such as justified them in resisting the King, in raising an army, in sending thousands of brave men to kill and to be killed. An act of attainder is surely not more a departure from the ordinary course of law than a civil war. An act of attainder produces much less suffering than a civil war. We are, therefore, unable to discover on what principle it can be maintained that a cause which justifies a civil war will not justify an act of attainder.

Many specious arguments have been urged against the retrospective law by which Strafford was condemned to death. But all these arguments proceed on the supposition that the crisis was an ordinary crisis. The attainder was, in truth, a revolutionary measure. It was part of a system of resistance which oppression had rendered necessary. It is as unjust to judge of the conduct pursued by the Long Parliament towards Strafford on ordinary principles, as it would have been to indict Fairfax for murder because he cut down a cornet at Naseby. From the day on which the Houses met, there was a war waged by them against the King, a war for all that they held dear, a war carried on at first by means of parliamentary forms, at last by physical force; and, as in the second stage of that war, so in the first, they were entitled to do many things which, in quiet times, would have been culpable.

We must not omit to mention that those who were afterwards the most distinguished ornaments of the King's party supported the bill of attainder. It is almost certain that Hyde voted for it. It is quite certain that Falkland both voted and spoke for it. The opinion of Hampden, as far as it can be collected from a very obscure note of one of his speeches, seems to have been that the proceeding by Bill was unnecessary, and that it would be a better course to obtain judgment on the impeachment.

During this year the Court opened a negotiation with the leaders of the Opposition. The Earl of Bedford was invited to form an administration on popular principles. St. John was made solicitor-general. Hollis was to have been secretary of state, and Pym chancellor of the exchequer. The post of tutor to the Prince of Wales was designed for Hampden. The death of the Earl of Bedford prevented this arrangement from being carried into effect; and it may be doubted whether, even if that nobleman's life had been prolonged, Charles would ever have consented to surround himself with counsellors whom he could not but hate and fear.

Lord Clarendon admits that the conduct of Hampden during this year was mild and temperate, that he seemed disposed rather to soothe than to excite the public mind, and that, when violent and unreasonable motions were made by his followers, he generally left the House before the division, lest he should seem to give countenance to their extravagance. His temper was moderate. He sincerely loved peace. He felt also great fear lest too precipitate a movement should produce a reaction. The events which took place early in the next session clearly showed that this fear was not unfounded.

During the autumn the Parliament adjourned for a few weeks. Before the recess, Hampden was despatched to Scotland by the House of Commons, nominally as a commissioner, to obtain security for a debt which the Scots had contracted during the late invasion; but in truth that he might keep watch over the King, who had now repaired to Edinburgh, for the purpose of finally adjusting the points of difference which remained between him and his northern subjects. It was the business of Hampden to dissuade the Covenanters from making their peace with the Court, at the expense of the popular party in England.

While the King was in Scotland, the Irish rebellion broke out. The suddenness and violence of this terrible explosion excited a strange suspicion in the public mind. The Queen was a professed Papist. The King and the Archbishop of Canterbury had not indeed been reconciled to the See of Rome; but they had, while acting towards the Puritan party with the utmost rigour, and speaking of that party with the utmost contempt, shown great tenderness and respect towards the Catholic religion and its professors. In spite of the wishes of successive Parliaments, the Protestant separatists had been cruelly persecuted. And at the same time, in spite of the wishes of those very Parliaments, laws which were in force against the Papists, and which, unjustifiable as they were, suited the temper of that age, had not been carried into execution. The Protestant nonconformists had not yet learned toleration in the school of suffering. They reprobated the partial lenity which the government showed towards idolaters, and, with some show of reason, ascribed to bad motives conduct which, in such a king as Charles, and such a prelate as Laud, could not possibly be ascribed to humanity or to liberality of sentiment. The violent Arminianism of the Archbishop, his childish attachment to ceremonies, his superstitious veneration for altars, vestments, and painted windows, his bigoted zeal for the constitution and the privileges of his order, his known opinions respecting the celibacy of the clergy, had excited great disgust throughout that large party which was every day becoming more and more hostile to Rome, and more and more inclined to the doctrines and the discipline of Geneva. It was believed by many that the Irish rebellion had been secretly encouraged by the Court; and, when the Parliament met again in November, after a short recess, the Puritans were more intractable than ever.

But that which Hampden had feared had come to pass. A reaction had taken place. A large body of moderate and well-meaning men, who had heartily concurred in the strong measures adopted before the recess, were inclined to pause. Their opinion was that, during many years, the country had been grievously misgoverned, and that a great reform had been necessary; but that a great reform had been made, that the grievances of the nation had been fully redressed, that sufficient vengeance had been exacted for the past, that sufficient security had been provided for the future, and that it would, therefore, be both ungrateful and unwise to make any further attacks on the royal prerogative. In support of this opinion many plausible arguments have been used. But to all these arguments there is one short answer. The King could not be trusted.

At the head of those who may be called the Constitutional Royalists were Falkland, Hyde, and Culpeper. All these eminent men had, during the former year, been in very decided opposition to the Court. In some of those very proceedings with which their admirers reproach Hampden, they had taken a more decided part than Hampden. They had all been concerned in the impeachment of Strafford. They had all, there is reason to believe, voted for the Bill of Attainder. Certainly none of them voted against it. They had all agreed to the act which made the consent of the Parliament necessary to a dissolution or prorogation. Hyde had been among the most active of those who attacked the Council of York. Falkland had voted for the exclusion of the bishops from the Upper House. They were now inclined to halt in the path of reform, perhaps to retrace a few of their steps.

A direct collision soon took place between the two parties into which the House of Commons, lately at almost perfect unity with itself, was now divided. The opponents of the government moved that celebrated address to the King which is known by the name of the Grand Remonstrance. In this address all the oppressive acts of the preceding fifteen years were set forth with great energy of language; and, in conclusion, the King was entreated to employ no ministers in whom the Parliament could not confide.

The debate on the Remonstrance was long and stormy. It commenced at nine in the morning of the twenty-first of November, and lasted till after midnight. The division showed that a great change had taken place in the temper of the House. Though many members had retired from exhaustion, three hundred voted; and the Remonstrance was carried by a majority of only nine. A violent debate followed, on the question whether the minority should be allowed to protest against this decision. The excitement was so great that several members were on the point of proceeding to personal violence. "We had sheathed our swords in each other's bowels," says an eye-witness, "had not the sagacity and great calmness of Mr. Hampden, by a short speech, prevented it." The House did not rise till two in the morning.

The situation of the Puritan leaders was now difficult and full of peril. The small majority which they still had might soon become a minority. Out of doors, their supporters in the higher and middle classes were beginning to fall off. There was a growing opinion that the King had been hardly used. The English are always inclined to side with a weak party which is in the wrong, rather than with a strong party which is in the right. This may be seen in all contests, from contests of boxers to contests of faction. Thus it was that a violent reaction took place in favour of Charles the Second against the Whigs in 1681. Thus it was that an equally violent reaction took place in favour of George the Third against the coalition in 1784. A similar reaction was beginning to take place during the second year of the Long Parliament. Some members of the Opposition "had resumed," says Clarendon, "their old resolution of leaving the kingdom." Oliver Cromwell openly declared that he and many others would have emigrated if they had been left in a minority on the question of the Remonstrance.

Charles had now a last chance of regaining the affection of his people. If he could have resolved to give his confidence to the leaders of the moderate party in the House of Commons, and to regulate his proceedings by their advice, he might have been, not, indeed, as he had been, a despot, but the powerful and respected king of a free people. The nation might have enjoyed liberty and repose under a government with Falkland at its head, checked by a constitutional Opposition under the conduct of Hampden. It was not necessary that, in order to accomplish this happy end, the King should sacrifice any part of his lawful prerogative, or submit to any conditions inconsistent with his dignity. It was necessary only that he should abstain from treachery, from violence, from gross breaches of the law. This was all that the nation was then disposed to require of him. And even this was too much.

For a short time he seemed inclined to take a wise and temperate course. He resolved to make Falkland secretary of state, and Culpeper chancellor of the exchequer. He declared his intention of conferring in a short time some important office on Hyde. He assured these three persons that he would do nothing relating to the House of Commons without their joint advice, and that he would communicate all his designs to them in the most unreserved manner. This resolution, had he adhered to it, would have averted many years of blood and mourning. But "in very few days," says Clarendon, "he did fatally swerve from it."

On the third of January, 1642, without giving the slightest hint of his intention to those advisers whom he had solemnly promised to consult, he sent down the attorney-general to impeach Lord Kimbolton, Hampden, Pym, Hollis, and two other members of the House of Commons, at the bar of the Lords, on a charge of High Treason. It is difficult to find in the whole history of England such an instance of tyranny, perfidy, and folly. The most precious and ancient rights of the subject were violated by this act. The only way in which Hampden and Pym could legally be tried for treason at the suit of the King, was by a petty jury on a bill found by a grand jury. The attorney-general had no right to impeach them. The House of Lords had no right to try them.

The Commons refused to surrender their members. The Peers showed no inclination to usurp the unconstitutional jurisdiction which the King attempted to force on them. A contest began, in which violence and weakness were on the one side, law and resolution on the other. Charles sent an officer to seal up the lodgings and trunks of the accused members. The Commons sent their sergeant to break the seals. The tyrant resolved to follow up one outrage by another. In making the charge, he had struck at the institution of juries. In executing the arrest, he struck at the privileges of Parliament. He resolved to go to the House in person with an armed force, and there to seize the leaders of the Opposition, while engaged in the discharge of their parliamentary duties.

What was his purpose? Is it possible to believe that he had no definite purpose, that he took the most important step of his whole reign without having for one moment considered what might be its effects? Is it possible to believe that he went merely for the purpose of making himself a laughing-stock, that he intended, if he had found the accused members, and if they had refused, as it was their right and duty to refuse, the submission which he illegally demanded, to leave the House without bringing them away? If we reject both these suppositions, we must believe, and we certainly do believe, that he went fully determined to carry his unlawful design into effect by violence, and, if necessary, to shed the blood of the chiefs of the Opposition on the very floor of the Parliament House. Lady Carlisle conveyed intelligence of the design to Pym. The five members had time to withdraw before the arrival of Charles. They left the House as he was entering New Palace Yard. He was accompanied by about two hundred halberdiers of his guard, and by many gentlemen of the Court armed with swords. He walked up Westminster Hall. At the southern end of the Hall his attendants divided to the right and left, and formed a lane to the door of the House of Commons. He knocked, entered, darted a look towards the place which Pym usually occupied, and, seeing it empty, walked up to the table. The Speaker fell on his knee. The members rose and uncovered their heads in profound silence, and the King took his seat in the chair. He looked round the House. But the five members were nowhere to be seen. He interrogated the Speaker. The Speaker answered, that he was merely the organ of the House, and had neither eyes to see, nor tongue to speak, but according to their direction. The King muttered a few feeble sentences about his respect for the laws of the realm, and the privileges of Parliament, and retired. As he passed along the benches, several resolute voices called out audibly "Privilege!" He returned to Whitehall with his company of bravoes, who, while he was in the House, had been impatiently waiting in the lobby for the word, cocking their pistols, and crying "Fall on." That night he put forth a proclamation, directing that the ports should be stopped, and that no person should, at his peril, venture to harbour the accused members.

Hampden and his friends had taken refuge in Coleman Street. The city of London was indeed the fastness of public liberty, and was, in those times, a place of at least as much importance as Paris during the French Revolution. The city, properly so called, now consists in a great measure of immense warehouses and counting-houses, which are frequented by traders and their clerks during the day, and left in almost total solitude during the night. It was then closely inhabited by three hundred thousand persons, to whom it was not merely a place of business, but a place of constant residence. This great capital had as complete a civil and military organization as if it had been an independent republic. Each citizen had his company; and the companies, which now seem to exist only for the sake of epicures and of antiquaries, were then formidable brotherhoods, the members of which were almost as closely bound together as the members of a Highland clan. How strong these artificial ties were, the numerous and valuable legacies anciently bequeathed by citizens to their corporations abundantly prove. The municipal offices were filled by the most opulent and respectable merchants of the kingdom. The pomp of the magistracy of the capital was inferior only to that which surrounded the person of the sovereign. The Londoners loved their city with that patriotic love which is found only in small communities, like those of ancient Greece, or like those which arose in Italy during the middle ages. The numbers, the intelligence, the wealth of the citizens, the democratical form of their local government, and their vicinity to the Court and to the Parliament, made them one of the most formidable bodies in the kingdom. Even as soldiers they were not to be despised. In an age in which war is a profession, there is something ludicrous in the idea of battalions composed of apprentices and shopkeepers, and officered by aldermen. But, in the early part of the seventeenth century, there was no standing army in the island; and the militia of the metropolis was not inferior in training to the militia of other places. A city which could furnish many thousands of armed men, abounding in natural courage, and not absolutely untinctured with military discipline, was a formidable auxiliary in times of internal dissension. On several occasions during the civil war, the train-bands of London distinguished themselves highly; and at the battle of Newbury, in particular, they repelled the fiery onset of Rupert, and saved the army of the Parliament from destruction.

The people of this great city had long been thoroughly devoted to the national cause. Many of them had signed a protestation in which they declared their resolution to defend the privileges of Parliament. Their enthusiasm had, indeed, of late begun to cool. But the impeachment of the five members, and the insult offered to the House of Commons, inflamed them to fury. Their houses, their purses, their pikes, were at the command of the representatives of the nation. London was in arms all night. The next day the shops were closed; the streets were filled with immense crowds; the multitude pressed round the King's coach, and insulted him with opprobrious cries. The House of Commons, in the mean time, appointed a committee to sit in the city, for the purpose of inquiring into the circumstances of the late outrage. The members of the committee were welcomed by a deputation of the common council. Merchant Tailors' Hall, Goldsmiths' Hall, and Grocers' Hall, were fitted up for their sittings. A guard of respectable citizens, duly relieved twice a day, was posted at their doors. The sheriffs were charged to watch over the safety of the accused members, and to escort them to and from the committee with every mark of honour.

A violent and sudden revulsion of feeling, both in the House and out of it, was the effect of the late proceedings of the King. The Opposition regained in a few hours all the ascendency which it had lost. The constitutional royalists were filled with shame and sorrow. They saw that they had been cruelly deceived by Charles. They saw that they were, unjustly, but not unreasonably, suspected by the nation. Clarendon distinctly says that they perfectly detested the counsels by which the King had been guided, and were so much displeased and dejected at the unfair manner in which he had treated them that they were inclined to retire from his service. During the debates on the breach of privilege, they preserved a melancholy silence. To this day, the advocates of Charles take care to say as little as they can about his visit to the House of Commons, and, when they cannot avoid mention of it, attribute to infatuation an act which, on any other supposition, they must admit to have been a frightful crime.

The Commons, in a few days, openly defied the King, and ordered the accused members to attend in their places at Westminster and to resume their parliamentary duties. The citizens resolved to bring back the champions of liberty in triumph before the windows of Whitehall. Vast preparations were made both by land and water for this great festival.

The King had remained in his palace, humbled, dismayed, and bewildered, "feeling," says Clarendon, "the trouble and agony which usually attend generous and magnanimous minds upon their having committed errors;" feeling, we should say, the despicable repentance which attends the man who, having attempted to commit a crime, finds that he has only committed a folly. The populace hooted and shouted all day before the gates of the royal residence. The tyrant could not bear to see the triumph of those whom he had destined to the gallows and the quartering-block.

On the day preceding that which was fixed for their return, he fled, with a few attendants, from that palace which he was never to see again till he was led through it to the scaffold.

On the eleventh of January, the Thames was covered with boats, and its shores with the gazing multitude. Armed vessels, decorated with streamers, were ranged in two lines from London Bridge to Westminster Hall. The members returned upon the river in a ship manned by sailors who had volunteered their services. The train-bands of the city, under the command of the sheriffs, marched along the Strand, attended by a vast crowd of spectators, to guard the avenues to the House of Commons; and thus, with shouts and loud discharges of ordnance, the accused patriots were brought back by the people whom they had served and for whom they had suffered. The restored members, as soon as they had entered the House, expressed, in the warmest terms, their gratitude to the citizens of London. The sheriffs were warmly thanked by the Speaker in the name of the Commons; and orders were given that a guard selected from the train-bands of the city, should attend daily to watch over the safety of the Parliament.

The excitement had not been confined to London. When intelligence of the danger to which Hampden was exposed reached Buckinghamshire, it excited the alarm and indignation of the people. Four thousand freeholders of that county, each of them wearing in his hat a copy of the protestation in favour of the privileges of Parliament, rode up to London to defend the person of their beloved representative. They came in a body to assure Parliament of their full resolution to defend its privileges. Their petition was couched in the strongest terms. "In respect," said they, "of that latter attempt upon the honourable House of Commons, we are now come to offer our service to that end, and resolved, in their just defence, to live and die."

A great struggle was clearly at hand. Hampden had returned to Westminster much changed. His influence had hitherto been exerted rather to restrain than to animate the zeal of his party. But the treachery, the contempt of law, the thirst for blood, which the King had now shown, left no hope of a peaceable adjustment. It was clear that Charles must be either a puppet or a tyrant, that no obligation of law or of honour could bind him, and that the only way to make him harmless was to make him powerless.

The attack which the King had made on the five members was not merely irregular in manner. Even if the charges had been preferred legally, if the Grand Jury of Middlesex had found a true bill, if the accused persons had been arrested under a proper warrant and at a proper time and place, there would still have been in the proceeding enough of perfidy and injustice to vindicate the strongest measures which the Opposition could take. To impeach Pym and Hampden was to impeach the House of Commons. It was notoriously on account of what they had done as members of that House that they were selected as objects of vengeance; and in what they had done as members of that House the majority had concurred. Most of the charges brought against them were common between them and the Parliament. They were accused, indeed, and it may be with reason, of encouraging the Scotch army to invade England. In doing this, they had committed what was, in strictness of law, a high offence, the same offence which Devonshire and Shrewsbury committed in 1688. But the King had promised pardon and oblivion to those who had been the principals in the Scotch insurrection. Did it then consist with his honour to punish the accessaries? He had bestowed marks of his favour on the leading Covenanters. He had given the great seal of Scotland to one chief of the rebels, a marquisate to another, an earldom to Leslie, who had brought the Presbyterian army across the Tweed. On what principle was Hampden to be attainted for advising what Leslie was ennobled for doing? In a court of law, of course, no Englishman could plead an amnesty granted to the Scots. But, though not an illegal, it was surely an inconsistent and a most unkingly course, after pardoning and promoting the heads of the rebellion in one kingdom, to hang, draw, and quarter their accomplices in another.

The proceedings of the King against the five members, or rather against that Parliament which had concurred in almost all the acts of the five members, was the cause of the civil war. It was plain that either Charles or the House of Commons must be stripped of all real power in the state. The best course which the Commons could have taken would perhaps have been to depose the King, as their ancestors had deposed Edward the Second and Richard the Second, and as their children afterwards deposed James. Had they done this, had they placed on the throne a prince whose character and whose situation would have been a pledge for his good conduct, they might safely have left to that prince all the old constitutional prerogatives of the Crown, the command of the armies of the state, the power of making peers, the power of appointing ministers, a veto on bills passed by the two Houses.

Such a prince, reigning by their choice, would have been under the necessity of acting in conformity with their wishes. But the public mind was not ripe for such a measure. There was no Duke of Lancaster, no Prince of Orange, no great and eminent person, near in blood to the throne, yet attached to the cause of the people. Charles was then to remain King; and it was therefore necessary that he should be king only in name. A William the Third, or a George the First, whose title to the crown was identical with the title of the people to their liberty, might safely be trusted with extensive powers. But new freedom could not exist in safety under the old tyrant. Since he was not to be deprived of the name of king, the only course which was left was to make him a mere trustee, nominally seised of prerogatives of which others had the use, a Grand Lama, a *Roi Fainéant*, a phantom resembling those Dagoberts and Childeberts who wore the badges of royalty, while Ebroin and Charles Martel held the real sovereignty of the state.

The conditions which the Parliament propounded were hard, but, we are sure, not harder than those which even the Tories, in the Convention of 1689, would have imposed on James, if it had been resolved that James should continue to be king. The chief condition was that the command of the militia and the conduct of the war in Ireland should be left to the Parliament. On this point was that great issue joined, whereof the two parties put themselves on God and on the sword.

We think, not only that the Commons were justified in demanding for themselves the power to dispose of the military force, but that it would have been absolute insanity in them to leave that force at the disposal of the King. From the very beginning of his reign, it had evidently been his object to govern by an army. His third Parliament had complained, in the Petition of Right, of his fondness for martial law, and of the vexatious manner in which he billeted his soldiers on the people. The wish nearest the heart of Strafford was, as his letters prove, that the revenue might be brought into such a state as would enable the King to keep a standing military establishment. In 1640, Charles had supported an army in the northern counties by lawless exactions. In 1641 he had engaged in an intrigue, the object of which was to bring that army to London for the purpose of overawing the Parliament. His late conduct had proved that, if he were suffered to retain even a small body-guard of his own creatures near his person, the Commons would be in danger of outrage, perhaps of massacre. The Houses were still deliberating under the protection of the militia of London. Could the command of the whole armed force of the realm have been, under these circumstances, safely confided to the King? Would it not have been frenzy in the Parliament to raise and pay an army of fifteen or twenty thousand men for the Irish war, and to give to Charles the absolute control of this army, and the power of selecting, promoting, and dismissing officers at his pleasure? Was it not probable that this army might become, what it is the nature of armies to become, what so many armies formed under much more favourable circumstances have become, what the army of the Roman republic became, what the army of the French republic became, an instrument of despotism? Was it not probable that the soldiers might forget that they were also citizens, and might be ready to serve their general against their country? Was it not certain that, on the very first day on which Charles could venture to revoke his concessions, and to punish his opponents, he would establish an arbitrary government, and exact a bloody revenge?

Our own times furnish a parallel case. Suppose that a revolution should take place in Spain, that the Constitution of Cadiz should be reëstablished, that the Cortes should meet again, that the Spanish Prynnes and Burtons, who are now wandering in rags round Leicester Square, should be restored to their country. Ferdinand the Seventh would, in that case, of course repeat all the oaths and promises which he made in 1820, and broke in 1823. But would it not be madness in the Cortes, even if they were to leave him the name of King, to leave him more than the name? Would not all Europe scoff at them, if they were to permit him to assemble a large army for an expedition to America, to model that army at his pleasure, to put it under the command of officers chosen by himself? Should we not say that every member of the Constitutional party who might concur in such a measure would most richly deserve the fate which he would probably meet, the fate of Riego and of the Empecinado? We are not disposed to pay compliments to Ferdinand; nor do we conceive that we pay him any compliment, when we say that, of all sovereigns in history, he seems to us most to resemble, in some very important points, King Charles the First. Like Charles, he is pious after a certain fashion; like Charles, he has made large concessions to his people after a certain fashion. It is well for him that he has had to deal with men who bore very little resemblance to the English Puritans.

The Commons would have the power of the sword; the King would not part with it; and nothing remained but to try the chances of war. Charles still had a strong party in the country. His august office, his dignified manners, his solemn protestations that he would for the time to come respect the liberties of his subjects, pity for fallen greatness, fear of violent innovation, secured to him many adherents. He had with him the Church, the Universities, a majority of the nobles and of the old landed gentry. The austerity of the Puritan manners drove most of the gay and dissolute youth of that age to the royal standard. Many good, brave, and moderate men, who disliked his former conduct, and who entertained doubts touching his present sincerity, espoused his cause unwillingly and with many painful misgivings, because, though they dreaded his tyranny much, they dreaded democratic violence more.

On the other side was the great body of the middle orders of England, the merchants, the shopkeepers, the yeomanry, headed by a very large and formidable minority of the peerage and of the landed gentry. The Earl of Essex, a man of respectable abilities and of some military experience, was appointed to the command of the parliamentary army.

Hampden spared neither his fortune nor his person in the cause. He subscribed two thousand pounds to the public service. He took a colonel's commission in the army, and went into Buckinghamshire to raise a regiment of infantry. His neighbours eagerly enlisted under his command. His men were known by their green uniform, and by their standard, which bore on one side the watchword of the Parliament, "God with us," and on the other the device of Hampden, "Vestigia nulla retrorsum." This motto well described the line of conduct which he pursued. No member of his party had been so temperate, while there remained a hope that legal and peaceable measures might save the country. No member of his party showed so much energy and vigour when it became necessary to appeal to arms. He made himself thoroughly master of his military duty, and "performed it," to use the words of Clarendon, "upon all occasions most punctually." The regiment which he had raised and trained was considered as one of the best in the service of the Parliament. He exposed his person in every action, with an intrepidity which made him conspicuous even among thousands of brave men. "He was," says Clarendon, "of a personal courage equal to his best parts; so that he was an enemy not to be wished wherever he might have been made a friend, and as much to be apprehended where he was so, as any man could deserve to be." Though his military career was short, and his military situation subordinate, he fully proved that he possessed the talents of a great general, as well as those of a great statesman.

We shall not attempt to give a history of the war. Lord Nugent's account of the military operations is very animated and striking. Our abstract would be dull, and probably unintelligible. There was, in fact, for some time no great and connected system of operations on either side. The war of the two parties was like the war of Arimanes and Oromasdes, neither of whom, according to the Eastern theologians, has any exclusive domain, who are equally omnipresent, who equally pervade all space, who carry on their eternal strife within every particle of matter. There was a petty war in almost every county. A town furnished troops to the Parliament while the manor-house of the neighbouring peer was garrisoned for the King. The combatants were rarely disposed to march far from their own homes. It was reserved for Fairfax and Cromwell to terminate this desultory warfare, by moving one overwhelming force successively against all the scattered fragments of the royal party.

It is a remarkable circumstance that the officers who had studied tactics in what were considered as the best schools, under Vere in the Netherlands, and under Gustavus Adolphus in Germany, displayed far less skill than those commanders who had been bred to peaceful employments, and who never saw even a skirmish till the civil war broke out. An unlearned person might hence be inclined to suspect that the military art is no very profound mystery, that its principles are the principles of plain good sense, and that a quick eye, a cool head, and a stout heart, will do more to make a general than all the diagrams of Jomini. This, however, is certain, that Hampden showed himself a far better officer than Essex, and Cromwell than Leslie.

The military errors of Essex were probably in some degree produced by political timidity. He was honestly, but not warmly, attached to the cause of the Parliament; and next to a great defeat he dreaded a great victory. Hampden, on the other hand, was for vigorous and decisive measures. When he drew the sword, as Clarendon has well said, he threw away the scabbard. He had shown that he knew better than any public man of his time how to value and how to practise moderation. But he knew that the essence of war is violence, and that moderation in war is imbecility. On several occasions, particularly during the operations in the neighbourhood of Brentford, he remonstrated earnestly with Essex. Wherever he commanded separately, the boldness and rapidity of his movements presented a striking contrast to the sluggishness of his superior.

In the Parliament he possessed boundless influence. His employments towards the close of 1642 have been described by Denham in some lines which, though intended to be sarcastic, convey in truth the highest eulogy. Hampden is described in this satire as perpetually passing and repassing between the military station at Windsor and the House of Commons at Westminster, as overawing the general, and as giving law to that Parliament which knew no other law. It was at this time that he organised that celebrated association of counties, to which his party was principally indebted for its victory over the King.

In the early part of 1643, the shires lying in the neighbourhood of London, which were devoted to the cause of the Parliament, were incessantly annoyed by Rupert and his cavalry. Essex had extended his lines so far that almost every point was vulnerable. The young prince, who, though not a great general, was an active and enterprising partisan, frequently surprised posts, burned villages, swept away cattle, and was again at Oxford before a force sufficient to encounter him could be assembled.

The languid proceedings of Essex were loudly condemned by the troops. All the ardent and daring spirits in the parliamentary party were eager to have Hampden at their head. Had his life been prolonged, there is every reason to believe that the supreme command would have been intrusted to him. But it was decreed, that at this conjuncture, England should lose the only man who united perfect disinterestedness to eminent talents, the only man who, being capable of gaining the victory for her, was incapable of abusing that victory when gained.

In the evening of the seventeenth of June, Rupert darted out of Oxford with his cavalry on a predatory expedition. At three in the morning of the following day, he attacked and dispersed a few parliamentary soldiers who lay at Postcombe. He then flew to Chinnor, burned the village, killed or took all the troops who were quartered there, and prepared to hurry back with his booty and his prisoners to Oxford.

Hampden had, on the preceding day, strongly represented to Essex the danger to which this part of the line was exposed. As soon as he received intelligence of Rupert's incursion, he sent off a horseman with a message to the General. The cavaliers, he said, could return only by Chiselhampton Bridge. A force ought to be instantly despatched in that direction for the purpose of intercepting them. In the mean time, he resolved to set out with all the cavalry that he could muster, for the purpose of impeding the march of the enemy till Essex could take measures for cutting off their retreat. A considerable body of horse and dragoons volunteered to follow him. He was not their commander. He did not even belong to their branch of the service. But "he was," says Lord Clarendon, "second to none but the General himself in the observance and application of all men." On the field of Chalgrove he came up with Rupert. A fierce skirmish ensued. In the first charge, Hampden was struck in the shoulder by two bullets, which broke the bone, and lodged in his body. The troops of the Parliament lost heart and gave way. Rupert, after pursuing them for a short time, hastened to cross the bridge, and made his retreat unmolested to Oxford.

Hampden, with his head drooping, and his hands leaning on his horse's neck, moved feebly out of the battle. The mansion which had been inhabited by his father-in-law, and from which in his youth he had carried home his bride Elizabeth, was in sight. There still remains an affecting tradition that he looked for a moment towards that beloved house, and made an effort to go thither to die. But the enemy lay in that direction. He turned his horse towards Thame, where he arrived almost fainting with agony. The surgeons dressed his wounds. But there was no hope. The pain which he suffered was most excruciating. But he endured it with admirable firmness and resignation. His first care was for his country. He wrote from his bed several letters to London concerning public affairs, and sent a last pressing message to the head-quarters, recommending that the dispersed forces should be concentrated. When his public duties were performed, he calmly prepared himself to die. He was attended by a clergyman of the Church of England, with whom he had lived in habits of intimacy, and by the chaplain of the Buckinghamshire Green-coats, Dr. Spurton, whom Baxter describes as a famous and excellent divine.

A short time before Hampden's death the sacrament was administered to him. He declared that, though he disliked the government of the Church of England, he yet agreed with that Church as to all essential matters of doctrine. His intellect remained unclouded. When all was nearly over, he lay murmuring faint prayers for himself, and for the cause in which he died. "Lord Jesus," he exclaimed, in the moment of the last agony, "receive my soul. O Lord, save my country. O Lord, be merciful to ——." In that broken ejaculation passed away his noble and fearless spirit.

He was buried in the parish church of Hampden. His soldiers, bareheaded, with reversed arms and muffled drums and colours, escorted his body to the grave, singing, as they marched, that lofty and melancholy psalm in which the fragility of human life is contrasted with the immutability of Him to whom a thousand years are as yesterday when it is passed, and as a watch in the night.

The news of Hampden's death produced as great a consternation in his party, according to Clarendon, as if their whole army had been cut off. The journals of the time amply prove that the Parliament and all its friends were filled with grief and dismay. Lord Nugent has quoted a remarkable passage from the next Weekly Intelligencer. "The loss of Colonel Hampden goeth near the heart of every man that loves the good of his king and country, and makes some conceive little content to be at the army now that he is gone. The memory of this deceased colonel is such, that in no age to come but it will more and more be had in honour and esteem; a man so religious, and of that prudence, judgment, temper, valour, and integrity, that he hath left few his like behind."

He had indeed left none his like behind him. There still remained, indeed, in his party, many acute intellects, many eloquent tongues, many brave and honest hearts. There still remained a rugged and clownish soldier, half fanatic, half buffoon, whose talents, discerned as yet only by one penetrating eye, were equal to all the highest duties of the soldier and the prince.

But in Hampden, and in Hampden alone, were united all the qualities which, at such a crisis, were necessary to save the state, the valour and energy of Cromwell, the discernment and eloquence of Vane, the humanity and moderation of Manchester, the stern integrity of Hale, the ardent public spirit of Sydney. Others might possess the qualities which were necessary to save the popular party in the crisis of danger; he alone had both the power and the inclination to restrain its excesses in the hour of triumph. Others could conquer; he alone could reconcile. A heart as bold as his brought up the cuirassiers who turned the tide of battle on Marston Moor. As skilful an eye as his watched the Scotch army descending from the heights over Dunbar. But it was when to the sullen tyranny of Laud and Charles had succeeded the fierce conflict of sects and factions, ambitious of ascendency and burning for revenge, it was when the vices and ignorance which the old tyranny had generated threatened the new freedom with destruction, that England missed the sobriety, the self-command, the perfect soundness of judgment, the perfect rectitude of intention, to which the history of revolutions furnishes no parallel, or furnishes a parallel in Washington alone.

END OF VOL. II.

www.ingramcontent.com/pod-product-compliance
Lightning Source LLC
LaVergne TN
LVHW020915110826
845150LV00004B/679

9781425555658